Global Entertainment Media

A critical cultural materialist introduction to the study of global entertainment media.

In *Global Entertainment Media*, Tanner Mirrlees undertakes an analysis of the ownership, production, distribution, marketing, exhibition and consumption of global films and television shows, with an eye to political economy and cultural studies. Among other topics, Mirrlees examines:

- Paradigms of global entertainment media such as cultural imperialism and cultural globalization.
- The business of entertainment media and trends in the global political economy of entertainment media.
- The "governance" of global entertainment media by state and non-state actors.
- The new international division of cultural labor (NICL), media work, runaway productions and international co-productions.
- The design features of blockbuster films, TV formats, lifestyle brands and synergistic media.
- The cross-cultural reception and effects of TV shows and films.
- The World Wide Web, digitization and convergence culture.

This book provides a conceptually rich, comprehensive, up-to-date survey of the globalization of entertainment media and the leading critical scholarship surrounding it.

Tanner Mirrlees is an Assistant Professor in the Communication Program at the University of Ontario Institute of Technology (UOIT).

Global Entertainment Media

Between Cultural Imperialism and
Cultural Globalization

Tanner Mirrlees

Routledge
Taylor & Francis Group

NEW YORK AND LONDON

First published 2013
by Routledge
711 Third Avenue, New York, NY 10017

Simultaneously published in the UK
by Routledge
2 Park Square, Milton Park, Abingdon, Oxon OX14 4RN

Routledge is an imprint of the Taylor & Francis Group, an informa business

Library of Congress Cataloging in Publication Data
Global entertainment media : between cultural imperialism and cultural globalization / Tanner Mirrlees.
    p. cm.
Includes bibliographical references and index.
1. Mass media and globalization.   2. Motion pictures and globalization.
3. Television and globalization.   4. Culture and globalization.   5. Motion picture industry—United States.   6. Television programs—United States.
7. Imperialism—Social aspects.   8. Globalization—Social aspects.   I. Title.
P94.6.M57 2013
302.23—dc23

2012034129

ISBN: 978–0–415–51981–6 (hbk)
ISBN: 978–0–415–51982–3 (pbk)
ISBN: 978–0–203–12274–7 (ebk)

Typeset in Sabon
by RefineCatch Limited, Bungay, Suffolk, UK

www.routledge.com/9780415519823

CONTENTS

CONTENTS

PREFACE

This book is a study of the increasingly transnational economic, political, and cultural forces that influence the production, distribution, marketing, exhibition, and consumption of films and TV shows. It presents a critical introduction to the theory, corporate ownership, state policies and regulations, texts and viewers of entertainment media in a world system.

This book is customized to suit the "culturally proximate" reading and watching habits of English-speaking communication, cultural, and media studies teachers, researchers, and students. Much of the book focuses on the power relationships between US-based transnational media corporations (TNMCs)—Disney, Time Warner, News Corporation, NBC-Universal, Viacom—and non-US media corporations, states, and cultures. This is because US-based media conglomerates and the films and TV shows they own are the most genuinely global. Although the book primarily focuses on US TNMCs, it also pays attention to national media corporations (NMCs) in parts of Europe, Latin America, the Middle East, East Asia, Africa, and elsewhere. Any reader/ watcher living in a country where their national TV networks and theater chains schedule and screen a lot of entertainment media exported by the US will therefore be likely to find this book informative or relevant to their own lives as workers, citizens, and consumers. While this book is intended for advanced undergraduate students, it has been written in a way that intends to also be accessible to non-academic and non-specialist readers such as cultural workers, activists, and citizens. This book aims to convey depth of understanding using popular langauge and intends to make difficult concepts palatable for readers who may not possess academic cultural capital. Part of the purpose of the book is to introduce "outsiders" to academic, state, and corporate "insider" terms, phrases, and acronyms. Key concepts that readers should know are included.

This book contributes to an already established field of critical political economy and cultural studies scholarship on the global media (Acland 2005; Artz and Kamalipour 2003; Bielby and Harrington 2008; Chakravartty and Zhao 2008; Curtin 2007; Grainge 2008; Grant and Wood 2004; Harvey 2006; Kraidy 2005; Lash and Lury 2007; McChesney 1997; McDonald and Wasko 2008; McMillin 2007; Miller et al. 2005; Parks and Kumar 2003; Scott 2005; Sparks 2007; Schiller 1976; Scott 2005; Thussu 1998, 2006, 2007; Thomas and Nain 2004). This book updates and extends many of Herman and McChesney's (1997) seminal arguments about global corporate control of the media, the decline of public broadcasting, the rise of neoliberal media policy, and the integration of non-US NMCs by US-based TNMCs. However, it also presents a much more focused account of the ownership, production, distribution, marketing and exhibition, politics, design, and consumption of entertainment media. This book supports many of the claims made by Miller et al.'s (2005) path-breaking work on Global Hollywood, but is more up-to-date. Though this book does not deal with entirely original topics, its organization, thoroughness, accessibility, and relevance are intended to make it a useful teaching and learning tool. This book is designed to be user-friendly. In fact, this book is an adaptation of fourteen lectures I delivered to a fourth-year undergraduate course on globalization and the media between 2006 and 2011. The book is thorough in its coverage of topics and key issues without losing depth of analysis. To illustrate key concepts, each chapter entails a number of context-specific examples of economic, political, and cultural practices surrounding entertainment media which will likely be familiar to readers.

The economic, political, and cultural significance of entertainment media raises many questions: does US cultural imperialism exist, or has it been eclipsed by a new set of processes called cultural globalization? How does capitalism influence the form and content of TV shows and films? What are the main business strategies employed by TNMCs and NMCs when they "go global"? Is the cross-border movement of entertainment media supported or stifled by the media polices and regulations of nation-states? Has the globalization of entertainment media strengthened or diminished state media policy imperatives to consolidate "imagined national communities" and national culture industries? Are national cultures and national culture industries withering or being re-established in the current era? Why are TV shows and films being produced by workers in many countries, and what conditions do the culture workers of the world face on a day-to-day basis? How do TNMCs and NMCs design TV shows and films to cross borders? Is the cross-border movement of entertainment media leading to global cultural homogenization, or is it deepening global cultural diversity? When local viewers consume global entertainment media, are they Americanized or culturally dominated, or is the situation more complex? Has digital technology revolutionized or fundamentally changed the world in which entertainment media circulates? Does the cross-border movement of entertainment media contribute to the strengthening or weakening of conditions amenable to social equality, cultural diversity, and democracy?

This book provides a range of ways of answering these and many more questions in the study of global entertainment media. Combining political economy and cultural studies approaches in order to forge a critical "cultural materialism," this book provides an up-to-date and example-rich introduction to the study of globalizing TV shows and films. It does so by examining the dominant paradigms of global entertainment media (cultural imperialism and cultural globalization); the business practices of the TNMCs and NMCs which own entertainment media; the state policies and regulations that govern the cross-border movement of entertainment media; the cross-border production of entertainment media within the new international division of cultural labor (NICL); the textual features of globally popular entertainment forms such as blockbuster event films, global-national TV formats, lifestyle brands, and synergistic media properties; and the cross-cultural consumption of global entertainment media products by local viewers.

Through an exploration of these and other relevant topics, this book reviews and contributes to global media scholarship. It introduces and evaluates key concepts by using relevant examples. Overall, this book aims to provide a conceptually rich, up-to-date, comprehensive, and accessible introduction to the critical study of global entertainment media. By doing so it hopes to foster an international or transnational outlook that moves beyond nationally bounded lenses. In an age when economies, polities, and cultures are interconnected by a number of asymmetrical power relations and processes, developing an acute understanding of the interdependencies between the national and the international spheres, the domestic and the foreign, the "here" and the "there," the local and the global, is of paramount importance. The study of global entertainment media provides one way of understanding these interconnections and interdependencies. Even though TV shows and films circulate in a world system of nation-states, they are shaped by economic, political, and cultural forces and relations that are no longer contained within national boxes.

ACKNOWLEDGMENTS

This book could not have been written without the hundreds of global media studies students I've had the pleasure and privilege of meeting, teaching, and learning from over the past five years. I am also grateful to the many teachers and colleagues who have contributed to my development over the past ten years. Going alphabetically, I would like to thank: Greg Albo, Amin Alhassan, Tariq Amin-Khan, Sedef Arat-Koç, Jody Berland, Mike Burke, Barbara Crow, Tuna Baskoy, Bob Hanke, Kevin Dowler, Greg Elmer, Bryan Evans, Grieg de Peuter, Scott Forsyth, Sam Gindin, Greg Inwood, Greg Klages, Joseph Kispal-Kovacs, Janet Lum, Ganaele Langlois, Pat Mazepa, John McCullough, David McNally, Colin Mooers, Leo Panitch, Ian Reilly, Beth Seaton, Mitu Sengupta, Sarah Sharma, John Shields, David Skinner, Aparna Sundar, Niel Thomlinson, and Scott Uzelman. I am also indebted to Jonathan Hardy, Paolo Sigismondi, and the four anonymous reviewers who provided the insightful revisions, comments, and suggestions which strengthened this book. I want to thank Erica Wetter and Margo Irvin for their patience, compassion and wonderful editorial support. Additionally, I appreciate the warmth of my new colleagues at the University of Ontario Institute of Technology (UOIT): Shahid Alvi, Aziz Douai, Shanti Fernando, Gary Genosko, Ganaele Langlois (again), Alyson King, Sharon Lauricella, Teresa Pierce, and Andrea Slane. I would like to thank Toronto's activist communities (SP, NS, IS), my family (Catherine, Jennifer, Sandi, Bill, Randy, Sheldon, Etti, Mia), and my cats (Karl and Scarfie) for their affection. And finally, I want to say thank you to Lauren Kirshner, who I love dearly and whose intelligence and writing ability continue to inspire me.

AVATAR IS GLOBAL ENTERTAINMENT MEDIA

Since its theatrical release in 2009, *Avatar* has been discussed by critics, journalists, and policy-makers in the US and around the world as a distinctly "American" Hollywood film. In fact, it proves difficult to read about *Avatar* without reading about its essential "American" provenance. Writing for the UK-based newspaper, *The Guardian*, Philip French (2010) says the "cinematic milestone of 2009 [. . .] is an American film called *Avatar*." Blogger Rich Johnston (2009) describes *Avatar* as "the most expensive American film ever." *Daily Telegraph* journalist Nile Gardiner calls it "one of the most left-wing films in the history of modern American cinema, and perhaps the most commercially successful political movie of our time." *The Times of India* journalist S. K. Jha (2009) says 2009 "was the year of the alien" in the Indian entertainment industry, a year "when an American film [called] *Avatar* completely took over our Bollywood filmmakers' psyche making them feel small, inadequate and incompetent." Wen (2010), of the China-based *Global Times*, worries that the "American film" *Avatar* "penetrated the whole of Chinese society" and has "been difficult for Chinese national power to deal with." Wen scolds Chinese viewers for failing to "resist" *Avatar*, a film whose financial success in China and elsewhere "shows us how vulnerable our national pride, confidence, and ambition to catch up with the US really are." In January 2010, the People's Republic of China (PRC) pulled *Avatar* from all 2-D screens and replaced it with *Confucius*, a state-produced film which supports Chinese nationalism by recounting the life of this important ancient Chinese philosopher (Jimbo 2010).

Seen through the eyes of certain reviewers, *Avatar* is a distinctly "American" Hollywood film, a product of an American—yet globalizing—culture industry and a force of American cultural imperialism abroad. *Avatar* is also classified as an "American" film by the country of origin codes that indicate the country in which a film is produced or financed. But what exactly is "American" about *Avatar*? How do reviewers and classifiers know the "America-nation-ness" of this film? What are the precise characteristics of national entertainment media? And is "cultural imperialism" an appropriate way to describe *Avatar*'s global presence? For some time, films and TV shows have been placed in nationalist boxes and classified as deriving from a specific country of origin. A national culture industry based in a specific territorial state creates national entertainment media—TV shows and films—that express or reflect an established "national identity" back to the resident population. Typically, nationally boxed entertainment media refers to films and TV shows that: 1) are owned and financed by a national business class/media firm based in one country; 2) are produced by one national media firm and created by cultural workers from one country; 3) are carriers of national stories which express/appeal to the national experiences and preferences of the viewers of one country; and, 4) are recognized and consumed by viewers in many countries as one country's "national" entertainment. For *Avatar* to qualify as strictly "American" entertainment media, it would have to fulfill the above criteria. It certainly does not.

Avatar is, in fact, the product of News Corporation (News Corp), a transnational media corporation whose owners are not all US citizens. News Corp's CEO and owner is Rupert Murdoch, a bi-national media mogul. In 1985, Murdoch chose to give up his Australian citizenship to become a US citizen. That switch enabled News Corp to buy Twentieth Century Fox, a Los Angeles-based film and TV studio. Though headquartered in New York City and listed on the NASDAQ as a US public company, News Corp currently boasts shareholders from many countries: the globe-trotting Murdoch family (38.74%), Saudi Arabia's billionaire Alwaleed bin Talal Alsaud (7.04%) and financial firms such as Invesco (1.8%), Bank of New York Mellon (1.19%), London-based Taube Hodson Stonex (1.07%), Dimensional Fund Advisors (0.71%), JP Morgan Chase (0.41%), Blackrock Group (0.35%), MFC Global Investment Management (0.35%), and Goldman Sachs Group (0.35%) (Bloomberg 2011). In addition to being owned by a globalizing investor class, *Avatar* was financed by transnational investors: the US-based Dune Entertainment and the UK-based investment and advisory group Ingenious Investments. Twentieth Century Fox's transnational distribution subsidiaries and other local distribution firms, including FS Film Oy (Finland), Bontonfilm (Czech Republic), Castello Lopes Multimedia (Portugal), Forum Cinemas (Estonia, Lithuania, and Latvia), Film 1 (Netherlands), and Nippon Television Network Corporation (Japan), licensed *Avatar* to theater chains and TV networks in many countries. Clearly, *Avatar* is not owned, financed, or distributed by one US business class or firm. Prior to *Avatar*'s release, Murdoch was confident the film "would lead the Christmas season" box office (cited in Cieply 2009). This turned out to be a modest assertion. Following its worldwide release (in more than 3,500 hundred theaters simultaneously) and $150 million dollar global marketing campaign, *Avatar* became the highest-grossing film of all time, generating nearly $3 billion ($2,782,275,172). Of *Avatar*'s total gross, 27.3 percent came from the North American box office (the US and Canada), while the remaining 72.7 percent came from the rest of the world (Box Office Mojo 2012).

Avatar was not manufactured solely by one US media firm or exclusively by US cultural workers. *Avatar* was conceptualized, written, and directed by James Cameron, a bi-national resident of the US and New Zealand, but also a Canadian citizen who withdrew his application for US citizenship after George W. Bush was re-elected in 2004. *Avatar* stars numerous US actors (Zoe Saldana, Sigourney Weaver, Stephen Lang, Michelle Rodriguez), but the film's lead is played by the English-born actor Sam Worthington. While much of *Avatar*'s production and post-production was handled by US-based firms, companies from all over the world also contributed to the film's assembly. The special effects were created by firms in the US (Stan Winston Studio, Giant Studio, Industrial Light and Magic), Canada (Hybride Technologies), New Zealand (Weta Digital), Great Britain (Framestore), and France (BUF). Production companies from New Zealand (Billionaire's Catering, Cunning Stunts, Human Dynamo, Izzat, Sideline Safety, Stone Street Studios, Weta Workshop), Great Britain (Codex Digital, Intelligent Media, Spitfire Audio, Synxspeed), and Japan (Panasonic) sold a variety of "below the line" services—catering, transport, lighting, equipment—to Twentieth Century Fox. Some sections of *Avatar* were shot in the US (Hawaii and California), but the film was largely a "runaway production" from the US to New Zealand, whose state Film Commission subsidized Twentieth Century Fox with its Large Budget Screen Production Grant and Post-Production Digital-Video Effects Grant. By shooting *Avatar* in New Zealand, Twentieth Century Fox received a grant worth approximately $45 million from the government (Voxy 2010). Twentieth Century Fox also traveled to New Zealand to buy the special effects services offered by Peter Jackson's famous Wellington-based firm, Weta Digital Studio (New Zealand 2009). The transnationality of *Avatar*'s "above the line" and "below the line" creative workers and the bi-national locations of its production complicates *Avatar*'s "American-ness."

Avatar is not a distinctly American "text." It is not a story about the US or written only for a US audience to appreciate. *Avatar* is certainly open to many nationally situated interpretations, but its manifest content does not represent the US territory, the US state, or US symbols. As a science fiction genre film, *Avatar* avoids the "cultural discount" associated with narrowly nationalistic and realistic stories. In *Avatar*, the year is 2154 and Earth's resources (not just the US's resources) have been exhausted. The human species (not just US citizens) faces extinction. The story has global resonance. Indeed, the film does not even imply the existence of the United States. In an attempt to stave off Earth's ecological disaster, an intergalactic (as opposed to US) mining corporation called the Resources Development Administration (RDA) colonizes Pandora, a jungle planet. The RDA is after a precious Pandoran mineral called Unobtainium, which it plans to exploit in order to fix Earth's ecological crisis and profit-maximize. The RDA does not raise the US flag on Pandora; its brand logo prevails. The RDA's goal to control Unobtainium creates conflict with Pandora's indigenous population, the Na'vi. Tall, blue-skinned, and feline, these creatures exist in spiritual harmony with nature. They worship Eywa, the "All Mother," an energy network that connects all life forms. The home of the Na'vi is a gigantic tree that sits above Pandora's largest Unobtainium deposit. The RDA wants the Unobtainium, but in order to get it they must induce the Na'vi to do what they will not do of their own volition: leave their communal, ancestral land.

To compel the Na'vi to get off their own land, the RDA employs a combination of persuasive and coercive power strategies. "Find a carrot to get them to move, or it's going to have to be all stick," says Selfridge. The RDA dispatches scientist-bio-ethnologists to convince the Na'vi to give up their land, followed by a privatized mercenary firm called Secops (not the US military) to use brute force to gain control of the Unobtainium.

The RDA initially uses persuasion to try to get the Na'vi to leave their homeland. On Earth, most strategies of persuasion entail human-to-human communication or mediated public relations efforts. But on Pandora, direct human-to-Na'vi communication is not possible because the air is poisonous to humans. To overcome this cross-species communications challenge, the RDA funds ethnologist-scientists to bio-engineer a cultural intermediary capable of traversing the boundaries between humans and Na'vis. In the RDA's laboratory, human and Na'vi DNA is spliced together to create half-human, half-Na'vi hybrid beings: Avatars. These giant life-size synthetic bodies look like Na'vi, but lack their own consciousness. Using complex neuro-connectors, RDA-employed humans control these Avatar bodies at a distance, from within pods. Plugged in to their Avatars, RDA personnel are visually and experientially immersed in Pandora's jungles as Avatar Na'vi. They communicate with and study the Na'vi population without ever putting their own bodies at risk of physical harm. The RDA's Avatar Na'vi to actual Na'vi persuasion campaign, however, proves ineffective. With the exception of the Avatar Na'vi operated by Dr. Grace Augustine (Sigourney Weaver), all Avatar Na'vi are expelled from the Na'vi community due to their cultural ignorance.

However, the RDA is desperate to remove the Na'vi and gain control of the Unobtainium, so Secops enlists an ex-marine and paraplegic named Jake Sully (Sam Worthington) to infiltrate Pandora's jungles as an Avatar Na'vi spy. Sully accepts the RDA job out of financial necessity. Earth's economy has collapsed and the RDA pays Sully a decent wage. Also, Sully's work for the RDA is motivated by his desire to make enough money to pay for an operation that will give him back the use of his legs: "Spinal cord injuries can be fixed, if you have the money" says Sully. Sully's mission is directed by the RDA's managerial elite. Secops mercenary-colonel Miles Quaritch (Stephen Lang) is convinced that a violent military conflict with the Na'vi is both inevitable and imminent, and so he is preparing to launch a pre-emptive "shock and awe" attack. He wants Sully to be his eyes, ears, and alter-ego in the jungles of Pandora and commands Sully to gather intelligence about the "hostile" and "savage" Na'vi. Selfridge, the RDA's sleazy CEO (Giovanni Ribisi), wants to dispossess the Na'vis of their land and expropriate the Unobtainium, but without slaughtering them. Selfridge is not morally opposed to exterminating the Na'vi, but worries that this course of action would diminish the RDA's public image and shareholder value: "exterminating the indigenous looks bad on the quarterly statement." To avoid a PR disaster, Sully is hired and dispatched by Selfridge to persuade the Na'vi to give the RDA the Unobtainium in exchange for a paternalistic RDA-sponsored modernization program (blue jeans, English-language courses, electricity).

Despite being employed by the RDA as a corporate scientist, Dr. Augustine still wants to conduct (and naively believes she can conduct) hard science for science's sake. She wants Sully to study the Na'vi's rituals, in order to develop a greater understanding and appreciation of their way of life, on their own terms. As *Avatar*'s narrative unfolds, the goals of militarism, capitalism, and science sometimes clash, but mainly coalesce. Sully begins his journey into the jungles of Pandora as nothing more than a cog in the RDA's intergalactic military-techno-science machine, but after falling in love with a female Na'vi warrior named Neytiri (Zoe Saldana) and learning about the Na'vi "way of life," Sully comes to identify with them. As Colonel Quaritch proceeds with the RDA's extermination campaign, Sully mobilizes Pandora's indigenous Na'vi population to defend their homeland. The film climaxes with a massive battle between the Na'vi and the RDA. Led by Sully's Na'vi Avatar, the Na'vi population defends itself against the RDA. In sum, *Avatar* was not written to be identified as a distinctly American text. As a science fiction film, *Avatar* represents a future-oriented time and fantastical place that are not reducible to the early twenty-first-century Earth's actual system of territorial nation-states. *Avatar*'s protagonists and antagonists are not US citizens, but an entirely different species and the employees of an inter-galactic mining corporation. *Avatar* is designed to have universal, as opposed to only American "national," appeal.

Avatar is a transnationally polysemic text which is open to and enabling of a diversity of interpretations by viewers in many countries. The film has been called an "all-purpose allegory" (Keating 2010) and 2009's filmic "ideological Rorschach blot" (Phillips 2010). In transnational and cross-cultural reception contexts, *Avatar* has been made meaningful by viewers who connect the film's themes and storyline to their own national histories, political circumstances, and cultural identities. US viewers on both the political Left and Right argue that *Avatar* is an allegory of US imperialism, old and new. Debbie Schlussel (2009) says *Avatar* is an allegory of the US's founding as a white colonial settler state: "It's essentially a remake of *Dances With Wolves* and every other movie where *we* evil Americans terrorize the indigenous natives, kill them, take their land, and are just all around imperialistically wicked and inhumane." Other conservative critics say *Avatar* is an allegory of the US's 2003 invasion of Iraq and evidence of so-called liberal Hollywood unfairly criticizing the US military. John Nolte (2009) says *Avatar* is "a thinly disguised, heavy-handed and simplistic sci-fi fantasy/allegory critical of America from our founding straight through to the Iraq War." Nile Gardiner (2009) claims that *Avatar* is:

> a critique of the Iraq War, an assault on the US-led War on Terror, a slick morality talk about the 'evils' of Western imperialism, a futuristic take on the conquest of America and the treatment of native Americans—the list goes on.

Not all conservatives agree with this interpretation.

A few neoconservative commentators contest these paleoconservative interpretations of *Avatar*'s meaning. They state that the film is not an allegory of US imperialism, but an empowering story about the universal value of American liberty. According to Ann Marlowe (2009), *Avatar* illustrates "the point we neo-cons made in Iraq: that American blood is not worth more than the blood of others, and that others' freedom is not worth less than American freedom." This peculiar reading of *Avatar* and bogus revisionist account of the US rationalization for invading Iraq (the US claimed it invaded Iraq because Iraq was allied with Al-Qaeda and possessed weapons of mass destruction) casts Sully as a benevolent US soldier who seeks to promote and protect the political liberty of everyone, everywhere (even on Pandora). "*Avatar* shows a man standing up for what is right, a quintessential American act," says Marlowe. Neoconservatives read Sully and the Na'vi as quasi American revolutionaries who fight for the universalization of political liberty against an authoritarian empire. In this respect, the film draws upon Hollywood narrative convention, pitting a freedom-loving band of underdog individuals (Sully and the Na'vi) against a corrupt, malevolent, hierarchical, and far more powerful economic and military institution: the RDA (Murphy 2010). US Marine Colonel Bryan Salas, says that by doing so, *Avatar* takes "sophomoric shots at our [US] military culture" and unfairly stereotypes the US military, instead of accurately depicting it "honorably fight[ing] and fall[ing] to win our nation's real battles today" (cited in Agrell 2010). Salas interprets Secops as representing the US Marines, even though Secops is not part of a state or a national organization.

Postcolonial feminists have a lot to say about *Avatar*. They criticize *Avatar* as a neo-Orientalist film in which a white man (Sully) "goes native" by assimilating with and then leading a native culture (the Na'vi) toward liberty (Newitz 2009). The theme of white men becoming the heroic leaders of those they had hitherto oppressed appears in many Hollywood films: *Dune, Indiana Jones and the Temple of Doom, The Last of the Mohicans, The Last Samurai,* and *District 9,* for example. Like those films, *Avatar* represents the colonial self (the RDA) and the colonized other (the Na'vi) through the lens of Orientalist stereotypes (Said 1979). In *Avatar,* the colonial self is portrayed as active, technological, modern, forward-looking, and rational, while the colonized other is depicted as passive, naturalistic, traditional, backwards, and spiritual. Applied to present-day cultural identity politics, "Stereotypes like this not only undermine the hard-won voice of marginalized peoples of color, but justify their continued marginalization" (Sengupta 2010). Newitz (2009) says *Avatar* is "a fantasy about race told from the point of view of white people," and interprets the film as an ideological resolution to "white guilt":

> Our main white characters realize that they are complicit in a system which is destroying aliens, AKA people of color—their cultures, their habitats, and their populations. The whites realize this when they begin to assimilate into the 'alien' cultures and see things from a new perspective. To purge their overwhelming sense of guilt, they switch sides, become 'race traitors,' and fight against their old comrades. But they go beyond assimilation and become leaders of the people they once oppressed. This is the essence of the white guilt fantasy, laid bare. It's not just a wish to be absolved of the crimes whites have committed against people of color; it's not just a wish to join the side of moral justice in battle. It's a wish to lead people of color from the inside rather than from the (oppressive, white) outside.

Sengupta (2010) agrees that "Cameron delivers his anti-modernity, pro-indigeneity and deep ecology parable through the most advanced cinematic technologies and the body of a handsome white man."

While *Avatar* is interpreted by many North American viewers as American entertainment media that allegorizes US imperialism and perpetuates Western Orientalist fantasies of the other, non-US viewers have presented more nuanced and sympathetic assessments of *Avatar* that take us beyond an American-centric reception box. Negative postcolonial critiques of *Avatar* are important, but by reducing the film to a conveyor belt for Orientalist ideology, postcolonial reviewers have overlooked its positive meanings and empowering uses in the actual geopolitical world, especially among indigenous peoples (Rao 2010). *Avatar* presents a potential oppressor (Sully) empathizing with others (the Na'vi), demonstrating solidarity with them in the face of oppression, and then fighting on their behalf. *Avatar* "unflinchingly indicts imperialism and corporate greed, defends the right of the oppressed to fight back, and holds open the potential for solidarity between people on opposite sides of a conflict not of their choosing" (Rao 2010). Senses extended through his Na'vi Avatar, Sully becomes a revolutionary hybrid that symbolizes "an uncompromising defense of the principle of self-determination and the right to resist exploitation and plunder" (Rao 2010). *Avatar* is much more than racist, neo-colonialist fluff. In order to understand this, scholars need to "develop a new attentiveness to all the implicit and explicit citations of radical content in mainstream culture" (Thompson 2010: 83). *Avatar*'s radical content resonated with people, providing an opportunity to turn cultural identification with science fiction into political action and resistance.

Activists in many different countries have appropriated and repurposed *Avatar*'s story for their own political activism (Jenkins 2010). The fictional Na'vi were transformed into symbols of the millions of people around the world oppressed by neoliberal governance, capitalism, and militarism. In December 2009, Chinese bloggers drew parallels between the plight of the Na'vi in *Avatar* and China's peasant population. They read the film as an allegory of the Chinese state's forcible removal of Chinese peasants from their land and the demolition of their homes to make way for capitalism with Chinese characteristics. Chinese bloggers on the website Chinasmack.com "found a striking similarity between the plot of *Avatar* and all kinds of forced evictions occurring on a regular basis in China" (661). In January 2009, Bolivia's first fully indigenous president, Evo Morales, praised *Avatar* for its "profound show of resistance to capitalism and the struggle for the defense of nature" (Huffington Post 2010). In February 2010, five Palestinian, Israeli, and international activists dressed up as Na'vi and marched through the village of Bilin in Palestine. They then posted a video of this performative political protest (and of Israeli soldiers shelling the Na'vi-dressed protestors with canisters of tear gas from behind a barb-wired fence) on YouTube. In that same month, The Dongria Kondh tribe of Eastern India said that the plight of the Na'vi in *Avatar* reflects their own struggle to stop a British mining company called Vedanta from opening a bauxite mine on their sacred land (Hopkins 2010). In Malaysia, a Penan man from Sarawak said that "the Na'vi people in *Avatar* cry because their forest is destroyed. It's the same with the Penan. Logging companies are chopping down our big trees and polluting our rivers, and the animals we hunt are dying" (cited in Teague 2010). In South Africa, a Kalahari Bushman, Jumanda Gakelebone, said "*Avatar* makes me happy as it shows the world about what it is to be a Bushman, and what our land is to us. Land and Bushmen are the same." In April 2010, Amazonian indigenous people asked James Cameron to support their struggle against the Brazilian state's construction of a dam. "What happens in the film is what is happening here," said José Carlos Arara, the chief of the Arara tribe (cited in Barrionuevo 2010). In Canada, an indigenous group living near the Athabaska Oil Sands in Alberta drew parallels between their own struggle against oil corporations in their territory and the struggle of the Na'vi. A $20,000 advertisement placed in the magazine *Variety*, and titled "Canada's Avatar Sands," said that Canada is "Where Shell, BP, Exxon, and other Sky People are destroying a huge ancient forest. Where giant Hell trucks are used to mine the most polluting, expensive Unobtainium oil to feed America's addiction" (cited in Rowell 2010).

Avatar's indigenized appropriations by activists in South and Central America, Africa, the Middle East, and Canada demonstrate the political openness and malleability of globalizing texts. Activists co-opted *Avatar*, and the hearts and minds of this film's transnational audience. They repurposed this text to draw attention to their own struggles against neoliberalism, capitalist dispossession, and war. They used *Avatar* to connect with mainstream entertainment consumers who may previously have ignored or simply failed to understand their struggles for justice, rights, and land. The cross-cultural political uses of *Avatar* highlight how popular culture is "one of the sites where the struggle for and against the powerful is engaged" (Hall 1998). *Avatar*'s text and reception also highlight the notion that all entertainment media produced by media conglomerates is not capitalist propaganda. Murdoch, a neoconservative and supporter of the 2003 US war in Iraq, did not command James Cameron to engineer *Avatar*'s text to forward his right-wing political agenda. Control of *Avatar*'s copyright and the revenue this film generated was surely more important to Murdoch than *Avatar*'s many textual meanings and viewer uses. Perhaps active transnational fan engagement with and mainstream debates about *Avatar* were functional to Twentieth Century Fox's viral marketing efforts, which put *Avatar* enthusiasts and fans around the world to work as unpaid and unwitting promoters ("prosumers") of the film. Viewer engagement and interactive immersion in the fantasy of *Avatar* contributed to the success of the overall entertainment franchise by creating more buzz about it. Though *Avatar*'s political-economic production context and cultural reception context are entwined in the same circuits of capital, they are not identical. Still, whether redeemed by a Leftist or trashed by a Conservative, *Avatar*—a globally popular film as opposed to a distinctly American entertainment film—ultimately served the profit goals of News Corp well.

Studied with reference to the transnational forces of ownership, financing, production, distribution, textual encoding, viewer decoding, and cultural use which surround it, *Avatar* is global entertainment media, a form of globally popular culture that complicates nationalist boxes. Like *Avatar*, this book moves across nationalist boxes by examining the economic, political, and cultural forces that influence the production, distribution, marketing, exhibition, and consumption of film and TV shows. It is a critical introduction to the political economies and cultures of global entertainment media.

GLOBAL ENTERTAINMENT MEDIA, CAPITALISM, AND CONSUMERISM: POLITICAL-ECONOMY AND CULTURE

The phrase "global entertainment media" is derived from three words: "global," "entertainment," and "media." According to *The Oxford English Dictionary*, "global" means "of or relating to the whole world." "Entertainment" refers to "an event, performance or activity designed to entertain others," or something that intends to provide "amusement or enjoyment" to others. "Media" is the main means of, and products of, mass communication. In this book, "global entertainment media" refers to media commodities produced, distributed, marketed, exhibited, and consumed in many different countries, and which intend to provide viewers with amusement and media conglomerates with profit. The types of global entertainment media this book primarily (though not exclusively) focuses on are TV shows and films. These audio-visual artifacts and products are shaped by and expressive of the political economies and cultures of numerous countries, big and small, rich and poor, neo-imperial and postcolonial. They are economically and culturally significant.

Since the turn of the millennium, the cross-border trade of TV shows and films has grown (WTO 2010). In fact, between 1998 and 2009, "every segment of the media industries has grown, except for newspapers and magazines" (Winseck 2011: 11). In 2008, the global value of the audio-visual sector was estimated to be US $516 billion. TV accounted for 68 percent of that total (US $352 billion), while film represented 16 percent (US $84 billion). The remaining 16 percent was accounted for by radio and music (WTO 2010). The audio-visual sector contributes to corporate profits, jobs creation in culture industries, and the Gross Domestic Product (GDP) of many countries. The cross-border movement of TV shows and films is part and product of a specific socio-economic system (capitalism) and is an agent of a particular cultural sensibility (consumerism).

TV shows and films are valuable products of the capitalist mode of production, a system in dominance worldwide. Marx (1848) famously described capitalism as a system that relied on permanent growth and territorial expansion: "the need of a constantly expanding market for its products chases the bourgeoisie over the whole surface of the globe. It must nestle everywhere, settle everywhere, establish connections everywhere" (476). Many of the economic trends described by contemporary analysts of globalizing capitalism—commodification, trade relations between countries, the international division of labor, the rise of cross-border finance and investment, the incorporation and integration of pre-capitalist societies into the system, time and space compression—have been part of the world since the 1840s, when Marx and Engels started examining capitalism's transformation of the world (Renton 2001). Since the fall of the Berlin Wall in 1989, the institutionalization of neoliberal policies of liberalization, deregulation, and privatization by states worldwide (Harvey 2007), and the revolution in information and communication technologies (ITCs), capitalist forces and relations have continually expanded worldwide, integrating national economies and states and leading to greater interdependency between them all. Global capitalism is surrounded by political controversy. Critics on the Left warn that global capitalism represents the rule of transnational corporations over sovereign states, the erosion of democracy, increasing inequality, and a deepening of the divides between rich and poor countries (Klein 2000; 2008; Robinson 2004). Proponents of globalization on the neoliberal Right champion global capitalism for "flattening the world" by spreading markets, opportunity, wealth, democratic ideas, creativity, and innovation everywhere (Friedman 2000; 2006).

Worldwide, TV shows and films have become an import sector of production and consumption. The territorial expansion of the Fordist factory system has been accompanied by the spread of post-Fordist culture industries that produce and distribute intangible and immaterial goods such as TV shows and films (InfoComm International 2010). From the maquiladoras of the Mexico-US border to the gigantic factory complexes of China, waged workers daily complete exhausting, Taylorized, and low-paid tasks like assembling standardized goods such as t-shirts, toasters, and computer screens. Growing alongside these Fordist-style jobs is waged work in post-Fordist service sectors including transport, retail, recreation, culture, and entertainment media (Dadush and Wyne 2011; Harvey 1989; World Bank 2009). The spread of these two production logics has been accompanied by the cultural ethos of consumerism, which presents shopping as the meaning and purpose of life and commercial goods as the main source of identity, community, and happiness (Barber 2008). The leisurely pleasures offered to people by consumerism offer temporary relief from the laborly compulsions demanded by employers. According to Vogel, "the term leisure is now broadly used to characterize time not spent at work (where there is an obligation to perform)" (2007: 4). Labor time and leisure time have gone global. From China to Chile to the Czech Republic, people work in all kinds of tedious waged jobs. In much of the time left over after waged work and sleep, people all over the world go shopping and watch a lot of TV shows and films made by domestic and foreign media firms.

The most powerful producers of entertainment media are transnational media corporations (TNMCs). Most of these firms—Time Warner, Walt Disney, News Corp, amongst others—are based in but not contained by the territorial borders of the United States. They straddle the globe, doing business in almost every country and selling entertainment media to consumers everywhere. The technological integration of country-specific media systems by satellites, the Internet, the World Wide Web, and convergent media, as well as the embrace of neoliberal policies that privatize state broadcasters and telecommunications systems, establish audio-visual free trade agreements, and remove cultural-nationalist protections, have increased and sped up the flow of entertainment media across borders. Daily, millions of people's eyes and ears are engaged by TV shows and films made inside and outside of their own country. Pay-per-view downloading services and peer-to-peer file-sharing sites like The Pirate Bay have enabled TV shows and films to cross borders in digital form, too. Worldwide, working people spend their wages and their leisure time on entertainment media. "Each year Americans cumulatively spend at least 140 billion hours and more than $280 billion a year on legal forms of entertainment. And globally, total annual spending is approaching $1 trillion" (Vogel 2007: xix). In 2010, US consumers spent $433 billion on entertainment products (Snider 2011). In that same year, consumers around the world spent $2 trillion on digital information and entertainment products and services (Haselton 2011). Superintended by the US superpower and courted by states worldwide, capitalist production models integrate people as waged workers while TNMCs meet and manage their emerging leisure time with spectacular media products.

In addition to being an integral part of the political-economies of many countries, entertainment media is an important part of many cultures, local and global, national and international. TV shows and films intersect with, represent, and may even influence entire "ways of life." The term "culture" is used by anthropologists to describe the "whole way of life" of a group of people. In many countries, entertainment media is a significant part of "culture": a complex of artifacts, "values, customs, beliefs and practices which constitute the way of life of a specific group" of people at a particular moment in time (Eagleton 2000: 34). A "whole way of life" includes the *artifacts, customs, beliefs and ideas, and practices* of a specific society, passed down from generation to generation (by industries, governments, legal systems, media and communication systems, religious institutions, families, and schools), which bind different and often geographically disparate people together, as one group.

TV shows and films are cultural artifacts produced by people within a complex division of labor. Yet why are TV shows and films produced? Obviously, these and other entertainment media are not created in order to sate basic human needs. Rather, entertainment media is produced to meet the profit goals of media corporations and a number of culturally constructed wants. People do not *need* to watch an episode of *Glee* to survive. Many people, however, *want* to watch *Glee* and participate in its online fandoms. People do not die when they stop watching films like *Toy Story 3* (2010). They will die if they are deprived of water and food. The cultural wants, desires and passions for entertainment media are powerfully influenced by media corporations, not people's subsistence needs. Interestingly, many people feel they can't live without TV shows and films. Media products are not only used by viewers—to relax after a day's work, to imagine or empathize with the lives of others, or to purge repressed emotions—but are also carriers of symbols that communicate something about cultures. People may gain a sense of themselves and the people in other countries by consuming the cultural symbols carried by TV shows and films.

Entertainment media is customary. TV shows and films are part of the dominant framework of customs—the common rules that a group uses for judging appropriate and inappropriate values, attitudes, and behaviors—not just in the US and other rich states, but all over the world. The consumption of TV shows and films during leisure time is taken for granted by many people. Entertainment media is also on many people's minds. Countless conversations—online, in pubs, in households, at school—are built around entertainment media. People have a range of different beliefs about TV shows and films, and they regularly communicate these beliefs to others—friends, family members, co-workers—while discussing what they watch. Fans of certain TV shows or films think, talk, and write about the fictional lives of certain characters. In addition to being thought about and talked about, entertainment media is also the site of day-to-day practices in many countries. The consumption of entertainment media is something ritualistically done by millions of people every day. It is woven into people's routines, often preceding, following, or occurring in tandem with the work day in a factory, retail outlet, or office. All TV shows and films imply a certain way of doing things with life, with time, and with space. The DVD box set or digital download, for example, asks us to spend time watching while seated in front of a TV set, or alternately while on the go with mobile media. In the absence of entertainment media, people might find something else to do with their time.

Globalizing TV shows and films may influence people, shaping the way they understand their social identities, their cultural communities, and the wider world in which they live, think, and act. TV shows and films do not reflect societies and cultures but, rather, construct the meaning of societies and cultures. Entertainment media conveys an array of representations of societies and cultures, which may shape how people perceive themselves and the world. In the twenty-first century, the representations carried all over the world by entertainment media often come between the objective world and people's subjective perceptions of it. They frame the world outside of people's immediate and local experiences, and are sometimes mistaken as reflections of the way things are and always will be. TV shows and films may shape the development of social identities and cultural communities by providing people with lifestyles to identify with and "ways of life" to emulate. TV shows and films show their viewers certain ways of being, thinking, and acting as people in society: how things are or ought to be. In sum, entertainment media is a significant agent of socialization (and acculturation). As such, TV shows and films are a source of explicit or tacit influence in society. They are a means of socializing a culture and used by people to develop a sense of themselves and others. Because entertainment media is an important and influential part of a culture policy-makers, media firms, citizens and consumers in many countries debate its purpose and effects.

In sum, global entertainment media is a substantial part of the political-economy of global capitalist-consumerism and is interwoven with the cultures of many people in many countries.

TOWARD A CRITICAL CULTURAL MATERIALIST STUDY OF GLOBAL ENTERTAINMENT MEDIA

This book's methodological and theoretical commitments support the "political-economy" and materialist "cultural studies" approaches to communication, media, and culture (Golding and Murdock 1991; Havens, Lotz, and Tinic 2009; McChesney 2008; Mosco 2008; 2009; Schiller 2007; Sparks 2007; Wasko 2003; Winseck and Jin 2011). Winseck (2011) says that:

> all approaches to the political economy of media take it as axiomatic that the media industries—the structure of the markets they operate in, their patterns of ownership, the strategies of key players, trajectory of development and so on—are important objects of analysis. (11)

Stuart Hall (1997) defines the study of culture as being "concerned with the production and exchange of meanings—the 'giving and taking of meaning'—between the members of a society or group" (2). Cultural studies scholars primarily, though not exclusively, examine the production, circulation, and consumption of meanings in particular contexts. This book employs political-economy and cultural studies approaches to the ownership, production, distribution and exhibition, policies, texts, and consumption of globalizing films and TV shows, as well as to the meanings and discourses surrounding these practices.

In this book, "political-economy" and "cultural studies" are employed as complementary critical approaches. This book affirms that the best practitioners of political-economy are those who integrate the insights of cultural studies, and the most interesting practitioners of cultural studies are those who are firmly grounded in political-economy. In fact, Babe (2009) argues that in the formative years of the political-economy of the media and cultural studies, these approaches "were fully integrated, consistent, and mutually supportive" (4). Williams (1981) makes a similar point about the "mutually supportive" relationship when calling for a "cultural materialist" approach to the media: "the analysis of all forms of signification [. . .] within the actual means and conditions of their production" (64–65).

This book is "cultural materialist." It analyzes the significations of globalizing entertainment media with reference to the actual, and increasingly transnational, economic and political means and conditions of their ownership, production, distribution, marketing, exhibition, textual design, and consumption. This book's cultural materialist approach takes it as axiomatic that entertainment media must be studied in relation to broader economic, political, cultural, and discursive contexts. Cultural materialism enables an examination of: 1) the capitalist base of the culture/creative industries (the ownership, production, distribution, exhibition, and marketing of entertainment media as a commodity by media corporations); 2) the state media policies and regulations that limit and enable the transnational production, movement, content, and consumption of entertainment media (the "governance" of the media); 3) the textual characteristics and design features of global entertainment media (media content, themes, stories, and representations); 4) the consumption, identifications, uses, and effects of entertainment media by viewers in various contexts of reception (meaning-making, indigenization, appropriation, ideological reproduction, etc.); and, 5) the discourses of—i.e., ways of representing, constructing meaning about, or signifying—the aforementioned processes and practices.

Furthermore, this book takes a "critical" approach to the study of global entertainment media. But being "critical" does not mean making a knee-jerk moral value-judgment about global entertainment media (as either good or bad for people, or good or bad for the world). Without even examining the specific business practices, state policies and regulations, texts, and viewer practices that influence the cross-border movement of entertainment media, pundits hastily frame this process as good and good for the world or, alternately, as bad and bad for it. Fraser (2003), a Canadian journalist, argues that the globalization of entertainment media:

> promotes values and beliefs that, while contentious, are ultimately good for the world. American entertainment—Hollywood, Disneyland, CNN, MTV, and Madonna—convey values that have made American great, such as an abiding belief in democracy, free enterprise, and individual liberties. (260)

Contra Fraser's apologia for cultural imperialism, many commentators in the Web 2.0 blogosphere (and in academic and cultural policy networks) claim that the globalization of entertainment media is bad for the world. A Yahoo! Answers forum entitled "Why is Hollywood a bad influence on the world?" contains a range of responses: "They glorify ways of life that many will never have, and create reality-defying works of fiction that delude people about the true nature of life"; "Because they distort reality, create false values and glamour, and tend to reduce everything to its simplest level; they portray a narrow and single minded view on the world"; "That in combination with the great spread of their material and social status of it pushes that narrow way of thinking into greater social groups. It narrows the horizon rather than broadens it." While it is easy to moralize about the effects of entertainment, it is much more challenging to understand the forces and relations that produce them.

While the author's moral view of global entertainment media will sometimes, tacitly or explicitly, be expressed in the following pages, overall this book encourages readers to come to their own moral position about global entertainment media, slowly and self-reflexively. The critical study of global entertainment media should begin not with superficial celebration or denigration, but with a deeper understanding of the actual political-economic, societal, and cultural forces and relations that bring entertainment media into the world. In this book, therefore, "being critical" does not necessarily mean being moralistic. This book does not directly affirm or attack global entertainment media, but instead encourages readers to grasp the worldly forces and relations that shape its existence. This book intends to be dialectical. It often puts opposing positions in dialogue and represents two conflicting positions on entertainment media simultaneously. The book is not overtly optimistic or glumly pessimistic. It tries to avoid one-dimensional screeds for or against global entertainment media and does its best to present a balanced approach. By taking a "middle range" position between two rival paradigms in global media studies—cultural imperialism (CI) and cultural globalization (CG)—this book encourages readers to avoid a simplistic good or bad view of global entertainment media. The world is far more complex than any single paradigm shows. By developing a cultural materialist, critical, and dialectical understanding of global entertainment media, readers may eventually develop their own moral critique of it and the kind of world system in which it exists. Films and TV shows are part and product of capitalism and need to be analyzed as such.

THE CHAPTERS

This book has six chapters. Each chapter focuses on a specific area of inquiry in global media and international communication studies relevant to the study of global TV shows and films.

Chapter 1—"Paradigms of Global Entertainment Media"—introduces and examines two of the most influential paradigms in the study of global entertainment media: cultural imperialism (CI) and cultural globalization (CG). At present, CI and CG are used by journalists, policy-makers, and scholars to make claims about a variety of processes and effects associated with transnational and cross-border movements of entertainment media. This chapter presents CI and CG as contested theoretical or paradigmatic discourses. It describes the history of these paradigms, why they emerged, their key claims, how they are used, criticisms of them, and their continued influence upon scholarly and practical agendas. The chapter addresses questions including: what is cultural imperialism? What is cultural globalization? What are the differences between the CI and CG paradigms? What are the strengths and weaknesses of each? How do the claims of each paradigm connect with the power relations of the actual world? What are the economic, political, and cultural dimensions of imperialism and globalization? Can the most significant insights of each paradigm be synthesized? An understanding of the history, claims, and counter-claims associated with the CI and CG paradigms is foundational knowledge in global media studies.

Chapter 2—"Capitalizing on Global Entertainment Media"—examines how capitalism shapes the existence of entertainment media, and looks at some current developments in the political-economy of global entertainment media. The first part of the chapter discusses the roles and goals of the major corporate stakeholders in the entertainment industry (producers, financiers, distributors, marketers, and exhibitors), highlights the unique characteristics of entertainment media commodities, examines the tension between competitive and concentrated, centralized, and controlled global entertainment markets, and describes horizontal and vertical integration strategies and synergistic entertainment media. The second part of the chapter examines the transnational political-economy of entertainment media. After distinguishing between positional and behavioral approaches to corporate power and discussing some of the features of national media corporations (NMCs) and transnational media corporations (TNMCs), I discuss the rise of "strategic alliances" between NMCs and TNMCs in the form of joint ventures, equity alliances, and licensing agreements. This chapter addresses several questions, including: what is capitalism? Who are the major corporate stakeholders in the entertainment industry? What makes TV and film commodities distinct from microwave ovens? What is the difference between a TNMC and an NMC? Which TNMCs control the lion's share of global entertainment media? What are vertical integration and horizontal integration, and how do convergent media strategies enable media corporations to profit-maximize? Does US cultural imperialism exist? An understanding of how the forces and relations of the capitalist mode of production influence global entertainment media is foundational knowledge in global media studies.

Chapter 3—"Governing Global Entertainment: The State, Media Policy, and Regulation"—examines how states govern the conduct of NMCs and TNMCs, and how they influence the bordered and cross-border production, distribution, exhibition, and consumption of TV shows and films. This chapter attends to the convergences and divergences of the de-territorializing goals of media corporations and the territorializing goals of states. By examining how state media policies and regulations influence media markets, this chapter challenges the view that global entertainment media flourishes above territorial governance. After defining media policy and regulation, this chapter examines liberal pluralist and power elite theories of the state and media policy-making processes. It then describes the main goals of media policy/regulation (nation-making, national culture/creative industry development, and "market failure" mitigation), examines the main areas of state intervention into the economy which influence the conduct of media corporations (intellectual property/ copyright, ownership, concentration/competition, content subsidization, content quotas, licensing, and censorship), and explores the key prescriptions of neoliberal media policy (liberalization, deregulation, and privatization) and global media governance. This chapter addresses questions such as: what is the state? What is media policy? What are the general purposes of media policy? On whose behalf is media policy made? What is the relationship between states and media corporations? What are the specific areas of media policy and regulation that govern entertainment? What is neoliberalism? Does the economic and cultural dominance of US-based TNMCs need to be curtailed in order for non-US media industries and cultures to flourish? The chapter conveys foundational knowledge about how politics influence global entertainment media.

Chapter 4—"Producing Entertainment Media in the New International Division of Cultural Labor"—examines the cross-border production of entertainment media by state and corporate actors in country-specific "media capitals." By engaging with and updating path-breaking scholarship on "global Hollywood," the chapter moves beyond the view that global entertainment media is produced by an essentially "American" industry, located in the US, owned by US businesspeople, and staffed by a predominantly US workforce. A new transnational space of entertainment production called the New International Division of Cultural Labor (NICL) has emerged (Miller et al. 2005). Film and TV commodities are assembled on a transnational (as opposed to "national") scale within local, regional, and national production zones. This chapter describes the general features of the NICL and then examines two important forms of cross-border entertainment production: the "runaway production" and the "international co-production." This chapter addresses questions including: which economic and political actors coordinate and control the NICL? Does the NICL destabilize or consolidate asymmetrical power relations between media capitals? Why are TV and film production companies moving from Los Angeles, California, to cities around the world? Which factors shape the offshoring and outsourcing of media production tasks? Do runaway productions and international co-productions help or hinder the development of national media industries and place-specific representations? What policies do states employ to attract runaway productions and participate in international co-productions? What are the benefits and costs of doing so? This chapter entails foundational knowledge in the study of cross-border entertainment production.

Chapter 5—"Designing Global Entertainment Media: Blockbuster Films, TV Formats, and Glocalized Lifestyle Brands"—examines the textual features of entertainment products that have been designed to travel across borders. To understand why certain TV shows and films are globally and transnationally popular, this chapter focuses on the business, textual encoding, and audience-targeting strategies of TNMCs. TNMCs strive to overcome the "cultural discount" by designing globally popular entertainment while simultaneously capitalizing on "cultural proximity" by designing TV shows and films for target audiences. Three forms of globally popular entertainment are analyzed: 1) blockbuster event films; 2) global-national TV formats; and 3) glocalized lifestyle brands. This chapter also examines "reverse entertainment flows" and the business and textual strategies used by non-US NMCs to get their TV shows and films exhibited in the US market. Questions addressed in this chapter include: what is the cultural discount? What is cultural proximity? What makes a specific entertainment text globally popular? Why might viewers in many different countries enjoy the same TV shows and films? What is a blockbuster event film? What is a global-national TV format? What is glocalization? Why are some films and TV shows so mobile? How do non-US NMCs break into the US market? This chapter provides foundational knowledge about the economics and texts of globally popular entertainment media.

Chapter 6—"Global Entertainment Media, Local Audiences"—explores five figures of the local audience for global entertainment media. In particular, the chapter analyzes neoliberalism's representation of the audience as a sovereign consumer, political-economy's representation of the audience as a commodity, cultivation and effects research on the audience as a cultural victim of Americanization and consumer-capitalist ideology; Cultural Studies research on the youthful audience as an active meaning-maker, identifier, and hybridizer of global TV shows and films, and New Media Studies' interactive prosumer. This chapter explores key issues within global media audience and cross-cultural reception studies apropos paradigm debates between

CI and CG scholars. Questions addressed in this chapter include: what is consumer sovereignty? Does consumer demand for entertainment media drive its production? What is the audience commodity? How is viewer attention sold to advertising corporations by TNMCs? What is branded entertainment? Does the transnational flow of entertainment cultivate pro- or anti-American sentiment? What are the effects of global entertainment media on the beliefs, ideas, and behaviors of viewers? Do local viewers uncritically internalize entertainment messages in predictable ways? Do the messages carried by globalizing entertainment media mean the same thing to everyone, everywhere? Does the global flow of entertainment media necessarily have negative local effects, or can media consumption be empowering? Have Web 2.0 and new media revolutionized the audience experience? This chapter presents the basics of global audience studies.

The concluding chapter—"Global Media Studies Between Cultural Imperialism and Cultural Globalization"—sums up the main points of the book and synthesizes the most salient features of the CI and CG paradigms.

CHAPTER 1

Paradigms of Global Entertainment Media

INTRODUCTION: GEORGE LUCAS ATTACKS US CULTURAL IMPERIALISM, PHILLIPPE LEGRAIN DEFENDS IT

On March 24, 2006, the *Sydney Morning Herald* ran a story entitled "George Lucas attacks US cultural imperialism." After receiving the Global Vision Award from the World Affairs Council in San Francisco, Lucas reportedly declared: "As long as there has been a talking Hollywood, Hollywood has had a huge impact on the rest of the world." Also, Lucas said the content of entertainment media, as it moves from the US to the world, shows:

> all the morality we [US citizens] espouse in this country, good and bad. [. . .] People see shows such as *Dallas*, about a wealthy Texas oil family, and decide they want the grand lifestyles portrayed [. . .]. They say this is what I want to be [. . .] That destabilizes a lot of the world. (AFP 2006)

For Lucas, globalizing Hollywood films and TV shows carry representations of America to the rest of the world, and he views the export of US entertainment as detrimental to the viewers on the receiving end of the flow. Globalizing US entertainment media exacerbates "a conflict going on for thousands of years between the haves and the have-nots" and shows "the have-nots what they do not have" (AFP 2006). Entertainment products "destabilize" non-US cultures by showing them a standard of living and style of life that they do not enjoy, possibly leading them to feel resentment or a desire to be like and live like "Americans." With no sense of irony or contradiction, Lucas bemoans the negative effects of US cultural imperialism while his *Star Wars* franchise (six global blockbuster films that rank among the top 100 highest grossing worldwide box office films of all time, video games, fast-food tie-ins, toys, clothing, board games, and remakes) travels the world. His attack on US cultural imperialism buttresses his liberal public image while downplaying the fact that Lucas is himself a beneficiary of this process.

In the summer of 2003, *The International Economy* magazine published an article by Phillippe Legrain called "In Defense of Globalization." Legrain, a special advisor to the World Trade Organization (WTO) and director of policy for the business lobby group Britain in Europe, views the cross-border flow of entertainment media differently than Lucas. While Lucas calls the US's export of entertainment media "cultural imperialism," Legrain refers to this process as "globalization," rejecting "fears that globalization is imposing a deadening uniformity" and the view that "local cultures and national identities are dissolving into a crass all-American consumerism" (Legrain 2003: 62). He says that globalization supports "an explosion of cultural exchange," and that "cross-fertilization is overwhelmingly a force for good" (62). Legrain believes that globalization is benign: it "frees people from the tyranny of geography" (62), "increases individual freedom" (62), "revitalizes cultures and cultural artifacts through foreign influences, technologies and markets" (62), enables "Cross-border cultural exchange" (64), and allows individuals to form "new communities, linked by shared interests and passions" (65) which fragment national cultures into "a kaleidoscope of different ones." He challenges the "myth that globalization involves the imposition of Americanized uniformity" (62) by claiming that "America is an outlier, not a global leader" (63), that "globalization is not a one-way street" (63), and that globalization enables "New hybrid cultures" to emerge. For Legrain, globalization is not US cultural imperialism in disguise or based upon unequal and asymmetrical economic and cultural power relations, but a force for good.

Lucas and Legrain hold very different views on the cross-border movement of US entertainment media. One assumes it is a destabilizing force of Americanization and cultural homogenization; the other views it as an empowering force of cultural exchange and diversity. Lucas and Legrain's comments reflect two of the most influential paradigms in the study of global entertainment media: cultural imperialism (CI) and cultural globalization (CG). A "paradigm" is a particular lens for looking at the world. Like Lucas and Legrain, scholars look at the world in which they live through different paradigms. A paradigm is a "generally accepted example" of an object or a process in the world, based on specific principles, implied empirical constants, and normative viewpoints (Fourie 2010: 18). No single paradigm provides a perfect vision of the world. Lucas's claim that the cross-border movement of entertainment is a destabilizing cultural force may be correct in some local reception contexts, but not all of them. Legrain's claim that the global spread of entertainment media leads to greater individual freedom, cultural exchange, and hybrid cultures may apply in some instances, but not in every one. Paradigms provide us with an "ideal type" construction of reality. A global entertainment media paradigm can be supported, contested, or modified by scholars through research and analysis.

This chapter contextualizes and reviews the claims and counter-claims of the CI and CG paradigms. At present, CI and CG are used by journalists, policy-makers, and scholars to describe a number of different processes and effects associated with the transnational or cross-border movement of entertainment media. Many diverse and varied meanings—connotative and denotative—flow from the signs of CI and CG. This chapter presents these meanings as integral parts of larger, contested discourses about the set of processes and effects associated with the cross-border movement of entertainment media. Following Hall (1996b), a "discourse" is (in the most general sense) a group of statements, produced by different institutions, agents, and groups, which provide a language for talking about—or a way of representing—a particular kind of knowledge about a topic, thing, or process (201). The CI and CG paradigms encourage different ways of talking about, making claims about, and representing the cross-border movement of entertainment media. An understanding of the history, claims, and critiques of the CI and CG paradigms is foundational knowledge in global media studies. This chapter contextualizes these paradigms and describes their key claims, criticisms, and continued influence.

CULTURAL IMPERIALISM (CI)

The CI paradigm in global media studies focuses on communication and media entertainment as an instrument of one nation-state's economic, geopolitical, and cultural power over others.

In the late 1960s and throughout the 1970s, critical communication and media studies scholars in the postcolonial states, the US, Canada, the UK, and elsewhere developed the concept of CI to examine the role that globalizing and corporate-controlled communication and electronic media systems played in establishing and maintaining unequal economic and cultural power relationships between imperial cores and peripheries, the global North and the global South, the rich and the poor countries. CI scholars argued that the structure of the world system was rigged to serve the geopolitical, economic, and cultural interests of wealthy developed states at the expense of poor underdeveloped ones (Boyd-Barrett 1977; Dorfmann and Mattelart 1975; Golding 1977; Hamelink 1983; Mattelart 1979; Murdock and Golding 1977; Schiller 1969, 1976; Smythe 1981; Tunstall 1977). These CI scholars were among the first within US and Western academia to critically examine how media corporations and their products could extend and reinforce unequal power relations between the US and others: not only between the US and poorer countries, but also between the US and wealthy Anglo-European states.

At present, "cultural imperialism" is a term used to refer to many different processes and effects: the building of a Wal-Mart store beside Aztec Ruins in Mexico (McKinley 2004); Starbucks' market competition with Taiwanese teahouses (Huang 2002); the spread of American-English, which causes "global language death" (Phillipson 2003); and the globalization of US Fordist mass production models (and the instrumental rationalities of McDonalds fast-food chains) (Ritzer 2002). Cultural imperialism can be criticized for its lack of a clear and singular definition (Fejes 1981). Sometimes, cultural imperialism is a cover for anti-American rhetoric. Beltran (1978) noted long ago how some critics of cultural imperialism take "recourse to slogans—catchphrases, mottos—which encapsulate their positions, serving them as quick and handy weapons" that "function as agents of emotion and dogmatic preconception, banning sensible dialogue in favor of aggressive monologue" (183). Despite these quibbles, it is possible to distill the key claims of a CI paradigm from the work of the radical political-economists of communication and the critical media scholars responsible for it (Beltran 1978; Boyd-Barrett 1977, 1998; Mattelart 1979; McPhail 1987; Schiller 1969; 1976; Tunstall 1977).

What is cultural imperialism? In the following, I contextualize the CI paradigm with reference to the economic, geopolitical, and cultural conditions of its making. I then review its main claims.

World Systems, Neo-Colonialism and Dependency Theory

Throughout the 1960s and 1970s, scholars from postcolonial states in the global South developed theories of the world system, imperialism/neocolonialism, and dependency. They gave ideological support to national liberation struggles in postcolonial states and challenged modernization theory's view that poor countries would "develop" automatically by embracing US and Western capitalist models (Amin 1977; Frank 1969, 1970, 1972, 1978, 1980; Nkrumah 1965; Wallerstein 1961, 1975, 1979). These theories were integral to the formation of the CI paradigm in communication and media studies.

Immanuel Wallerstein (1974) developed "world systems theory" to examine capitalism's uneven geographical development, the rise, fall, and rivalries between different empires, the international division of labor, and racial, sexual, and class oppressions and inequalities between and within nation-states. According to Wallerstein (1974), the world system consists of three zones: the core, the semi-periphery, and the periphery. The core state and its corporations rule the world system, serving their own geopolitical and economic interests at the expense of the semi-peripheral and peripheral zones. These zones are not static, but shifting. Nevertheless, in every period, a core state exists and benefits economically and politically from an unequal and exploitative exchange relationship with semi-peripheral and peripheral states. Between 1500 and 1800, the first truly world system of capitalist market relationships was established by Western colonial states—Portugal, Spain, Holland, and later, France and England. "Empire" was a Western state policy, practice, and ideology. Core states organized the world system to serve their own economic and geopolitical interests. During this period, imperialism was the extension of one state's sovereignty over a territory beyond its borders, or colonization. Settler colonies entailed the mass immigration and settlement of populations. Exploitation colonies were established for the sole purpose of resource extraction and exploitation, but without large-scale population settlement. On behalf of industrialists, core imperial states conquered and controlled colonial peripheries to produce a system of unequal and exploitative relations that benefitted them. The colonized existed solely for the benefit of the imperial countries. According to world systems theorists, the "development" of imperial cores—Spain, Portugal, the Netherlands, France, and England—relied upon the "underdevelopment" of the colonized peripheries (Rodney 1981).

Following World War II, the old European empires began to crumble. The world system's center of gravity shifted from Europe to the US, which became a new kind of postcolonial empire that ruled markets through sovereign states. In his 1952 essay "Great Britain, The United States, and Canada," Harold Innis (1995) presciently stated that the US empire was "made plausible and attractive in part by the insistence that it was not imperialistic" (283) and warned against "the threat of Americanization" (287). The US emerged from World War II as the indisputable economic, political, and military superpower, locked into rivalry with the ominous, yet slightly less powerful, Soviet Union. While both the US and Soviet empires sought to influence world affairs, the United States had greater capacity to do so. Following World War II, the US was the world's economic dynamo. It established the General Agreement on Tariffs and Trade (GATT), the International Monetary Fund (IMF) and International Bank for Reconstruction and Development, pegged international currency to the US dollar, and held the biggest share of gold. American industrial and financial corporations dominated world markets. In addition to being an economic powerhouse, following World War II the US became a military juggernaut: the national security state grew, the US arsenal and military bases expanded, and the North Atlantic Treaty Organization (NATO) put the US defense establishment in charge of international security. The US established the Marshall Plan and the Act for International Development in order to rebuild Western Europe, whilst also aiding decolonizing regions to modernize along US-sanctioned developmental lines. The NSC-68 doctrine outlined the general objective of US foreign policy for the second half of the twentieth century: to actively extend and defend US-style liberal democratic capitalist developments and to defeat the Soviet Union and all associated socialist developments. From 1945 to 1991, the Cold War was fought by the two superpowers and their proxy states in a series of small "hot wars" in postcolonial countries.

During the Cold War, the colonial empires of Western Europe were falling, but the achievement of state sovereignty by formerly colonized peoples did not mitigate the unequal economic and political relations between the rich core countries and the poor peripheries. A new "neo-colonial" relationship between the US and other states was emerging. In *Neo-Colonialism: The Last Stage of Imperialism*, Ghana's socialist leader Kwame Nkrumah (1965) observed that "the essence of neo-colonialism is that the State which is subject to it is, in theory, independent and has all the outward trappings of international sovereignty. In reality, its economic system and thus political policy is directed from outside" (ix). Nkrumah said that postcolonial states gained sovereignty after ousting the Western colonial powers but, nevertheless, they remained subject to the military oversight and aid, political meddling and influence, and economic exploitation of corporations of the former colonialist and new imperial powers. Neo-colonialism referred to a new US-led form of de-territorialized economic rule through formally sovereign postcolonial states. The US and Western states promoted the profit-interests of their corporations within postcolonial countries and were supported by a local comprador class. An unequal neo-colonial relationship was facilitated by outwardly "sovereign" states.

Dependency theorists built upon critical studies of neocolonialism. They argued that the embrace of capitalist modernization by postcolonial states in Latin America, Asia, Africa, and the Middle East was not initiating their rapid economic and social "development," but was instead exacerbating their "underdevelopment" (Amin 1974, 1977, 1988; Cardoso and Faletto 1979; Frank 1969; Furtado 1964; Smythe 1981). The US Marxist Paul Baran (1957) argued that the impoverishment of postcolonial countries had little to do with traditional personality types or backwards infrastructure. For economic development to occur in poor countries, the bulk of the surplus generated through business transactions would need to be re-invested into the local economy to benefit local businesses and populations. But this was not happening. Instead, the profit generated was being absorbed by US and Western multinational corporations or hoarded by self-serving comprador elites. US and Western modernization was not aiding the development of poor countries, but was instead reproducing an unequal relationship in which postcolonial states remained in subordinate positions vis-à-vis the world system's old Anglo-European powers. The development of the core relied upon the "underdevelopment" of the peripheries. The enrichment of a few nation-states was based upon the poverty of the many (Young 2001: 51). As Frank (1972) argued, "the expansion and development of capitalism throughout the world has simultaneously generated—and continues to generate—both economic development and structural underdevelopment" (9). To escape the "development of underdevelopment," many autocratic leaders tried to de-link from the world system's power centers and pursue self-reliant development. Their attempts to cut their ties with formerly colonialist and neo-colonial states met with little success.

Theories of the capitalist world system, neo-colonialism, and dependency were taken a priori by many CI scholars, who sought to understand how communication technology and media were central to the growth, power, and administration of empires, past and present. Schiller (1976) thus defined CI as broadly being "the sum processes by which a society is brought into the modern world system and how its dominating stratum is attracted, pressured, forced, and sometimes bribed into shaping social institutions to correspond to, or even promote, the values and structures of the dominating center of the system" (9). According to Schiller, US communication and media corporations were the US empire's Trojan horse. They entered postcolonial countries, and then integrated them into the center of US geopolitical, economic, and cultural power. For Schiller, US media corporations established a networked technological infrastructure for US financial investment and transnational commodity production, distribution, and marketing while US commercial entertainment products ideologically reinforced this process by transmitting "in their imagery and messagery, the beliefs and perspectives that create and reinforce their audiences' attachments to the way things are in the system overall" (30). A number of scholars contributed to critical work on cultural imperialism by developing definitions of their own.

Some political-economists felt that Schiller's broad definition of "cultural imperialism" lacked methodological and conceptual precision, and so they developed the more narrow concept of "media imperialism" (Murdock and Golding 1977; Tunstall 1977) to focus upon the political-economy of media industries in a world system. Boyd-Barrett (1977) described media imperialism as:

> a process whereby the ownership, structure, distribution or content of the media in any one country are singly or together subject to substantial pressure from the media interests of any other country or countries without proportionate reciprocation of influence by the country so affected. (117)

Boyd-Barrett's media imperialism concept enables the comparative study of media industry relations between two or more countries. It attends to the pressure that US media corporations put on the media systems of postcolonial countries, the unequal exchange of communication technology and media products between the US and other countries, the adoption of the US commercial media model, the diffusion of US business, managerial, and professional norms and values, and the modeling of local news and entertainment media on commercial forms originating in the US. Boyd-Barrett (1998) later reformulated the concept of media imperialism to mean the "colonization of communications space" during "periods in which access to or control of any dimension of media activity is controlled by any one nation or group at the expense of others" (163). Cultural and media imperialism scholars present historicist, political-economic, and policy-oriented analyses of the non-reciprocal and imbalanced flow of entertainment media between countries.

THE CLAIMS OF THE CULTURAL IMPERIALISM PARADIGM

The CI paradigm is associated with the following claims about the cross-border movement of media and the nature of the world system in which TV shows and films circulate.

First, the CI paradigm views cultural imperialism as part and product of imperialism. As Beltran (1978) says:

> It is logical to expect a nation exerting economic and political influence over other countries to exert a cultural influence as well. When the influence is reciprocal with those of such countries, the case is one of balanced, legitimate and desirable intercultural exchange. But when the culture of a central and dominant country is unilaterally imposed over the peripheral countries it dominates at the expense of their cultural integrity, then the case is one of cultural imperialism. (185)

Here, cultural imperialism is a by product of Western and US imperialism, a corollary of the economic, military, and technical growth and dominance of empires, old and new. While Great Britain ruled the world communication system during the nineteenth and early twentieth century, by the end of World War II, the US was the new communication superpower. "The old communication system centered on London, which had served Great Britain well for seventy years, began to disintegrate along with the empire it had served" (Headrick 1991: 267). Over the course of World War II, the US broke away from the British telecommunications monopoly; Hollywood dominated the international film trade; US radio broadcasters built a domestic TV industry that would soon go global; and US news corporations started to rule world news services (Headrick 1991; Hills 2002).

Observing these trends, Schiller (1969) analyzed the centrality of communications technology and media industries to the burgeoning US empire: "American power, expressed industrially, militarily and culturally has become the most potent force on earth and communications have become a decisive element in the extension of United States world power" (206–207). Schiller also argued that "each new electronic development widens the perimeter of American influence, and the indivisibility of military and commercial activity operates to promote even greater expansion" (80). In the contemporary era, Schiller's view of US empire and communications may seem controversial. But during World War II, this view was "common sense" to influential US media moguls. In a 1944 *Life* article entitled "World Communications," Henry Luce emphasized the centrality of communications technology and media to US imperial power: "Upon their [communications systems] efficiency depends whether the United States will grow in the future, as Great Britain has in the past, as a centre of world thought and trade" (cited in Schiller 1992: 45). Even in the mid-1990s, US foreign policy elites praised US media dominance. In his article "In Praise of Cultural Imperialism?," David Rothkopf, former managing director at Kissinger Associates, declared that the US is the indispensable nation-state in the management of global affairs and, as such, should actively globalize liberal capitalist democracy and multiculturalism in order to overcome a possible "clash of civilizations" between Western and Eastern cultures. To achieve this goal, the US state was to join forces with US media corporations to "win the battle of the world's information flows, dominating the airwaves as Great Britain once ruled the seas" (1). Rothkopf continued: "just as the United States is the world's sole remaining military superpower, so is it the world's only information superpower" (5). In sum, a major claim of the CI paradigm is that cultural imperialism is part and product of the US empire and capitalist imperialism.

Second, the CI paradigm represents the world system as comprising a strong or "dominant" media center (the US) and much weaker or "dominated" peripheries (non-US countries). What happens in the US media center—i.e., what the US-based TNMCs and US nation-state do—influences what happens everywhere else. As the center of the world system's media production, distribution, and marketing, the US has long been home to the world's most powerful media corporations. In the post-World War II era, military-industrial communication corporations dominated transnational technology production and distribution, while the Hollywood studios and the Big Three TV networks (CBS, NBC, and ABC) ruled the world's entertainment flow. Throughout the 1960s and 1970s, US media corporations entered countries in Latin America, Asia, Africa, and the Middle East. The US-based Radio Corporation of America (RCA) and the National Broadcasting Company (NBC) sold technology to state and private TV networks in Latin America, Africa (particularly Nigeria and Egypt), Syria, and Saudi Arabia (Segrave 1997). Also, supported by the US state, US media companies trained media executives, managers, and personnel in the running of postcolonial media firms. Nigeria's first TV network, for example, was built with the assistance of NBC. A Nigerian TV producer spent four months in the United States on a state department-sponsored tour (Segrave 1998: 34). US media corporations established themselves in postcolonial states through the "institutionalization of the cultural industries in those countries" (Jin 2007: 768). This enabled them to exert economic and cultural influence within postcolonial states through their national media systems.

Third, the CI paradigm says that audio-visual trade between rich and poor countries is not reciprocal, and that the US is the central and most influential source of entertainment media worldwide. Cultural imperialism is defined by a largely one-way or uni-directional flow of media entertainment from the US to the rest of the world. Most entertainment media travels from "North" to "South" and from "West" to "East" without much of a diverse counter-flow or reciprocal exchange (Nordenstreng and Varis 1974; Varis 1984). Many countries import US entertainment media, but the US does not import many TV shows and films made elsewhere. In an important study of this imbalance, Varis (1984) found that in Africa, 40 percent of TV programs were imported, with 50 percent of those imports coming from the US. A largely one-way media flow between the US and other countries is caused by a number of factors. Following World War II, many countries established TV networks but lacked TV and film production studios, a large cultural working class (scriptwriters, directors, actors, technicians), and means of financing the production and distribution of national entertainment (Boyd 1984). Non-US media executives needed to fill their schedules with content, and the US industry had a lot of it to offer and at a low cost. After recouping production costs and turning a profit by selling to the home market, US media firms slashed prices for the world market. They sold TV shows to

US networks as part of an exclusive first run deal, sold them as re-runs to local affiliates of the big TV networks, and then sold them to non-US networks at a discounted price. American TV shows typically cost non-US TV networks between one-quarter to one-tenth of the cost of making their own TV shows (Feigenbaum 1996). In 1974, *Variety* estimated that a US TV program shown on a Hong Kong TV network cost between $60 and $75; in Costa Rica, between $35 and $45, and in Kuwait, between $60 and $90. In 1981, a Philippines TV network could import a 13-part US TV series for $2,500, whereas a locally produced TV series that ran for the same time would cost $10,400 (Boyd 1984). Schiller (1969) noted that the US could sell a TV show to a UK broadcaster for $4,200, yet sell the same TV show to a Kenyan TV broadcaster for $22. By slashing prices, US media corporations gave non-US TV networks an incentive to license entertainment media from them instead of producing their own content. This undercut the development of strong TV and film production sectors outside of the US and contributed to the one-way flow. Hence, Ogan (1988) described media imperialism as:

> a process whereby the United States firms [. . .] produce most of the media products, make the first profits from domestic sales, and then market the products in Third World countries at costs considerably lower than those the countries would have to bear to produce similar products at home. (94)

Fourth, the CI paradigm states that the global expansion of the US media industry relies on the universalization of the capitalist media model and the dismantling of publicly owned media systems. Schiller (1969) was a proponent of national public broadcasting. He believed that both US citizens and the citizens of postcolonial states were under-served by the commercial media model, and that an informed and critical-thinking citizenry was both a prerequisite for a functioning democracy and a force of progressive change in all societies. He argued that a public broadcasting model organized to support values of national education, information, and citizenship—as opposed to mass consumerism—would benefit US and non-US citizens alike. Schiller (1969) believed that a public media system, not a commercial one, was the most conducive to democracy. This public choice rested upon "the willingness and ability of scores of weak countries to forego the cellophane-wrapped articles of the West's entertainment industries and persistently, to develop, however much time it takes, their own broadcast material" (Schiller 1969: 122). Schiller viewed the US commercial model as a threat to public broadcasting, democracy, an informed and engaged citizenry, and cultural sovereignty.

Fifth, the CI paradigm claims that the universalization of the commercial media model and the growth of media corporations are *structurally functional* to the spread of, and the ideological legitimization of, capitalism. Following World War II, US industrial corporations saw the global expansion of US media corporations as crucial to the growth of new markets. Entertainment media—advertising-supported commercial TV, in particular—manufactured the desire for commodities while showcasing the American "consumer way of life" to the world. As vice president of ABC International Donald Coyle said:

> It is highly desirable from the standpoint of the economies of these [postcolonial] countries themselves that television be brought in—so that it can fulfill its natural function as a giant pump fuelling the machine of consumer demand, stepping up the flow of goods and services to keep the economy expanding. We have learned that television, through its sight, sound and motion, creates the emotion to buy. [. . .] By doing this, television opens new markets. New and better products, designed to meet new needs, creates wider prosperity. Television advertising not only lubricates the wheels of the economy, but actually adds new wheels and generates the energy to make them run.
> (cited in Segrave 1998: 11)

For Coyle (and CI scholars), the global entrenchment of the US commercial media model helps US industrial corporations avert a crisis of profitability by stimulating and maintaining transnational consumer demand. Globalizing entertainment media sells consumer-capitalism as a "way of life" to people everywhere. TV shows and films help US corporations expand their markets across national boundaries and "facilitate the flow of consumer images to help organize the aspirations of potential customers around the globe" (Curtin 1993).

Sixth, the CI paradigm says that the US government actively supports the dominance of US media corporations, the expansion of the US corporate media model, and the cross-border flow of entertainment media by means of a foreign media policy called the "free flow of information doctrine" (Schiller 1969: 3). Proponents of the free flow doctrine argue that all national media systems should be open and run on a commercial basis. State broadcasters are to be opposed, as are barriers to the cross-border flow of information. In state-corporate rhetoric following World War II, the "free flow of information" was represented as a means of building a free, democratic, and peaceful world order based on cultural pluralism and exchange (Rosenberg 1984: 215). In practice, the free flow doctrine was employed to make the US corporate media system appear to be the most free and most democratic, while framing those that did not emulate the US model as un-free and un-democratic. Furthermore, the free flow doctrine "championed the rights of media proprietors to sell wherever and whatever they wished" (Thussu 2006: 55–56). By the mid-1980s, this had become an argument for the "free trade" in audio-visual products (Comor 1997). The US government saw the free flow of US media as a means of ideological influence too. In support of this point, Schiller (1969) quotes a 1967 paper published by a US Congressional Committee: "Winning the Cold War: The American Ideological Offensive."

Seventh, the CI paradigm states that the content of US corporate and/or state-produced entertainment represents American nationalist and/or consumerist-capitalist ideologies. CI scholars say US ownership of the media and the production of TV shows and films for the US territorial market results in entertainment content that idealizes and glorifies "The American Way of Life." Exported abroad, such entertainment is an agent of Americanization. CI scholars also argue that most TV shows and films communicate a consumer-capitalist ideology. Schiller (1979), for example, claims that globalizing US media products represent:

what has come to be recognized [. . .] as the capitalist road to development. [. . .] the media [. . .] are the means that entice and instruct their audiences along this path while concealing the deeper reality and the long term consequences that the course produces. (31)

Schiller (1969) also notes that commercial media "material from the United States offers a vision of a way of life [. . .] The imagery envelops all viewers and listeners within the range of electronic impulses patterned after the American [capitalist] model" (3). Many CI scholars believe that globalizing TV shows and films promote "America" and American consumer-capitalist ideology, advertise consumer goods and services, and glorify consumer lifestyles. Schiller (1976) recognized how US media firms glocalized or adapted TV shows to the cultural preferences of different audiences, but noted that, overall, "the content and style of the programming, *however adapted to local conditions*, bear the ideological imprint of the main centers of the capitalist world economy" (10).

Eighth, the CI paradigm claims that entertainment media is a means by which the strong states and the corporations headquartered in them (in this context, the US and US-based media corporations) influence, change, or erode the local cultures of other, weaker states. Strong imperial states use TV shows and films as instruments of power in world affairs. In some instances, CI scholars view US entertainment media as a tool for coercively imposing foreign (American) or corrosive (consumer-capitalist) values upon non-US cultures. Beltran (1978), for example, defines cultural imperialism as "a process of social influence by which a nation *imposes* on other countries its set beliefs, values, knowledge and behavioral norms as well as its overall style of life" (184). CI scholars worry that globalizing US TV shows and films subvert or threaten national and local cultures. They are concerned that entertainment media acts as an agent of cultural diffusion and is bringing about the cultural Americanization or homogenization of the world. Cultural diversity and difference are the casualties of cultural imperialism, and CI scholars argue that the spread of US capitalist media models and US commercial entertainment make the world increasingly similar and "synchronized." Hamelink (1983), for example, claims that:

In the second half of the twentieth century, a destructive process [. . .] threatens the diversity of cultural systems. Never before has the *synchronization* with one particular cultural pattern been of such global dimensions and so comprehensive. (4)

BOX 1.1

HOW TO READ DONALD DUCK

An interesting study of the consumer-capitalist ideology communicated by US entertainment media is Dorfman and Mattelart's (1975) *How to Read Donald Duck: Imperialist Ideology in the Disney Text*. This text needs to be read in relation to its historical and political context.

BOX 1.1 (Continued)

In the early 1970s, Chile, a country whose economy was ruled by US corporations and whose state was influenced by the US for many years, underwent a socialist revolution. The US state and US media corporations supported counter-revolutionary ideological operations in Chile. In response to the near presidential victory of Salvador Allende (a socialist), the CIA began supporting local political movements and cultural organizations committed to undermining socialist sentiments (Blum 2004: 207–208). Nevertheless, by 1970, Salvador Allende's socialist Popular Unity Government prevailed over the US-backed political opposition and was democratically elected by a slim majority of Chileans. Three years later, (September 11, 1973), Allende was un-democratically deposed in a CIA-backed coup led by the Chilean dictator General Pinochet. Tens of thousands of Chilean socialists and political opponents of Pinochet were murdered as a result (Blum 2004). During its short-lived revolutionary period, Allende's Popular Unity Government attempted to counter the ideological effects of what was widely perceived by locals as US cultural imperialism. Until 1970, Chile's most popular TV network imported half of its content from the US; without the capacity to develop an indigenous cinema, more than 80 percent of its films were imported from the US; the major Chilean newspapers and magazines were owned by US Pepsi-Cola president, Agustín Edwards Eastman; the leading daily, *El Mercurio*, was funded by the CIA as part of its anti-socialist cultural front (Kombluh 2003; Kunzle 1991:12). Against these forces, the Popular Unity Government developed a national publication house called Quimantu, which became part of a socialist cultural counter-offensive. Pinochet's military coup, however, destroyed nearly all traces of Chile's revolutionary culture. Many of Chile's cultural producers—artists, intellectuals, authors—were jailed, killed, or forced into exile. Ariel Dorfman and Armand Mattelart, the authors of *How to Read Donald Duck: Imperialist Ideology in the Disney Text* (1971), survived.

In their book, Dorfman and Mattelart examine how Disney comic books communicate neo-colonialist ideologies. The authors argue that Disney narratives represent pro-business, pro-individualist, pro-consumer-capitalist ideologies which conflicted with Chile's burgeoning socialist values of egalitarianism, democracy, and collectivism. Disney comic narratives, like those found in so many European colonial discourses, constructed non-American countries as exotic or backward paradises inhabited by dumb, ugly, inferior, or criminal indigenous people (Kunzle 1991: 17). *How to Read Donald Duck* linked the exploitative conditions of Disney comic-book production within the company's metropolitan animation factories to the ideological effects of consuming these commodities in postcolonial states. For Dorfman and Mattelart, Chilean consumers and Disney's cultural workers had a common class interest in confronting their shared oppressor: the Walt Disney Corporation. During the coup, Dorfmann and Mattelart were exiled. *How to Read Donald Duck* was quickly banned by Pinochet. The book is perhaps the first lengthy postcolonial Marxist critique of US imperialist ideology in global entertainment media. It is a counter-hegemonic text that not only speaks back to the objective conditions of US state and corporate ideological warfare, but also attempts to articulate an alternative to US economic and political expansion in the form of democratic socialism.

Ninth, the CI paradigm claims that US entertainment media has "effects" upon local audiences and that these effects are negative. Some CI scholars present the local viewers of imported US entertainment as a bunch of passive consumers that are forced to consume foreign TV shows and films. Critics of cultural imperialism—cultural nationalists, religious groups, state policy-makers—worry about the psychological and cultural consequences of entertainment media in local reception contexts. The advertising which accompanies media entertainment indoctrinates people with false consumerist wants for products they do not need. When juxtaposed with the real conditions of poverty and class inequality that limit opportunities, entertainment's images of affluent consumerist lifestyles and permanent upward mobility cultivate mass angst and resentment. Globalizing entertainment media leads elite upper-class groups in poor countries to align themselves with the US and the West at the expense of their own cultures and the needs of the populations they are responsible for governing. At the same time, globalizing entertainment encourages working-class people to judge themselves and their own cultures according to foreign ideals, reject the culture they were born into, and aspire to be part of a another nation.

Schiller (1976) believes that US media corporations are ideologically influential and powerful, but does not depict all local viewers as passive, helpless, gullible, or apolitical dupes. He says that humans possess the agency to think critically about the world in which they live. Schiller (1989) also challenged the "hypodermic syringe" model of media effects: "The transfer of cultural values is a complex matter. It is not a one-shot hypodermic inoculation of individual plots and character representations" (149). He (1976) also wrote: "Audiences do, in fact, interpret messages variously. They may also transform them to correspond with their individual experiences and tastes" (155). He did not dispute the fact that people actively interpret globalizing media texts, he simply sought to balance an account of the interpretive power of viewers with an understanding of the structural power of media corporations. Schiller (1976) even hoped that global media influence might foster a critical consciousness and "arouse those who are now dominated to increase their efforts at resistance and to extend the area of conflict to a more visible arena" (76). However, Schiller did not believe that the power of consumers to make specific TV show and film texts meaningful in their own ways was tantamount to "resisting" transnational corporate power and the system which supported it. His (1991) response to his critics is worth recalling:

> There is much to be said for the idea that people do not mindlessly absorb everything that passes before their eyes. Yet much of the current work on audience reception comes uncomfortably close to being apologetics for present-day structures of cultural control. (25)

Schiller did not reject the idea of viewer agency; instead, he contextualized the agency of viewers and the political efficacy of their meaning-making practices in relation to broader structural determinations.

Tenth, the CI paradigm is postcolonial. Young (2001) presents a masterful consideration of how critical concepts travel, particularly those concepts now identified with postcolonialism, which developed "dialogically in a syncretic formation of western and tri-continental thought" between "particular anti-colonial emancipatory politics" (64) in the tri-continental states and the social upheavals of the 1960s in the West led by New Left civil rights activists, pacifists, and radicals (Harvey 2005: 60). During this time, "radical forms of knowledge and experience that had been created in earlier eras of resistance and struggle" (Young 2001: 64) migrated to Western metropolitan academies, destabilizing and challenging existing orthodoxies and neo-colonial ideologies. Schiller and other CI scholars viewed the world through a "postcolonial optic" (Kelsky 2001).

They attended to "the continuing adjustments and permutations of colonial power relations" and "the ways that the power differentials embedded in older colonial projects still exert[ed] their effects even when the formal colonial relationships" were over (Kelsky 2001: 25). The CI paradigm emerged between struggles for national liberation in tri-continental states and the production of radical scholarship by supportive US and Western communication scholars. While Schiller's "defense" of national cultures against US and Western media corporations is sometimes read as support for a paternalistic state that dictates the meaning of a national culture or of a cultural purity that does not exist, Schiller's advocacy for "national culture" against cultural imperialism is much more complex than is often understood by his critics. Some context is needed.

Schiller was writing about cultural imperialism at a time when national liberation struggles were sweeping the globe. Nationalism was the most significant form of anti-colonial resistance in the twentieth century. While nationalism has been criticized as derivative of bourgeois Western Enlightenment discourses (Hobsbawm 1994: 199–201), patriarchy-affirming, elitist, homogenizing, and exclusionary (Spivak 1993; McClintock 1995), racially essentialist (Chrisman 2004: 192–193), and a temporal paradox (Chatterjee 1986; McClintock 1995; Anderson 1991), it should nonetheless be remembered that nationalism was the political form taken by all African, Asian, Middle Eastern, and Latin American anti-imperial struggles in the post-World War II period (Sivandan 2004: 45). Said (1993) writes: "it is a historical fact that nationalism—restoration of community, assertion of identity, emerging of new cultural practices—as a mobilized political force instigated and then advanced the struggle against Western domination everywhere in the non-European world" (218). Through heterogeneous and unevenly developed violent and non-violent struggles for national liberation, decolonization commenced post-World War II, and continued until the mid-1970s. During the tumultuous period of decolonization, struggles for national *political* independence were accompanied, and sometimes strengthened, by struggles for cultural independence from Western "cultural domination." Indeed, anti-colonial cultural politics—for liberation and against domination—played a tremendously important role in the struggle. Young (2001) states that "cultural activism, often deployed alongside the development of modes of resistance with which to meet force, was designed to counter the ideological assumptions, justifications, and sense of inferiority that colonists propagated upon subject peoples" (164). There is no room here to discuss all of the diverse theorizations of cultural-nationalist politics that emerged during this conjuncture. A review of two classic anti-colonial texts—one produced at the beginning of the 1960s and one that marked the end of the colonial era—captures the complexity of anti-colonial cultural nationalism.

Frantz Fanon, the Martinique-born psychiatrist and intellectual freedom-fighter with the Algerian National Liberation Front, delivered his influential speech "On National Culture" to the Second Congress of Black Writers and Artists in Rome in 1959 (the speech was published two years later in *The Wretched of the Earth*). Fanon criticized the cultural dimension of colonial domination, on the basis that it "manages to disrupt in spectacular fashion the cultural life of a conquered people" (236) and it makes "every effort [. . .] to bring the colonized person to admit the inferiority of his culture" (236). Under colonial domination, the destruction of expressions of national culture "are sought in systematic fashion," (237) and due to racist dehumanization, "the poverty of the people, national oppression, and the inhibition of culture" become "one and the same thing" (238). Instead of validating negritude's essentialist and nostalgic return to a pre-colonial cultural past as the appropriate political response to Western cultural domination, Fanon proposed something much more radical: a forward-looking anti-colonial nationalist "culture of combat" which reflects, and is made by and for the oppressed through their struggles for cultural liberation and "the renaissance of the state" (244). Eleven years after Fanon's speech, Amilcar Cabral, agronomist and Secretary-General of the African Party for the Independence of Guinea and the Cape Verde Islands (PAIGC), delivered "National Liberation and Culture," the Eduardo Mondlane Lecture at Syracuse University, New York. This explicitly Marxist theorization of cultural resistance, set in the context of the Portuguese-ruled Guinea and Cape Verde Islands, considered how the coercive dimension of colonial rule (military force) is combined with "the permanent and organized repression of the cultural life of the people concerned" (139) (political consent). For Cabral, "imperialist domination, denying to the dominated people their own historical process, necessarily denies their cultural process" (143). Like Fanon, Cabral did not put forth a romantic account of local cultures as timeless, essentially unified, or devoid of internal problems, contradictions, and inequalities, but instead envisaged demands for cultural autonomy and projections of collective cultural difference as a countervailing force to the complete assimilation and homogenization of the colonized. Cabral proposed that a revolutionary national culture would emerge through an ongoing struggle, a dialectic which would work through "the essential and secondary, the positive and negative, the progressive and reactionary, the strengths and weaknesses" (150).

Fanon and Cabral were just two of the many opponents of colonial cultural dominance and proponents of anti-colonial cultural resistance in the post-World War II conjuncture. For each of them, the new national culture was not something already given or known, but something imagined and forged through the struggle of the people for liberation from below. Schiller's defense of the national cultures of the formerly colonized is largely indebted to Fanon and Cabral's theories of national culture and the revolutionary national liberation struggles against colonial cultural dominance which occurred in the tri-continental states. In the final chapter of *Communication and Cultural Domination* ("National Communications Policies: A New Arena for Social Struggle"), Schiller cites Fanon's *Wretched of the Earth* and Cabral's "National Liberation and Culture" in proposal of a cultural revolution that is borne, not of a nativist escape to traditionalism, but through national communication and cultural policy. Taking his cue from Fanon and Cabral, Schiller stated that "National communications policy making is a generic term for the struggle against cultural and social domination in all its forms, old and new, exercised from within or outside the nation" (96). Schiller and other cultural imperialism scholars supported the sovereign rights of postcolonial states to develop and govern their own communications and media systems and, in turn, determine their own national cultures, free of unwanted external influences. They tied communication and cultural sovereignty to political sovereignty.

Schiller's "theory" of cultural imperialism was linked to his communication and cultural policy activism. In the early 1970s, Schiller traveled to Chile to assist Salvadore Allende's Popular Unity Government. In the mid-1970s, Schiller contributed directly to the Non-Aligned Movement's (NAM) battle for a New World Information and Communication Order (NWICO) at UNESCO by participating in many international symposiums and research teams (including the MacBride Commission) (see Chapter 3). His support for national communication and cultural sovereignty in postcolonial states was never naïve about the risks of such a project. He self-reflexively warned of nationalist elites using the language of cultural imperialism in self-serving and politically opportunistic ways. Schiller was also frustrated by the lack of social class analysis in the NWICO struggle (Maxwell 2003: 70). He criticized NWICO's professionalization and hierarchical decision-making process. Following discussion about a UNESCO move to set up national communications policy councils staffed with political leaders, technicians, media elites, and social scientists, Schiller (1976) rhetorically asked his readers: "Where are the working people? Where are the non-professionals?" (95). He favored a democratic and inclusive communications and cultural policy-making process: "Communications-cultural planning cannot be formulated by experts and delivered to the rest of the population as a legislative gift" (96). Schiller argued that national communications and cultural policy would have to be made by "the fullest participation of the total community," as anything else would "make the likelihood of diversion and atrophy inevitable" (96).

Schiller supported the goal of communication and cultural sovereignty in postcolonial states by documenting, criticizing, and struggling to bring about a fundamental transformation of the economic and political barriers to the achievement of this goal. The majority of the postcolonial states that emerged after World War II were wedged between the European colonialist communication networks and globalizing US media corporations. The past structures of Western colonial communications and the present structures of US corporate media expansion posed difficulties for postcolonial communication and cultural sovereignty. The power to control the lion's share of the media belonged to a handful of media corporations based in the West and the US, and this thwarted the sovereign cultural goals of those revolutionary groups that struggled on the terrain of the nation from below, and posed problems for the postcolonial state elite, which eventually sought to manufacture a national culture from above. The communications and cultural sovereignty of postcolonial states was further undermined by US propaganda agencies such as the United States Information Agency (USIA), The Bureau of Educational and Cultural Affairs (BECA), and the Voice of America Radio (VOA). Alongside violent CIA-counter-insurgency incursions, these state propaganda agencies promoted US capitalism and liberal democracy as "modernization" in postcolonial states throughout the 1950s and 1960s as "an ideological counterpart to Marxist-Leninist theories about imperialist attempts to dominate the new nations of Asia, Africa, and Latin America"(Dizard 2004: 84). During this period, the US state sought to deter anti-colonial revolutions from becoming anti-US socialist movements.

Cultural imperialism scholars saw the global profit-goals of US media corporations and the campaigns of US state propaganda agencies fettering a postcolonial state's development of its own communication and media system. US media corporations and the US state undermined the communication and cultural sovereignty of postcolonial states through their enclosure of the space available for sovereign imaginings of a post-colonial national identity. Schiller believed that before the ideals of cultural sovereignty and cultural exchange could be realized, the dominance of US and Western corporate and state communication structures, and the extent to which they compromised cultural sovereignty and exchange, would have to be transformed. However, Schiller's criticism of cultural imperialism was not motivated by a Western desire to see essential, traditional, unitary, or pure national cultures sheltered from cultural mixing. Apropos Fanon and Cabral, Schiller saw the postcolonial "nation" as a terrain of struggle between elite and popular blocs, something which the formation of was fought over by incipient imperial comprador classes and counter-hegemonic nationalist movements. Cultural imperialism scholars felt that "this process of cultural struggle and transformation" should occur "free of neocolonial intervention" (Schiller 1996: 100). At their best, cultural imperialism scholars did not lament the loss of a pre-formed national culture, but conceptualized the globalization of US media corporations and US state propaganda as a threat to the right and capacity of postcolonial publics and states to determine their own sense of national identity, by and for themselves. Cultural imperialism scholars were fighting with, and for, the sovereign right of people in the tri-continental states to imagine and realize their own national cultures.

In the late 1970s, Schiller and others did not simply outline the cultural imperialism paradigm; they also put forward "a thesis of resistance to cultural imperialism" (Maxwell 2004: 62). Schiller argued that the negative effects of CI could be countered by sovereign national communication and cultural policies that protected and promoted national communication and media systems from unwanted and deleterious foreign influence and control. CI was just one of many concepts used by postcolonial leaders and sympathetic metropolitan academic-activists, not only to reactively speak back to European cultural colonialism and the new US communication empire, but also as a tool in the struggle to advance an alternative to them. Set in this postcolonial context, CI is conceptually counter-hegemonic relative to the dominant discourse of US media corporations, the US state, and the academic field of international communication in the 1960s and 1970s (Sparks 2007). Cultural imperialism scholars challenged the free-flow of information doctrine and "the dominant paradigm" of development communication in US academia ("modernization"). Both of these positions were fully aligned with US foreign policy objectives, and ethnocentrically represented the US as the apex of world-historic development (Bah 2008). In sum, the CI paradigm helped destabilize the metropolitan fantasy that everyone in the world actively courted US media, illuminated the international divisions and disparities in the capacity to produce, distribute, and consume media, prompted a consideration of the potentially negative impact of global TV shows and films on local cultures, and offered public broadcasting as a democratic alternative to commercial media.

CULTURAL GLOBALIZATION (CG)

The CI paradigm presents a critical, political-economic, and postcolonial account of the power and influence of entertainment media in a world capitalist system of unevenly developed nation-states. From the early 1980s, throughout the 1990s, and to the present-day, the Marxist world systems, imperialism, and dependency models on which the CI paradigm was based faced much criticism. During this time, the CI paradigm was complicated (and in many instances, caricaturized) by business journalists, policy-makers, and communication studies scholars both inside and outside of the US. While Schiller (1991), Boyd-Barrett (1998), and other critical scholars such as Herman and McChesney (1997) rethought and revised parts of the CI paradigm from within, many scholars did not. Outside of the paradigm, some of CI's problems were illuminated and scrutinized. However, rather than updating or extending the CI paradigm with reference to contemporary changes, many scholars "threw out the baby with the bath-water," dismissing it as an outmoded relic of the past. As result, CI became "far less fashionable a critical position in academic circles in the 1990s than it was during the 1970s and 1980s" (Tomlinson 1999: 79). Kraidy (2005) contends that "though cultural imperialism was the reigning thesis since the 1960s and the 1970s, numerous critics have, since the 1980s, alleged that it no longer reflects the complexity of intercultural relations" (4). In an attempt to grasp the complexity of intercultural relations in a rapidly changing world, scholars developed new theories of globalization and cultural globalization (CG). Sparks (2007) states that the "globalization paradigm is today still far and away the most popular and influential way of thinking about the world, and the world of media and communication in particular" (190).

What does globalization mean? And what does it say about the world, especially the world in which entertainment media is produced, distributed and consumed? In the following sections I contextualize globalization with reference to its economic, polit-ical, cultural and technological, and media dimensions. I then distinguish between "strong" and "weak" paradigms of globalization, and review and respond to the key claims they make against the CI paradigm.

Globalization

Mody (2003) says that "globalization" was the primary intellectual theme in the social sciences and a buzzword in trade and industry throughout the 1980s and 1990s (vii). Like cultural imperialism, globalization can be defined in a variety of ways (Hopper 2007). Throughout the 1980s and 1990s, "globalization" meant many different things to many different people. The term is not value-neutral, but is fought over by a number of different actors and interest groups. The anti-capitalist activist who promotes the union rights of workers in the maquiladoras of Juarez Mexico will likely hold a very different view of globalization than the CEO of the corporation that sub-contracts low-waged tasks to and exploits those same workers. Globalization is a contested concept and the site of intense debate over its causes, historical antecedents, and effects (Christopherson, Garretsen, and Martin 2008: 343). For some, globalization eludes a precise definition. As Hafez (2007) says: "Again and again, attempts to systematize the field of globalization scholarship have shown a lack of empirical clarity and of a work-able theoretical concept" (5). Jameson (1998) says globalization is "the modern or postmodern version of the proverbial elephant, described by its blind observers in so many diverse ways" (xi).

Though "globalization" can mean many things, it often functions as a "periodizing" term (Denning 2004: 24). The processes associated with globalization have a long history

(Pieterse 2003), but in much "news-worthy" discourse, the term globalization functions as a synonym for the economic, political, and cultural trends which have occurred since the end of the Cold War (Cox 2001). Throughout the 1990s, politicians, economists, journalists, and social theorists used the term "globalization" to describe the main dynamics of the new world system or "order" that was being consolidated following the collapse of the Soviet Union. What had changed? What was new? Capitalism seemed triumphant; the spread of liberal democracy and increasing political interdependence through institutions of global governance seemed unstoppable; borders were being opened to flows of money, technology, people, media, and ideas; the Internet, the World Wide Web, and media corporations were stitching everyone together, everywhere, driving a hybridized, post-national, and cosmopolitan global culture. Throughout the 1990s, the surface novelty of present-day trends, not the depth of the historical past, filled the pages of numerous books, articles, and op-ed pieces on globalization. Even in the post-9/11 period of the so-called US global war on terror, globalization continued to be a way to periodize the present. "Everyone agrees that we live in a more 'globalized' world, but views differ as to what this means and whether it is a trend for good or ill" (Christopherson, Garretsen, and Martin 2008: 343).

Though globalization is largely a periodizing term, it also refers to a variety of interrelated economic, political, cultural, and technological processes said to be *integrating* the world, leading to greater *interdependency* and *interconnectedness* between all countries.

Economic globalization: the geographical expansion of capitalist market relations and actors (waged labor, commodification, trade corporations, and financial institutions) around the world. This process is driving the economic integration of formerly sovereign national economies. Friedman (1999), a staunch proponent of free trade, describes globalization as "the spread of free-market capitalism to virtually every country in the world." Over the past thirty years, interlocking financial systems and trade arrangements have been established (e.g., the North American Free Trade Agreement (NAFTA) between Canada and the US). The World Trade Organization (WTO), the World Bank (WB), the World Intellectual Property Organization (WIPO), and the International Monetary Fund (IMF) enforce global market rules. Transnational corporations outsource jobs from Northern to Southern economies, coordinate the manufacture of goods and services across many countries, treat the world as one market to buy from and sell to, and strive to maximize global shareholder value. Despite growing global economic integration, "There is no 'global economy' abstracted from the particular local, national, and regional economies that constitute it, or from the relations among them, whether among major capitalist powers or between imperialist powers and subaltern states" (Wood 2002: 17). At present, global capitalism exists in, and is coordinated by, states within a hierarchical world system.

Political globalization: the growth of transnational linkages between states and non-state actors in the world system. The day-to-day relationships and bilateral and multilateral agreements and treaties between nation-states, inter-governmental organizations (IGOs) (e.g., United Nations), non-governmental organizations (NGOs) (e.g., Reporters without Borders, UNICEF, Greenpeace), and transnational corporations (TNMCs) (e.g., Coca-Cola), drive global political interdependencies. As the functions of sovereign states are uploaded as supranational forms of governance and downloaded to a plurality of non-state actors, the traditional connection between territory and political power is said to be transformed. Held and McGrew (2000) note that "the modern state is increasingly embedded in webs of regional and global interconnectedness permeated by quasi-supranational, inter-governmental and transnational forces, and unable to determine its own fate" (13). The sovereign "capacity of nation-states to act independently in the articulation and pursuit of domestic and international policy objectives" is said to be being eroded by these global-local forces (Held and McGrew 2000: 14). The notion that state sovereignty is in decline, however, is a global "myth" (Hirst and Thompson 1999). At present, states still define the "national interest" and pursue those interests in domestic and foreign affairs; they lay claim to the monopoly of legitimate physical violence within their territories; they are the locus of juridical power; they exert police and surveillance powers over a geographically situated citizenry; they are responsible for a national currency; they provision social services; and they support national culture. State sovereignty may be changing due to sub-national and transnational actors but, with the exception of those deemed to be "failures," most states hold sovereignty over territories, economies, populations, and cultures. Global capitalism has not undermined the sovereignty of states. Rather, global capitalism is facilitated and legitimized by sovereign states (Aronowitz and Bratsis 2002; Jessop 2002; Panitch 1994, 1996, 2004).

Cultural Globalization: "the process of cultural flows across the world" and how "contacts between people and their cultures—their ideas, their values, their way of life—have been growing and deepening in unprecedented ways" (Kumaravadivelu 2008: 37–38). Cultural globalization refers to face-to-face and mediated interactions between people from many different countries, the exposure of people to values and ideas other than their own, the mixing of these values and ideas, and the means by which "ways of life" are changing and hybridizing as result of these integrative processes. Tomlinson (1999) says that "globalization lies at the heart of modern culture; cultural practices lie at the heart of globalization" (1). In the current era, no one culture is an island, totally cut off from cultural others. Cultures—groups of people and ways of life—which have previously been insulated or separated from values and ideas other to them, face increased exposure and transformation. "The global cultural economy" (Appadurai 1997: 27) is one of the most influential paradigms of cultural globalization. Appadurai believes that cultures are always in a state of flux, changing and mutating as opposed to being fixed in place for all time, and that the contemporary world is full of opportunities for cultural mixing and meaning-making. Appadurai's "global cultural economy" is not defined by state-based power geopolitics and economic rivalries in a world capitalist system of imperial cores, semi-peripheries, and peripheries, but by cross-border cultural flows of interacting and disjunctive "scapes": financescapes, ethnoscapes, ideoscapes, technoscapes, and mediascapes.

Financescapes refer to the industrial and service corporations (Wal-Mart, ExxonMobil, Toyota, General Electric, Samsung Electronics, McDonald's, Unilever, Coca-Cola) and financial institutions (Deutsche Bank, BNP Paribas, Citigroup, ING Group, Fannie Mae) which move across borders in pursuit of profit on behalf of CEOs and shareholders. These financescapes operate in two or more countries. They spread market relations, investment, waged labor, production models, and commodification to virtually every country in the world, integrating places and people through capitalist logics. *Ethnoscapes* refer to the individuals or groups of people that move from one country to others. People are moving further, faster, and more frequently across borders than in previous eras. Tourists move for pleasure, thrills, and new experiences; migrant laborers travel to meet their subsistence needs; middle-class professionals migrate in pursuit of socio-economic mobility or to re-connect with family in diaspora; CEOs travel to attend business meetings; victims of war and genocide flee death and persecution. *Ideoscapes* refer to big systems of ideas and beliefs such as liberal democracy, Christianity, and Islam. These ideas move across borders, from one or several places to many more. *Technoscapes* refer to the technological systems (hardware and software) that connect two or more geographical locales. Information and communications technologies (ICTs) constitute material and immaterial networks of satellite links, telecommunications, fiber-optic cables, computer networks and highways, and ocean and air routes. *Mediascapes* refer to media corporations, print and electronic mediums, and their content (newspapers, magazines, comic books, TV shows, films, video games).

Appadurai (1997) states that these scapes flow across borders in greater quantities and with greater speed than occurred in the past, resulting in new cultural connections, mixes, and interdependencies. The cultural effects of these scapes are not uniformly experienced everywhere, and thus Appadurai encourages scholars to study the inter-actions between these scapes of flows, and the culturally heterogeneous mixings and meanings that result from those interactions. Appadurai is interested in the micro-level cultural experiences and meanings made by individuals and groups of people immersed within the flows and scapes: "imagination is now central to all forms of agency, is itself a social fact, and is the key component of the new global order" (31). The flows of scapes constitute "imagined worlds, that is, the multiple worlds that are constituted by the historically situated imaginations of persons and groups spread around the globe" (36). Appadurai says mediascapes act as "resources for experiments with self-making in all sorts of societies, for all sorts of persons" and "provide resources for self-imaging as an everyday social project (34). Appadurai claims that the people in "all sorts of societies" that imagine themselves and the wider world through their local contact with globalizing mediascapes are not victims of Americanization: "Globalization does not necessarily or frequently imply homogenization or Americanization, and to the extent that different societies appropriate the [media] materials of modernity differently, there is still room for the deep study of specific geographies, histories, and languages" (17). Appadurai implies that the world is more culturally heterogeneous precisely *because* of the disjunctive mash-ups created by the flow of scapes.

Cultural globalization scholars also focus on the connections and interconnections between the "here" and the "there," the domestic and the foreign, the local and the global, the national and the international. Giddins (1990) says "Globalization is the intensification of worldwide social relations which link distant localities in such a way that local happenings are shaped by events occurring many miles away and vice versa" (64). The pleasure the brand-loyal Apple consumers of the world feel while playing with their Apple iPads, for example, is linked to the distant drudgery of the Chinese peasant workers who assemble Apple iPods, iPhones, and iPads at Foxconn plants for $9 a day. The billions of dollars in annual profits generated by the California-based Apple Inc., relies upon the worldwide consumption of Apple-trademarked commodities by the youth of many countries. Baylis and Smith (2005) say that globalization is the "process of increasing interconnectedness between societies such that events in one part of the world more and more have effects on peoples and societies far away" (9). When the US financial system crashed in 2008, for example, the effects were felt by people in every country connected with it. Affected states launched a transnationally coordinated political response. Tomlinson (1999) states that cultural globalization refers to "complex connections between societies, cultures and individuals worldwide" (170) and encourages the study of the ways in which distant global events impact upon present experiences and local identities (9).

Technological and Media Globalization: the movement of ICTs and electronic media across and between borders, establishing networks that enable many people in a variety of different locations to build new relationships, communities, connections, and experiences. ICTs and electronic media are viewed as the chief enablers of the political, economic, and cultural integration and interdependence of economies, nations, and cultures. As O'Hara and Stevens (2006) claim:

> Critical to the process of globalization is ICT. Indeed, ICT forms a necessary component of the onward march of globalization. Without the technological developments of recent decades, the much-trumpeted closer union of national economies, politics and cultures would be impossible. (119)

Lule (2011) argues that "globalization could not occur without the media, that globalization and media act in concert and cohort, and that the two have partnered throughout the whole of human history" (5). These technological and media determinist scholars depict ICTs and electronic media—as opposed to people and the social power relations between them—as the cause of world change. Although the globalization of ICTs and electronic media is largely influenced and utilized by the large-scale economic and political organizations that own them, they have supported novel forms of integration and interdependence.

De-territorialized and mediated sociality. ICTs and electronic media have increased the range of possibilities for mediated socialization between and among people located in many different places, and through de-territorialized social spaces of interactivity. Traditionally, one's social experiences and interactions with others were tied to a territorial place. Face-to-face communication happened with our partners, family members, co-workers, and friends, in place-based contexts. Although most human activity is still tied to a territorial location or place, globalization scholars say that territory no longer constitutes the sole or total "social space" in which human interaction takes place. Due to innovations in ICTs and the cross-border flow of electronic media, social experiences and interactions can now be detached from place, or "de-territorialized." Thompson (1995) notes that electronic media "creates new forms of action and interaction and new kinds of social relationships—forms that are different from the kind of face-to-face interaction which has prevailed for most of human history" (81). Indeed, social experiences have become more mediatized and de-territorialized than in the past. As Rantanen (2005) says "Globalization is a process in which worldwide economic, political, cultural and social relations have become increasingly mediated across time and space" (8). De-territorialized socialization occurs daily, between people who, while physically separated, are connected by ICTs. Family members in diaspora—some in Toronto, some in Mumbai, and others in Chicago, for example—interact through Facebook. Exchange students from China studying in New York City use Skype to converse with family members in Beijing. Business managers employed by local subsidiaries of global marketing corporations hold conferences in virtual boardrooms generated by tele-conferencing systems. These forms of de-territorialized and mass-mediated com-munication connect two or more people who are not located in the same physical place, *simultaneously*. Giddens (1991) calls this mediated intertwining of absence and presence "distanciation." People are physically absent, yet visually present. Far away, but virtually near.

The Global Village, or, the world is shrinking. ICTs and electronic media have connected different parts of the world, establishing what some call a "global village." Marshall McLuhan coined the "global village" to describe how the advent of radio communication brought people from many nations into faster and more intimate contact with each other. He believed that the transition from an individualist print-based culture to one immersed in electronic media communication (radio and TV) heralded a new age of "electronic interdependence" (McLuhan and Powers 1989). Observing the globalization of TV, McLuhan (1964) announced: "Today, after more than a century of electric technology, we have extended our central nervous system itself in a global embrace, abolishing both space and time as far as our planet is concerned" (19). At present, ICTs and electronic media connect people in many parts of the world via screens, increasing the visual, auditory, and oratory interconnections between them. As O'Neill (1993) argues: "communications technology always influences human organization [. . .] As the speed of communication rises, social distance shrinks and ever larger numbers of people, widely separated by space, are drawn together into common experiences" (24). ICTs and electronic media visually expand local horizons while compressing the world into media images. They blur the previous perspectival distinctions between domestic and foreign, here and there, near and far, local and global, national and international. Satellite TV and digital media platforms such as YouTube domesticize foreign events, make here seem there, collapse near and far, localize the global, and "mash up" the national and international spheres. The result is a feeling that the world is one, that everyone is connected with everyone else. Robertson (1992) says that globalization "refers to both the compression of the world and the intensification of consciousness of the world as a whole" (8). ICTs and electronic entertainment media enable the time-space compression of experience and create the feeling that we are living in a global village. However, despite the rise of placeless spaces of social interaction and feelings of global villagism, locality still matters to people. The feeling of belonging has long been attached to a locale, a place. The global village is the horizon of national, regional, and local villages. And differences between villages are still pronounced due to the uneven development of capitalism (Harvey 2006: 100–101). As Gray (1998) says: "the increased interconnection of economic activity throughout the world accentuates uneven development" (55–56). Furthermore, due to the digital divide, genuinely "global"—that is, universally accessible—villages, communities, and mediated spaces may not even exist (Sparks 1998).

Clearly, "globalization" refers to many economic, political, cultural, and techno-logical processes, the effects of which seem to be greater integration, interdependence, and interconnection between countries. The spread of capitalism and markets; state interaction at global, national, and regional levels of governance; the movement of money, technology, people, media, and ideas across borders; cross-border and intercul-tural mixing and meaning-making; and the rise of information and communication technology and electronic media-supported forms of connectivity, de-territorialized sociality, and global villagism: these are all contemporary processes, trends, and trans-formations which are interesting, and worthy of study. The tendency among globaliza-tion scholars to think outside the box of the CI paradigm by contemplating things that do not add up to imperialism, Westernization, or Americanization is refreshing: when we view the world exclusively through the CI paradigm, we risk reducing all transna-tional relationships, practices, and processes to expressions of Western or US economic, political, and cultural power and thereby fail to recognize the plurality of non-US inter-ests that are also important parts of the world. Strong CG scholars present interesting observations about the contemporary world and highlight processes, trends, and changes that do not align with CI.

Do the globalization processes, trends, and transformations described by CG scholars necessarily reflect a fundamentally new post-imperial period? Do the imperial economic and political structures built over the past five hundred years or so still exist? Has global-ization heralded the demise of the world capitalist system and the associated asymmet-rical power relations between imperial core zones, peripheries, and semi-peripheries? Are there no longer any dependency relations between countries in the global North and global South? Is the spread of free markets and YouTube making the capitalist geography of the world "flat" (Friedman 2006) as opposed to unevenly developed? (Harvey 2006). Do global-local political relations and governmental regimes crush the sovereign powers of territorial states? Have the movements of ICTs and electronic media across borders eroded national cultures by spreading cosmopolitan ideals and globalist values? Do these ideals and values provide for a full-blown global culture that has the same kind of popular resonance as nationalism? Do forms of de-territorialized sociality and mediated commu-nication spaces eclipse territorial and place-based forms of affiliation? Does globalization negate or extend imperialism and cultural imperialism?

The answers to these questions largely depend upon whether one subscribes to a strong or weak paradigm of globalization. Sparks (2007) distinguishes between "strong" and "weak" paradigms of globalization in terms of their application to global communication and media studies. The "strong" CG paradigm claims that we have entered a brand new period, in which the world system has become or is fast becoming fundamentally different to the past. Old theories are anachronistic, and completely new theories are needed in order to grasp these "new times." The "weak" CG paradigm emphasizes continuity with the past while attending to what is new, and retains "many of the features of the old imperialism paradigm" (Sparks 2007: 191). The strong CG paradigm says everything is new and that the old is moot, while the weak CG paradigm recognizes that some things are new, but that the past still weights upon the present.

The "global cultural economy" is a strong paradigm of cultural globalization, and one that departs from older Marxist theorizations of world systems, colonialism/imperialism, and dependency. Appadurai (1997) notes that "Even the most complex and flexible theories of global development which have come out of the Marxist tradition [. . .] are inadequately quirky" (32). For its proponents, Appadurai's model represents:

> a new, fundamentally transnational world system [. . .] that no longer has Wallerstein's visualizeable, Euclidean, center-periphery structure, but can be described as an appeal to chaotics [. . .] a comprehensive, complexly interacting system that is by definition not totalizeable or deterministic, one that is bewilderingly heterogeneous and heterogenizing at a multitude of sites. (Buell 1994: 313)

This model represents the dynamics of the world as being fundamentally new or different than before: the divisions and oppositions between core, semi-periphery, and periphery no longer hold; the US empire and its brand of liberal capitalist imperialism is over; nation-states have lost their sovereignty to the free flow of people, ideas, technology, media, and money across borders (which, in turn, empowers individuals!); ICTs and electronic media generate new and primary spaces for social interaction and indigenized identifications; and national cultures are diminishing due to hybridizing interplays of global-local scapes. Media corporations are not agents of the US empire, nor do they culturally dominate other peoples or countries. They support cultural diversity by selling the symbolic resources for self-making. Whereas the CI paradigm focuses on the macro-level political and economic structures of the world system, Appadurai's strong CG paradigm focuses on micro-level cultural identifications and the play of meanings.

The strong account of CG presented by Appadurai and other post-structuralist and postmodernist social theorists tries to "move beyond" what they perceive to be a totalizing CI paradigm. Though their cosmopolitan and post-national outlook may broaden intellectual horizons, the strong CG scholar's conceptualization of the world has many shortcomings. The claims made in the name of strong CG (especially those pertaining to global communications and media) derive from social theory, and not from grounded research into media corporations, state media policies, market structures, and all of the other stuff serious communication studies require. Strong CG scholars "operate at a very abstract level, and are not much concerned with evidence about the world they are discussing, or even with formulating their ideas in ways that might be subject to evidential review" (Sparks 2007: 127). The strong CG paradigm is theory-heavy and evidence-light. Hesmondalgh (2007) states that "there is an almost spectacular lack of evidence in the work of commentators [. . .] associated with globalization theory" (177). CG theorists may nod their heads and say "yes" when asked if the world system has changed fundamentally, even in the absence of any evidence that supports the radical changes they imply. Their claims of world-historic change are hyperbolic and function more as "a popular rhetoric than a guide to serious analysis" (Sparks 2007:184).

Furthermore, the strong CG paradigm's rejection of the CI paradigm's political-economic research method, avoidance of concrete policy problems, and abandonment of radical aspirations for social change leads to an uncritical affirmation of the world as it is. Sparks (2011) says "globalization theories have, in the main, been celebratory. They have explored the complexities of the production, trading and consumption of media artifacts without any serious attempt to locate these within structures of differential wealth and power" (5). Also, the rebuttal "of the 'everything is worse' perspective of cultural imperialism" too often leads to an uncritical embrace of an "an affirmative, 'everything for the best' view of globalization" and research that is out of touch with "radical history, economics and political studies" (Curran 2002: 182). Borderless media movements, diasporic cultural mixings, and cosmopolitan imaginings are affirmed, while attention to the persistence of worker exploitation, cultural dispossession, and virulent ethnocentrism is displaced. Hybridity, post-national subjectivity, and fluidity cause global merriment, while the pain of cultural conflict based on essentialism, the perpetuation of provincial and nationalistic mindsets, and the rootedness of the world's poor in destitute and desperate slums are neglected (Davis 2006). Strong accounts of CG normalize an idealistic image of the world and accept global corporate wish-fulfillment as fact.

Additionally, the strong CG paradigm may be linked to US imperial exigencies. Anglo-American intellectuals were the most prolific authors of globalization discourse. Tunstall (2007) claims that the concept of globalization was "developed by various Anglo-American authors and public relations people in the 1980s," and was followed by a "big flood of globalization books around 1990–92" (321). Henwood (2003) links globalization discourse to US foreign policy exigencies. He says that the concept of "globalization" gained currency in tandem with the Clinton Administration's liberal-internationalist foreign policy speeches, which represented a globally integrated and interdependent post-industrial information economy (145). Gowan (2002) avers that "at the very heart of the Clinton administration's approach to [foreign policy] strategy is the concept of globalization" (20). What kind of ideological work do some accounts of "globalization" perform? According to Bacevich (2004), the affirmative and universal-izing meta-narrative of globalization masked the persistence of US power:

> Across the globe, US policy was emphasizing the value of open markets, open investments, open communications and open trade. [. . .] But the creation of an open world was not in the first instance a program of global uplift. [. . .] The pursuit of openness is first of all about Americans doing well; that an open world might also benefit others qualifies at best as incidental. (102)

While the US foreign policy establishment and its affiliated think-tanks deployed the idea of globalization to organize the consent of rival states to the Washington consensus, some strong CG scholars may have unintentionally reproduced the US state's ideological framework in their theories. For this, they have been accused of "cultural imperialism." Pierre Bourdieu and Loic Wacquant (1999: 41) argue that "Cultural imperialism rests on the power to universalize particularisms linked to a singular historical tradition by causing them to be misrecognized as such." For these scholars, "The strongly poly-semic notion of globalization" was one such de-historicized, particularistic concept being mass-produced within US universities and exported to the whole planet in the 1990s. When used in academic and political discourses, globalization "ha[d] the effect, if not the function, of submerging the effects of imperialism in cultural ecumenism or economic fatalism and making transnational relationships of [corporate and geopolitical] power appear as a neutral necessity" (42).

Bourdieu and Wacquant's reduction of the meaning of the concept of globalization to a cultural imperialist mask or an ideological rationalization for US imperial foreign policy is unfair. "Globalization" means many different things to different scholars. Some theories of globalization and the associated research may support US foreign policy objectives, but there is plenty of critical research on globalization that contests and challenges US and transnational corporate power. The notion that all theorizations and studies of globalization conform to the dominant ideological worldview or "ruling class interests" of the US state and corporate power is dubious. There is a significant body of globalization research within communication, cultural, and media studies that is conceptually savvy yet empirically grounded, historicist yet perceptive of present-day trends, politically-minded but not tendentious, critical though not dogmatic, and attuned to the dialectic of continuity and change in the world system. This kind of research falls into what Sparks (2007) refers to as the "weak" CG paradigm. While strong CG claims are direct counterpoints to the CI paradigm, the weak ones complicate, qualify, work against the grain of, and extend the CI paradigm in novel directions. In what follows, I review the "strong" and "weak" claims of the CG paradigm, as they relate directly to the claims of the CI paradigm, critiquing some of the "strong" CG claims while heeding the "weak" ones.

THE CLAIMS OF THE CULTURAL GLOBALIZATION PARADIGM

The CG paradigm is associated with the following key claims about the cross-border movement of media and the nature of the world system within which TV shows and films circulate. For the most part, these claims do not add up to a coherent paradigm; rather, they contribute to the problematization of the claims that tend to be associated with the CI paradigm.

First, the strong CG paradigm claims that the age of empires and imperialism is over and that the world system is fundamentally different than before. The world is no longer divided between dominant imperial superpowers and dominated peripheries. Rival states and corporations are no longer the main agents which drive capitalist and political integration. In the conclusion to a book-length critique of CI, Tomlinson (1991) says that "globalizing modernity" heralds the end of imperialism and the rise of "a different configuration of global power that is a feature of these new times" (175). Tomlinson calls this new configuration of global power "globalization," which is "distinguished from imperialism." Globalization is claimed to be "a far less coherent or culturally directed process" than imperialism, which was "a purposeful project" or "the intended spread of a social system from one center of power across the globe." Tomlinson states that globalization refers to the "interconnection," "interdependency," and "integration" of all areas in the world system, but without a state or set of states directing the process. More importantly, "the effects of globalization are to weaken the cultural coherence of *all* individual nation-states, including the economically powerful ones: the imperialist powers of a previous era" (175).

The notion that globalization is an agentless set of integrative processes that are not directed by any imperial state or set of states and that globalization itself is a causal agent of major economic, political, and cultural change is problematic. Rosenburg (2001) says that scholars take globalization as *explanans* (a force that determines and explains the changing character of the world) rather than as *explanandum* (the effect or outcome of some pre-existing set of economic, political, or cultural determinations). Whereas the CI paradigm linked change to the forces and relations of capitalist imperialism within a hierarchically organized and unevenly developed world system of nation-states, Tomlinson depicts "globalization" itself as a powerful agent for change which has effects everywhere. By attributing agency to globalization, as opposed to the concrete interests of organizational actors, strong CG theorists overlook the continuing "directive" and "purposeful" power goals of corporations and nation-states in an unevenly developed world capitalist system. Furthermore, the notion that the US is no longer the world system's center of power is not true. Many historians, international relations scholars, and Marxists argue that throughout the 1990s the US continued to be the imperial superpower of the world system, economically, militarily, and culturally (Ahmad 2004; Anderson 2002; Bacevich 2002; Harvey 2004, 2005; Panitch and Gindin 2004). In the 1990s and in the present era, the concepts of US empire and capitalist imperialism continue to hold "real relevance for understanding the media" (Hesmondhalgh 2008). The US is not the superpower it once was, but it is still a powerful center (militarily, economically, and culturally). In the twenty-first century, information and communication technology (ICTs) and media corporations continue to be pillars of US power. Not every transnational or cross-border media relationship, practice, or flow is reducible to cultural imperialism or "Americanization." There is more going on in the world than US cultural imperialism. But the sun has not set on the US empire or US-based media conglomerates. While not all studies of globalizing TV shows and films need to begin and end with the US, the US state and US-based media conglomerates will likely show up somewhere along the way as influential creators and gatekeepers of the flow.

Second, the CG paradigm complicates the CI paradigm's "David and Goliath model" of the US center dominating weak peripheries and US media corporations holding cultural dominion over unwitting dependencies. This dominator/dominated binary obfuscates a more complex and interactive power relationship between the US and other states in the contemporary world (Golding and Harris 1997: 6). To account for these power relationships, Straubhaar (1991) developed the concept of "asymmetrical interdependence," which attends to "a variety of possible relationships in which countries find themselves unequal but possessing variable degrees of power and initiative in politics, economics, and culture" (39). Straubhaar (1991) agrees with CI's view that not all countries have the same (i.e., equal) ability to produce and distribute entertainment media worldwide, but says that almost all countries do have national media industries which produce national TV shows and films. Straubhaar "recognizes the limits placed on many nations' media systems by operating within subordinate positions in the world system, but it also recognizes and gives analytical emphasis to the distinct dynamics of each nation's or industry's historical development." Straubhaar does not deny the power of US media conglomerates, but nonetheless "suggest[s] a larger gamut of possibilities, from dependence to relative interdependence, in media relations" (56) than is often comprehended by the CI paradigm. National media industries, supported by national states, exist. Straubhaar says scholars should study them and the politics of "conflicts between domestic and transnational elites," the "interests of key national [media and political] elites," "the agendas and actions of key production personnel," and "the effects of state intervention, particularly as policy-maker, provider of infrastructure and advertiser." Asymmetrical interdependence presents a useful alternative to a *strict* CI paradigm because it enables analysis of non-US states and media corporations as competitors and collaborators, both with the US and with each other.

Third, some CG scholars represent the US as one media center—as opposed to the only media center—in a world system of multiple, shifting media centers and peripheries. While CI scholars focus on a unipolar world system of centralizing US economic and cultural control, CG scholars attend to the de-centralizing dynamics of a multipolar world system in which diverse and multiplying media centers based in hitherto "peripheral" zones exist. The past thirty years have seen a diversification of and increase in the number of non-US media centers, or what Curtin (2003: 205) aptly describes as "media capitals." In many countries, media corporations exhibit localizing, regionalizing, and nationalizing characteristics; they target an audience of viewers who prefer to consume entertainment made by and featuring people "who look the same, talk the same, joke the same and behave the same" as they do (Tunstall 2008: xiv). A plurality of regionally based media capitals of entertainment finance, production, distribution, and marketing exist, customizing TV shows and films for "culturally proximate" audiences. Hong Kong, Cairo, Bombay, and many other media-capitals, for example, exhibit "extensive entertainment distribution networks, market maturity and economies of scale—all features of Hollywood's global dominance in film and television" (Keane 2006: 835). Countries once viewed by CI scholars as weak peripheries—such as Australia, Brazil, Canada, and India—now exhibit strong media production capabilities (Reeves 1993; Sinclair, Jacka and Cunningham 1996; Sparks 2007; Tracy 1988). The political-economy of global entertainment media is no longer dominated solely by US-based TNMCs. Tunstall (2007) notes that "Hollywood and the US media have lost market share because of a huge growth in national media output since the 1980s" (322). The US may indeed have lost some of its global market share, but it still controls the greater market share relative to other media-exporting countries. The rise of non-US "media capitals" has not occurred in tandem with the immediate decline of the US media capital (Los Angeles) in the world system. The US remains the world system's media power center (Sparks 2007). The world system has many competing media capitals, but the US is still "numero uno" (Chalaby 2006; McChesney and Schiller 2005; Miller et al. 2005; Morley 2006).

According to CG scholars, the rise of regional media capitals has led to a shift away from the one-way flow of TV shows and films from the US media center to the consumption markets of nearly every other country to multi-directional flows between many countries. Thussu (2007) says that there now exists a wide variety of media flows—multi-vocal, multi-directional, and multi-media—that circulate as "mainstream commercial commodities to be consumed by a heterogeneous global audience, and as alternative messages and images—emanating from a wide range of actors" (10).

Entertainment media no longer *only* flows from the global North to global South and from West to East, but often from the South to the North and from the East to the West as well (Murdock 2006). TV shows and films move between culturally proximate countries while chasing viewers in diaspora from their country of origin to the many countries they migrate to. Appadurai (1997) says that "the United States is no longer the puppeteer of a world system of images, but is only one node of a complex transnational construction of imaginary landscapes" (31). But this strong CG claim is unhelpful. The multi-directionality of flows can be studied without losing sight of the centrality of the US as a media "node." Thussu (2007) is careful not to downplay the persistent flow of media products from the global North (the US media core) to the South, but notes that "contra flows" originating from "the erstwhile peripheries of global media industries" (11) do exist and should be analyzed. The existence of multi-directional flows between many countries, however, does not imply the non-existence of near one-way flows from the US to the rest of the world. Multi-directional and contra flows can be studied without losing sight of US media dominance.

Fourth, some CG scholars say the state is not necessarily the sole source and savior of national culture. CI scholars regularly condemn the vices of the US commercial media model while championing the virtues of state-owned "public" broadcasters. To resist the negative influence of "cultural imperialism," CI scholars encourage states to de-link their national media systems from the world's dominant power centers, reject the commercial media model, and strengthen state broadcasting initiatives. CG scholars problematize the notion that the state and state broadcasting are best suited to promote and protect national culture. They highlight how states often define national culture according to their own ideological agendas. At worst, state broadcasters promulgate a national culture which reflects the beliefs and values of the dominant groups which rule the state while excluding the beliefs and values of everyone else (Sparks 2007: 211). By representing Americanization as a threat to national cultures, communist and theocratic states have justified media censorship and propaganda in the name of national security (Ma 2000; Nain 2000; Mowlana 1996). To protect national culture (and its industry) from US media intrusion, states and their presumably paternalistic elites enact un-democratic and authoritarian media policy controls (Curran and Park 2000: 5). In the hands of some states, the discourse of cultural imperialism can support oppressive and un-democratic policy outcomes. Flew (2012) says that "cultural imperialism stokes the fires of moral outrage more than unequal cultural terms of trade" does, and that "anti-Americanism has always had a certain emotional appeal, not least to the political and cultural elites who wish to lecture their citizens on the unhealthy nature of their popular culture consumption diets." That being said, not all state initiatives to protect or promote "national culture" are oppressive, un-democratic, or anti-American. While strong CG scholars promulgate an anti-statist and pro-market view that supports the neoliberal business ideology of media conglomerates and their lobbyists, the best of the weak CG scholars caution against the use and abuse of cultural imperialism discourse by state elites. The state, media policy, and the nation itself are most usefully conceptualized as "terrains of struggle" whose resources, capacities, and meanings are fought over by a number of interested actors. Furthermore, the state can create positive cultural outcomes when the media market fails to do so (Grant and Wood 2004). As

Boyd-Barrett (1997) says: "there is no other credible route [than the state] available for the resolution of significant media issues in the twenty-first century, unless we are prepared to believe that the 'free' market is the best regulator" (xi).

Fifth, some CG scholars criticize the structural functionalist models of society which privilege economic forces and relations as the primary determinants of all cultural phenomena (Sreberny-Mohammadi 1997: 50). They say CI scholars rely on a Marxist base/superstructure model of society that tends to reduce culture to the base logics of the capitalist mode of production. Media corporations produce culture as a commodity, and this culture is determined by, expressive of, and functional to the structural imperatives of capitalism. As commodities exchanged within markets, conveyers of consumer-capitalist ideology, and tools used by media firms to capture audience attention to be sold to advertisers, cultural products are structurally functional to capitalism. By adopting this view, the CI paradigm always comes to the same conclusion: global TV shows and films are commodities of the capitalist system and, as such, ultimately serve its goals. "Selling products is above all the role of popular culture in an age of transnational corporate market domination," claims Schiller (1992). Though true—and perhaps an effective way of rallying people to challenge the capitalist status quo—this claim does not always make for detailed research on the complexities and contradictions of capitalist cultural production (Hesmondalgh 2007: 5–8). "[T]he shortcoming of the cultural imperialism thesis is not that it neglects the interplay between these various forms of [economic and cultural] power: the shortcoming is that it offers an impoverished and ultimately reductionist account of this interplay" (Thompson 2001: 174). The relationship between capitalist media industries and culture is highly mediated. Media corporations and the commercialized TV shows and films they sell may influence culture, but they are not in themselves identical to culture. US-based media corporations do not always manufacture entertainment media products whose imagery and messages represent US "national culture." A media corporation headquartered in one country may have a centralized and concentrated national base, yet still produce and distribute TV shows that represent different cultures. Media corporations may even produce cultural content that is critical of consumer-capitalist ideology. People experience the cultural products of capitalist media industries differently (Tomlinson 1991). Activists often appropriate commodified culture in order to challenge it. The CI paradigm's focus on the macro-level trends, structures, and functions of capitalist culture should be balanced with micro-level analysis of the conduct of specific media institutions, production rituals, media texts, and viewers (Hesmondalgh 2007). That being said, the strong CG notion that culture is autonomous or exists in a completely disjunctive relationship to economic and political power structures is not feasible. Capitalist culture is complex and contradictory, but we cannot understand the "workings of contemporary culture without recognizing the close alliances between political and economic power that characterize the contemporary phase of capitalism" (Sparks 2009: 9)

Sixth, CG scholars present a mixed assessment of the sovereign power of states. Strong CG scholars claim that the nation-state is being undermined by or losing sovereignty to cross-border flows of scapes (Appadurai 1997). However, unlike CI scholars, they seem to uncritically celebrate the decline of the state without attending to what has been lost in the process. The most politically savvy, weak CG scholars attend to the continued cultural "gatekeeping" role of states vis-à-vis external states, TNMCs, and entertainment media. Worldwide, states are important markers of different "languages, political systems, power structures, cultural traditions, economies, international links and histories" (Curran and Park 2000: 11–12). States perform a variety of "national" media functions: they subsidize media firms, establish content quotas for broadcasters, give licenses to networks, censor content and promote and protect national cultures. Curran and Park (2000) say that states are tremendously "influential in shaping media systems," "largely determine who has control over television and radio," "frame the laws and regulations within which national media operate," and "have a range of informal ways of influencing the media" (12). Against the notion that globalization heralds the decline of the nation-state, Curran and Park (2000) claim that "media systems are shaped not merely by national regulatory regimes and national audience preferences, but by a complex ensemble of social relations that have taken shape in national contexts" (12). Hence, the weak CG paradigm attends to how the profit-interests of transnational media corporations are both restricted and enabled by national gatekeeping strategies, including the media policies of state political elites, the priorities of national media owners, and the specific tastes and preferences of local viewers (Chadha and Kavoori 2000: 428).

Seventh, CG scholars say that media products are not necessarily transmission belts for monolithic images of America and consumer-capitalist ideologies. CG scholars take issue with the CI paradigm's static view of "The American Way of Life" which is supposedly exported to the world by TV shows and films. Through analysis of media content and texts, they show how the image of the American Way of Life carried by globalizing TV shows and films is not always unitary, standardized, and predictable (Gray 2007). US media conglomerates may control the largest supply of TV shows and films circulating in global markets, but these media products represent many different "Americas" and not all of these "Americas" give ideological support to hegemonic views of the nation (Gray 2007). Additionally, CG scholars say that the CI paradigm places "too much emphasis on the role of consumerist values" in TV shows and films while neglecting "the enormous diversity of themes, images and representations which characterize the output of the media industries" (Thompson 1996: 171). Furthermore, CG scholars address the new post-Fordist media production logics such as glocalization and lifestyle segmentation. By studying the actual content of TV shows and films, CG scholars complicate the CI paradigm's view that global entertainment always imparts un-complicated images of America.

Eighth, strong and weak CG scholars emphasize that people all over the world actively consume globalizing entertainment media, and they focus on what people "do" with TV shows and films in their reception contexts. CG scholars scrutinize the notion that local viewers are dominated, victimized, or coerced by global entertainment media. They challenge the CI paradigm's reliance on an outdated transmission model of communications that privileges the position of the Sender as the source and originator of meaning and action, the center from which both the spatial and social integration of the passive Receiver is effectuated through linear and deliberate transmission (Ang 1996: 369). They criticize the CI paradigm and say it "makes a leap of inference from the simple presence of cultural goods to the attribution of deeper cultural or ideological effects" (Tomlinson 1999: 84). They affirm that people select, adapt, indigenize, mix, and redeploy globalizing entertainment media (Ang 1985; Appadurai 1997; Buell 1994; Classen and Howes 1996; Liebes and Katz 1990; Fiske 1988; Morley 1992; Tomlinson 1991). They say that the consumption of entertainment media is a complex and contradictory process and examine how viewers select TV shows and films from a smorgasbord of national and multinational media sources. Though non-US viewers watch a lot of imported US TV shows and films, they also watch culturally proximate entertainment that reflects their local language and style of life (Straubhaar 1991). Worldwide, people's domestic entertainment diet is supplemented with entertainment media imported from the US and culturally proximate countries. Yet, viewer selectivity and audience activity do nothing to challenge the political-economic structures of CI or rectify imbalances in audio-visual flows between countries. Hesmondhalgh (2008) says it is "unfair for critics to claim that concepts such as active audiences and cultural hybridity demolish the notion of cultural imperialism" (107). The agency of viewers can be recognized and studied without abandoning political economy.

BOX 1.2

THE GLOBAL MEDIA EVENT

Building on McLuhan's (1964) notion of the "global village," Meyrowitz (1986) argues that cross-border electronic TV flows have transformed the traditional relationship between physical location and social interaction. Physical location has long been the key site of social interaction, culture, and identity. The immediate "here and now" was the paramount container of identity, but cross-border electronic media flows now enable social experiences to become de-territorialized and increasingly mediated through TV screens and other ICTs. Satellite television turns viewers into "audiences to performances that happen in other places and give us access to audiences who are not physically present" (7). Electronic media bring "information and experience to everyplace from everyplace" as presidential speeches, military invasions, and sports events become "dramas that can be played on the stage of almost anyone's living room" (118). Meyrowitz (1986) believes that new "communities without propinquity" are being established by people in and through their relationships to the fictions of TV shows, films, or news media events. Media products are referents for common cross-border experiences. A globally popular TV show may make the world feel like one single, interconnected space, and may encourage people to develop an awareness of how their own local, regional, and national experiences are connected to the local, regional, and national experiences of others. Global media events are excellent examples of this phenomenon.

A "global media event" is a happening or occurrence that becomes the site of intense, repetitive, and regularized coverage by media organizations and which is consumed by viewers in many different countries. Global media events are watched by millions of people from many different countries. Global media events focus on topics of collective importance, such as war and peace, miracles and disasters, and broader universalistic dramas about sport, celebrity, and royalty (Couldry, Hepp, and Krotz 2009). Global media events attract a transnational audience, as opposed to a national audience. Although the event may happen in one country or place, it is viewed worldwide via global satellite TV and web-based communication. Ribes (2010) says that global media events are "mediated through new technologies, which produce their own emotional climate" and have "spectacular collective ritual performances" (1). Wark (1994) states that global media events foster a new virtual geography constructed entirely by technology and mediated information flows.

In the twenty-first century, global media events are regularized. They attract media corporations to triumph and trauma, advertisers to media corporations, and viewers to commercial events. The September 11, 2001 terrorist attacks on the US were watched by people all over the world, as was the 2003 US "shock and awe" bombing of Baghdad. The 2006 FIFA World Cup Final was watched by 715 million people (Harris 2007). The 2008 Summer Olympics opening ceremony in Beijing was watched by between one and four billion people (Dean and Fong 2008). Nielsen Media Research claims that 4.7 billion individual viewers (70 percent of the world's population) watched at least some part of the 2008 Summer Olympics on TV. The 2010 rescue of thirty-three trapped Chilean miners was watched by millions of people online (CBC 2010). The 2011 Cricket World Cup semi-final between India and Pakistan was watched by about one billion people (Marks 2011). The wedding of Prince William and Catherine Middleton drew 47 percent of the world's population in 180 different countries into its monarchical spectacle (BBC News UK 2011). All of these global media events established a transnational visual and affective connection between millions of different people from many different countries and cultures. People were united by the shared exposure to and ritualistic consumption of the same content.

Ninth, the CG paradigm challenges essentialist notions of territorially based or contained local or national cultures. In some accounts, cultural imperialism depicts Western and US TV shows and films as spreading a Western and American "culture" around the world, corrupting or violating local cultures in the process. Some CI scholars present a reductive notion of Western-American "culture" and a simplistic view of the local cultures ostensibly dominated or destroyed by Western-American TV shows and films. CG scholars criticize the conflation of entertainment media with culture, the view that "national" culture is the main source of identity, and territorialist and essentialist account of "cultures."

CG scholars criticize those who conflate entertainment media and national culture. Tomlinson (1991) says the relationship between "media" and "culture" should be viewed as a "subtle interplay of mediations" (61). TV shows and films do represent the meaning of culture for viewers in partial and selective ways, but culture is not reducible to entertainment media; it is also formed and reproduced through the actual or lived experiences of people. "With or without media channels," says Morris (2002), "people find ways of maintaining traditions that are meaningful to them" (285). A distinctive culture may thrive in the absence of a strong national media industry because culture does not always rely on electronic media for its expression or reproduction. CG scholars say that culture should not be equated with people's daily electronic media diet, and that people do not necessarily lose interest in their own culture when they areexposed to foreign entertainment. Also, contact with global entertainment media sometimes fortifies local and national identities. "Media can provide models to push against by kindling enhanced awareness of local values and symbols through contrast with images of foreign practices" (Morris 2002: 285). Watching US TV shows and films may enable people to compare and contrast their "national cultures" with those of the US as a way of re-affirming their sense of belonging to a nation.

CG scholars also scrutinize some CI scholars for representing national culture—bound by borders, composed of the same parts, and linked to territory—as the primary source of cultural identity. Kraidy (2004) identifies an "unarticulated assumption that guided much of early cultural imperialism work: culture conceived as a holistic, organic entity, usually identified with the nation-state" (250). While national identity is an important source of identity, and one which establishes a "group's sense of belonging to a particular collective with shared attributes (of place, language, culture) and a sense of exclusivity" (McQuail 1992: 264), it is not the only or the most significant source of cultural identity in the modern world. Tomlinson (1991) contends that within and between states, there exist patterns of cultural identification which are quite different to, and often in direct conflict with, the (ostensibly homogenous) "national culture" (68–69). Massey (1991, 1992) argues that territories are not culturally homogeneous, but are in fact "spaces of interaction" in which a variety of different identifications and identities are constructed from media and material resources which are developed locally and trans-locally. Ang (1990) says that "The transnational communications system [. . .] offers opportunities of new forms of bonding and solidarity, new ways of forging cultural communities" (252) that are not contained by territorial borders. Diasporic communities, ethno-linguistic struggles for recognition, indigenous particularisms, and anti-capitalist counter-nationalisms flourish, problematizing simplistic views of internally unified national cultures. On the individual and micro-community levels, people's day-to-day cultural identifications are not always contained or controlled by the symbolisms of nation. As Ang (1990) notes, the concept of national identity is problematic because "it tends to subordinate other, more specific and differential sources for the construction of cultural identity" (252). People worldwide identify with and against their fellow national citizens through subcultures, gender roles, religions, social classes, familial obligations, brand lifestyles, and political ideologies. By privileging nation-ness as the main source of identity, some CI scholars overlook the multiplicity of people's cultural identifications and the fact that the nation is never given, but always constructed.

CG scholars also challenge the view that essential, pure, or authentic national cultures are being lost, polluted, corrupted, or changed as result of contact with global entertainment media:

> Statements about the negative effects of imported media on identities are based on the assumption that something from outside—media—will corrupt something inside—identity. This, in turn, is based on the often-unrecognized assumptions that identity is dependent on fixed traditions and symbols, and that identity and its unadulterated expressions originated from some early point in a group's existence. (Morris 2002: 280)

Some accounts of cultural imperialism—though not Herbert Schiller's—depict US entertainment media destroying a country's national culture, which is presumed to be the site of "pristine cultural authenticity" (Ang 1996: 153). They presume "the existence of a pure internally homogenous, authentic, indigenous [national] culture, which then becomes subverted or corrupted by foreign influence" (Morley 1994: 151). They can be faulted for suggesting that prior to US media contact, the national cultures of postcolonial nation-states were untouched by foreign influences (Hannerz 1996: 66; Massey 1992: 9; Thompson 1995: 169; Tunstall 1977: 57–59). In this respect, some accounts of CI espouse a tacit "cultural essentialism": the belief that singular cultures exist and that cultures are internally unified by distinctive, fixed, and static traits, qualities, or characteristics.

CG scholars also complicate the totalizing view of American and Western culture represented by some CI scholars, who often use terms like "America" and "the West" interchangeably to denote a unified, homogeneous, and universalizing culture. But countries and entire geo-political regions—the US and the West—do not have pure, authentic, and unitary cultures. "Americanization" and "Westernization" are problematic categories that connote many different things: capitalism, scientific and technological rationality, liberal political ideology, consumer culture, the English language, certain styles of dress, food preparation and consumption habits, architecture, urbanization, religion, and so on (Tomlinson 1996: 25). Where do these American–Western cultural elements begin and end? The territory of the United States? The members of the EU? New York City? Qatar? In the twenty-first century, concepts such as "the West" and "America" lump together a hodgepodge of economic, political, and cultural elements that are no longer tied to or bound by any one geography. "The West" and "America" are ideological terms. "The West acts as an ideological category, an imperial fetish, an alibi in the determinate absence of a plausible conceptualization of capitalism and imperialist social relations" (Lazarus 2002: 57). "America" can be just as mystifying. Unitary notions of America conceal divisive social relations of class, racial, and sexual inequality in the US.

To move beyond monolithic and essentialist accounts of Western and American identity, CG scholars use the concept of *hybridity*. This concept posits all cultures as heterogeneous, mixed up, and changing (Pieterse 2003; Parmeswaran 1999; Tomlinson 1991, 1996). Kraidy (2002) says that hybridity is an umbrella concept for cultural mixing, such as creolization and syncretism, and that this term encompasses "the postcolonial cultures in Africa, Latin America, Asia and the diaspora in the West" (319). Cultural hybridity is the synthesis of two or more cultural elements from different sources. When one culture meets another, they mix, forming something new or different. CG scholars say that cultures are always hybrid in nature. "[E]very culture," notes Morley (1994), "has ingested foreign elements from exogenous sources with the various elements becoming 'naturalized' within it" (151). Garcia-Canclini (1997) says that "diverse intercultural mixtures" are found in modern society among traditional and modern, high, popular, and mass cultures, as well as across geographical borders (11). Pryke (1995) claims that "culture is not a timeless source of purity, but is, in general conditions, subject to constant absorption and adaptation" (68). Morris (2002) argues that

> identity and the practices and symbols that express it are never pure and uncorrupted, [and] that nothing comes solely from the 'inside' a culture, and that symbols and traditions—whether invented, imposed, emergent, constructed, begged, borrowed, or stolen—change all the time. (280)

As a result of the global cultural economy, opportunities for cultural mixing have increased. Through mixing, one culture can change another. Instead of viewing culture as something that is authentic, pure, closed, and unified, CG scholars argue that culture is plastic, impure, open, and ever-changing. As Said (1993) affirms, "All cultures are involved in one another: none is single and pure, all are hybrid, heterogeneous, extraordinarily differentiated and un-monolithic" (xxv). Throughout history, "all cultures (if to different degrees) have routinely absorbed and indigenized elements from other sources" (Morley 2006: 37). Hybrid cultural identities are constructed, not given. And cultural exchanges are infrequently reciprocal; hybridity often results from asymmetrical and unequal power relations between states, media firms, and groups of people. Some countries—the most powerful ones—have a greater capacity for spreading their cultural elements around the world than do others. Hybridization is not always a happy process.

Tenth, CG scholars take issue with the CI paradigm's apparently neo-colonial "discourse of domination" and warn scholars in metropolitan academia against the use and abuse of such terms. In a classic deconstruction of the CI paradigm, Tomlinson (1991) argues that "cultural imperialism" is a Western (ostensibly American-centric) discourse of cultural domination, contending that:

> The discourse we're concerned with is inescapably lodged in the culture of the developed West [. . .] Cultural imperialism is a critical discourse which operates by representing the cultures whose autonomy it defends in its own (dominant) Western cultural terms. It is a discourse caught up in ironies that flow from its position of discursive power. (2)

Tomlinson's concern with CI is not whether or not the discourse points to something actually existing in the real world (i.e., a form of cultural domination) but, rather, a sense that by speaking and writing about cultural imperialism as the "domination" of a weaker country by a stronger country, scholars reproduce the very process their writing seeks to challenge: "there is danger of the practice of cultural imperialism being reproduced in the discussion of it" (11). Tomlinson says that when CI critics claim that non-US cultures are "dominated" by US media corporations, they affirm the dominant power of the US media over non-US cultures. Tomlinson's concern about "who speaks for whom" in discussions of cultural imperialism demonstrates a self-reflexive awareness of the relationship between intellectual knowledge, power and privilege, the geopolitical location of institutional power/knowledge, and the politics and potential effects of representation.

Fredrick Buell (1994) extends Tomlinson's criticism of the concept of cultural imperialism. Buell takes issue with CI scholars' infrequent use of the phrase "cultural penetration" (when describing the process of strong US media corporations entering weaker non-US peripheries to off-load their media goods). Cultural penetration is read as the "unconscious use of gender-significant rhetoric" (2), which makes US audio-visual trade in non-US countries tantamount to rape. The US is framed as a hyper-masculine criminal rapist; the Rest are framed as feminized victims of rape. For Buell, the notion that media corporations penetrate local cultures is inappropriate; it conveys a woeful disregard of the agency of the people being talked about: "it repeats the gendering of imperialist rhetoric by continuing to style the First World as male and aggressive and the Third as female and submissive" (2). Buell continues: the "portrayal of the cultural helplessness of the Third World repeats what it opposes: it too readily assumes the imperial viewpoint that Third World cultures are weak and defenceless"

(3). Buell's reading of the CI paradigm is inspired by numerous postcolonial criticisms of the gendering of colonial subjects and the sexualization of colonized geographies by Orientalist discourses, whose binary strategies were a constitutive part of the European colonialist project (Said 1979). By talking about cultural domination, US metropolitan intellectuals (like the European colonialist intelligentsia in a different conjuncture) risk producing a disparaging discourse about inferior, passive, and weak non-US others which, in turn, affirms (and constitutes) the identity of the US as superior, active, and strong. Inserted into Buell's analytical frame, which conjoins the ideological determinations and effects of nineteenth-century colonial poetics to post-colonial international relations, CI scholars (with their fantasy of US media corporations penetrating peripheries) are rendered as ignorant intellectuals whose discourse of cultural domination is meta-textually and geopolitically on the side of US and Western cultural imperialism.

Tomlinson and Buell's concern about speaking for others, their social constructivist bias, and their binary-breaking meta-criticism of the concept of cultural imperialism establish two claims. The first concerns the geographical origin and usage of the concept of cultural imperialism (cultural imperialism originates as part of an essentially Western academic discourse in the metropolitan academy to be used by, for, and among metropolitan intellectuals). The second claim concerns the political identity of the concept of cultural imperialism, and the ideological effects of the usage of this concept (it is oppressive and its users are in some way—consciously or otherwise—complicit with the process they oppose).

Both of these claims are unfair. As mentioned earlier, CI is a postcolonial concept that emerged *against* Western colonialism and US neo-colonialism. Critics of the CI paradigm have "taken the notion out of context, abstracting it from the concrete historical conditions that produced it: the political struggles and commitments of the 1960s and 1970s" (Mattelart and Mattelart 1998: 137–8). Cabral (1973), Fanon (1963), and Thiong'o (1986) all criticized cultural imperialism and emphasized the centrality of anti-imperial cultural politics. The discourse of CI is not lodged, as Tomlinson imagines, in the intellectual culture of the West. It emerged through anti-colonial struggles, and was then more carefully theorized by Western anti-imperial intellectuals like Schiller, after he spoke with and then on behalf of those voices which his own nation-state's political and economic elite so frequently ignored. The attempt to excise the discourse of cultural domination from communication theory, and the deconstruction of the culturally dominant/culturally dominated dichotomy, risks flattening the global field of power of relations and disavowing the fact that the world continues to be a systematically and fundamentally unequal place. Some states and corporations have greater power at their disposal to get what they want from others. The world system underlying the "global cultural economy" is not flat, equal, or socially just.

CONCLUSION: BETWEEN CULTURAL IMPERIALISM AND CULTURAL GLOBALIZATION

This chapter has contextualized, reviewed, and discussed the main claims associated with the CI and CG paradigms in global media studies. The goal of this chapter has not been to legitimize CI or CG as the best, truest, or most adequate paradigm for studying global TV shows and films. Rather, this chapter put these two paradigms in dialogue. While quite a lot of scholarship on global entertainment media tends to side with either the CI paradigm *or* the CG paradigm, this book contends that the insights of both paradigms are relevant and useful. The CG paradigm presents a useful counterpoint to some of the gloomier, underdeveloped, and polemical discussions of CI. Though the CG paradigm has been embraced by scholars who wish to "move beyond" or "modify" the original CI paradigm, many of the CI paradigm's core claims are still valid (Curran and Park 2000; Harindrath 2002; Morley 2006; Sparks 2007, 2012; Van Elteren 2003). While the CG paradigm's focus on what's new is compelling, there is still a need to examine how the old political-economic structures of imperialism haunt the present. As Morley argues: "Unfashionable as it has become in some circles, it may still be that we should take Schiller's argument for the continuing existence of North American cultural imperialism very seriously" (2005: 33). The CI paradigm's critical political-economic approach to global entertainment need not be exchanged for the CG paradigm's focus on discourse, cultural complexity, consumption, and the play of meanings. Political economy and critical cultural studies can be used in a complimentary fashion. This is the point of "cultural materialism."

A challenge for twenty-first century global media studies may be the development of a middle ground paradigm that does not tirelessly or naively defend the supposed claims to truth of the CI paradigm or the CG paradigm. Too often, these two paradigms appear in literature reviews and skirmishes between ideologues on the Left and Right as caricatures or straw men, when the research associated with each paradigm is often more supple, complex, and nuanced. A cultural materialist middle-ground paradigm mobilizes the best of the radical political-economy and critical cultural studies approaches of the CI and CG paradigms in a complimentary fashion. The CI and CG paradigms can be employed in a mutually supportive way; CI scholars can learn from critical cultural studies scholars, just as CG scholars can learn from radical political economists. Moran and Keane (2006) suggest that instead of substituting one paradigm or "research totality" for the other, scholars should perform more "median kinds of studies and investigations" (72) that are grounded, contextual, and focused on power relations.

Although the CI and CG paradigms emerged in different historical periods, they are not trapped in those periods; both paradigms remain significant and useful to scholars. While the CI paradigm emphasizes continuity with the past, the CG paradigm attends to change associated with present-day trends. Though the CI paradigm is often said to be irrelevant and therefore necessarily replaced by the CG paradigm, this book contends that the adequacy or inadequacy of each paradigm can only be determined by case-specific cultural materialist research on the production, distribution, marketing, exhibition, textual design, and consumption of specific globalizing TV shows and films. A modified CI paradigm or a "weak" CG paradigm which attends to imperial history, political-economic structures and cultural power asymmetries, is committed to social justice, and grapples with the dialectic of continuity and change is favored by this author. But this book encourages scholars to participate in the global paradigm debate by testing the claims of each paradigm through research. Students and scholars may support, contest, complicate, extend, or synthesize these paradigms through localized and contextually specific research. The chapters which follow work in and between the CI and CG paradigms: some tacitly side with the CI paradigm while others support positions connected with the CG paradigm. Debates between the proponents of each paradigm have been going on for a long time, and these paradigms will likely continue to inspire interesting research. The remainder of this book does not seek to close down the debates arising from the CI and the CG paradigms, but instead aims to provide an accessible and engaging contribution to them.

CHAPTER 2

Capitalizing on Global Entertainment Media

INTRODUCTION: ENTERTAINMENT INCORPORATED

Entertainment is produced within a capitalist mode of production. A mode of production refers to the ways in which production is organized in society. Capitalism is the world's dominant mode of production; it is the dominant mode of producing and distributing entertainment in nearly every country on the planet. Capitalism is an economic system in which goods and services are produced for sale (with the intention of making a profit) by a large number of separate firms using privately owned capital goods and wage-labor (Bowles and Edwards 1985: 394). In the twenty-first century, TV shows and films are made by waged workers employed by a number of production firms and sold (or licensed) as a commodity to consumers (i.e., other media corporations and viewers). The means of producing, distributing, marketing, and exhibiting most TV shows and films are owned by media conglomerates, not by governments or the workers themselves. The studios in which workers create and assemble entertainment are private property; so too are the distribution and exhibition channels that carry entertainment to consumers. Audiences are transformed into commodities by media corporations and sold to advertising clients. Media corporations coordinate TV and film commodity production, distribution, marketing, and exhibition using technology, labor, and financial resources within and between many nation-states. All media corporations—whether based in China, Canada, India, South Korea, France, Poland, or the US—produce and sell entertainment as a market commodity. In order to maximize their profit, media corporations are "consciously denationalizing from their domestic origins in the course of developing genuinely global strategies of operation" (Sklair 2001: 48). Entertainment media is primarily produced, distributed, exhibited, and consumed as a commodity within a world system in which media corporations compete to control the copyright to TV shows and films, the means of media production, distribution and exhibition, and audience attention.

Which basic capitalist logics influence the production of entertainment media in society? Who are the main corporate players in entertainment industries, and what are the relations between them? Which economic and cultural processes shape the actual production, distribution, marketing, and exhibition of TV shows and films as commodities? What are the distinctive qualities of entertainment commodities? How do media corporations attempt to profit-maximize at the expense of rivals by competing to control markets? What is convergence? How do horizontal and vertical integration strategies shape entertainment content? What is the difference between a transnational media corporation (TNMC) and national media corporation (NMC)? Where are the world's most powerful media firms based? What is the power relationship between US and non-US media corporations? To answer these questions, this chapter discusses the capitalist entertainment industry and some relevant topics and developments in the transnational capitalist economy of entertainment media. Curtin (2005) argues that "further development of the scholarly literature regarding media globalization will require more careful attention to the institutional logics of media organizations" (156.) This chapter examines how entertainment media is shaped by capitalist logics and the goals of media corporations.

The first part of this chapter discusses how some of capitalism's basic logics shape the existence of entertainment media, describes the roles and goals of the major corporate stakeholders in the capitalist entertainment industry (producers, financiers, distributors, marketers, and exhibitors), highlights the unique characteristics of entertainment media commodities, examines the tension between competition and concentrated, centralized, and controlled entertainment markets, and discusses convergence, horizontal and vertical integration strategies, and synergistic entertainment media. The second part of the chapter examines the transnational political economy of entertainment media. After distinguishing between "positional" and "relational" approaches to power and describing the characteristics of national media corporations (NMCs) and transnational media corporations (TNMCs), I discuss the rise of "strategic alliances" between TNMCs and NMCs based on joint ventures, equity alliances, and licensing agreements. An understanding of how the forces and relations of capitalism and powerful media corporations influence entertainment media is foundational knowledge in global media studies.

ENTERTAINMENT MEDIA IN CAPITALISM: MEDIA CORPORATIONS, CLASS DIVISION, COMMODITIES, AND PROFIT

Entertainment media is an integral part and product of many capitalist societies in the present age. In all capitalist societies, profit-seeking media corporations own the means of media production and distribution, a class division between media owners and waged cultural workers exists, and commoditized media goods are made to be bought and sold in markets.

In capitalist societies, privately owned *media corporations*—not governments—are the dominant owners of the means of producing, distributing, and exhibiting entertainment media in society (Chan 2005a; Epstein 2006; Flew 2007; Scott 2005; Meehan 2010; Wasko 2003). The goal of all media corporations is profit-maximization. In order to generate profit, they bring money, technology, media, and hundreds (if not thousands) of people together in productive social relations. Though media corporations comprise many people, they are recognized by law as one person, with rights and responsibilities. Viacom employs thousands of people, but is recognized as one person. So too are Walt Disney and Time Warner. The legal fiction of the media corporation as a singular person allows CEOs, board members, and shareholders to enjoy limited liability for the conduct of the corporations they govern. As rights-bearing people, media corporations can exercise their rights against other people (and governments).

Though media corporations exist to profit-maximize on behalf of their CEOs and shareholders, they have privileges and liabilities distinct from those of their owners. To diminish concerns about their power, they do many things to build a positive public image. Viacom donated $1 million tax-deductible dollars to support the construction of a Martin Luther King Jr. memorial on the National Mall in Washington, DC (Robertson 2007). In 2010, Disney donated more than $198 million tax-deductible dollars to various children's charities. Through the media platforms they own, media corporations regularly represent themselves as good corporate citizens, but it is important to note that they are primarily organized in order to, and are legally obligated to, maximize profit.

Media corporations pursue the goal of profit within a class-divided society in which the ownership of, and access to, private property is unequal. All capitalist societies are divided between the financial and industrial owners of the means of production ("the ruling class") and the people who must sell their labor in exchange for a wage ("the working class"). A mere one percent of the world population controls at least forty percent of the world's total wealth (Stiglitz 2011). The richest one percent of the US population controls at least twenty-three percent of all US wealth (Reich 2010). Media corporations are institutionalized expressions of the class divisions in capitalist societies. The representation of the corporation as a single person conceals the thousands of waged working people that are employed by them, and the specific contributions that they make. The structure of media corporations is based upon a *class division* between the owning class (the few people who own and manage the corporation) and the working class (the many people who sell their labor power to that corporation in exchange for a wage).

The *owning class* is a small group of people who own the property rights to entertainment media, and the means of producing, distributing, and exhibiting it. This class includes the chief executive officers (CEOs) and shareholders of media corporations. Rupert Murdoch, the founder, chairman, and CEO of News Corporation—the world's second largest media conglomerate—is a member of the owning class. *Forbes* magazine says that Murdoch is the 38th richest US citizen and the 117th-richest person in the world. His net worth is $7.6 billion dollars. Media owners have power. They possess the exclusive right to create, control, rent, sell, and use the entertainment capital they own in whatever way they choose. The owning class—shareholders and CEOs—live off the profits generated by the media corporations they own and the labor of the thousands of waged workers they employ.

Distinct from the owners of media corporations is the *working class*. Unlike owners, the majority of cultural workers do not own the means of entertainment production, distribution, and exhibition. They do not own studios, TV networks, retail systems, or the copyright to the TV shows and films they produce. The majority of News Corporation's more than 50,000 employees do not own the conglomerate. The almost 50,000 animators in China, India, Singapore, South Korea, and the Philippines that Walt Disney, Time Warner, and Sony regularly outsource jobs to do not own the animation studios they toil within (Mukherjee 2011). Cultural workers live by selling their labor power—the mental and manual capabilities required to achieve specific tasks—to media corporations as a commodity in exchange for a wage. Like all workers, the workers employed by media corporations need an income to fund their base subsistence needs. They sell their labor power to their employers in exchange for the money they need to pay their rent/mortgage and utility bills and to buy food and clothing. They also use their wages to sate cultural wants: a ticket for the latest blockbuster film, a copy of a new video game, or admission to a play.

There is nothing manifestly "coercive" about the exchange relationship between media corporations and workers. The market treats media corporations and workers as "free and equal" individuals, buyers and sellers of commodities (labor-power and finished entertainment products). But the outcome of this manifestly "free and equal" exchange relationship is a situation that favors the power and profit-interests of media corporations. Through this exchange relationship, media corporations gain control over the labor power of their workers for a set period of time. Once hired and under contract, workers are legally obliged to submit to the media corporation's right to direct their skills and talents in whatever way they decide. A finished entertainment product—a TV show or film—is the result of the exchange relationship between media corporations and the workers they employ. Many waged workers collaboratively produce TV shows and films, but they do not "own" them: the media corporation they are employed by does. Intellectual property law enables media corporations to divest workers of the creative products of their intellect and effort and exert proprietary control over what workers produce: TV shows and films.

The world's most powerful media corporations are gigantic holding companies for copyrighted TV shows and films—the commodities produced by the waged cultural workers they employ. Marx (1977) deems the "cell form" of the capitalist mode of production to be the *commodity*: something produced for exchange in a market. Schiller (2007) defines commodity as:

> a resource that is produced for the market by wage labor. Whether a tangible good or an evanescent service, universally enticing or widely reviled, a consumer product or a producer's good, a commodity contains defining linkages to capitalist production and, secondarily, to market exchange. (21)

Media corporations hire waged workers to produce TV shows and films to be exchanged in markets as commodities. The ownership of TV shows and films by media corporations and the exchange of these as commodities in markets depend on copyright: a set of state-granted exclusive rights that regulate the reproduction and use of a particular creative expression (see Chapter 3).

In order to profit-maximize, media corporations sell TV shows and films in many commodity forms through various market exhibition "windows" to many consumers in many countries over time (Wasko 2003). *Profit* is the difference between the total amount of money a media corporation spends to produce an entertainment commodity (costs) and the total amount of money generated by a media corporation through the sale, licensing of the rights to, or reproduction of entertainment (revenue). If the amount of money a media firm accumulates by selling an entertainment commodity (revenue) exceeds the amount of money spent in making it (cost), profit is made. Time Warner's HBO, for example, profited by selling *Game of Thrones* (2011), a medieval fantasy TV series, to TV networks in many countries. HBO spent approximately $50 million dollars making *Game of Thrones*; it charged TV networks in many countries about

$2.5 million for every episode they broadcast (Szalai 2011). The revenue HBO collected by selling the global rights to *Game of Thrones* far exceeded the cost of manufacturing it: HBO profit-maximized.

With profit, CEOs can do a number of things: they can engage in price wars with competitors to reward brand-loyal consumers with low prices, discounts, or perks, or they can increase the wages of their workers to reward them for a job well done. But what they usually do is pay dividends to shareholders. A dividend is a sum of money derived from profit which a media corporation pays to shareholders. In 2011, for example, Viacom, CBS, Time Warner, and Walt Disney paid big dividends to shareholders (Szalai 2011). "Returning value to shareholders is a commitment we take very seriously," said CBS president and CEO Leslie Moonves (cited in Szalai 2011). The CEOs of media corporations also take a huge cut of profits by paying themselves massive salaries and bonuses. In 2010, the world's thirty highest-paid media CEOs earned an average of nearly $22 million each, an increase of thirteen percent over 2009 (James 2011). Seven of the top ten highest paid people in the US are media CEOs. In 2011, Viacom Inc.'s CEO, Philippe Dauman, was paid $84.5 million. CBS Corporation CEO Leslie Moonves took $57.7 million, including a $27.5 million bonus. Liberty Media Corp's CEO Gregory B. Maffei accumulated $87.1 million (Lublin 2010). Discovery Communications' CEO David Zazlav raked in $42.6 million; Brian Roberts, CEO of Comcast, received $31 million; Roger Iger, CEO of Walt Disney, took home $28 million; Jeff Bewkes, CEO of Time Warner, banked $26.1 million (Hagey 2011). In addition to paying themselves immense sums of money, CEOs re-invest a portion of their profit back into the means of production through mergers, acquisitions, and capital upgrades.

THE INDUSTRY STRUCTURE, OR WHO DOES WHAT?
CAPITALIST CIRCUITS AND VALUE CHAINS

Private ownership of the means of production and distribution, a social class division, the commodification of media content, and the pursuit of profit shape the social existence of entertainment media in all societies that have been integrated into global capitalism. According to Marx (1977), capitalism is not a reified thing, but a system in motion. At its most basic, capitalism is a dynamic "circuit" that entails the following practices: corporations use money (M) to purchase as commodities (C) the means of production (P) (labor, technology, and resources) to produce commodities (C') that are sold for more money (M') on the market. Part of the total money generated through the sale of commodities is retained as profit (shareholder dividends and CEO salaries and bonuses); another part is re-invested back into the means of production. This basic circuit underlies the production of TV and film commodities. Media corporations use money (M) to purchase as commodities (C) the means of production (P) (labor power and technological resources) to produce new entertainment commodities (C') that are sold for more money (M') to consumers. Part of the total money generated through the sale of entertainment media as a commodity is retained as profit; another part is re-invested back into the means of production. Pressured by market competition, media corporations accelerate this circuit, turning money into entertainment commodities, and then back again, into more money.

Marx's circuit model of capitalism is a useful starting point for conceptualizing the dynamic set of processes through which media corporations use money to produce TV show and film commodities, sell them to consumers in markets, and resultantly generate more money to start the production cycle anew. There are many media corporations involved in the production, distribution, marketing, and exhibition of any one TV show or film in all societies. All media commodities are produced by numerous media corporations, which interact in a number of interdependent circuits and through a set of interacting stages. Porter (1985) conceptualizes the stages involved in making commodities as a "value chain." TV shows are conceptualized, physically assembled (produced), packaged and marketed, distributed to exhibitors, and then transmitted or carried to consumers. Films are created, shot and produced, marketed and distributed, and exhibited to viewers through a variety of exhibition windows such as theater chains, DVDs, and digital files. The chain of activities that bring TV shows and films into the social world as commodities is not coordinated by individual consumers, but by many corporate stakeholders.

Hundreds of profit-seeking corporate "players" are intermediaries in the circuits that comprise the overall value chain. They conduct "the business" of entertainment media. The main players who bring TV shows and films into the world are production companies, financiers, distribution companies, marketing companies, and exhibition companies. Before being released for public consumption, a TV show or film will have already been influenced by the business calculations and cultural perceptions of production companies, financiers, distributors, marketers, and exhibitors. In the following sections, I describe how the structural roles and goals of these players shape the existence of entertainment media.

Production companies conceptualize, produce, and sell TV and film content. They organize and administer the financial and physical infrastructure for producing media content. They raise financing for projects, hire waged cast and crew members, manage a division of cultural labor, and schedule and monitor tasks from pre- to post-production. Many production companies are subsidiaries of larger media conglomerates: "independent" production companies often operate under contract as affiliates to large conglomerates. Within production companies, executives, directors, or a group of writers propose and pitch story ideas. The story may be original or derived from an existing work such as a novel, comic book, video game, TV show, or film. *Avatar* (2009), for example, was based upon an original screenplay written by James Cameron. The globally popular *Hunger Games* (2012) film was derived from science fiction novels written by Suzanne Collins. The *Resident Evil* film franchise takes its story from the popular Japanese survival-horror video game by the same title. The *A-Team* film (2010) was adapted from a popular US TV series that was originally broadcast to US and transnational viewers in the mid-1980s. Christopher Nolan derived the story and characters of *Batman Begins* (2005), *The Dark Knight* (2008), and *The Dark Knight Rises* (2012) from DC comic books. No cultural worker employed by a production company is a completely autonomous creator: they do not get to make whatever TV show or film they want to make. In fact, the creative autonomy of every cultural worker hired by a production company—directors, actors, script writers, and others—is constrained by external financial pressures.

Some of the world's largest audio-visual production companies are based in the US. These include ABC Studios (Walt Disney), Warner Brothers Television and CBS Television Studios (Time Warner), Fox Entertainment Group (News Corporation), Paramount Pictures and MTV Films (Viacom), and Universal Studios (NBC-Universal). But audio-visual production companies are based elsewhere too: Cuatro Cabezas (Argentina), Crawford Productions (Australia), Globo Filmes (Brazil), Brightlight Pictures (Canada), Orange Sky Golden Harvest (China), Vision Quest Media (France), Grundy UFA (Germany), Balaji Telefilms (India), Cinecittà (Italy), Nordisk Film (Iceland), Kadokawa Pictures (Japan), Esperanto Films (Mexico), Motek (Netherlands), Regal Entertainment (Phillipinnes), VID (Russia), Five Star Production (Thailand), Abu Dhabi Media (Abu Dhabi), and Film4Productions (United Kingdom) are all examples of non-US production companies.

All production companies, regardless of where they are located, are reliant upon financing. A production company's transformation of a story concept into a TV show or film commodity depends upon access to money. TV shows and films cannot and will not be made unless financiers seed a large sum of money to the production. A *financier* invests money in entertainment production with the expectation that a finished TV show or film will generate a return sum of money—over time and space—that exceeds their original investment. Financing is the single most important factor determining whether or not a TV show or film story concept will be made into a commodity, because TV shows and films are very expensive to manufacture. Screenplay development costs money; the labor of directors, screenwriters, and actors costs money; set building, wardrobe development, make-up, and transport cost money; special effects and musical score design cost money; editing costs money. TV shows and films cannot be manufactured without a tremendous amount of money behind them. Thus, before production can begin, executive producers—the people in charge of production companies, and who are responsible for securing financing—must consult with a number of potentially interested financial players—conglomerates, banks, venture capitalists, states, and advertisers—about the profit-potential of the story concept and whether or not they would be interested in supporting it. The production of TV shows and films is "financialized": it is subject to a host of pre-emptive financial valuations and speculations which instrumentalize entertainment media as a means of increasing returns for investors. Like other industrial sectors, the entertainment and culture industries are integrated into world financial markets and geared toward serving the goals of a number of financial actors.

Entertainment financing comes from a variety of sources. A significant amount of financing for entertainment media is provided "in house" by the vertically and horizontally integrated media conglomerates which "parent" a large number of production and distribution companies. Large media conglomerates own distribution companies as subsidiaries, which act as financers to production companies. Film and TV distribution companies are quasi-banks to production companies: they lend money to them in return for content rights. They incur huge debts in order to finance production because they expect that, over time and space, the finished TV show or film will generate financial returns that far exceed the debt. A portion of the required finance can also come from "out-of-house" sources such as banks, governments, and even advertisers

(Basu 2010; Vogel 2007). Global banks, private equity firms, and venture capitalists invest in, operate hedge funds for, and grant lines of credit to TV and film production companies (Avery 2006; CFO Staff 2005). In early 2012, Sun Media Group and Harvest Fund Management established Harvest Seven Stars Media Private Equity, an $800 million Chinese equity fund that supports the production of entertainment media in China and in other countries, with the goal of maximizing returns for investors. This equity fund provided financing to the 2012 global hit film, *Mission Impossible: Ghost Protocol* (Cieply 2012). State-supported TV and film financing agencies such as the United Kingdom's EM Media and Germany's Bavarian Film & Television Fund also provide financing to production companies (Epstein 2005). Advertising companies may co-finance production through product placement deals. On behalf of their clients, ad firms pay production companies to display or feature a branded product in a finished film or TV show. Advertising companies indirectly finance TV shows by paying TV networks to expose targeted audience groups to the advertisements scheduled between TV shows. Thus, advertising firms—the primary source of revenue for TV networks—influence the kinds of TV shows conceptualized, produced and exhibited.

All financiers—studios, TV networks, distributors, financial institutions, states, and advertisers—want and expect a financial return on their entertainment investment. If a film or TV show is profitable, financiers receive back their principal and a percentage of their initial investment or, alternately, take a percentage of the overall profit. Advertisers are paid with quantified and commercialized audience attention. However, there is no guarantee that a film or TV show will turn a profit or capture an audience. The decision to finance entertainment is always a gamble. In an attempt to minimize risk and maximize returns, financiers try to figure out in advance whether or not a TV show or film will be a hit. Before fronting money, financiers speculate about the profit-potential of a TV show or film. They may ask and attempt to answer some or all of the following questions: which countries and which audience demographic (mass and/or niche) will this TV show or film target (what is the likelihood of this entertainment product connecting with particular audience segments in many countries)? Will this TV show or film serve the needs of advertising corporations (will this product also attract the viewers that advertising firms want to display their ads to)? Which exhibition platforms will be used, and where and when (what exhibition windows will this TV show or film be circulated by, and in what time frame)? How will consumer demand for this TV show or film be cultivated (how will this product be marketed to viewers, at what expense, and through which channels)? Will state media regulators and policies limit or enable the flow of this TV show or film (how might content quotas affect the cross-border movement of this product)? Will cultural conditions impede or accelerate popular receptivity to this TV show or film (will cultural-linguistic differences deter or encourage consumers to watch)?

A combination of economic and cultural considerations bears upon the decision to finance, and ultimately to produce, TV shows and films. The economic and cultural concerns of financiers influence both the creative autonomy of cultural workers and the entertainment content they create. Given that production companies largely depend upon ongoing and amicable relations with financers, many of the TV and film concepts they propose for production will be those they anticipate will impress or be approved by financiers. In an attempt to minimize risk and maximize a return on their investment, financiers will try to influence the content—the genre, the narrative, the ideology, the aesthetic, and the cast—of the TV shows and films they choose to support. Financiers put up money for entertainment projects they believe—or have been persuaded to believe—will maximize financial returns, while shirking and stymying projects they fear will not. By proposing projects they believe financiers will support, and heeding financiers' content concerns, many production companies find that their creative autonomy is substantially curbed. Christopherson (2011) says the cultural workers employed by production companies "cannot produce what they want (at least to earn a living). They must respond to what the conglomerates [and financing entities] want to distribute" (133). The power of financiers to seed money to production companies through a complex deal-making process gives them a significant amount of influence over cultural creativity and media content. Standardized TV shows and films designed to serve the profit goals of financiers are often the result. Yet, innovative TV shows and films with an "edge" (risky, non-traditional, and taboo content) are also produced (Curtin 1999). Despite industry pressures, cultural workers do have some creative autonomy (Hesmondhalgh 2007). Production companies create both standardized and innovative media content, not one or the other.

If and when a deal is made between a production company and its financiers, a contract is signed and the production of a story into a TV show or film commodity is "green-lighted." In the pre-production stage, the story concept is further developed by writers, and every step of the ensuing production of the TV show or film is meticulously planned. The executive producer hires a managerial crew for the project, including a production manager, director, assistant director, casting director, location manager, cinematographer, sound designer, art director, costume designer, storyboard artist, choreographer, and many others. Starring and supporting actors are signed for the production. As the story concept goes into principal photography—the point of no return for financiers—more waged cultural workers are hired from a New International Division of Cultural Labor (NICL) to complete a number of tasks (see Chapter 4). Studio sets are designed or constructed. Shooting locations are arranged. The actual production and filming of TV shows and films happens over weeks, months, and, in some instances, years, and often in more than one country. In post-production, scenes are cut, added, and further enhanced with special effects, soundscapes, animations, and other elements. The TV show or film is edited. The completed or finished TV show or film is then prepared for distribution.

Distribution companies act as intermediaries between production companies and exhibition companies. Distribution companies are basically wholesalers of entertainment content. They buy the rights to distribute TV shows and films from production companies and then sell these rights to exhibition companies for a set period of time. The terms of the business deal between a distribution company and a production company are stipulated by a distribution agreement. This legal document grants the distributor the right to distribute, license, and reproduce a TV show or film in specific territories, languages, and exhibition markets for a set period of time. All production companies must transact with distribution companies if they want their products to be screened in theaters, broadcast on TV, and sold as DVDs in retail outlets. Distributors play a significant role in influencing where TV shows and films will be released, when they will be released, and how they will be released to viewers. A distributor's decision to acquire a TV show or film's distribution rights for a particular country is shaped by locational factors such as the size of the market, whether or not similar TV shows or films have been well received by viewers in the past, the availability of exhibition outlets, the release schedules of competing products, and the cultural intricacies of state policy. Distribution executives decide what entertainment media will be watched and why, based upon business calculations and cultural assumptions about the cultural-linguistic tastes and preferences of viewers in the various countries they target (Havens 2008).

Some of the world's most powerful distribution firms are owned by large US-based media conglomerates such as Walt Disney (Disney Media Distribution), Sony (Columbia TriStar Motion Picture Group and Sony Pictures Television), Viacom (CBS Television Distribution and Paramount Pictures Corporation), and News Corporation (Fox Filmed Entertainment). But smaller distribution companies also exist all over the world: Pachamama Cine (Argentina), Titan Viwe (Australia), Imagem filmes (Brazil), Mongrel Media (Canada), Greater China Film and Television Distribution Company (China), Gaumont Film Company (France), Constantin Film (Germany), JCE Movies Limited (Hong Kong), Continental Content Distribution (Kenya), Dharma Productions (India), Toho (Japan), CJ Entertainment (South Korea), Sandrew Metronome (Sweden), Global Agency (Turkey), and Venevision (Venezuela).

Distribution companies are TV show and film marketers too. Havens (2003) says that in order to minimize the uncertainties surrounding the demand for TV shows and films, "numerous sales and marketing executives are necessary actors [. . .] to ensure that the products receive favorable critical evaluations and that they are sufficiently differentiated from and promoted against competitor's products" (22). Distribution companies cultivate demand for the TV shows and films they license by marketing these products to TV network acquisitions agents, theater chain buyers, and potential consumers at exhibition markets. Marketing can be handled by the distributors themselves, and/or contracted out to other marketing firms. In addition to conducting research on viewers to try to predict which TV shows or films will be profitable, *marketing companies* try to generate consumer interest in TV shows and films. They spend incredible sums of money and use a number of strategies to attract people to TV shows and films. They place ads in newspapers, news websites, and culture industry trade magazines such as *Variety* and *Hollywood Reporter*, pay for ads to be broadcast by TV and radio networks, buy film trailer time and space from theater chains, and place poster promotions on walls and billboards. Marketing companies generate buzz about TV shows and films by mobilizing unpaid advertisers like film and TV critics, reviewers, and brand-loyal consumers themselves. They release press kits (with detailed plot summaries, images, biographies of star actors, production notes, etc.) to the public with the expectation that people will voluntarily recirculate this material via their own personal communication networks. They arrange for star actors to talk up the product they appear in by giving interviews on soft TV news programs and talk shows. They "give away" promotional material such as buttons, posters, and t-shirts to fans, who then becoming walking, talking ads. They construct and monitor interactive websites to crowdsource viral advertising functions to fans, who actively create, cut and paste, and repurpose TV show and film PR through their own private blogs, Facebook pages, Twitter feeds, and YouTube channels.

Prior to, in tandem with, and after the marketing blitz commences, the finished TV shows and films start flowing into exhibition markets. Distributors sell the right to publicly exhibit copies of original TV shows and films to a number of *exhibition companies* (i.e., theater chains, TV networks, retail outlets, and Web stores). The cross-border movement of entertainment media is mediated by business transactions between international distributors (sellers) and national exhibition chains (buyers). Exhibition companies buy TV shows and films from distributors. The acquisitions agents for exhibition firms select content with the profit-interests of their employers in mind. Their decision to buy is shaped by a number of additional considerations: will it cost more or less to acquire a foreign TV show or film than to support or develop a homegrown TV show or film? Will the acquired product draw a large audience and thereby attract advertising clients to generate revenue for the exhibitor? Compared with other available products, does the TV show or film possess high-quality production values?

TV distributors and exhibitors conduct business at global TV trade fairs such as NATPE (National Association of Television Programming Executives), MIPCOM (Marche International des Films et des Programmes pour la Television, la Video, le Cable et le Satellite), and MIP-TV (Marche International des Programmes de Television) (Havens 2003). At these and other TV trade fairs, TV shows are showcased and promoted, TV licenses are bought and sold, and global-local networks are formed. TV distributors license the rights to transmit or sell a TV show to broadcast TV networks, pay cable TV, video on demand (VOD) services, and pay-per view (PPV) service providers for a set period of time. After that period of time expires, the TV show rights are returned to the distributor, which then sells them again to other exhibitors. Prices are determined by the distributor according to the buyer's ability to pay and assumptions about the cultural and economic value of the TV show (Havens 2008).

Film distribution companies sell the right to screen reproduced films to theater chains as exhibition licenses. This legal agreement between a distributor and theater chain specifies the date of a film's theatrical release and for how long (i.e., how many weeks) it will be screened. A few months after a film's theatrical release (and sometimes in tandem with its theatrical release) it will be sold in DVD or Blue-Ray Disc commodity forms by rental outlets (Blockbuster Video and a host of smaller stores) and big-box retailers (Best Buy, Future Shop, and Wal-Mart). In 2011, Wal-Mart sold $3.5 billion worth of DVD commodities (*Financial Times* 2011). Major airlines also license and exhibit filmed entertainment. A few months after its theatrical release, a film can be watched by individual flyers using on-demand in-flight entertainment platforms on seat-back screens. Usually a year or two after its theatrical release, a film is released as a TV program through licensing deals with TV firms. Theater chains and TV firms (broadcast, cable, and pay-per view) are traditional exhibitors of entertainment media, and are perhaps the most widely used.

Due to growing corporate and technological convergence, new media has become a significant exhibition platform for TV shows and films. Vertical and horizontal integration strategies, combined with the transformation of film and TV content into digital data (the 1s and 0s that make up binary code), paved the way for digital exhibition through personal computers and web sites, video game consoles, mobile devices, and tablets. Film and TV distributors license digital copies of entertainment media to Web-based media companies, which deliver them it to users. Apple's iTunes and the online stores for the Sony Playstation 3, Microsoft Xbox 360, and Nintendo Wii enable users to pay-to-download digital copies of TV shows and films. Major TV networks stream licensed TV episodes from their own websites and link to Facebook, Twitter, and MySpace to share promotional TV show and film material with fans. Since 2008, major and minor US TV networks—NBC, ABC, Fox, PBS, USA Network, Bravo, and Syfy—have digitally exhibited TV shows to viewers through the video website Hulu. com. Netflix, a subscription-based exhibitor of on-demand Internet-streamed entertainment media, digitally exhibits licensed TV and film content to viewers all over the world. In April 2011, Netflix announced it had 23.6 million subscribers in the United States and over 26 million subscribers worldwide in Canada, Latin America, the Caribbean, the United Kingdom, and Ireland. In the digital media age, corporate-controlled Web exhibitors aim to profit-maximize by managing and commercializing a user's uploading and downloading of TV shows and films.

Google-owned YouTube is an important yet informal means of digitally exhibiting TV show and film clips (Strangelove 2010). In 2010, 14.6 billion YouTube videos were streamed per month and the typical YouTube user watched approximately 100 videos per month. Against predictions that YouTube's user-generated content will displace attention from entertainment media produced by established media conglomerates, Hilderbrand (2007) argues that YouTube's popularity relies, at least in part, upon recirculated TV and film clips, old and new. The media corporations that own the TV shows and films from which the content clips are cut have an ambivalent relationship with YouTube. They sanction YouTube's exhibition of some clips and try to stop the flow of others. Pirate Bay, ISO Hunt, and other BitTorrent websites are informal (yet massively used) digital exhibition platforms that media corporations (and many governments) want to shut down (Fernandez 2012). Although the Web is a relatively new source for TV show and film exhibition, it does not herald the decline of traditional exhibition platforms. The new media cannibalize the old media, but do not kill it. In the current era, "multiple platforms" (Doyle 2010) co-exist and interact in a variety of ways. Worldwide, TV shows and films are exhibited through many platforms—theater chains, TV networks, airlines, retailers, the Web—in a variety of commodity forms and by way of carefully timed "windowing" strategies (Vogel 2007). Using a variety of exhibition platforms, media corporations circulate TV shows and films in different commodity forms and at different prices in order to tap the presumed willingness of a range of different people to pay different prices for copies of the same content.

In sum, TV shows and film content are brought into the world as commodities by a number of corporate stakeholders in overlapping and interdependent capitalist circuits and industry value chains: production companies conceptualize and manufacture entertainment content; financers seed money to production companies; distribution companies buy the licensing rights to finished content from production firms and lease the use of entertainment content to exhibitors (theater chains, TV networks, digital and actual rental outlets and retailers); marketing companies stir up demand for TV shows and films, which a number of exhibitors deliver to consumers. All of the corporate stakeholders involved in this complex process are in pursuit of profit: production companies make money by selling content rights to distribution companies; financers make money from their investment in entertainment; distribution companies make money from selling to exhibitors; marketing companies make money by creating consumer interest in and demand for TV shows and films; exhibitors make money by selling copies to consumers (and by selling consumer attention to advertisers). Every mediating circuit in this value chain of transactions is influenced by strategic economic calculations and cultural considerations.

CONTENT IS KING! THE CHARACTERISTICS OF ENTERTAINMENT MEDIA COMMODITIES

As discussed in the previous section, entertainment media content is produced and made to be consumed as commodities in exhibition markets. Copyrighted TV and film content (or "property") is a significant asset of all media corporations. "Content is certainly where most consumer and investor attention is typically focused" says Vogel (2007: 41). Many media corporations believe "content is king." Coined by Viacom CEO Sumner Redstone in the late 1990s, this phrase represents the view that control of copyright is essential to corporate profitability. At Time Warner, "content is king" says Weil (2011), linking 70 percent of the firm's cash flow to the corporation's cable TV library. At Walt Disney, "Content is King" claims Seitz (2011), reporting on Disney-ABC Television Group's lucrative deal with Amazon.com and Netflix to stream Disney's digital TV content. "Great content is king" says Philippe Dauma, CEO of Viacom (S. Olsen 2008). "We have vast libraries of content, and we are able to find new audiences thanks to emerging distribution. People in Asia are discovering *Beavis and Butt-head* and it hasn't been in the United States for seven years," Dauma adds. "For us, it's about finding more and more places to put it" (cited in S. Olsen 2008). By putting content in "more and more places" over time, media corporations try to make more and more profit. "Content is king" because of the capacity of media corporations to sell that content through a variety of different exhibition windows.

The TV shows and films produced to be sold by media corporations in exhibition markets, however, have characteristics that are both similar to and different from other commodities. Like all commodities produced in capitalism—automobiles, refrigerators, and microwave ovens, for example—TV show and film content is manufactured to be exchanged in and for a market as a commodity. Content is given a price tag, a monetary worth, an *exchange-value*. Although TV shows and films are produced to be sold as commodities in a market, they possess characteristics that distinguish them from most commodities. Winseck (2011) notes that "information and communication are 'strange commodities' " (12). Indeed, TV shows and films have unique characteristics: they are intangible, have public good qualities, are reproducible at minimal additional cost, express a cultural value that is not reducible to market exchange, and have societal externalities.

First, entertainment commodities are *intangible*. Tangible goods can be physically touched, picked up, put down, or destroyed. TV shows and films are not like tangible commodities. You cannot drive an episode of *The Simpsons* to the mall, store leftover pizza in a digital file of *Downton Abbey*, or pop corn with *Fringe*. Though films and TV shows are not intrinsically tangible, they can take tangible commodity forms: DVDs, comics and toys, for example. Teenagers may buy a DVD copy of *Pirates of the Caribbean: On Stranger Tides* (2011); an angry comic fan can rip a page out of an *X-Men* comic book; a child may mash together a plastic Batman toy and a Joker toy during play-time. While tangible entertainment commodities such as these have physical properties and an exchange-value, intangible entertainment commodities have no physical properties, but have an exchange value nonetheless. A digitally downloaded copy of *Pirates of the Caribbean*, purchased from iTunes and temporarily stored on a computer hard drive, cannot be touched: it can only be watched and listened to. The *X-Men: First Class* (2011) story cannot be incinerated. The concept of the *Batman* character does not fit in the palm of one's hand. Though they can be bought and sold just as easily as tangible entertainment commodities, intangible entertainment commodities are not inherently physical. The core of the value of entertainment is content, i.e., the immaterial story concept or idea caged by a number of tangible and intangible commodity forms.

Second, TV shows and films have public good qualities (Baker 2004). The two core characteristics of a public good are non-rivalry and non-excludability.

Non-rivalry. Many goods create rivalries. If Ravinder purchases a laptop computer from Best Buy on Friday, that means there is one less laptop computers available at the store for Derek to buy. If Dallas, Abigail, and John want to play the first-person shooter war game *Call of Duty: Black Ops* (2010) all day and night, then they will each have to each buy their own Playstation 3, Xbox, or Wii console. Most goods are not easily shared or sharable. But some goods are: A US consumer's enjoyment of a TV broadcast of the London 2012 Olympics, for example, does not reduce the availability of that TV show for consumption by millions of other people in other countries. One person's enjoyment of a digital episode of *Dexter* does not limit that TV show's availability to others. As a public good, media is a "product that is not 'used up" in consumption" and "can be consumed over and over again without additional units having to be produced" (Napoli 2009: 164).

Non-excludability. In addition to being non-rivalrous, media goods are non-excludable. Many people are excluded from certain goods because they do not have the means to pay for them. If Ravinder and Derek are deprived of the cash needed to buy a new laptop computer, they do not get to own one. If Dallas, Abigail, and John do not each have enough money to buy a new video game console, they will not get to play video games all day and all night. Price prohibits many people in many countries from using computers and playing video games. Some goods, however, do not naturally exclude people from enjoying them. It is difficult to exclude people from enjoying sunlight or air. A broadcast TV series does not naturally exclude people, nor does a digital copy of a TV show. Like sunlight and air, once a TV show exists in the world (and especially as a digital copy on the Web), it is very difficult—if not impossible—to exclude anyone from enjoying its benefits, even people who will not pay for the privilege of doing so (Vogel 2007: 19). A DVD copy of a blockbuster film can be rented from a video store, ripped to digital file, and then uploaded to Pirate Bay, where it is accessible to anyone who wants to consume it. A TV series box set can be shared, lent or, given by a friend to a friend. Participants in creative commons and gift economies protect and promote the public good qualities of TV shows and films while media corporations and their intellectual property lawyers use the force of copyright to turn such goods into rivalrous and exclusionary commodities. Although copyright tries to obliterate the public good qualities of TV shows and films, media firms and their lawyers are often outflanked by people who like to share.

Third, entertainment commodities are easily reproduced in mass quantities but at a marginal cost. Media corporations spend a lot of money producing TV shows and films, and they do so with no guarantee of recouping production costs or generating revenue. They do not know how many licensing deals will be arranged or the number of digital downloads consumers will pay for. The cost of producing the entertainment commodity is "fixed" or "sunk" (i.e., a sum of money is already spent and should be presumed as being unrecoverable) (Vogel 2007). But once a media corporation has sunk a large investment into the original product, each additional unit entails little extra marginal cost to reproduce. Once a copy of a TV show or film is produced, reproduction costs very little. BMW must spend additional money for every copy of a Mercedes-Benz it manufactures; a Nike sweatshop must put up a small sum of money for every copy of a pair of Nike shoes its impoverished workers stitch together; every iPad assembled in China's Foxconn adds to Apple Inc's production costs. A TV or film distributor, however, does not need to spend much to reproduce a TV show or film. TV shows and films can be made and remade, sold and resold, without incurring significant additional manufacturing costs. As result of digitization, entertainment media can be reproduced as bits of information for next to nothing. TV shows and films are expensive to produce (high sunk costs), but are incredibly cheap to reproduce. After the high cost of producing the first copy of a TV show or film is absorbed, the cost of reproducing it drops to zero, especially through digitization. This distinguishes entertainment media from most other goods.

Fourth, entertainment media has cultural use-values that are not reducible to exchange-values. TV shows and films are valued as property by copyright valuators using cash-nexus schematics. They are also valued culturally as communicative vehicles for stories, ideas, and images that represent, intersect with, and shape ways of life in incalculable and irreducible ways. TV shows and films are regularly valued for exchange by the media corporations that own them. However, their cultural use value is difficult to discern in monetary terms. Entertainment commodities are valued "both by those who make them and by those who consume them, for social and cultural reasons that are likely to complement or transcend a purely economic evaluation" (Throsby 2008: 219). TV shows and films are "experiential goods" that people consume to fulfill experiential and emotional wants (pleasure, thrill, excitement, catharsis) as opposed to purely utilitarian or base subsistence needs (Cooper-Martin 1991). The opening weekend box office net of *Kung Fu Panda 2* (2011) in China is calculable ($19.3 million); the way each member of China's film audience felt about global Hollywood's humorous representation of Chinese culture while watching *Kung Fu Panda 2* is not. The production budget of *Captain America: The First Avenger* (2011) is $140 million;

the feelings of national pride or angst felt by the US citizens who watched the film is hard to valuate. *Rise of the Planet of the Apes* (2011) cost $93 million to make; the film's contribution to animal rights activism eludes pricing mechanisms. TV shows and films have, and are given, cultural values and uses that are not easily (if at all) reducible to economic criteria. They provide the symbolic materials that define people and give them a way to define themselves.

Fifth, TV shows and films have externalities. An externality is the effect or impact that the production and consumption of a commodity has on one person (individual) or an entire group of people (society) who did not choose to produce or consume it (Baker 2004). According to Hoskins, McFadyen, and Finn (2004), an externality "is a cost or benefit arising from an economic transaction that falls on a third party and that is not taken into account by either parties (i.e., the seller [producer] or buyer [consumer]) to the transaction" (290). No externalities could be said to exist if a media corporation that sells a media product and the consumer that buys it are the only ones that receive a cost or benefit from this exchange, but this is never the case because markets are part of societies. Media corporations and media consumers interact with children, citizens, family and religious groups, and governments that do not have an immediate stake in the production and consumption of certain media products but who are nonetheless affected/afflicted by them. You may not watch Fox News Channel, but the viewers that do and the TV programs it airs might contribute to the election of a president that steer the country in a direction you oppose. You may have zero interest in seeing, hearing, or talking about *The Dark Knight Rises* (2012), but you will be made aware of it by every billboard poster, TV ad, web banner, newspaper, retail outlet, and person that markets, reviews, sells, or talks about it. TV shows and films are not part of "free-markets" that hover above social power relations between people; they are part of the social world we live in. As such, TV shows and films may have unintended societal effects that no one of us is solely responsible for, but which nonetheless affect all of us in ways we may not like and have not chosen.

The social externalities of TV shows and films can be both *positive* and *negative*. Positive externalities are those effects that people would want and probably pay for if given a choice (a benefit of some kind). For example, the circulation of quality watchdog journalism may encourage corporations and governments to be more transparent and accountable to the public. Documentary TV programs about significant topics that are of collective importance may enhance a citizen's understanding of the world they live in and encourage them to participate in making major decisions that affect their lives. Good governance and active citizenship are the positive externalities of these media products. While few commercial TV shows and films have civic and democratic benefits, many have negative externalities, i.e., effects that third party actors would likely not want or purchase (a cost of some kind). One negative externality arising from the production of a Hollywood blockbuster film, for example, is pollution. Hollywood firms pump out approximately 127,000 tons of ozone and diesel emissions a year (CBC Arts 2006). Ultra-violent, anti-intellectual, and crass TV shows may contribute to the public's desensitization to violence, a collective "dumbing down," a degradation of culture, and a diminishment of the quality of social life. While many people pay to watch violent and anti-intellectual TV shows, most people would not choose or pay to live in a society full of violence-prone, ignorant, ahistorical, non-participative, and seemingly irrational citizens.

In sum, TV shows and films have special qualities that distinguish them from most other commodities in the market. What form does the market in which these strange commodities are touted take? And how do the media corporations which own them try to control their flow?

OLIGOPOLISTIC ENTERTAINMENT MARKETS: COMPETITION, CONCENTRATION, CENTRALIZATION, AND CONTROL

Capitalism is supposedly based upon the ideal of market *competition*, such as the competition between the many media corporations that produce entertainment commodities to be sold to consumers. Fierce competition between a number of rival media corporations—a few based in the US and many based elsewhere—all struggling to produce and sell TV shows and films that consumers may want to watch, is a much vaunted capitalist ideal. In Vietnam, competition between cable TV companies is reported to be "fierce" (no author 2011b). A *Variety* article about international film festivals also declares that competition between national screen industries is "fierce" (Wright 2011). In India, *The Hindustan Times* reports a "fierce" Bollywood global box office rivalry between the science-fiction superhero action film *Ra. One* (2011) and *3 Idiots* (2009). Bounce TV, a new TV network targeting African Americans, is reported to be in "fierce" competition with KIN TV, which offers a "'wide range of programming designed to entertain, inform and inspire a broad audience of modern African-American viewers" (Style News Wire 2011). Competition between Univision (US-based), Telemundo (US–Puerto Rico-based), and TV Azteca (Mexico-based) for Spanish-speaking US and non-US viewers is also said to be "fierce" (Hartlaub 2002).

Cheerleaders for capitalism are enthusiastic about market competition; it is what motivates media corporations to develop exciting and high-quality entertainment commodities (after all, how would a media corporation stay in business if it produced TV shows and films that most viewers rejected?). Ideally, competition reduces the price of high-quality entertainment commodities for consumers (Cowan 1997). In neoclassical economic theory, a market works best when no one seller has extraordinary or significant control over the production and distribution system, the conduct of its competitors, or the price of goods. A competitive market is one in which a specific media corporation cannot act or intervene in ways that transform or change the basic competitive forces faced by either itself or another firm. In a competitive market, the fate of all media corporations—their rise and fall—is determined by market forces that none control. Interestingly, media corporations do everything they can to thwart so-called "free-market" competition: this occurs as result of "competition" and presumably "competitive" practices. Here, the meaning of competition is not derived from neoclassical theories (Albarran 2010), but from the cut-throat practices of media corporations themselves. Competition refers to the strategic attempt by one media firm to out-perform and outmatch rival media firms by gaining and leveraging control of material and symbolic resources, consumers, revenue, and markets. While competition is, in theory, the general characteristic of capitalism, in practice it leads to control. Though some firms may enjoy rivalry with others, most strategize to minimize competition, which is a source of financial risk and uncertainty.

In order to profit-maximize, media corporations try to gain as much control over markets as possible by establishing or reinforcing barriers to entry that aim to minimize competition (Knee, Greenwald, and Seave 2009: 34). In their struggle to gain a competitive advantage over their rivals, media corporations compete to control tangible and intangible resources (Habann 2000; Landers and Chan-Olmsted 2004; Miller and Shamsie 1996). They compete to control audience attention and ad dollars by cultivating brand-loyal consumers and devising strategies for customer lock-in. In turn, the competition for audience share motivates corporations to try to control access to entertainment content, and the means of producing it (technology and human labor). Because content is worthless if it cannot be made available to consumers, media firms also compete to control the means of distributing and exhibiting entertainment (Waterman 2005). The end-game of market competition is control of audiences, intellectual property, and the means of media production, distribution, and exhibition by a few firms. In sum, market control is a contradictory yet immanent consequence of capitalist competition between rival firms.

Competition and control are two sides of the same capitalist coin. According to Marx (1976), capital accumulation leads to *concentration* (as firms grow larger and more powerful by re-investing a portion of their profits back into the means of production) and *centralization* (as large firms grow even larger and more powerful by absorbing, taking over, or merging with smaller ones to stave off the threat of rivalry). Marx (1976) says that competition leads to "the ruin of many small capitalists, whose capitals partly pass into the hands of their competitors, and partly vanish completely" (80). The outcome of concentration and centralization is the erosion of competitive markets (many sellers of goods and low barriers to entry) and the consolidation of oligopolistic markets (a few sellers of goods and high barriers to entry). In many countries, much entertainment media is controlled by concentrated and centralized firms which enjoy oligopoly power. Media corporations seek oligopoly power because it as good as guarantees their profitability: it enables them to influence or set prices for entertainment commodities, deter or limit the ability of new rivals to enter or compete for audience share and revenue within the market, and coordinate a cartel-like relationship with other firms. As Gomery (2000) notes:

> Oligopolists are mutually interdependent. When they cooperate they can act like a monopolist; yet cooperation comes only with a handful of issues such as expanding the marketplace possibilities for all or keeping out new and powerful competitors. [. . .] Simply put, oligopolists tend to see and agree on an informal set of rules for competition, restructuring the game of profit maximizing to themselves. (514–515)

Over the past thirty years, competition has led to corporate control of media markets in the US and around the world (Bagdikian 2004; McChesney and Schiller 2003; Noam 2009; Schiller 2007). In the first edition of *The Media Monopoly*, Bagidikian (1983) listed fifty dominant US media corporations. Year after year, the number of dominant media corporations was reduced as result of concentration: twenty-nine firms in 1987;

twenty-three in 1990; ten in 1997; six in 2000; and five in 2004 (Hesmondhalgh 2007: 170). Bagdikian (2004) notes that the five largest US media conglomerates—Disney, News Corporation, Time Warner, Viacom, Bertelsmann—operate "with many of the characteristics of a cartel" and "own most of the newspapers, magazines, book publishers, motion picture studios, and radio and television stations in the US media" (3). Though the share of the total US market controlled by these five conglomerates doubled from 1984 to 2005 and media concentration is happening, the US is not a monopolistic media market (Noam 2009). According to Noam (2009), the US is an oligopolistic—as opposed to a monopolistic—media market. Currently, media ownership concentration is happening in the US and many other countries (Fuchs 2010; Winseck 2008). Many country-specific media markets are now "oligopolies, where a very small number of firms account for the majority of market share" (Flew 2011). A 2005 report by the European Federation of Journalists (2005), *Media Power in Europe: The Big Picture of Ownership*, documents media concentration in twenty-five EU member states. Mastrini and Becerra (2011) also document the high level of media concentration in Argentina, Brazil, Chile, and Uruguay—the Southern Cone countries of Latin America.

Horizontal and Vertical Integration: Convergence and De-Convergence

The concentration, centralization, and control by media conglomerates of the means of producing, distributing, and exhibiting media content has been driven by "convergence" strategies which have caused a significant structural change in the media industry overall.

In the pre-convergence era, media companies tended to operate in a single industry sector. Time Inc., for example, was primarily a publishing company. News Corporation was mostly a news company. Film studios produced and sold films. Viacom was, for the most part, a TV syndication and cable company. Most "media companies focused on their core business areas, partially because government policies, including antitrust laws and cross-ownership restrains, sought to define them distinctly and to keep them separate" (Jin 2011). From the 1980s onwards, and due to neoliberal media policy transformations and new business models, media companies that previously operated in one sector began acquiring a range of media firms in many other sectors, merging and "converging" them. Hardy (2010) notes that "we are now so far from that world where media companies tended to own discrete media with few having a significant cross-media portfolio" (xv).

In 1986, News Corporation gained full control of Twentieth Century Fox film studios and launched Fox TV. In 1989 Time and Warner merged, and in 1991 they launched the WB TV network. In 1995, Disney acquired ABC. In 1999, Viacom merged with CBS, bringing together film and TV production studios, broadcast TV stations, and cable networks, video exhibitors, and publishing houses. In 2001, Time Warner took over AOL. In 2004, General Electric-NBC bought Universal Studios (Winseck 2011: 15). In 2011, Comcast Corporation took over NBC Universal (Adegoke and Levine 2011). However, corporate convergence is not a distinctly US phenomenon: it is spreading around the world. China 2010: Want Want China Times Group, owner of numerous Chinese newspapers, magazines, publishing houses, and TV news channels, took over China Network Systems, a cable TV outfit (Lee 2011). Canada 2010: Bell Canada Enterprises (BCE), Canada's largest telecommunications company, bought CTV, giving it control of twenty-seven TV stations, thirty specialty TV channels, and numerous web platforms and radio stations (Marlow 2010). India 2011: the News Corporation-owned Star TV, an Asian-focused cable TV company, and Zee Turner, India's largest entertainment distribution company, formed Media Pro Enterprise India, a joint distribution venture (Ramachandran 2011). South Korea 2011: CJ E&M was consolidated by way of a five-way merger between film importer and developer CJ Entertainment, TV broadcasters CJ Media and OnMedia, video game development firm CJ Internet, and music publisher and broadcaster Mnet Media (Lee 2011). Poland 2011: the Paris-based conglomerate Vivendi's Canal+ (a French film and TV production and distribution firm) merged its pay TV services with TVN, Poland's largest TV broadcaster, to form a strategic partnership (Krajewski 2011).

Corporate convergence is often accompanied and rationalized by "technological convergence." Media corporations often represent their mergers and acquisitions as a natural response to technological change. But media and telecommunications corporations themselves are the primary agents pushing for technological convergence (Jin 2011; Schiller 2007). As corporations converge, an array of communication mediums for distributing, marketing, exhibiting, and consuming content converge too. In the past, a specific kind of medium corresponded with a specific kind of content: the TV set was the "go to" technology for TV shows; movies formatted for VHS, DVD, and Blue-Ray disc were reliant upon VCRs and DVD players; taped songs were played on tape decks, while those on compact discs (CD) were played on CD players; gamers immersed themselves in digital games using video game consoles or personal computers. Technological convergence, however, has decoupled the longstanding one-to-one relationship between a medium and media content (Brooker 2001; Kackman and Binfield 2010). McLuhan (1964) once noted that "the content of any medium is always another medium" (305). Now, however, a single medium can carry many different kinds of content and a specific kind of content can be accessed through many different mediums. Jenkins (2006) notes that technological convergence has blurred "the lines between media" (10). Many mediums have been bundled together: video game consoles are now used to play games, store and watch movies and TV shows, listen to music, surf the Internet, and shop in virtual malls; mobile phones are used daily to converse with friends, play music, exhibit pictures, check the time, send and receive text messages, and record and play videos; all kinds of entertainment media can be accessed, watched, listened to, and played on personal computers. People now retrieve different kinds of media content from a single device or retrieve a specific kind of media content from many mediums.

As a result of corporate and technological convergence, a small number of powerful media conglomerates have gained control over almost every sector, circuit, and medium of the entertainment industry as a whole. As media mogul Ted Turner (2004) declared, "Today, the only way for media companies to survive is to own everything up and down the media chain [. . .] Big media today wants to own the faucet, pipeline, water and the reservoir." In order to "own everything up and down the media chain," media conglomerates are using horizontal and vertical integration strategies (Ahn and Litman 1997; Albarran 1996; Fu 2009; Jin 2011; Riordan and Saliant 1994; Waterman 2005). We can ask, therefore, what distinguishes horizontal integration from vertical integration and how effective are these strategies at maximizing profits?

Horizontal integration enables a media corporation to control one kind of media product in one type of media market. A media corporation in the TV market which owns a TV production studio, a broadcast TV network, and a cable TV network is a horizontally integrated TV conglomerate. Time Warner's TV holdings exemplify horizontal integration: it owns Twentieth Century Fox Television, a major TV production studio, and it also owns Twentieth Century Television, a major TV distributor. This distributor licenses (or sells the rights to broadcast) TV shows to the Time Warner owned TV Fox Broadcasting Company (a major TV network). Time Warner is a horizontally integrated TV conglomerate; it owns TV production studios, TV distribution, and TV exhibition companies.

Vertical integration occurs when one media corporation grows by acquiring or merging with other media corporations which cover the entire production, distribution, and exhibition spectrum of many different kinds of media products. Vertical integration allows a media corporation to control numerous kinds of media products in many types of media markets. A media corporation that produces and sells entertainment commodities in many different media markets—TV shows, films, news content, books and magazines, video games, music—is a vertically integrated media conglomerate. Viacom is a vertically integrated media conglomerate: it owns film and TV production studios, TV networks, TV stations, cable TV stations publishing firms, radio firms, and amusement and theme parks.

Horizontal and vertical integration are routine processes in day-to-day business transactions between media conglomerates in oligopolistic media markets, not just in the US, but around the world. Why are so many media conglomerates in so many countries integrating horizontally and vertically? Prior to the rise of these integrated media conglomerates, each step in producing entertainment media involved a degree of uncertainty. Would enough capital be raised to finance production of a particular TV show or film? Would a production company be able to hire the desired director, screenwriters, and actors? Would the story concept be effectively translated into a finished commodity? Would the finished TV show or film be picked up by a distributor and purchased by an exhibitor? How would the TV show or film be marketed, and through what channels? When the TV show or film was finally brought to market by exhibitors, would people even want to watch it? All entertainment media requires a substantial start-up investment, but the amount of revenue generated by finished TV shows or films is always uncertain. In order to mitigate such uncertainty, and the financial risk associated with it, media conglomerates developed horizontal and vertical integration structures and strategies. This gave them maximum control of every circuit of capital involved in the making of entertainment media. Owning the production companies, the distribution companies, and the exhibition platforms gives media conglomerates a number of advantages.

First, this strategy allows media conglomerates to *minimize financial risk*. If one production subsidiary loses money on a project, the other subsidiaries can be relied upon to create a product to offset the loss. For example, if one of the film studios owned by a media conglomerate produces a "flop" and loses money, the other studios it owns can be pressured to make up that financial loss by producing a global box office hit. Media conglomerates tend to operate with an "80:20" rule: 80 percent of their revenue or profit comes from 20 percent of the entertainment commodities they produce and distribute (Vogel 2007: 41). Of any ten major films produced, only three or four will be profitable. For every ten prime-time TV series made, six or seven will be canned. An integrated media conglomerate can lose substantial sums of money on unsuccessful film or TV properties, but can then offset the loss by exploiting one successful or "hit". Integration enables a media conglomerate to take financial risks with reduced fear of bankruptcy should an exorbitantly high-cost film or TV series fail to "have legs." It enables media conglomerates to withstand the short-term financial losses which result from flops.

Second, the integration strategy allows media conglomerates to benefit from *economies of scale*. This term refers to how the per unit cost of producing a good or service diminishes when the volume of its output increases (*The Economist* 2008). On average, a TV show costs between $1.5 and $2 million to make (Steele 2008), which is a huge "sunk cost" (a cost that will not necessarily be recovered by a production firm or its financiers). But the cost of reproducing the TV show is very low, especially in the digital age. Once a TV show is made, it can be reproduced for next to nothing and sold (licensed) to consumers for whatever price the company decides without incurring additional production costs. Integrated media conglomerates can afford the huge "sunk" costs of creating high quality TV shows and films. They then generate revenue through successive rounds of low-cost exploitation based on windowing strategies (Litman 2000), integrated for a variety of different commodity forms.

Third, integrated media conglomerates benefit from *economies of scope*: i.e., when firms are able to "engage efficiently in multi-product production and associated large-scale distribution operations" (Lipsey and Chrystal 1995: 880). Warf (2007) states that "economies of scope exist if one firm can produce two separate products more efficiently [less expensively] than two firms can produce them separately" (95). Integrated media conglomerates are able to spread the costs associated with making a TV show or film internally over the numerous production, distribution, and exhibition subsidiaries they control. Inter-firm business transactions keep money circulating within the firm and create substantial cost efficiencies. Furthermore, economies of scope allow the cost of business transactions—from financing, to research and development, to pre- and post-production, to distribution deals to marketing—to be handled internally between companies that are owned by the conglomerate. This relieves the conglomerate of the need to find, negotiate with, monitor, or resolve disputes over the terms of the deal, licensing agreements, labor rates, and so on, with external media firms. Within a horizontally and vertically integrated structure, firms buy from and sell to each other. As a result, any TV show or film created by a production company within a larger conglomerate will be assured distribution and mass marketing by other companies owned by that conglomerate.

Fourth, the integration strategy gives media conglomerates access to the capital they require to launch expensive and large-scale multi-platform marketing campaigns.

Media conglomerates want to generate as much revenue as possible by selling TV shows and films to consumers who are willing to pay, while simultaneously diminishing the ability of their rivals to do the same. But consumer behavior is always a source of uncertainty, so media conglomerates use marketing to channel consumer attention toward their TV shows and films, cultivate consumer demand, and try to create a brand-loyal audience. The huge marketing budgets of media conglomerates contribute to their oligopolistic power. In 2010, News Corporation spent $1.37 billion and Time Warner spent $1.19 billion on marketing (Szalai 2011). By outspending competitors on advertising, media conglomerates try to deter people from consuming the less-hyped TV shows and films sold by smaller firms, which cannot afford to compete with the gargantuan marketing budgets controlled by giants. Media conglomerates are also promoters of their own media brands (Hardy 2010).

In sum, horizontal and vertical integration enables media conglomerates to minimize financial risk, maximize control over financing, production, distribution, and exhibition, and establish very high barriers to entry for smaller and independent media firms. Media conglomerates can afford the huge "sunk" costs of creating, distributing, marketing, and exhibiting high-quality TV shows or blockbuster films. Smaller firms most often cannot. High-budget TV shows and films tend to be more effective at attracting viewers than low-budget entertainment (Wildman 1994). By controlling all of the circuits of media capital, media conglomerates ensure that their TV show or film will enter many markets. Control of these circuits also enables media conglomerates to block or limit the access of smaller firms to the market, significantly reducing their ability to compete. Integrated media conglomerates relegate smaller media firms to subordinate positions as subsidiaries, affiliates, or contractors. Centralized media conglomerates are now at the core of a decentralized (and global) network of "in house" subsidiary and "out of house" contractor media firms (Arsenault 2011). As Wayne (2003) observes:

> the new corporate structures are characterized by *decentralized accumulation* where the dominant logics of capital are mediated through a multi-divisional corporate structure in combination with a web of subsidiary and subcontractor modes which give the appearance of plurality and autonomy in the marketplace. (84)

Very often, the small media firms that are owned by, and affiliated to, the big media conglomerates are pitted against each other as competitive rivals. As a result, they compete for project work by offering to do more for less pay and with fewer workers. These independent companies often strive to be acquired by the media conglomerate. In sum, the integrated media conglomerate decreases competition and source diversity. As Foster (2000) says, "there is no longer a life-or-death competition threatening the survival of the mature capitalist enterprise [. . .] Rather, the giant corporations that dominate the contemporary economy engage primarily in struggles over market share." Competition in media markets most often happens within and between the most powerful media conglomerates.

THE COMING DE-CONVERGENCE?

Although vertical and horizontal integration buttresses the market dominance and control of media conglomerates, there are some instances when "convergence" fails to pay off. These instances are beginning to be examined by global media studies scholars. Flew (2011) notes that:

> a great deal of attention is given to the original decision to expand a media corporation or take over another, and far less attention is given to how the merged entity actually performs, meaning that we may well be prone to overstate the success of conglomeration strategies in the media and entertainment industries.

Flew (2011) also says there are "potential downsides of media conglomeration" that need to be examined:

> rather than taking corporate media managers at their word on proclaiming the success of media synergies. [. . .] There is very often a gap between what is presented as the favourable outcomes of such strategies at the time of their gestation [. . .] and what actually materializes in practice.

Jin (2011) presents a thoughtful study of the downsides of convergence, noting how many of the most powerful media conglomerates that converged at the turn of the millennium—Viacom-CBS, AOL-Time Warner, AT&T-Liberty Media—began to "de-converge" soon after, as represented by "the sale of profit-losing companies, spin-offs, and split-offs and massive layoffs." While de-convergence is happening in the US and elsewhere, it is unlikely that this process signals the decline of horizontally and vertically integrated media conglomerates. Subsidiaries that serve their parent's profit-maximization goals will be retained, while those that do not will face liquidation. Convergence and de-convergence will co-exist in the near future. One strategy does not precede or follow the other; corporations are always buying and selling resources. That's capitalism.

SYNERGISTIC ENTERTAINMENT MEDIA: CONVERGENT COMMODITIES

Corporate and technological convergence has been leveraged by media conglomerates to produce, distribute, and exhibit "synergistic entertainment media." Hardy (2010) observes how, since the 1980s, "there has been a marked growth of synergistic practices whereby media firms have sought to maximize profits through the co-ordinated promotion, diffusion, sale and consumption of media products, services and related merchandise" (xv). According to Grainge (2009), synergy is "a principle of cross-promotion whereby companies seek to integrate and disseminate their products through a variety of media and consumer channels, enabling brands to travel through an integrated corporate structure" (10). Herman and McChesney (1997) say that synergy enables "the exploitation of new opportunities for cross-selling, cross-promotion, and privileged access" (54). Murray (2005) observes how the commercial motivation behind synergy is "content streaming": "content parlayed into multiple, cross-promoting formats owned by a single conglomerate creates multiple revenue streams from essentially fixed production costs" (417). Entertainment media is now routinely designed to synergistically move across or stream from one medium to the next, collecting revenue every step of the way. Synergistic entertainment media are the ideal commodities of convergent capitalism.

BOX 2.1

PROFILES OF THE LARGEST THREE HORIZONTALLY AND VERTICALLY INTEGRATED MEDIA CONGLOMERATES

	WALT DISNEY	TIME WARNER	NEWS CORPORATION
Film-TV Production Studios	*The Walt Disney Studios* Walt Disney Motion Picture Group: Walt Disney Pictures, Touchstone Pictures, Hollywood Pictures, Marvel Studios, Marvel Animation, Dreamworks Pictures, Disneynature, ESPN films, Walt Disney Animation Studios, Pixar, DisneyToon Studios, Skellington Productions, Miravista Films, Pantagonik Film Group (joint venture between Disney and Artear Argentina); TV: ABC Studios, Walt Disney Television Animation, Disney-ABC Domestic Television, Walt Disney Television, BVS Entertainment/ Saban Entertainment, Disney-ABC International Television, Disney Educational Productions, It's a Laugh Productions	Warner Brothers, Warner Communications, Warner Brothers Animation, New Line Cinema, Castle Rock Entertainment	Twentieth Century Fox, Fox Filmed Entertainment, Fox Searchlight, Blue Sky Studios
Film TV Distribution	Walt Disney Studios Motion Pictures, Walt Disney Studios Home Entertainment		
Cinema Chains/ Theatrical Exhibition	El Capitan Theatre	UCI (50%), WF Cinema Holdings (50%)	
TV Networks	Disney-ABC Television Group:ABC, Inc., ABC Television Network, ABC Daytime, ABC Entertainment (Greengrass Productions, Victor Television Productions), ABC Kids, ABC News; International: Disney Channel Worldwide (25 channels); Playhouse Disney (9 channels), Disney Cinemagic, Hungama, Super RTL (joint venture between Disney and Germany-based RTL Group),	WB Network	Fox Broadcast Company

BOX 2.1 (Continued)

	WALT DISNEY	TIME WARNER	NEWS CORPORATION
TV Stations	ABC Family, Disney Channel, Toon Disney, ESPN, Soap Net, A&E, Lifetime, Lifetime Movie Network, History Channel, E! Entertainment	HBO, Cinemax, TW Sports, CNN, Comedy Central, TBS, TNT, TCM, Cartoon Network, Turner Classic Movies	Fox News, Fox Kids, Fox Sports, Fox Movies, FX, National Geographic (50%)
Cable Networks	Disney Channel, Disney Junior, Disney XD, ABC Family, SOAPnet (37.5%), Lifetime Entertainment Services and A&E Television Networks (joint venture between Disney, Hearst Corporation and NBC Universal, ESPN Inc. (80% joint venture with Hearst Corporation 20%)	Time Warner Cable	
Satellite Broadcasts			DirecTV, BSkyB, Sky Italia, Sky Brazil, Innova, Perfect TV Japan, Phoenix, Star TV
Print	Disney Publishing Worldwide Magazines: US Weekly (50%), Discover, Wondertime, Family Fun, Disney Adventures, ESPN Magazine, Talk (50%)	Time Inc., Time Life, DC Comics, People, MAD Magazine, IPC	Gemstar TV Guide, Weekly Standard, InsideOut, New York Post, The Times, The Sun, News of the World, 100s of local newspaper titles
Publishing	Hyperion, ABC Daytime Press, ESPN Books, Hyperion East, Hyperion Audiobooks, VOICE, Marvel Publishing (Marvel Comics, Icon Comics, Max, Ultimate Comics, Marvel press)	Little, Brown & Co, Warner Books, Time Life books, Book of the Month Club (50%)	HarperCollins, Marrow-Avon
Radio	Radio Disney: 100s of stations in the US and worldwide		
Recorded Music	Disney Music Group, Walt Disney Records, Hollywood Records, Mammoth Records	Atlantic, Elektra, Maverick, Rhino, WEA, Columbia House (50%), Quincy Jones Entertainment Co. (37%)	

Internet/Web	Hulu (27% owned by ABC), Disney Online, D23, Disney Auctions, ABC.com, ABCnews.com, ESPN.com, ESPNsoccernet, Go.com, Familyfun.com, Wondertime.com, Family.com, TouchstonePictures.com, BVOnlineEntertainment.com, Muppets.com, Hollywoodrecords.com, LyricStreetRecords.com, ABCFamily.com, Video.com, SOAPnet.com, Oscar.com, ClubPenguin.com	Adult Swim Video, Cartoon Network Video, Court TV Extra, Crime Library, DramaVision, TheFrisky.com, GameTap, CallToons, Play On! Powered by ACC, Select, Super Deluxe, The Smoking Gun, TNT Overtime, Toonami Jetstream, Very Funny Ads, CNNStudentNews.com, CNN.com, CNN Mobile, CNN Newsource, CNN to Go, CNNMoney.com, SI.com, PGA Tour.com and PGA.com, CNN Pipeline, NASCAR.com, Bamzu.com
Video Games	Disney Interactive Studios: Avalanche Software, Black Rock Studios, Fall Line Studios, Junction Point Studios, Playdom, Wideload Games, Tapulous	
Dramatic Performance/ Theater	Disney Theatrical Productions: Hyperion Theatrical, Disney Live Family Entertainment, Disney on Ice	
Theme Parks, Amusements, Resorts	Walt Disney World Resort (Florida, US), Disneyland Resort (Anaheim California, US), Tokyo Disney Resort (Tokyo, Japan), Disneyland Paris (France), Hong Kong Disneyland resort (Penny's Bay, Hong Kong), Disney Cruise Line, Disney Vacation Club, Disneyland Paris	Warner Brothers theme park in Australia
Retail Consumer Products and Shopping	Disneyshopping.com, Disneystore, World of Disney Store, Disney Apparel Accessories & Footwear, Disney Food, Health & Beauty, Marvel Toys	

Jenkins (2004) conceptualizes the synergistic entertainment product as a wheel. At the "hub" of the wheel lies the copyrighted creative concept (the story, the characters, the imagined worlds, etc.). The "spokes" that spread out from the wheel's hub are the many different commodity forms: films, TV shows, comic books, video games, websites, product tie-ins, and merchandise. "Everything about the structure of the modern entertainment industry was designed with this single idea in mind—the construction and enhancement of media franchises" (Jenkins 2006: 106). Following the logic of synergistic franchising, a book owned by a media conglomerate becomes a TV show licensed to a TV network owned by the conglomerate, which is then turned into a film, which is produced by a studio and released by a theater chain, both of which are also owned by the conglomerate. A film soundtrack is then issued on a record label owned by the conglomerate, and released in tandem with a video game developed by a games studio owned by the conglomerate. The book, the TV show, the soundtrack, and the video game are all heavily promoted by the magazines, newspapers, TV networks, and websites owned by the conglomerate. Characters from the book, TV show, and video game become children's clothing, posters, action figures, lunch boxes, and promotional tie-ins with fast-food restaurants. Synergistic entertainment media is at the forefront of what Hardy (2010) calls "cross-media promotion": "the promotion of one media service or product through another" (xv).

Media conglomerates design synergistic entertainment products to generate as much revenue from one hub as possible. Unlike traditional storytelling, wherein one story is contained by one media form (i.e., a TV show or a film), synergistic franchises—or "trans-media stories"—spread across many platforms (Gillan 2010; Jenkins 2006; Lotz 2007). "[T]here are strong economic motives behind transmedia storytelling," notes Jenkins (2006: 106). Media conglomerates design one single media property to be exploited and delivered to consumers through a plurality of exhibition platforms. According to Jenkins (2006), this expands the potential market for one entertainment product and attracts consumers who may only be comfortable with one particular medium into additional mediums. It is no longer enough to be a *Spider Man* comic book fan: in order to capitalize on the *Spider Man* synergistic entertainment franchise, firms encourage consumers to pay for the toys, the comic books, the films, and the video games. Synergistic entertainment media products try to get consumers to move from screen to screen, store to store, platform to platform, spending money along the way.

MEDIA CORPORATIONS IN THE WORLD SYSTEM

Now that some of the general conditions that determine the existence of TV shows and films in capitalist societies have been discussed, I would like to focus on structural and relational approaches to the "power" of and between media conglomerates in the world system.

A structural approach to power analyzes the positions of the political and economic organizations and institutions of a society which control the most resources. "These positions are held to be central to the control of resources that are the basis of power, and the occupants of these positions are the central actors in the exercise

BOX 2.2

HARRY POTTER AS SYNERGISTIC ENTERTAINMENT MEDIA

Harry Potter—a series of fictional books about the adventures of a young wizard by British author J.K. Rowling—is one of the most commercially successful synergistic entertainment products in the world. Rowling owns the rights to the Potter idea, and Scholastic owns the book publishing rights. Rowling's fictional fantasy about the struggles, quests, and adventures of adolescent wizard Harry Potter form the conceptual hub of an ever-expanding *Potter* multi-media universe. Rowling's eight best-selling books have been translated from English into more than sixty-nine other languages. US-based TNMC Time Warner owns the rights to the films and all licensing, franchising, and merchandising deals. In 2001, AOL and Time Warner merged into the massive horizontally and vertically integrated TNMC. *The Economist* (2001) notes how AOL-Time Warner used "different platforms to drive the movie, and the movie to drive business across the platforms." *Potter* was AOL-Time Warner's premier synergistic entertainment franchise: Warner Bros Pictures, owned by AOL-Time Warner, produced the film; Warner Bros Music Group label Atlantic Records made the soundtrack; Time Warner owned *Entertainment Weekly* and *Time Magazine* published features and promotional *Potter* articles (*The Economist* 2001); and, additionally, *Potter* was promoted through AOL-controlled websites using interactive games, user contests, sneak previews, and participatory fan boards. In 2009, the merger between AOL and Time Warner ended, but Time Warner continued to control the *Potter* franchise and its many sources of revenue. The hub—*The Harry Potter* story and characters—now spreads across a number of spokes: films, websites, video games, toys, clothing lines. The *Potter* films are global blockbusters, and *Potter* video games are spun off from the films. Lego develops *Potter*-themed sets. Clothing companies sell *Potter* t-shirts, nightgowns, and pants. Candy manufacturers sell candy copies of snacks that appear in the film, including Bertie Bott's Every Flavour Beans and Chocolate Frogs. Gigantic theme parks are engineered around *Potter* images: at the Universal Orlando resort in Florida, The Islands of Adventure Theme Park USA stars "The Wizarding World of Harry Potter." Potter fans are invited to "experience pulse pounding rides including Dragon Challenge, Flight of the Hippogriff and Harry Potter and the Forbidden Journey," and to buy a few more ancillary products derived from these thrilling amusements—collectibles, t-shirts, and games—as they dizzily exit through the gift shop. Horizontal and vertical integration enabled Time Warner to design *Harry Potter* is a synergistic entertainment franchise.

of power" (Scott 2012: 70). Applied to the study of media corporations, a structural approach to power analyzes the position and identity of those media corporations which exert the greatest degree of ownership and control over the means of producing, distributing, marketing, and exhibiting media products. According to the structural approach, the most powerful media corporations are those that own or control the majority of the material and symbolic resources required to produce, distribute, market, and exhibit media products in many countries around the world. The power position of a media corporation in a structural hierarchy is determined by its control of material resources (capitalization and revenue, the number of production and distribution subsidiaries it owns, the size of its intellectual property library, the geographical extent of its operations, and so on) and symbolic resources (a positive public perception of its business operations, conduct and products, the knowledge and know-how of its workforce, its prestige and brand image in many markets).

This structural approach is implied by McChesney's (2004) "three-tier model" of corporate power, which ranks the power position of media corporations in a hierarchical world system. This is the "who owns what?" approach. In McChesney's model, the top or "first-tier" consists of six to ten media conglomerates, most of which are based in the US but have transnational operations (i.e., Walt Disney, Comcast-NBC-Universal, News Corporation, Time Warner, Viacom-CBS, Sony, Vivendi, Bertelsmann, Thomson Reuters). The middle power or "second-tier" media firms refer to fifty or sixty media corporations, based in the US and in other countries, which are national and regional giants (i.e., Al-Jazeera, Abril, Astral Media, BBC, Bell Media, Bennet, the Cisneros Group, Coleman, CCTV, Clarin, Fuji, the Globo Group Grupo Televisa, Hearst, Mediaset, Naspers, Phoenix TV, Prisa, RedeGlobo, Telmex, Telefonica, Televisa, Shanghai Media Group, Zee, etc.). The bottom or "third-tier" level is filled with hundreds (or even thousands) of smaller scale commercial, public, and independent media firms (i.e., Warsaw Documentary Film Studio, Zimbabwe Broadcasting Corporation, Daily Times of Nigeria, Welland Tribune, Warwick Video Production, Māori Television, National Indigenous Television, Birthmark Films, Baghdad TV). McChesney's "three-tier" model presents a useful structural approach to the "who's who" of media corporations in the world system. Before studying the world's most powerful media corporations in the world, we first must identify them. This is what a structural approach to power enables us to do.

Though useful for documenting which media corporations own the most material and symbolic resources at any given time, McChesney's structural approach to power poses some methodological challenges. One such challenge is that of accurately collecting data about, describing, and evaluating the material and symbolic resources that a media corporation controls. Many media corporations do not release data about their internal affairs to public, state, or academic analysts. Another challenge rests in determining what resources should be the focus of enquiry and how data about those resources should be interpreted. Ranking the structural position of a media corporation always entails selecting specific power resources as a point of focus. But what are the most significant resources possessed by a media firm? The total value of its shares? The number of skilled "above the line" cultural workers it employs? The business savvy of its CEOs? Its track record of producing and distributing global blockbuster films? Stats about children in various countries expressing affinity to its corporate logo? The number of copyrighted TV shows a firm controls? All of the above? The structural approach freezes the power position of a media corporation vis-à-vis other corporations in a hierarchy. It is a snapshot or image of structural power at a given moment in time. But this macro-level reification of power does not grasp the micro-level dynamics and ever-changing power relations between media corporations in the world system.

The starting point for any critical political-economic study of the power of media corporations in a world system is the structural approach, but critical studies of the power of media corporations need not begin and end here. The structural approach to power can be supplemented by a relational approach (Jessop 2012). Here, power is not conceptualized as static or concretized in resources, but in the relationships between two or more entities; it is the ability of one entity to get another to do what they would not otherwise do. In some instances, power is the ability of one entity to get another to do what they ordinarily do (Jessop 2012). The relational approach grants that structures exist and that the power of a media corporation is linked to the material and symbolic resources it controls, but, additionally, it analyzes *power relations* between a media corporation and other actors, the goals of a media corporation, and the strategies it employs to achieve them. Here, power is not just the control of resources, but the ability of a given media corporation (or a group of media corporations) to get other actors (governments, media corporations, cultural workers, consumers) to do what it wants them to do. Media corporations are daily engaged in power relations with others: the states they lobby and depend on as regulators, media corporations in other circuits of capital, the waged cultural workers they hire or employ, and the consumers they target and sell TV shows and films to.

Always engaged in power relations with others, media corporations struggle to control, reproduce, or change existing situations to support their interests and achieve their goals (to get others to do what they might or might not otherwise do of their own volition). In order to achieve their interests and goals, media corporations use strategies that are both coercive and persuasive. While "hegemony" is a term often reserved for the analysis of how dominant capital blocs rule societies through outwardly sovereign state apparatuses (Gramsci 1971), the term can also be used when analyzing how media corporations struggle to rule the markets of many countries. Media corporations are not only significant contributors to the hegemony of the existing ruling capital blocs, but are also hegemonic actors in their own right. Artz (2003), for example, says that global corporate media hegemony is "an institutionalized, systematic means of educating, persuading and representing subordinate classes to particular cultural practices within the context of capitalist norms" (16–17). Using strategies of force and consent, media corporations compel and cajole a number of public and private actors to do what they want them to do in order to control, reproduce, or change situations to their advantage.

Coercive strategies refer to a media corporation's use of threats, punishments, and fear to get governments, other media firms, workers, and citizens to act in ways that align with the media corporation's goals. For example, a media corporation may threaten a government with the movement of its core operations to another country as a way of getting that government to provision maximal subsidies or heed a number of neoliberal policy demands. A TV network may threaten to downsize its operations as a way of getting a government regulatory agency to relax or abolish national content quotas. A film studio may threaten to punish a subsidiary production firm with reduced financing if the films and TV shows it makes do not perform well at the global box office or in international TV markets. A distribution company may threaten to deprive exhibitors of the content they want unless they agree to schedule and screen the TV shows and films the distributor chooses. A production company may threaten to outsource and offshore tasks if cultural workers unionize or strike, thereby reducing worker expectations for fair wages and secure jobs.

In addition to using the above coercive strategies, media corporations may use a variety of *persuasive strategies* to get what they want. Persuasive strategies refer to consent-building activities. These strategies strive to attract others to the corporation. They are used to get others to want what the media corporation wants and do what it wants them to do. A media corporation may employ a lobby group to convince a government agency or group of citizens that the neoliberal policies of privatization, deregulation, and liberalization which primarily serve its own particular profit-interests will support the general interests of an entire country. A TV network may run a series of ads or programs that convince citizens that TV content quotas undermine or are hurting local TV. A film studio may encourage a production company to continually manufacture high-quality content by awarding it financial incentives or rewarding it for a job well done. A production company may secure financing by convincing a distribution firm that its TV show or film concept, once produced, will be a hit in many national markets. A distribution company may organize the consent of many exhibitors to purchase its content (as opposed to that of competitors) by offering discounts. A TV network may convince young college graduates that by taking an unpaid internship for half a year, they will one day get a full-time job.

Structural and relational approaches to the positional and hegemonic power of media corporations in the world system can be used in complimentary, as opposed to mutually exclusive, ways. A media corporation's control of material and symbolic resources shapes its capacity to act toward others using strategies of coercion and persuasion. A media corporation's position in the overall world hierarchy enables and limits its ability to achieve its goals. Now that power has been defined, I will discuss the world system's most structurally powerful media corporations and their relations with other media firms.

TRANSNATIONAL MEDIA CORPORATIONS (TNMCS)

The world system's most structurally powerful media entities are *transnational media corporations* (TNMCs) (Chan-Olmsted 2005; Fuchs 2010; Gershon 1993, 1997; Herman and McChesney 1997; McChesney and Schiller 2003; Rantanen 2005; Schiller 1991; Sklair 2002; Sreberny 2006). Schiller (1991) observed the rise of TNMCs at the end of the Cold War, and described the transformation of distinctly US national media corporations into "huge, integrated, cultural combines," "conglomerates," and "transnational enterprises" which controlled the means of producing and distributing "film, TV, publishing, recording, theme parks, and even data banks" (14). He said that TNMCs manufactured "a total cultural environment" and sold it "to a global as well as a national market" (14). In this period, the growth of TNMCs represented "a phenomenal expansion of transnational capitalism and its seizure of global communication facilities—nationally based, to be sure—for its marketing and operational and opinion controlling purposes" (15).

Schiller's (1991) account of TNMCs has been echoed by many scholars. Warf (2007) notes that "[A]cross the planet, the market for media services has become dominated by a few giants that have established powerful production and distribution networks" (89). Fuchs (2010) says that the transnationality of a media corporation is indicated by "the average share of foreign assets in total assets, the average share of foreign sales in total sales, the average share of foreign employment in total employment, and the share of foreign affiliates in total affiliates" (44–45). A TNMC is a nationally headquartered company that has a diverse range of business operations (assets, sales, employment, and affiliates) in many different countries. Though registered in one state or "home country," TNMCs have many offices, connections, and subsidiary branches in numerous countries or "host countries." They are often controlled by a transnational owning class (a complex web of transnationally located shareholders and multiple passport holding directors and CEOs). TNMCs produce and distribute global, national, and glocalized entertainment media to both mass and niche viewers in many countries. They "are organized around a global network of multimedia corporations that extend from a core of diversified multi-national media organizations, to large national and regional companies, and to their local affiliates in different areas of the world" (Arsenault and Castells 2008: 707).

The world's most structurally powerful TNMCs are based in the US. "The rise of the [media] cartel has been a long time coming," argues Crispin-Miller (2002). "It represents the convergence of the previously disparate US culture industries—many of them vertically monopolized already—into one global super-industry providing most of our 'imaginary content' " (1). The top US-based TNMCS are: Walt Disney, Comcast-NBC-Universal, News Corporation, Time Warner, Viacom, CBS Corporation, Liberty Media, and a few others. These US-based "first-tier" TNMCs control the lion's share of the US and cross-national circuits of producing, distributing, marketing, and exhibiting entertainment media. Between 2001 and 2008, US-based TNMCs accumulated unprecedented profits, and in 2010 the US copyright industries accounted for $134 billion in foreign sales and exports, a sum greater than that generated by aircraft and agriculture in the same year (Block 2011). In 2010, the top five companies in the audiovisual industry were based in the US and derived most of their revenue from there (Westcott 2011). Furthermore, these five US-based companies—Comcast, Google, Walt Disney, Time Warner, and Direct TV—together generated $143.2 billion in revenue. In 2011, this sum represented 30 percent of the combined revenue of the top fifty media corporations in the world (Westcott 2011).

The US and US-based TNMCs occupy the dominant or top power position vis-à-vis other countries and media firms in the world system's hierarchy. According to Winseck (2011), the US is the world's largest media market and "is in fact larger than the next four media markets combined: Japan, Germany, China and the United Kingdom" (36). While it is true that "the US is not the only centre of media production, it remains by far the most important, both in terms of its absolute size and dominance in audio-visual trade" (Sparks 2007: 220). US-based TNMCs are at the top of the "world media pecking order" and are the only genuine exporters of entertainment media to almost every country worldwide (Tunstall 2008: 235). From the 1980s to the present day, the US has been the world's number one exporter of films and TV shows (Chalaby 2006; Nye 2004: 33; Thussu 2004: 140). US TNMCs rule the media markets of Europe, Asia, Latin America, and Africa (Morley 2006: 35). They have "cultural primacy" in nearly every major media market (Chalaby 2006). As Fu (2006) says:

> The international trade in audiovisual products resembles a mismatched boxing contest [in which] a small league of heavyweight countries dominates the export of film and television programs to the import markets of other countries, whereas the latter have only a

featherweight trade capability or none at all. Within the heavyweight league, the United States is by far the most prevalent contender. (813)

The world system's major entertainment flow continues to be owned by US-based TNMCs. TV and film flows between the US and other countries are not only one way, but are also imbalanced and un-reciprocal. The US continues to export a far greater number of TV shows and films than other countries, while importing only a small amount of "foreign" media content. The US accounts for nearly half of the world's total audio-visual trade (WTO 2010) and has an audio-visual trade surplus with every country (Chalaby 2006; Nye 2004: 33; Thussu 2004: 140). In 2008, the US exported film and TV shows worth US $13,598 million to other countries, but imported only US $1,878 million worth of non-US film and TV shows (Jin 2011).

US TV is genuinely "global" TV. According to the European Audiovisual Observatory, the number of hours of American TV shows scheduled by major European TV networks in 2000 was about 214,000. In 2006, American TV's presence in Europe grew by nearly 50,000 hours to more than 266,000 hours (Arango 2008). The European Union has an audio-visual trade deficit with the US of $8–9 billion, and half of this sum is accounted for by TV content (Doyle 2012). Warner Brothers CEO Barry M. Meyer says "The [international] demand for American-produced television shows is stronger than it has ever been." US TNMCs license TV shows to exhibitors in the US market (the largest TV market in the world) and then sell additional copies of those TV shows at a much lower cost to exhibitors in other countries (Doyle 2012). In 2006, Canada's audio-visual trade deficit with the US, for example, was $1.2 billion. Much of this was incurred by the Canadian TV networks which broadcast US TV shows. In 2007–2008 they spent a record $775.2 million on foreign programming, principally US TV drama, and only $88.3 million on the production of "Canadian" TV. In 2008, the world's three most popular TV shows in sixty countries were US exports: *House* (81.8 million viewers), *Desperate Housewives* (56.3 million viewers), and *The Bold and the Beautiful* (24.5 million viewers) (*Foreign Policy* 2009). In 2010, NBC-Universal licensed the hit show *House* to 250 territories worldwide: in France, *House* averaged 9.3 million viewers per episode; in Italy, 4.7 million; in Germany, 4.2 million; in Poland, 3.3 million; and in the Netherlands, 793,000 viewers. Other US TV shows such as CBS's *CSI: Las Vegas* and *CSI: Miami* attracted more than 50 million viewers each (Adler 2010).

Hollywood films are genuinely "global" films. Between 1999 and 2009, Hollywood majors achieved record global growth, increasing their global box office revenue by 5 percent from $17.6 billion to $29.5 billion (MPAA 2010). In many countries, Hollywood films routinely take more than 50 percent of the market share (WTO 2010: 9); in 2009, 62 percent of global box-office revenues were accounted for by just six Hollywood studios (USITC 2011), and in that same year, US studios accounted for 64 percent of the box-office revenues generated by the top 100 distributors across the whole of the European Union, which is the second largest film producing region in the world (Hancock and Zhang 2010). Of the top thirty all-time highest-grossing films worldwide, only one (*Spider-Man 3*) was *not* made by a film studio owned by a US-based TNMC (Sony) (Box Office Mojo 2012). In 2008, Hollywood films took in

16.4 billion rubles at the Russian box office, five times more than was generated by Russian films (*The Economist* 2011d). In the People's Republic of China, only thirty-four foreign-made films are allowed to be screened per year, yet of the top ten 2012 box office hits in China, nine were Hollywood films: *Titanic 3-D, Mission Impossible: Ghost Protocol, The Avengers, Men In Black 3, Journey 2: The Mysterious Island, Battleship, John Carter, Sherlock Holmes: A Game of Shadows*, and *Wrath of the Titans. Painted Skin 2: The Resurrection* was the only "made in China" hit.

The industries of information and communication technology (ICTs) which facilitate the flow of TNMC-owned entertainment media content across borders are predominantly centered in the US too (Boyd-Barrett 2006). ICT hardware and software ownership and the pipelines and protocols of the Internet and the World Wide Web (and now Web 2.0) are largely, though not exclusively, controlled by US-based digital corporations. This is increasingly becoming a concentrated industry (Noam 2009). Throughout the 1980s and 1990s, US-based ICT corporations globalized (McChesney and Schiller 2003: 19). As of 2011, five of the world's top ten ICT hardware companies—Dell, Intel, HP, Apple, and Cisco—were based in the US. The other five are based elsewhere: Samsung in South Korea, Foxconn in Taiwan, LG Electronics in South Korea, Nokia in Finland, and Toshiba in Japan (Hardware Top Ten 2011). Seven of the world's top ten software companies—Microsoft, IBM, Oracle, HP, Symantec, Activision Blizzard, and EMC—are US-based. The remaining three are Germany-based SAP, Sweden-based Ericsson, and Japan-based Nintendo (van Kooten 2011). While the US faces rivalry in the ICT sectors from Chinese and Indian firms (Boyd-Barrett 2006: 21; Thussu 2005: 93), it is still home to five of the world's largest companies: Hewlett-Packard, AT&T, Apple Inc., IBM, and Verizon. China's Glam Media, Tencent, Baidu, NetShelter Technology, and Alibaba are powerful digital corporations, but according to Nielsen NetRatings (2012), the world's most profitable Web companies—Google, Microsoft, Facebook, Yahoo!, Wikimedia Foundation, eBay, Amazon, InterActive Corp, Apple Computer, and AOL Inc.—are all US-based (Nielsen 2011).

The rise of new and convergent media is often represented as giving "power to the people," destabilizing existing hierarchies, and tearing down old state and corporate structures. But US TNMCs are using convergent media to give their commodities new exhibition/consumption windows, reproduce power hierarchies, and build new structures which function to serve profit-goals. The technological integration of country-specific media systems by satellite, the Internet, the World Wide Web and convergent mobile media, neoliberal policies of privatization, deregulation, and liberalization, and the growth of web-based exhibition services and bit Torrent sites have increased and sped up the flow of digital copies of TV shows and films across borders. However, a large volume of the entertainment media content circulating through convergent media "is effectively recycled or reflects multiple versions of narratives being generated out of the same individual stories and content properties" (Doyle 2010). Much of the digitized TV show and film content uploaded and downloaded, bought and stolen, traded and trafficked, was made by US TNMCs.

On the World Wide Web, US TV shows and global blockbuster films are perhaps the most available and the most widely consumed digital media products. They are the most pirated, too. As of May 2012, the top ten most pirated films of all time were owned by US-TNMCs: *Avatar, The Dark Knight, Transformers, Inception, The Hangover, Star Trek, Kick-Ass, The Departed, The Incredible Hulk*, and *Pirates of the Caribbean: At World's End* (The Daily Bits 2012). Downloaded more than 25 million times from public torrent sites, the second series of the HBO Network's *Game of Thrones* ranks as the most globally pirated TV show of 2012 (Greenberg 2012). In 2011, the top ten pirated TV shows were all American too: *Dexter, Game of Thrones, The Big Bang Theory, House, How I Met Your Mother, Glee, The Walking Dead,*

BOX 2.3

GLOBAL MEDIA OWNERSHIP

Top Ten audio-visual corporations in the world (by revenue)

NAME	COUNTRY	SECTOR	2010 REVENUE ($BILLION)
Comcast	USA	Cable Operator	35.6
Google	USA	Internet Portal	29.3
Walt Disney	USA	Diversified Media Company	27.3
Time Warner	USA	Diversified Media Company	26.9
DirecTV	USA	Pay TV Operator	24.1
Sony	Japan	Diversified Media Company	23.5
News Corp.	USA	Diversified Media Company	22.7
Time Warner Cable	USA	Cable Operator	16.8
Vivendi	France	Diversified Media Company	16.6
NBC-Universal	USA	Diversified Media Company	16.4

Source: IHS Screen Digest 2010

Top Ten Broadcasting and Cable Corporations in the world (by revenue)

NAME	COUNTRY	FORBES RANKING	2011 MARKET VALUE ($BILLION)
Comcast	United States	104	687.7
Walt Disney	United States	110	81.5
News Corp	United States	149	45.5
Time Warner	United States	163	39.7
DirecTV	United States	314	36.3
Vivendi	France	146	33.8
Viacom	United States	294	27.3
CBS	United States	474	16
Liberty Media	United States	684	10.3

Source: Forbes Global 2000 Leading Companies

Though most TNMCs are based in the US, Sony is headquartered in Tokyo, Japan, and is registered there. Sony Pictures Entertainment (SPE) is Sony Corporation's primary audio-visual production firm. It is not headquartered in Tokyo, but in Culver City, California. The chief executive officer (CEO) of Sony Entertainment is not a Japanese citizen or an American citizen, but a British citizen named Howard Stringer. SPE produces and distributes motion pictures and television programming, manages TV channels, develops and markets entertainment franchises and merchandise, and operates a variety of studios worldwide. SPE's organizational structure is characterized by centralized and decentralized accumulation. SPE entails high concentrations and centralization of capital within a multi-divisional corporate structure which employs a combination of relatively autonomous subsidiary and subcontractor firms, the better to enable flexibility in the production, marketing, and distribution of a variety of entertainment commodities. Indeed, SPE oversees Columbia Tristar Motion Picture Group (CTMPG), a centralized structure connected to three flexible film acquisition, production, and distribution firms: Columbia Pictures (specializing in blockbuster and mass circulation films); Sony Pictures Classics (specializing in independent and niche-market US and foreign films); and Tristar Pictures (specializing in genre-specific films). SPE co-owns Metro-Goldwyn-Mayer studios with Comcast, another US-based conglomerate. Sony Pictures Digital (SPD) entails customized production studios for SPE media commodities, including Sony Pictures Imageworks (SPI) (a visual effects and digital production studio), Sony Pictures Animation (an animation and digital content generation studio), and SonyPictures.com (an online and mobile content studio). SPE's main film production studio is Sony Pictures Studio (SPS), located in Culver City, California. With twenty-two gigantic sound stages, this US-based motion-picture mega-complex is Sony Corporation's world audio-visual production center. Sony Pictures US (SPUS) and Sony Pictures Releasing International (SPRI) are responsible for selling, distributing, and marketing SPE's finished entertainment commodities in sixty-seven territories worldwide.

Terra Nova, *True Blood*, and *Breaking Bad* (Saltzman 2011). Instead of threatening the economic and cultural dominance of US-TNMCs, the global growth of convergent media platforms and the World Wide Web provides more windows for offloading copies of their media products. In addition to establishing greater source diversity and media selections, the Web enables greater global exposure to entertainment media sourced by US TNMCs.

NATIONAL MEDIA CORPORATIONS (NMCS)

US-based first-tier TNMCs are the world system's most structurally powerful media owners, and US entertainment media is the most genuinely global. Yet, "second-tier" and "third-tier" national media firms (NMCs) in media capitals all over the world have influence as well. A national media corporation (NMC) is a nationally headquartered company with business operations that are mainly, though not exclusively, focused on one country or region market. NMCs are often owned and managed by a national political and/or business class (i.e., the shareholders, directors, and CEOs are citizens of one country), employ a nationally situated workforce, focus on competing within and controlling a "national" media market, produce and distribute "nationalistic" TV shows and films in the local language, and target a nationally or regionally based audience. Flew (2011) says that "nationally based incumbent media continue to have significant advantages in their own markets, regardless of the superior resources and brand leadership of the big global media companies." NMCs possess intimate knowledge of national and regional audience tastes and preferences, understand advertiser demands, can tap cultural workers and national celebrities, boast links with non-media businesses, and have amicable relations with political parties and states. All of this gives them market advantages and policy privileges. Due to the dialectics of market competition and market control discussed earlier, many second- and third-tier NMCs are striving to become first-tier TNMCs.

For much of the twentieth century, NMCs—public and private—ruled national media markets, but during the 1980s and 1990s, this began to change. Many NMCs expanded their operations and moved into other countries in search of new investments, new waged labor to exploit, new production and distribution systems to acquire, and new consumer markets for the sale of their commodities (Herman and McChesney 1997). In the world system, a "second-tier of perhaps a hundred national and regional companies also plays an important role in the trans-nationalization process" and typically allies "with the leading transnationals behind a politics stressing convergence and industrial consolidation" (Schiller 2007: 121). Of the top fifty "second-tier" NMCs, those not based in the US are located in Japan (NHK, TV Asahi, Nippon TV, Tokyo Broadcasting System, TV Tokyo, Fuji Television), the United Kingdom

---

BOX 2.5

MCOT AS AN NMC

MCOT is a Thailand-based NMC that owns and operates Modernine TV (TV broadcaster), the Panorama Worldwide Company Limited and Seed MCOT (news, music TV, and film production studios), sixty-two radio stations, and the Thai News Agency (TNA) wire service. MCOT is headquartered in Bangkok, the city-capital and largest urban area of Thailand. The Thai government (the Ministry of Banks) owns 77 percent of MCOT; the remaining 23 percent is owned by Thai capital. MCOT's president and board of directors are Thai citizens. Most were educated in Thailand, but a few were educated in the US (at the University of Pennsylvania, Indiana University, Fordham University, University of California, and Pine Manor College). MCOT employs Thai creative workers, news journalists, technicians, and more. It is a national media powerhouse which reaches urban and rural viewers with national news and edutainment products. Modernine TV reports that it is improving TV products by "inserting [into their content] more modernity, strength, content and entertainment under a theme of 'Trendy Place for Content-based Entertainment in the Family'." Modernine TV broadcasts comprise 36.62 percent news TV shows, 21.38 percent shows conveying information and knowledge, 33.39 percent entertainment content, 5.68 percent sports TV, and 2.92 percent TV public service and program promotions. MCOT produces and circulates nationally popular TV entertainment such as *Yok Siam Program* and *The Star* (game shows), *I Love Thailand* and *Woody Talk program* (variety and talk shows), and *Kob Nok Kala, Khun Phra Chuay*, and *Khon kon Khon* (family sitcoms).

Although MCOT is based in Thailand and is mainly Thai-focused, it also has international ambitions.

(BBC, Pearson, ITV), France (Vivendi), Germany (Bertelsmann), Canada (BCE-CTV, Rogers Communication, Shaw Communication, Quebecor), Italy (Mediaset), India (Bennet Coleman, Zee), Brazil (RedeGlobo, Abril), Mexico (Groupo Televisa, TV Azteca), and China (CCTV, Shanghai Media Group, Phoenix TV) (Arsenault and Castells 2008). In 2010, the world's top fifty media corporations took in $470.5 billion in revenue, an incredible sum of money that exceeds the gross domestic product (GDP) of many countries (Mitchell 2011).

POWER RELATIONS BETWEEN US-TNMCS AND NON-US NMCS

A number of scholars argue that second-tier NMCs challenge, or at least pose substantial rivalries to, first-tier TNMCs (Giddins 1999; Chadha and Kavoori 2000; Fraser 2003; Sonwalker 2001). Discussions about second-tier NMCs acting as rivals to the first-tier firms based in the US are not entirely new (Tunstall 1977). The rise of NMCs and the growing audio-visual production and export capacity in developing countries complicates the CI paradigm's view that the world TV and film market is ruled solely by US-based TNMCs. The global market share for audio-visual exports held by developing countries rose from 27.6 percent in 1994 to 44.6 percent in 2002 (Sauve 2006: 14). But to speak of the power of US-based TNMCs as being undermined by non-US NMCs is absurd, especially when considering that they have dramatically expanded their operations and their profits *within* developing countries over the past forty years. Undoubtedly, many NMCs produce their own TV shows and films for national and regional markets and some do have transnational ambitions. In many East Asian countries, for example, NMCs conduct business in national and regional markets to sate the viewer preference for entertainment content that is "closer to home" than the stuff exported by US-based TNMCs (Kean, Fung and Moran 2007): Brazil's Rede Globo exports TV shows to regional markets in South America; Venezuela-based TeleSUR broadcasts TV shows throughout Latin America; India's Bollywood makes hundreds of films each year; Netherlands-based Endemol and London-based Freemantle Media export non-scripted media formats throughout Europe and to the US (Sigismondi 2011). While powerful and transnationally oriented non-US media firms exist, they do not currently outmatch US TNMCs.

Second-tier NMCs compete with US TNMCs for market share, but they do not currently rival them, nor do they challenge their capitalist logics. Herman and McChesney (1997) point out that the rise of NMCs does not compromise US cultural imperialism:

> The crucial incursion is the implantation of the model; the secondary developments of importance are the growth, consolidation, and centralization of the commercial systems, their increasing integration into the global system, and the gradual effects of these processes on economies, political systems, and the cultural environment. (153–154)

Second-tier NMCs replicate and extend the US corporate media model. They reproduce and support the capitalist logics of US-based TNMCs by pursuing profit-maximization, perpetuating the post-public US capitalist ownership form, exploiting waged cultural workers, selling audiences to advertisers, re-transmitting US TV shows and films to local viewers, and modeling their entertainment products on those made by US-based

TNMCs (Morley 1996). NMCs replicate US-originated entertainment styles, forms, and narratives because of their global familiarity. TV shows and films made by US-based TNMCs remain the standard of excellence against which NMCs evaluate the "production value" or "quality" of their own commercial content. Also, second-tier media companies often have politically conservative owners who bias media output toward elite global-local agendas (Curran and Park 2000). Venezuela's Univision, for example, is owned by local pro-US media magnate, Gustavo Cisneros. Like many US allies, Cisneros was educated in the US, and he is a good friend of former US President, George W. Bush (Ruiz 2004). Cisneros's Univision supported the 2002 US-backed coup against Venezuela's socialist president, Hugo Chavez (Fraser 2003).

US-TNMCs continue to be the structurally dominant media players in the world system. But do they "dominate" non-US media systems, as some critics of cultural imperialism say? Do Viacom, Walt Disney News Corporation, Time Warner, and others coerce non-US theater chains and TV networks into screening and scheduling US entertainment media? The power relationship between US TNMCs and non-US NMCs is not based on coercion, but on persuasion. And media corporations are not "cultural imperialists" in their own right. In the twenty-first century, both first-tier and second-tier media conglomerates are organized as capitalist organizations. They compete to control market share but also collaborate within them. In fact, first-tier US-based TNMCs regularly establish and enter into strategic alliances with second-tier NMCs (Oba and Chan-Olmsted 2007). There is often a mutually beneficial (as opposed to hostile) relationship between the executives of first-tier US-based TNMCs and second-tier NMCs. TNMCs and NMCs profit-maximize by working with, not against, each other. TNMCs "push" through borders to enter media markets outside the US, while NMCs "pull" TNMCs into strategic alliances with them. US-TNMCs do not dominate NMCs: the power relationship is one of "asymmetrical interdependence" (Strauhbhar 1991), not coercive domination.

Why do TNMCs partner up with NMCs? TNMCs can globalize either by establishing a new subsidiary corporation in the country in which it seeks to do business or by forming a strategic alliance with an existing firm that is already headquartered in the target country (Oba and Chan-Olmsted 2007). A strategic alliance refers to those instances when a TNMC cooperates or collaborates with an NMC by sharing resources such as financing, production and distribution systems, knowledge and skills, and copyrighted entertainment. The strategic alliance's goal is a global-local synergy. Instead of establishing an entirely new and highly capital-intensive subsidiary in another country, TNMCs form strategic alliances with NMCs. By doing so, TNMCs gain a national business partner which possesses established distribution systems and knowledge about the state and market (the media policies and regulations of the state and the place specific cultural codes, tastes, and preferences of viewers). This enables the TNMC to spread the risk of business around, and to flexibly adjust its conduct to local market conditions (Pathania-Jain 2001).

NMCs competitively pull TNMCs into alliances as a way to capture foreign direct investment (FDI), technology, managerial expertise, and knowledge. They also pull TNMCs to acquire their entertainment content. Second-tier media firms often consume and re-circulate US entertainment commodities domestically, while simultaneously linking up with US-TNMCs as a way to get their own entertainment media distributed in the US (McChesney and Schiller 2003: 11; Sinclair 2003). As Arsenault and Castells (2008) observe: "local and regional players are actively importing and/or re-appropriating foreign products and formats while corporate transnational media organizations are pursuing local partners to deliver customized content to audiences" (708). In a study of the strategic global-local alliances formed between TNMCs—Time Warner, News Corporation, Walt Disney Corporation, Viacom, and NBC Universal—and NMCs from 2001–2005, Oba and Chan-Olmsted (2007) found that "TNMCs have intensified their expansion into many emerging economies amid saturating media demand in developed countries, especially the US, and with the help of local partners in these markets" (22). Schiller (2007) similarly observes that:

> A scattering of conglomerates domiciled in countries such as South Korea, China, India, Mexico, Brazil and Venezuela have thereby joined those based in the United States and a few other wealthy nations in widening and deepening the culture market—and extending the entire industry's transnational orientation. (120)

The strategic global-local business alliance between US-based TNMCs and non-US NMCs take the form of joint ventures, equity alliances, and licensing agreements (Liu and Chan-Olmsted 2002).

A *joint venture* is when a TNMC and NMC together establish an entirely new media corporation. They then share expenses, assets, and revenues. Artz (2007) says that joint ventures are:

> enterprises that produce within one nation but are jointly owned by multiple corporations from multiple nations [. . .] and have no national allegiance and bring together capitalist classes from two or more nations for the purpose of producing and profiting from media commodities. (148)

In 2010, for example, Walt Disney Corporation formed a joint venture with South Korean telecommunications provider SK Telecom Corporation as a means of launching a Korean-language, Disney-branded TV channel (Reuters 2010). In 2010, Walt Disney Corporation also formed a joint venture with the Russian UTH in order to start an advertising-supported free-to-air Russian version of the Disney Channel. The channel broadcasts a mix of Russian TV shows and Disney Channel TV shows to more than 40 million households in fifty-four Russian cities. It also reaches rural regions (Chmielewski 2010). "International expansion is a key strategic priority for our company and Disney Channel has proven to be invaluable in building the Disney brand around the world," said Robert A. Iger, Walt Disney Corporation's president and CEO. "We are excited about increasing Disney Channel's presence in Russia and delivering exceptional family entertainment to this important growth market" (cited in Chmielewski 2010).

An *equity alliance* is when a TNMC acquires a percentage of an existing or new NMC by investing in it. For example, in 2009 Time Warner established an equity alliance with Central European Media Enterprises Ltd (CME) by investing US $241.5 million in CME. This alliance gave CME, one of Central and Eastern Europe's most powerful NMCs, an investment that enabled it to expand its operations. In return, Time Warner gained 19 million shares in CME, appointed of two of its own executives to CME's board of directors, and launched a TV channel to distribute films and TV shows from its Warner Brothers intellectual property portfolio. This equity alliance resulted in a synergy. As CME founder Ronald S. Lauder said:

> I'm confident that this alliance with Time Warner will accelerate CME's future development and take it to levels I could only dream of fifteen years ago. The combination of CME's market leading positions and Time Warner's brands will enhance the prospects of both companies as we work together. (cited in CME 2009)

Time Warner Chairman and Chief Executive Officer Jeff Bewkes said:

> This transaction with CME is a unique opportunity for us to invest in—and partner with—the leading media company in Central and Eastern Europe. [. . .] The investment advances our strategy to create, package and deliver high-quality programming on multiple platforms globally. (cited in CME 2009)

A *licensing agreement* is when a TNMC (licensor) which owns a copyrighted TV show or film authorizes an NMC (the licensee) to distribute the TV show or film to its own viewers. Through licensing-distribution agreements, TNMCs distribute the entertainment media they own through the TV networks and outlets that are owned by its NMC partner. Many TV shows and films scheduled by second-tier NMCs are supplied by US-based TNMCs (Morley 1996). For example, in 2010, NBC Universal established a TV and film distribution licensing agreement with Viasat Broadcasting, which is owned by the Modern Times Group. This Swedish media conglomerate uses Viasat Broadcasting, based in London, to target viewers in Nordic and Baltic countries such as Sweden, Scandinavia, Norway, Estonia, Denmark, Latvia, Finland, Lithuania, and Slovenia. The licensing agreement gave Viasat Broadcasting's TV1000 premium channels the exclusive pay-TV rights in Sweden, Norway, Denmark, and Finland to Hollywood films such as *Robin Hood, The Wolfman*, and *Green Zone*. "The pay-TV agreement with NBC Universal is new for TV1000 and it further strengthens TV1000's position as the leading premium movie channel brand in the Nordic region," said Hans Skarplöth, CEO of Viasat Sweden (cited in Clover 2010). Second-tier NMCs license a tremendous amount of entertainment content from US-based TNMCs—sometimes more than they want. NMCs regularly load their schedules with and broadcast US entertainment media instead of allocating cash to the production of high-quality national entertainment (Jin 2007).

Non-US NMCs also license TV show and film content to US-TNMCs. For example, Hong Kong's IMAGI International Holdings Limited and Creative Power Entertaining Limited Liability Company recently licensed 100 episodes of the *Pleasant Goat and Big Big Wolf* TV series to Disney-owned Buena Vista International, which will license this TV show in forty-six countries, including Macau, Taiwan, South Korea, India, Singapore, Malaysia, and Thailand (IMAGI 2012). Soh Szu Wei, CEO of IMAGI, said: "We are delighted to further strengthen our partnership with Disney. This alliance has enabled *Pleasant Goat and Big Big Wolf* to further penetrate the international market." While Disney content "penetrates" China, a Hong Kong NMC "penetrates" the global market by linking with and capitalizing on a US-TNMC's chain of distributors and exhibitors.

BOX 2.6

BLOCK BOOKING FILM AND TV

The licensing strategy employed by US TNMCs to flood NMC schedules is called *block-booking*. Torre (2009) argues that block-booking began in the late 1920s and early 1930s. Hollywood was made up of the "Big Five" studios (Paramount, MGM, Twentieth Century Fox, Warner Brothers, and RKO) and the "Little Three" studios (Universal, Columbia, and United Artists). Members of the "Big Five" owned the means to produce (studios) and exhibit film (theater chains). Paramount Pictures bought the Paramount-Publix theater chain (1,200 screens) and then insisted that theater house operators buy "block" packages of Paramount films. Hollywood moguls grouped together a bunch of high-quality and lower quality feature films. In order to acquire the high-quality films, theater owners had to buy the lower quality films too. The logic of the Hollywood block-book deal was this: "If you want this film you have to take all of these other films too." Block-booking guaranteed a film would reach an audience. It was also a way of controlling markets and undermining the competition. Since the 1960s, US TV distribution companies have used the block-booking strategy worldwide. They compel non-US TV network buyers who want to acquire a hot TV series to buy it bundled with a block of lower quality TV shows. Therefore, for a non-US TV network to obtain a top-rated US TV series, they must also purchase lower-rated TV shows. So, for every popular TV show purchased, three or more unpopular TV shows are booked with it (Segrave 1998: 115). The "international output deal"—when a US TV distributor creates packages of a few high-quality TV shows with less desirable TV shows for sale to non-US TV networks—is the most recent term for block-booking in transnational business relations between US TV distributors and non-US TV networks (Torre 2009). Output deals occur when buyers for TV networks agree to purchase and exhibit all of a distributor's TV shows over a period of time (Havens 2011: 148)

In sum, first-tier TNMCs do not dominate local second-tier NMCs, but the emergence of second-tier NMCs does not currently pose a substantial rivalry to the US-based TNMCs. TNMCs actively court NMCs in pursuit of business goals, and NMCs eagerly and actively enter into strategic alliances with TNMCs to better serve their local profit interests. Cultural imperialism, to the extent that it presumes the coercive domination of one national media industry by another, is not an appropriate description of the global-local power relationship between TNMCs and NMCs. Arsenault and Castells (2008) state:

> While a few media organizations form the backbone of the global network of media networks, local and national media are not falling like dominos under the ruthless expansion of global media organizations. Rather, global companies are leveraging partnerships and cross-investments with national, regional, and local companies to facilitate market expansion and vice versa. (722)

Joint ventures, equity alliances, and licensing agreements are not based on coercive power relationships between exploiter and exploited, oppressor and oppressed, dominant and dominated. In many countries, corporations exploit workers and dominate nature, but in transnational media trade, the media bourgeoisie work together to achieve the goal of accumulation. The outcome of this strategic alliance may be the economic dominance of TNMCs, but this dominance is fully supported by the CEOs of NMCs. TNMCs operate within and through NMCs. TNMCs and NMCs synergistically coordinate entertainment media financing, production, distribution, marketing, and exhibition in order to meet the profit-maximization goal of global and local media owners. As Schiller (2007) points out: "National capital has often claimed a significant role in implanting and reorganizing this enlarged trans-national complex" (120). Indeed, in 2006, sales by affiliates of US-based TNMCs totaled US $23.7 billion (WTO 2010: 6).

CONCLUSION: US MEDIA IMPERIALISM CONTINUED

This chapter has employed a political-economy and critical media industry studies approach in order to describe and examine the many ways that capitalism and capitalist logics shape the production, distribution, marketing, and exhibition of entertainment media as a commodity. It has also examined the main trends in the transnational political economy of the media.

Although capitalist media logics have gone global, the US remains the world system's media center. US TNMCs continue to be the most structurally dominant in the world system. In virtually every country, first-tier US-based TNMCs have increased their economic presence and cultural influence. They rule global audio-visual markets. More countries import more entertainment from the US than ever before. The flow of TV shows and films between the US and other countries is not reciprocal; audio-visual trade is imbalanced. US viewers consume far less "foreign" content than do non-US viewers. Boyd-Barrett (1977) defines media imperialism as:

> a process whereby the ownership, structure, distribution or content of the media in any one country are singly or together subject to substantial pressure from the media interests of any other country or countries without proportionate reciprocation of influence by the country so affected. (117)

This definition remains relevant. The "pressure" exerted by US TNMCs in many countries may thwart the development of strong non-US TV and film production/distribution sectors, resulting in a situation that further strengthens the power position of the US at the expense of others.

That being said, the dominance of US TNMCs is not based on a coercive power relation. US TNMCs do not dominate non-US TNMCs, and non-US countries are not forced to open their markets to US media owners, distributors, exhibitors, or TV show and film content against their will. The power relation between US TNMCs and non-US NMCs is persuasive, not coercive. Whereas in the past it may have been appropriate to speak of US-based TNMCs as agents of "the sum processes" bringing non-capitalist societies closer to the US center, in the twenty-first century, almost all societies have been integrated into and have adopted the capitalist model. Though capitalism continues to be unevenly developed and differentially governed (Harvey 2006), it is a universal phenomenon. Many country-specific "media capitals" are home to powerful second- and third-tier NMCs which conduct business transactions in an asymmetrically interdependent power relationship with US TNMCs. US-based TNMCs and non-US NMCs compete and collaborate to control markets. They support the "sum processes" which promote and reproduce consumer-capitalist social relations and the commercial media model everywhere.

The US is the world system's dominant media center, home to the world's most powerful TNMCs. But this dominance may be gradually diminishing due to the rise of non-US media capitals and NMCs:

> In 1998, the US media market accounted for one half of all worldwide media revenues; in 2010, the figure was less than a third. The four largest Anglo-American markets—United States (1), United Kingdom (5), Canada (8), and Australia (12)—still account for about 44 percent of media revenues worldwide, but this is a strong drop from 60 percent in the late 1990s. (Winseck 2011: 38)

US "media imperialism" continues, but is unlikely to last forever. Capitalism influences entertainment media and structures the global power relations between media corporations, but de-territorializing capitalist logics intersect with the territorial interests of states. This will be examined in the next chapter.

CHAPTER 3

Governing Global Entertainment Media
The State, Media Policy, and Regulation

**INTRODUCTION: ENTERTAINMENT MEDIA FLOWS IN
A WORLD SYSTEM OF NATION-STATES**

States within the European Union compel their national TV broadcasters to commit a portion of the daily schedules to "European" entertainment. In Kenya, the Kenya Broadcasting Corporation (KBC) strives to "provide quality TV" programs that preserve indigenous values and promote "universal access to information for all" (Kenya Broadcasting Corporation 2011). In Sri Lanka, the Sri Lankan Ministry of Mass Media compels the Sri Lanka Broadcasting Corporation (SLBC) to:

> secure the Sri Lankan identity and national heritages in the modernized technological environment and to establish and maintain an ethical media practice in the country while contributing directly towards the development of the country and preserving the right of the people to have access to correct information. (Media Centre for National Development of Sri Lanka 2011)

Japan's Japanese Agency of Cultural Affairs subsidizes Japanese "arts, entertainment and cultural properties," while NHK Japan Broadcasting Corporation airs Japanese TV shows and films (Visiting Arts 2008). In post-Saddam Iraq, the Iraqi Communications and Media Commission (ICMC) monitors TV broadcasters to ensure that they support Iraqi economic development and national cohesion. In Jamaica, the Jamaican Broadcasting Commission regulates TV broadcasting to ensure that broadcasts represent salient national issues. In the United Kingdom, Ofcom monitors entertainment content in accordance with "British values." Around the world, states use media policies and regulatory agencies to support, influence, and censor entertainment media. The cross-border production and distribution of entertainment media by NMCs and TNMCs does not happen above, below, or between states, but within their territorial borders. The conduct of all NMCs and TNMCs is shaped by state media policies and regulations.

The relationship between states and media corporations, however, is often under-examined. The CG paradigm sometimes imagines states to be in decline or suffering a crisis due to globalizing flows. Appadurai (1997), for example, claims that "the nation-state as a complex modern political form, is on its last legs" (19). Too often, states are rendered moot entities that are undermined by global-local market interactions between

TNMCs and consumers (Morris and Waisbord 2001: ix). The CI paradigm, meanwhile, represents states as either comprador allies of TNMCs, who "sellout" national culture, or as helpless victims of TNMCs, who must fight heroically to save national culture. Yet, the notion that "transnational media flows undermine the stability of the nation-state by their very capacity to connect corporations to consumers bypassing national borders, derives from a romantic, liberal market logic" (McMillan 2007: 216). TNMCs dream of a seamlessly integrated world market that allows them to profit-maximize without the need to attend to the particularities of specific places, political regimes, and cultures. In the actual world, all entertainment media is governed by states (Artz 2003:4; Price 2002: 227; Sparks 2007: 184). Curtin (2005) says that TNMCS are "grounded by a set of forces" which influence their conduct, namely, the political forces of the territorial state.

This chapter examines how states govern the conduct of NMCs and TNMCs and influence the cross-border production, distribution, exhibition and consumption of entertainment media. It attends to the convergences and divergences between the goals of territorial states and de-territorializing media corporations. This discussion of the power relationships between states and media corporations shows how significant territorial states are vis-à-vis de-territorializing media corporations. This chapter examines how states court and contest the profit-maximization goals of NMCs and TNMCs in national and international contexts. In a hierarchical world system, states are central to the facilitation and legitimization of capitalism. Though states are distinct from NMCs and TNMCs, they perform a variety of functions that buttress, and in some instances, constrain, business interests. By examining how states shape the conduct of media corporations, this chapter challenges the view that global entertainment media flourishes above territorial governance. Worldwide, states govern media corporations and gatekeep the flow of entertainment media between borders.

What is the state? What is media policy? On whose behalf is media policy made? What are the general purposes of media policy? What are the specific areas of media policy that govern entertainment? Does the economic and cultural dominance of US-based TNMCs need to be curtailed in order for non-US media industries and cultures to flourish? The first section of this chapter defines media policy; it then examines liberal pluralist and power elite theories of the media policy-making process. The second section describes the main goals of media policy: nation-making, national culture/creative industry development, and "market failure" mitigation. The third section examines forms of state intervention into the media market: intellectual property/copyright, ownership, concentration/competition, content subsidization and quotas, and censorship. The fourth section discusses the key prescriptions of neoliberal media policy regime (liberalization, deregulation, and privatization) and global media governance. The final section explores the pitfalls and promises of nationalist media policy.

Sovereign States: Media Policy

Since the emergence of capitalism, states have not operated independently of "market forces," nor have market forces existed independently of "political forces" (Wood

2004). Capitalism (as a mode of production) has always entailed a specific mode of political regulation, a set of governmental institutions, policies, laws, regulatory agencies, and practices that support the accumulation of capital (Harvey 1989; Steinmetz 2003). That mode of political regulation is the state, the universal form of political order in the modern world. "The modern state is an institutional complex claiming sovereignty for itself as the supreme political authority within a defined territory for whose governance it is responsible" (Hay and Lister 2006). The earth's landmass is divided up into spheres of governmental influence by 192 states, each of which claims sovereignty as the supreme political authority over territorialized populations, economies, and cultures (Hay and Lister 2006). The state is "a distinct set of political institutions whose concern is with the organization of domination, in the name of the common [national] interest, within a delimited territory" (McLean and McMillan 2003: 512). As Morris and Waisbord (2001) claim: "States remain fundamental political units in a world that continues to be divided along Westphalian principles of sovereignty according to which states are supreme authorities within their borders" (x). Worldwide, states are responsible for law-making, legitimated violence, and order within the territories they govern. They strive to exercise sovereign power over their internal territories and when dealing with external others.

Media sovereignty (Price 2002) refers to the power of states to manage, support, filter, promote, or limit the flow of informational and entertainment media within their territorial borders. In practical terms, media sovereignty is the right and the ability of states to develop and enact policies which influence the conduct of NMCs and TNMCs. States and media corporations occupy distinct spheres in society: the political and the economic. But, according to McChesney and Schiller (2003), "What is inadequate and wrong about this conventional framing [the separation of the state and the media corporation] is the notion that [. . .] state-media relations naturally tend to be antagonistic" (2). In fact, the history of states and media corporations is one of accord, not conflict. As Curtin (2007) explains:

> markets are subject to political interventions that enable, shape and attenuate the
> dynamics of media capital [. . .] market forces are in fact meaningless without
> self-conscious state interventions to fashion a terrain for commercial operations.
> Markets are made, not given. (22)

Entertainment media markets are also made, and most often with immense state assistance. States "ultimately hold the power to pass legislation that affects domestic media industries" (Morris and Waisbord 2001: x–xi) and regularly enact regulations to govern them.

Media policy scholars make a useful contribution to the study of how state policies and regulations govern the actions of and interactions between media corporations and citizen-consumers in society. Policy refers to those state or corporate decisions and actions which guide certain kinds of conduct in society. In practice, policy influences, controls, or changes people, institutions, and situations. Media scholars present useful definitions of media policy as a tool of governance. Garnham (1998) describes media policy as "the ways in which public authorities shape, or try to shape, the structures and practices of the media" (210). Sarikakis (2004) defines media policy as "the general principles which guide decisions of authorities, usually governments, about the function of the mass media." Raboy (2002) says media policy encompasses "the full range of attempts to influence the orientation of these [media] systems by [state and non-state] social actors mobilizing whatever resources they can in order to promote their respective interests" (2). Freedman (2008) states that "media policy refers to the development of goals and norms leading to the creation of instruments that are designed to shape the structure and behaviour of media systems" (14).

Until recently, media policy was distinguished from cultural policy (Bratich, Packer, and McCarthy 2003; Lewis and Miller 2003; McGuigan 2003 and 2004; Miller and Yudice 2002). As Hesmondhalgh (2005) says, "Cultural policy has usually been strongly associated with the subsidized arts sector, whereas media and communication policy has tended to be analyzed in terms of economics and politics (in the narrow sense of the latter term)" (95). Garnham (2005) elaborates:

> Historically, there was a clear division between [cultural] policy towards the arts,
> based broadly on the principles of patronage and enlightenment and on assumptions
> of an inherent opposition between art and commerce, and [media] policy towards
> the mass media, and therefore, the provision of mass or popular culture. (16)

However, the emergence of horizontally and vertically integrated media firms and convergent culture industry, media industry, and telecommunication markets has rendered the distinction between media policy and cultural policy problematic, if not irrelevant. Both "media" and "cultural" policy focus on the relationship between politics, the means of producing and distributing symbolic products, and national identity (McGuigan 2004). I define media policy inclusively as those policies that aim to influence the conduct of all organizations—public and private—which produce, distribute, and exhibit media goods.

This inclusive definition enables a study of a state's governance of all of the media corporations that own and control the means of media production, distribution, and exhibition in society ("the culture industry"; "the creative industry"; "the communication industry"; "the media industry"). Media policy scholarship focuses on the state policies and regulations that govern the NMCs and TNMCs which own, media products (TV shows, films, video games, digital content) and represent and shape ways of life ("culture"). Media policy is a state instrument for governing the NMCs and TNMCs which create the media commodities that represent and influence ways of life.

While media policy represents the will and the ways of governing NMCs and TNMCs, state regulatory agencies and regulation are the means of doing so. As Freedman (2008) says, "If media policy suggests the broader field where a variety of ideas and assumptions about desirable structure and behaviour circulate, then regulation points to the specific institutional mechanisms for realizing these aims" (13). Abramson (2001) similarly claims that regulation is policy in practice: "where policy sets out the state's role in bringing its preferred mediascape into being, regulation is the instrument through which the state supervises, controls or curtails the activities of non-state actors in accordance with policy" (301–302). All countries have state regulatory agencies which monitor NMCs and TNMCs to ensure that they operate in accordance with law and established policy. There are many examples: The US regulatory agency is the Federal Communications Commission (the FCC); Canada's regulatory agency is the Canadian Radio-Television and Telecommunication Commission (CRTC); the United Kingdom: Ofcom (short for Office of Communication); China: General Administration of Press and Publication (GAPP) and the State Administration of Radio, Film, and Television (SARFT); India: The Ministry of Information and Broadcasting; Saudi Arabia: Ministry of Culture and Information; Zimbabwe: Ministry of Media, Information and Publicity; Ireland: the Commission for Communication Regulation; Russia: Ministry of Culture and Mass Communication of the Russia Federation; Portugal: Autoridade Nacional de Comunicações (ANACOM). While all states have regulatory agencies that are mandated to enforce policy, no two conduct media policy and regulation in exactly the same way. Every country has its own internal media policy and regulatory history and structure that should be examined on a case-by-case basis.

Politics and Power in Media and Cultural Policy-Making

In every country, the state plays a significant role in establishing national media policies and enacting and enforcing them through a regulatory agency. Media policy and regulation is not just technical (i.e., committed to solving problems), but also *political*. Freedman (2008) claims media policy is "the systematic attempt to foster certain types of media structure and behaviour and to suppress alternative modes of structure and behaviour," "is a deeply political phenomenon," (1) and that media policy-making is "a battleground in which contrasting political positions fight both for material advantage [. . .] and for ideological legitimization" (3). Raboy (2007) contends that "the terrain of media policy—is hotly contested; it is a battleground, a field of tension and struggle rooted in social history and the natural law that technologies are not neutral but emerge out of particular political circumstances"(344). Media policy is power: it is a means by which a state gets others to do want what it wants them to do, a site of decision-making about the allocation of resources in society, and a way of intervening in and acting upon society in order to change it.

Though states formulate media policy on behalf of the general "national interest," many policies actually support the particular interests and values belonging to a national interest group (or coalition of groups). Which interest groups shape media policy and regulatory frameworks? How do struggles for power between different groups shape media policy and regulatory practices? Which particular group's media policy interest does the state generalize as the national interest? Which interest groups are most able to influence state media policy? How, and why, do they do so? These questions are central to critical media policy studies. As Garnham (1998) says: "We always need to ask the question why this policy in this form now and in whose interest it is designed? Neither policies nor their presentation should ever be taken at their face value" (210). According to McChesney and Schiller (2003), "the question is not whether the government plays a role in establishing communication systems, because it plays a foundational role. The question is whose interests and what values do government communication policies encourage?" (3). Liberal pluralist and power elite theories of the state present useful yet diametrically opposed answers to this question.

In mainstream political science, pluralism is probably the most dominant theory of state policy-making. Many policy analysts employ a pluralist framework. Pluralists hold a benign view of the state: they view the state as the highest expression of liberal democratic ideology and as a mechanism for political organization and change. First, pluralists believe that in liberal democracies, pluralism is a guiding principle which permits the peaceful coexistence of different interest groups with an array of values, beliefs, and lifestyles. Second, pluralists say that society comprises hundreds of special interest groups, and that citizens are rarely part of one single interest group: they move between many different interest groups based on ethnicity, culture, gender/sex, occupation, religion, lifestyle, and so on. Third, pluralists argue that interest groups come together around, and compete with, other groups to shape state policies. These interest groups are not static or fixed in place for all time, but are contingent and time-bound. Fourth, pluralism claims that power is not the property of any one interest group, dominant class, or power elite. Resources are broadly (though unequally) distributed among many interest groups, which compete with each other to influence policy agendas. Fifth, the pluralist believes that due to competition between many interest groups, policy-making is always a negotiated process. The struggle of one interest group to realize its interests is always constrained by opposing interest groups. Seventh, the pluralist says that the state is a value-neutral arbiter of competitions between diverse interest groups. The state is genuinely pluralistic, open to all. State policy-making is not partial to the interests of any one single group but, rather, reflects negotiations and compromises between many interest groups. Eighth, the pluralist says that states make policy with the goal of consensus and conflict resolution. Pluralists argue that the state settles conflicts to the mutual benefit of all contending interest groups.

Pluralism represents a normative view of media policy-making. In liberal democracies, a number of different interest groups with an array of values, beliefs, and lifestyles strive to shape media policy. For example, NMCs and TNMCs strive to shape media policy through the lobbyists they pay; unions, citizen watchdog groups, consumer activists, and many other interest groups do the same. These interest groups form around a number of issues related to the conduct of NMCs and TNMCs in society and compete with other interest groups to shape media policies. No one interest group has total power to determine the media policy-making process. NMCs and TNMCs are one interest group among many. They compete to shape the media policy agenda: due to competition between many media policy interest groups, media policy-making is always a negotiated process. The struggle by corporate lobbyists to put the interests of the NMCs and TNMCs they serve on the state's policy agenda, for example, is always constrained by the union, citizen, and consumer interest groups that may oppose them. The state is not structurally biased to one interest group (e.g., media corporations) or another (e.g., the media unions). When the state makes media policy, it does not do so on behalf of one group. Nor does the state exclude any interest group from the media policy-making process: the state is genuinely pluralistic, open to the media policy interests of all. The outcome of the policy-making process—media policy/regulation—represents compromises between many interest groups. Media policy represents a bargained consensus; no one interest group gets everything it wants from the state or gets every media policy outcome it desires at the expense of other groups. Media policy represents a settlement of conflicts between contending interest groups.

Power elite theorists argue that the liberal pluralist account of state policy-making is misleading (Domhoff 2007; Mills 1956), and that the liberal democratic state primarily exists to serve elite interests, most often the interests of business. They say that society is not based upon the peaceful coexistence of different groups; for them, society is based upon conflict between two antagonistic groups: the rulers and the ruled, the elite and the non-elite, the bourgeoisie and the proletariat (Domhoff 2009; Mills and Wolfe 2000). While society is comprised of hundreds of identity-based interest groups, the fundamental division is between the elite owning class (the minority) and the working class (the majority). In capitalism, one percent of the world's population—liberal and conservative—controls at least forty percent of the world's total wealth (Stiglitz 2011). In the US, one percent of the US population controls approximately twenty-three percent of total US wealth (Reich 2010). Power elite theorists say that, while many interest groups do compete to shape state policies, the elite business class is the most powerful interest group and influencer of policy. The elite is able to achieve its interests through the state because its members occupy positions of institutional decision-making power, which enable them to directly establish policies or indirectly pressure state policy-makers to do their bidding. There may be competition between many interest groups to shape the policy agenda but, most often, state policy serves the short- and long-term interests of the elite. Power elite theorists say that the state is not a neutral power-broker, but is biased toward elite business groups. When pressured or facing a legitimacy crisis, states do sometimes make concessions to the working poor, but most often they are partial to the elite interests of business. The outcome of policy-making is not consensus, but conflict.

The power elite theory represents a critical counterpoint to liberal pluralist views of media policy formation. NMCs and TNMCs are elite interest groups: "Everywhere, these industries seek to influence the government to improve their competition position both internally and internationally" (Sparks 2007; 207–209). NMCs and TNMCs are more able to influence media policy-making processes than are other interest groups. As Freedman (2008) says:

> Media policy ought to be a field that is open to resource-poor groups with competing
> voices and different objectives but, in reality, it is not; it is a process that, for all
> its conflicts, is ultimately dominated by those with the most extensive financial,
> ideological and political resources who are best able to mobilize their interests against
> their rivals" (23)

NMCs and TNMCs dispatch lobbyists to court, co-opt, and persuade politicians and policy-makers to do their bidding. The Motion Picture Association of America (MPAA) and the International Intellectual Property Right Association (IIPRA), for example, are powerful lobby groups formed to advance the interests of US-based TNMCs (Bettig 1996: 226; Segrave 1997; Tunstell 2000: 51). In many countries, state policy-makers

BOX 3.1

THE US STATE AS BOOSTER OF CORPORATE POWER

The US state serves the profit interests of NMCs and TNMCs. Corporatism, not unfettered free-market capitalism, underpins the power and prosperity of US-based media corporations. Many US state agencies secure the profit interests of US TNMCs. The US Treasury, US Congress, the Department of Defense, the Commerce Departments, the National Telecommunications and Information Administration, the US Patent and Trademark Office, the Federal Communications Commission (FCC), the White House Office of the US Trade Representative, and the State Department all take part in media policy-making and regulatory practices that tend to benefit media firms. Many US state agencies have been "captured" by powerful lobbyists for NMCs and TNMCs, including the Motion Picture Association of America (MPAA), The National Association of Broadcasters (NAB), the Newspaper Association of America (NAP), and the International Intellectual Property Rights Association (IIPRA) (Bettig 1996: 226; Herman and McChesney 1997; Schiller 2000; Segrave 1998; Tunstell 2000: 51). As result, the US state's media policies and regulatory agencies facilitate and legitimize the profit-interests of the media firms, often privileging concentration, oligopolistic markets, and stringent copyright regimes at the expense of media democracy, cultural diversity, and the public interest (McChesney and Schiller 2003). "The history of Big Government and Big Corporations is more one of accommodation than of confrontation" (8) writes Bagdikian (1997). For McChesney (2003), the political issue at stake is not state intervention/regulation versus corporate freedom/de-regulated markets, but, to the contrary, state intervention/regulation to serve the public as opposed to the corporate interests that captured the state.

and regulators are "captured" by NMCs and TNMCs. As Freedman (2008) observes: "Key [media policy] decision-makers operate in close ideological conformity with the broad interests of one key constituency—that of business" (104). In sum, power elite theorists posit that state policy serves the interests of NMCs and TNMCs. State policy-makers view the prosperity of NMCs and TNMCs as a vital source of Gross Domestic Product (GDP), tax revenue, and job creation. States are most often not neutral power-brokers between a plurality of interest groups and radically different visions of media policy: they are biased toward the interests of NMCs and TNMCs.

Basically, the pluralist theorist says that decision-making is located in the framework of government, but that many special interest groups use their resources to influence policy-makers. The power elite theory of the state says that state decisions are influenced by, expressive of, and most often partial to the interests of elite groups—and in the case of media policy, media corporations.

THE GOALS OF MEDIA POLICY

Why do states develop media policies? Media policies are attached to a number of state goals:

> to garner support from particular class fractions [i.e. media corporations or media unions] or in response to a perceived need to manage the changing, competing pressures arising from broader restructurings within societies [i.e. the transition from industrial to post-industrial information, creative and knowledge economies]. (Gray 2007: 205)

States publicly justify their support for media policy by stressing the media's instrumental value to the achievement of other policy objectives. In state after state, the media and culture are rendered strategic "resources" of extra-media and cultural policy objectives. The specific instrumental goals of media policy are: 1) making nations; 2) making national culture/creative industries; and, 3) mitigating media market failures/negative social externalities.

Making nations. States use media policy to make national identities. McQuail (1992) defines national identity as "a group's sense of belonging to a particular collectivity with shared attributes (of place, language, culture) and a sense of exclusivity" (264). In this respect, media policy is cultural policy. As Ahearne (2009) observes: "Any political order needs the means to maintain its symbolic legitimacy [. . .] In this sense, we might say that 'cultural policy' represents a trans-historical imperative for all political orders" (143). States are not the same as nations, though they often appear as such (hence the "nation-state" concept): "state" refers to those bureaucratic administrative entities which govern; the nation is the symbolic means by which the state elicits loyalty from its citizens and provides citizens with a sense of a territorially-distinctive cultural identity. The nation binds people separated by vast geographical distances and with many different linguistic, socio-economic, and cultural characteristics to a larger collective sense of "We" or "Us" within a specific territory. The symbols of nation give people a sense of a collective past, present, and future, a sense of where they come from, who they are, and where they may be going. The meaning of national identity is not something that is unchanging or fixed in place for all time, but is something that is made and remade through politics (and often through struggles for hegemony) (Ahmad 1996).

There is no natural relationship between the state and the nation. Yet, the state and the political blocs that seek to rule it daily claim to represent and act on behalf of "the national interest." To the public, the nation represents a mythical and fictive image of cultural homogeneity, singularity, and unity. Yet, in every nation, there is a wide spectrum of heterogeneity, difference, and conflict along social class, ethnic, race, and sexual lines. The nation is a way of resolving differences, a means by which states and political actors try to construct and maintain cohesion and order within the territories they govern. "States ambitiously scheme and relentlessly strive to render natural and obvious 'national culture' and 'national history' due to their central positionality in fostering a sense of cohesion among people over space and time" (Khattab 2006: 352). States employ media policy to make and remake—with, and sometimes without, the populations they govern—nation-ness. As a tool of governance, media policy fixes in place what and where a nation essentially is and what and where it is not, and who the citizens of a nation are and who they are not. Media policy is a form of "communicative boundary maintenance" (Schlesinger 1991) which claims to promote and protect national cultures that are bound by the borders of sovereign states.

Though states employ media policy to make nations, nation-ness is reproduced in the hearts, minds, and bodies of citizens through their everyday rituals of imagining with and through entertainment media. Anderson (1991) famously claimed that nations are "imagined communities." They are imagined in the literal sense that "members of even the smallest nation will never know most of their fellow-members." They are also imagined, in the minds of their subjects, to be "limited": that is, having "finite, if elastic boundaries, beyond which lie other nations"; to be "sovereign" in that they "dream of being free"; and to be a "community" in that "regardless of the actual inequality and exploitation that may prevail in each, the nation is always conceived as a deep, horizontal comradeship" (6–7). Nations are imagined because their members will never know, meet or even hear most of their fellow members, "yet in the minds of each lives the image of their communion" (6). Entertainment media is central to the imagining of nations. Goff (2007) says that films and TV shows:

> are a powerful medium through which opinions are formed and identities defined. They provide the most visible prism through which national values and customs are refracted. They are potentially both imbued with and constitutive of the common meanings that undergird the societies of which they are a product. (18)

When viewing nationally inflected TV shows and films, people may perceive themselves to be part of a larger national collective, despite the fact that they may never know, meet, or see most of the other people who are also watching. Entertainment media conveys symbols and stories of nationhood to viewers, providing them with a visual connection to a much bigger national Self. Billig (1995) describes identification with the mundane and taken-for-granted media representations of the nation as "banal nationalism." TV shows and films flag people as members of a distinctive nation, soliciting their identification with a national "I." Banal nationalist entertainment media does not reflect the nation, but, instead, represents the meaning of a national "Us," a collective national "We." In the world system, entertainment media daily tells people who they are and who they are not.

Media policy is integral to the media's making of and the public's imagining of national identities. As Morris and Waisbord (2001) say: "The promotion and maintenance of national and cultural identities is a prominent reason why governments regulate certain aspects of the media. Nationally produced media can be used to promote local values and identities" (xiv). States employ media policy to ensure that media corporations will represent the nation in order to reinforce public identification with nation-ness and maintain social cohesion within the territories they govern. State media policy initiatives are often rationalized as a means of securing, defending, or protecting a distinct "way of life" from the threat of a foreign—often American—Other. In response to fears of "Americanization," states worldwide, in countries as diverse as Canada, Korea, France, Ireland, Australia, South Africa, and Jamaica, have established content regulations that seek to promote and protect the "nation" (Feigenbaum 2003). In response to the popularity of films like *Avatar* (2009) and *Transformers 3* (2011), Chinese President Hu Jintao strengthened China's film and TV production capabilities to secure Chinese national culture from the threat of Westernization (Wong 2012). In sum, state officials use media policy to bind diverse and geographically distanced citizens together, as one nation (Schudson 1994: 656).

Making national culture/creative industries. States also use media policy to build national culture/creative industries (Throsby 2008). In this respect, media policy is a kind of industrial policy. The "culture industry" concept was coined by Frankfurt School theorists Max Horkheimer and Theodore Adorno following World War II in order to critique the commodificiation of culture. Once a pejorative Marxist concept, the "culture industry" is now enthusiastically taken up by media policy-makers as a strategic priority (Milz 2007; Throsby 2001). Attached to neoliberal governancy the culture industry concept rescued cultural policy "from its primordial past and catapulted it to the forefront of the modern forward-looking policy agenda, an essential component in any respectable economic policy-makers development strategy" (Throsby 2008: 229). The culture industry concept has recently been supplemented by the more voguish "creative industry" concept. These concepts are often used synonymously but lately, the "creative industry" is the preferred term (Potts 2008). Banks and O'Connor (2009) note that:

> The apparent break with the notion of "cultural industries"—with its problematic connotations of art and politics—precipitated an intensified commodification of artistic activity and the purposeful integration of creativity (and "useful" forms of culture) into a variety of economic and social policy initiatives. (365)

In the past, culture, arts, media, and heritage were viewed as state-subsidized sectors vis-à-vis the real capitalist economy, but current policy-makers depict the culture or creative industries as a significant means of producing commercial ideas, innovations, and processes which contribute in substantial ways to a state's economic base, and which have ripple effects across markets.

Media policy-makers portray the development of culture/creative industries as central to the economic development of societies that are undergoing a "transition" from industrial to post-industrial capitalism: i.e., from a mode of production based on the production of tangible things to a mode of production driven by the production of intangible yet exploitable ideas. The culture and creative industries—and the NMCs and TNMCs that own them—are viewed by state policy-makers, arts and heritage ministers, and neoliberal economists as engines of capitalist prosperity, long-term growth, and job creation. As the United Nations Conference on Trade and Development (UNCTAD) *2010 Creative Economy Report* says: "culture and creativity are powerful engines driving economic growth and promoting development in a globalizing world." A 2007 report from the Conference Board of Canada commissioned by the Heritage Department entitled *Valuing Culture: Measuring and Understanding Canada's Creative Economy* declares: "the cultural sector helps drive the economy." These industries are viewed as having economic and cultural benefits. In a period of economic downturn, they generate tax revenue, create jobs, contribute to Gross Domestic Product, and attract international tourists to service sectors in stagnating cities. They also promote regional and national social cohesion, recognize and represent cultural diversity, and aid human development initiatives. Furthermore, these industries fuel domestic and foreign investment in telecommunications, digital technology, and consumer electronics infrastructures. Media policy-makers worldwide are gearing their populations to labor within creative capitalism. They present culture/creative industry development as being integral to economic development. The value of culture is no longer explicitly tied to the moral uplift of citizens, the achievement of social goals, or the fostering of cultural nationalism, but is frequently measured in terms of economic growth. Statesmen now do everything in their power to realize culture's exchange value. In sum, media policy is a form of industrial policy that provides ideological and concrete support to the growth and profitability of media corporations. The evidence abounds.

According to the MPAA's Michael O'Leary, who calls on the state to support Hollywood:

> In a struggling economy that has 9 percent or more unemployment, America's creative community—those whose jobs and businesses are involved in the production of movies, music, books, and other forms of intellectual property—can be a driving force for putting Americans back to work. (Block 2011)

A 2010 European Commission publication entitled "Unlocking the potential of cultural and creative industries" claims that the European creative industries employ 5.8 million workers, account for 2.6 percent of Europe's total GDP, and are "not only essential for cultural diversity" but also have "an important role to play in helping to bring Europe out of the crisis" (cited in European Commission 2010). The Scottish Government's 2011 report "Growth, Talent, Ambition: the Government's strategy for the Creative Industries" outlines a strategy for building and maintaining support for the creative industries, which "generate billions of pounds each year for the Scottish economy and support more than 60,000 jobs" (Scottish Government 2011). Canadian Minister of Arts and Culture, James Moore, says that "arts and culture represents over 630,000 jobs in Canada and Canada's culture industries represent $46 billion in the Canadian economy" (Moore 2011). China is trying to shed its "made in China" label as an export-processing zone for industrial commodities and establish a new post-Fordist "created in China" image based on digital entertainment media; the Hong Kong Council for Technology & Creation (HKCTC) supports the development of China's creative and high-tech industries, which in 2010 exported US $84 billion in cultural commodities. In 2010, Japan's Ministry of Economy, Trade and Industry (METI) established a "New Growth Strategy" and "Industrial Structure Vision 2010." Using the slogan "Cool Japan," it established the Mission of the Creative Industries Promotion Office to promote the creative industries as a strategic sector for Japan. The office seeks to support the globalization of these industries and spur a fivefold increase in cultural exports by 2020 to $140 billion—almost as much as Japan earns from car exports (*The Economist* 2011b). Since 2010, the National Creative Economy Policy Committee of the Thai Government has sought to develop the country's creativity sector, enhance the competitiveness of the creative industries at the national level, and increase the industry's potential to integrate into the global economy (UNESCO 2010).

Mitigating Market Failures. In many countries, states use media policy to make nations and national culture/creative industries. Yet, media policy is not only a tool of top-down nationalism or culture industry development on behalf of elite political-economic interests. When media markets fail to produce benefits and cause social, cultural, and political problems (i.e., inequality and exclusion, cultural loss or disruption, or un-democratic deficiencies) media policy can be used to mitigate the negative externalities (Leys 2001; Garnham 2000). Media policy can be used by the state to pre-empt or correct "market failures" or negative externalities resulting from the conduct of media corporations. Media policy can be used to create positive social, cultural, and political externalities when TNMCs and NMCs and the products they sell fail to do so

BOX 3.2
ENTERTAINMENT MEDIA PRODUCTION LOCALES AS GLOBAL TOURIST ATTRACTIONS

Tourism is a global industry and leisure activity. In 2011, 983 million people reportedly traveled to and stayed in places outside their home territory, spending their money at restaurants and hotels and on a variety of leisure, cultural, and entertainment experiences (UNWTO 2012). Tourism contributes to gross domestic product (GDP) and generates service sector jobs. It also benefits the corporations that own hotel chains and property developers, who exploit people, cultures, and environments for their own commercial gain. At present, tourist industry development is viewed by many state cultural and media policy-makers as means of kick-starting or continuing economic and social development. Tourism is a post-Fordist "modernization" strategy. To develop tourist industries, states engage in "nation branding" exercises that use a variety of media—TV ads, films, posters, websites—to manufacture a version of history, place, heritage, and national identity. State policy-makers construct and promote nation brand images to the world. In competitions for trade, foreign direct investment, and tourist dollars, nation-states "are identifying themselves as unique, competitive brands in the global economy" (de Mesa (2007). States are leveraging their culture and creative industries as part of their tourist industry development and nation branding campaigns. Culture industry development, tourism, and nation branding are intertwined. Nurse (2007) notes that in many major cities, "cultural tourism is estimated to be as high as 40 percent of annual visitor arrivals" and that "cultural tourists tend to spend more on local goods and services than the average visitor."

Entertainment media has recently been integrated into state strategies of attracting cultural tourists to stay and shop in their countries. In the post-industrial creative economy, states capitalize on the transnational thirst for the experience of different locales and cultures by turning their geography, history, and populations into market-ready tourist attractions based on global entertainment fictions. As competition for foreign tourist dollars intensifies due to the standardization of tourist development strategies everywhere, the global goodwill people feel toward hugely appealing media brands has become an integral resource for national publicity. The local places of global entertainment production—the cities, landmarks, and territories in which films and TV shows are shot— are converted into spectacular cultural heritage sites in a worldwide entertainment-based tourist industry. Nationally specific landscapes and places are made-over as entertaining images. Guides with titles like *The Worldwide Guide to Movie Locations* (Reeves 2007) and *On Location: Cities of the World in Film* (Hellman 2006) offer tourist-fans "a light-hearted, round-the-world tour of famous movies so you, too, can go 'on location'." New Zealand, offers tours of "Middle Earth" to jet-setting Tolkien fans. Select places in the United Kingdom where *Harry Potter* was shot receive visitors by the thousands. At platforms 4 and 5 at London's King's Cross Station, fans may try to board the Hogwarts Express by walking through a brick wall. This site is marked by a shopping trolley disappearing into a wall marked, as per *Potter*'s fictional world, "Platform 9 ¾." This mass attraction to the sites where *Potter* was shot represents how the places of entertainment production, and not the work of entertainment itself, has been invested with new meaning. These sites capitalize on consumer desire for communion within a fictional universe, allowing tourist-fans to imaginatively and ritualistically partake in cults of copyrighted character, while leaving no trace of the workers that engineered *Potter*'s magic tricks.

(Freedman 2008; Napoli 2006). State intervention on these grounds can be used to support the public "right to communicate," "cultural diversity," and "civic media products."

Intervention to ensure the "right to communicate." Media policy can ensure that the right of citizens to access the means of producing, distributing, and receiving entertainment media and informational products ("the right to communicate") is protected and promoted (Dakroury, Mahmoud, and Kamalipour 2009; Fisher 2002; Hamelink and Hoffmann 2008; Hicks 2007; Raboy and Shtern 2010). The right to communicate is a universal human right. All citizens, in every country, regardless of their class, race, gender, or creed, have a fundamental human right to make, share, and acquire media products. But media corporations only grant access to information and communication technology (e.g., telecommunication, mobile devices, Internet connection) and media products (flows of information and entertainment media) to those that can pay for it. Those millions of people who cannot pay are denied the right to communicate. In response, media policy can be used to ensure that all citizens have *access* to the means of producing, distributing, and receiving informational products. A media policy guided by the right to communicate would ensure that all citizens have access to the means of seeking, receiving, and imparting expressions so that they can see, hear, and read others and others can see, hear, and read them. The right to communicate is not the same as "freedom of expression." While freedom of expression is guaranteed largely to those citizens who own the means of producing, distributing, and exhibiting expression in society (i.e., the media corporations), the right to communicate grants all citizens access to such means.

Intervention to support "cultural diversity." Media policy can also be used to ensure that there is a diversity of media products available to be consumed in any place, at any given time (Napoli 2006: 11–12). According to UNESCO, the promotion and protection of diverse audio-visual and cultural products such as indigenously and nationally made TV shows and films, is integral to societal cohesion, cultural pluralism, and democracy (Doyle 2012). If TNMCs and NMCs fail to produce a diversity of indigenous media products, media policy can attempt to do so. Driven by market logics, NMCs acquire cheap but attractive TV shows and films from US-based TNMCs, schedule them during prime-time, draw a large audience and generate advertising revenue. This local-global business transaction stifles the production and distribution of indigenously made and nationally inflected entertainment goods. What's good for NMCs and TNMCs (profit-maximization) in the market is not always good for society: the representation of diverse local and national cultures. Grant and Wood (2004) argue that media policies are needed to promote and protect the production and distribution of diverse national media products to curtail US media dominance: a lack of state subvention often results in a reduction in non-US media sources and diminishes the supply of culturally and linguistically diverse media products. According to Napoli (2006), media policies in support of cultural diversity "are instituted in large part to protect or preserve domestic cultures in the face of the importation of cultural products (most often, media products) produced elsewhere, typically from the United States, which dominates the global cultural marketplace" (12–13).

Intervention to Support "Civic Media." Media policy can support the production and distribution of high-quality and civically minded media products when markets do

not. Proponents of consumer sovereignty say that the media market gives consumers what they want. Yet, the TV shows and films people want may not always contain what they need in order to participate in democracy as civically minded and astute citizens. Democracy works better when all citizens are informed, engaged, and participating. However, many TV shows and films do not inform, engage, and encourage people to participate as sovereign citizens in democracy. They distract and deter people from public and political life. Teenagers may be titillated by watching rituals of fictional bloodletting in *Scream 4* (2011), but a documentary about the actual bloodletting in the Congo or Sudan might better prepare them to act as citizens of the world. The gamer may feel some kind of cathartic release when killing thousands of digital Russian soldiers in *Modern Warfare 2*, but this interactive game will not help them develop a deeper understanding of Cold War history. The media market circulates an abundance of entertainment products that give consumers what they think they want but a media policy which supports the production of public, intellectually enriching civic media products might be better able to give people what they need to function as citizens, at home and while abroad.

In sum, the main goals of media policy are nation-making, national culture/creative industry development, and the mitigation of negative externalities resulting from market failures.

AREAS OF MEDIA INTERVENTION

States employ a range of media policy and regulatory tools to achieve political, economic, and cultural goals. The main areas of state policy/regulatory intervention in media markets are: intellectual property/copyright, ownership, concentration/competition, content subsidization and content quotas, broadcast licensing, and censorship.

Intellectual Property Rights/Copyright

States protect the property rights of media corporations. Property rights include ownership, possession, and the right to sell, destroy, and give away. Without a state, property rights would not exist. Woods (2003) argues that "The nation state has provided that stability and predictability by supplying the elaborate legal and institutional framework, backed up by coercive force, to sustain property relations of capitalism" (17). Worldwide, states are expected to protect the intellectual property rights of media corporations while disciplining and punishing those individuals and groups who violate them. As Sparks (2007) says: "The enforcement of intellectual property rights is one obvious, and extremely important, contemporary example of how the global market depends for its functioning on the preparedness of states to enforce a common set of laws and regulations" (160). Intellectual property—the legal base of creative capitalism—only exists insofar as the state recognizes and daily enforces it on behalf of media corporations.

Copyright is a significant form of intellectual property. Copyright gives media corporations (and other corporate "authors") the exclusive right to enable or prohibit others from using or copying their entertainment media. It also gives them the right to sell, license, or trade these rights to others. Copyright holders can prohibit or authorize the reproduction ("copying") of an entertainment property in various forms, including

DVDs and digital files, theatrical and musical performances, radio and TV network broadcasts, and adaptations in other forms as well. News Corp (owner of Twentieth Century Television and Gracie Films Production, Fox), for example, holds the copyright to *The Simpsons*, one of the world's most popular entertainment properties. This gives News Corp the exclusive right to allow or restrict *The Simpsons* property (and all characters, imagery, and sounds associated with *The Simpsons*) from being used. News Corp sells the broadcasting rights to *The Simpsons* TV series to TV networks worldwide, and licenses *The Simpsons* concept to comic book publishers, film studios, music labels, and video game publishers. News Corp also capitalizes on a multi-billion dollar merchandising industry of *The Simpsons* magazines, t-shirts, posters, board games, and more. Fox's executive vice president of licensing and merchandising, Peter Byrne, says that *The Simpsons* is "without doubt the biggest licensing entity that Fox has had, full stop, I would say from either TV or film" (cited in Bonné 2003). Control of copyright enables News Corp to capitalize on *The Simpsons*. "Copyrights afford corporate owners monopoly power for a span of many decades over an increasing list of cultural properties" (Schiller 2007: 47).

All media corporations rely on state-supported copyright regimes that they publicly justify with reference to economic and moral criteria. The economic justification for copyright is this: copyright gives media corporations an economic incentive to produce and distribute new entertainment commodities based on the opportunity for ownership and profit. Copyright gives media corporations a legal assurance that the money they sink into entertainment production will result in a TV show or film that they own and can exploit for commercial gain. While individual artists create new works for a variety of reasons (and not necessarily commercial ones), media corporations create to own and profit-maximize. The defender of copyright argues that the media corporations which create new TV shows and films are entitled to a financial return on their investment and should be financially compensated for what they produce. If there was no way of legally safeguarding their property and revenue, media corporations would likely not spend such vast amounts of time and money in making new movies and TV shows. Without copyright's promise of ownership and exploitation rights, media corporations would be unlikely to invest large sums of money in the production of new entertainment media. In sum, state-supported copyright regimes support markets by giving media corporations an incentive to invest time, waged labor, and money into the creation of TV shows and films.

In addition to providing media corporations with an economic incentive to create new products, defenders of copyright say that it is a means to protect the moral rights of individual authors. Moral rights refer to the right of a creative person to be publicly recognized for the work they produce, and also the right of an author to oppose changes to their creative work which might harm its aesthetic integrity or their public reputation. This copyright justification emerged in eighteenth-century England alongside the growth of the publishing industry and the new concept of the "individual author." Copyright was formed around the notion that individual authors were special kinds of people, uniquely attached to their creative work (Schiller 2007). Twenty-first century copyright lawyers employed by TNMCs often cite the moral rights of the individual author when suing others for copyright infringement. Warner Bros Entertainment Inc.

and J. K. Rowling, for example, successfully sued RDR Books for copyright infringement when this Michigan-based publishing company tried to publish and sell *The Harry Potter Lexicon*. Rowling's testimony against Vander Ark (assembler of the *The Harry Potter Lexicon*) elicited sympathy from the jury by claiming that her moral rights to her corpus had been violated (Eligon 2008; Neumister 2008). Prior to selling the *Star Wars* franchise to The Walt Disney Company, George Lucas employed the "moral rights" argument when tinkering with and changing the original *Star Wars* films against the wishes of *Star Wars* fans (Kelly 2011). "Moral rights" are also invoked by Lucas's corporate lawyers when they send "cease and desist" letters to fans who violate copyright by creating non-commercial *Star Wars* websites, publishing fan fiction and fan videos, and organizing fan movie-marathons (Wenn 2011). Publicly justified by appeals to economic incentives or the moral rights of corporate authors, copyright is the precondition for a multi-billion dollar litigation industry.

In this respect, copyright violation by pirates has become a significant business opportunity for copyright lawyers, especially for those currently employed by or contracted to US-based TNMCs. Piracy has been called "a global scourge," "an international plague," and "nirvana for criminals" (Bodo 2011). New information and communication technology (ICTs) and digital media platforms have fueled entertainment piracy in the US and around the world, especially in developing countries (Bodo 2011). Making copies of TV shows and films and then distributing them is relatively easy and inexpensive to do. Pirates record debut films in theaters using hand-held camcorders, exchange TV shows and films using Bit Torrent software and peer-to-peer file-sharing sites like ISO Hunt and The Pirate Bay, and stream copyrighted content through on-line video platforms. While a global commons of digital sharing has emerged, unrestricted copying has undermined the ability of US-TNMCs to extract maximum revenue from their TV shows and films. In response, US-based TNMCs are lobbying the US and all other states to clamp down on global digital piracy. The MPAA is currently on a global mission to: 1) attack peer-to-peer (P2P) piracy through cyber lockers, video streaming, and user-generated content sites by encouraging states to establish and enforce legal protections for digital copyright; 2) stop piracy of motion pictures in theaters by pressuring states to adopt anti-camcording legislation and define the camcording of motion pictures in theaters a criminal offense; and, 3) criminalize piracy by ensuring all new audio-visual trade agreements contain high standards of intellectual property protection appropriate to the digital environment and make states comply with the terms of existing trade agreements and the World Intellectual Property Organization (WIPO) Internet agreements (MPAA 2010).

The high cost of privatized entertainment experiences and the low wages of the world majority, combined with the diffusion of digital technology, may contribute to media piracy (Bodo 2011). Global piracy may be an effect of global poverty. For millions of people, especially in poor countries, US TV shows and films are luxury goods that are far less important to daily life than access to clean drinking water, a nutritious meal, and shelter. Nonetheless, poor people all over the world are exposed, on a daily basis, to advertisements that tell them that they "must see" TV shows and films made in the US. Although they do not possess the means to pay for such goods,

they have been persuaded that they want the experience. If media distributors and exhibitors lowered the cost of access, it is possible that the number of copyright violations around the world would begin to diminish. If people earned higher wages, perhaps they would pay for entertainment media instead of "stealing" it. Or maybe not. Many people—poor and rich alike—reject, or at least find ways of subverting, copyright. Digital piracy is prevalent in Canada, the United Kingdom, and Korea—wealthy countries.

Copyright faces many criticisms. Copyright presumes that a creative expression is entirely original. Yet, there may be no such thing as an original expression because all entertainment is produced and consumed in shared social contexts. Most entertainment texts are inter-texts of other works and, to a greater or lesser extent, "derivative" of themes, ideas, and symbols from society. Furthermore, copyright privileges the individual author as the source of original meaning, but entertainment products are not produced solely by one individual. Copyright was originally developed alongside the culture industry to encourage and protect the rights of an individual author to own, control, and profit from the use of their work (Schiller 2007), but all TV shows and films are collaboratively produced by numerous waged cultural workers. Furthermore, in the court of law, the individual "author" protected by copyright is most often the TNMC. Also, while copyright is intended to protect and promote creativity, it can undermine and close down creativity by depriving cultural workers of the materials they need to innovate new works (Lessig 2004). Copyright may create a chilling effect that deters creative people from creating new works by instilling in them a fear of being sued for the use of a copyrighted idea or expression. Finally, US-based TNMCs have drastically expanded their juridical power over creativity. When the US was founded, copyright lasted for fourteen years; it could then be renewed, but for only fourteen more years. But from 1974 to the present day, TNMCs have expanded the duration of copyright (from thirty-two to ninety-five years), the scope of copyright (from publishers to everyone), the reach of copyright (from print to digital content), and the limits of control (from original to derivative works) (Lessig 2004). Worldwide, NMCs and TNMCs now expect states to establish and enforce copyright so that fines can be collected, revenue can be accumulated, and compliance with profit-maximization can be enforced.

BOX 3.3

WALT DISNEY AND COPYRIGHT CASES

Walt Disney regularly sues others for violating its copyright. In 2002, Walt Disney sued Swedish-based Harlequin Trade when it tried to sell 25,000 "knock off" "Winnie the Pooh" stuffed bears. Walt Disney won the case and the bears were destroyed (Associated Press 2002). In 2007, Walt Disney teamed up with Twentieth Century Fox, Paramount Pictures, Columbia Pictures, and Universal Studios to sue Beijing based Jeboo.com, which claimed to be China's largest film and TV downloading site (Francia 2007). In 2011, Walt Disney and Starz Entertainment sued Satellite TV provider Dish Network for providing its 14 million subscribers with unlicensed access to Walt Disney films and TV shows (Adegoke 2011). In 2011, Disney Enterprises and Hanna-Barbera Productions sued Costume World for selling "Buzz Lightyear" and "Sully the Monster" Halloween

costumes without permission (Pacenti 2011). Disney sues, but it is also sued. A New York named Queen Mother Dr. Delois Blackely claims that Disney stole her 1987 auto-biography *The Harlem Street Nun* in order to make *Sister Act* (1992) (Shoard 2011). April Magolon, a woman from Pennsylvania, is seeking more than $200,000 in damages from Walt Disney for negligence, battery, negligent infliction of emotional distress, and inten-tional and reckless infliction of emotional distress. Magolon accused a Walt Disney employee dressed as Donald Duck of groping her breast at the Epcot Center in 2008. The lawsuit says when Magolon requested an autograph, "Donald Duck proceeded to grab her breast and molest her and then made gestures making a joke indicating he had done something wrong" (cited in Pacheco 2010). In 2011, a British screenwriter named Jake Mandeville-Anthony sued Walt Disney and Pixar. Mandeville-Anthony claims that Walt Disney's animated films *Cars* (2006) and *Cars 2* (2011) are derived from a script he wrote in the early 1990s called *Cookie & Co.* and *Cars*, which included a sample screenplay, forty-six animated car character descriptions, ten cars character sketches, and a marketing-merchandising strategy (China Daily 2011). Walt Disney's copycatting of works without permission and without compensating the original creator is not unprecedented. Walt Disney's first commercial animated hit *Steamboat Willie* (1928) was derived from Buster Keaton's silent film, *Steamboat Bill*. Derivative works of this kind were very common in 1928, and no cause for litigation. The rigid copyright laws Walt Disney now pushes on the world would have likely stifled its initial growth as a media corporation and undercut its ability to compete.

Ownership

Public, Private, and Mixed. States use policy to shape the form that media ownership takes in society. Media systems are owned. The form ownership takes is not pre-determined, but is the outcome of state policy. The moment of every national media system's emergence involved a political choice: would the media be publicly or privately owned (or entail a combination of both)? Following World War II, three different ownership models co-existed: the private ownership model, the public ownership model, and the mixed public-private model (or "single system" model). Some states developed publicly owned media systems; some choose completely privately owned media systems; others favored a mix of public and private media ownership forms.

The public ownership model refers to a society in which all media corporations are entirely publicly owned. State broadcasters are financially supported by the citizens (through taxation or licensing). In this model, the purpose of broadcasting is to serve the public interest by informing, educating, and enlightening citizens. Broadcasting exists to serve the "public good," not by giving citizens the media content they may want, but by providing the kind they are assumed to need in order to become engaged and intellectually competent members of society. Quality information is privileged over lowest common-denominator content. Free from corporate control, competition for ad revenue, and ideally at "arm's length" from direct political influence, publicly owned broadcasting corporations are mandated to produce informational and entertainment content that is intended to be inclusive by representing the interests and concerns of all citizens within a territory, regardless of their social class position, race, or creed. Publicly owned broadcasters ideally represent a forum that enables viewers to learn about and reflect upon significant national matters so that they may participate as informed citi-zens in a democracy. Following World War II, the public ownership model was the global norm. Public broadcasters existed in all Western European nation-states and in several other countries, including Canada, Australia, New Zealand, Japan, and India.

However, since the 1980s, the public ownership model has been criticized. Neoliberals heap scorn on public broadcasters, regarding them as state instruments for the propagation of elitist, paternalistic, and exclusionary nationalist media products. The public ownership model is far less popular than it was sixty years ago, and many public broadcasters are privatizing and commercializing their operations in order to compete with private firms. Banerjee and Seneviratne (2006) report that:

> public service broadcasting around the world has witnessed intense competition and pressures from commercial broadcasters as well as a whole range of new media channels [. . .] public service broadcasting has been under siege from a new breed of commercially oriented and profit-seeking broadcasters. (2)

That being said, as recently as 2003, "in 97 countries, the state controlled on average nearly one-third of newspapers, 60 percent of TV stations and 72 percent of top radio stations" (*The Economist* 2003). Public broadcasters still play a role in the global cultural economy. Many public broadcasters produce diverse, edgy, or enlightening media products not supported by ad-dependent NMCs, and preserve a space for imagining the nation in periods of change. However, as Feigenbaum (2009) notes:

> whatever the orientation of such programming, elite, local, or international, no programming protects the national culture and national identity if no one watches it. Thus public broadcasters may need to strike a balance between high art and culture with mass appeal. (236)

While the future of public broadcasting is uncertain, the global dominance of private ownership is not. The private model treats media broadcasters as part of a for-profit industry and the means of producing and distributing entertainment products as a necessarily capitalist venture. The private ownership model places a premium on profit-maximization, and not on public dialogue, democracy promotion, citizen cultivation, or nation-building. The private ownership model does not produce entertainment media to enlighten the intellectually lacking masses or to integrate people into a mythical nation (though some entertainment may in fact achieve this). If an identifiable audience wants a certain type of entertainment product, media corporations will provide it. In practice, the entertainment products created under the private model most often privilege the tastes and preferences of the affluent groups targeted by advertising firms. In the aftermath of World War II, there were only eleven states that subscribed to the private ownership model. In the twenty-first century, the private model is the dominant model worldwide (Tracey 1998). Many states support media capitalism and accept the neoliberal mantra that there is no alternative to capitalism (even though the system is in crisis).

Nonetheless, no state in the twenty-first century has a wholly publicly owned or entirely privately controlled media system. Completely socialist countries have completely state-run media corporations (none exist in the world today). Completely capitalist countries have comprehensively capitalist-run media corporations (none exist in the world today). Most countries in the world system exhibit a *combination* of public and private media firms. For example, in the US and Canada we find both privately owned media corporations (Walt Disney Corporation and Rogers Communications) and publicly owned media (the PBS and the CBC). In communist-capitalist China, there are privately owned media corporations such as Viacom, CNN, and Star TV, and state-owned companies including China Central Television. In the United Kingdom, there is the publicly owned BBC and the privately owned ITV. In Spain there is public broadcaster Radio-Television Española (RTE) and private broadcasters including Telecinco and Antena 3. Italy's state-owned broadcaster RAI competes with the Berlusconi family media giant, Mediaset. South Africa's state-owned South African Broadcasting Corporation (SABC) operates alongside Multichoice, the country's oldest pay TV and satellite TV firm. Public broadcasters will likely co-exist with private firms for some time.

Ownership: Competition vs. Concentration. States use media policy to encourage or discourage competitive or concentrated media markets. In many countries, state policy-makers have enabled market concentration. State elites have actively dismantled the ownership regulations that were intended to protect market competition and have supported the vertical and horizontal integration of media firms. The push toward media concentration started in the US following Congress's passing of the 1996 Telecommunications Act. Prior to 1996, the Federal Communications Commission (FCC) prevented media conglomerates from "owning multiple TV stations in the same community, TV stations in every community in the nation, or TV stations and radio stations and newspapers and cable TV systems in the same community." Lobbyist pressure and influence led to the overturning of this longstanding FCC regulation, giving a few US-based TNMCs the right control all and any media sector they chose and greatly diminishing the diversity of media sources (Herman and McChesney 1997; Schiller 2000). The US model of media concentration was reproduced in many other countries, where media lobbyists pressured their respective states to also dismantle restrictions on concentration. In 1996, Canada's CRTC overturned regulations which prevented the owners of broadcasting, newspaper, and telecom corporations from merging; as a result, large Canadian media conglomerates grew larger through a plethora of mergers and acquisitions. In the UK, the 2003 Communications Act reduced media ownership regulations. In China and India, News Corp expanded its Star Satellite network into these countries' respective media markets after lobbying state policy-makers for favorable deregulation (Thussu 2007). By significantly reducing or eliminating the regulations set up to prevent media concentration, many policy-makers enabled NMCs and TNMCs to grow more powerful.

States, however, still possess the power to curb ownership concentration and monopolistic media markets. Critics worry that media ownership concentration reduces source diversity and the diversity of cultural expression. Baker (2002) says that "monopoly is intrinsically objectionable" because it threatens media pluralism and democracy (176). Freedman (2008) says that monopoly power "is always problematic because it is apt to reduce diversity, squeeze out the regional and local, and stifle dissent" (105). To pre-empt one media conglomerate or a small group of them from monopolizing the total media environment and preserve the diversity of media sources, states can use anti-trust legislation and regulation to place limits upon how many media sources one firm can own (Baker 2002).

Galvanized by media democracy activism, states can and do stifle the monopoly goals of media owners. For at least ten years, McChesney (2004) and likeminded Free Press media democracy activists have fought for "a well-funded, structurally pluralistic, and diverse non-profit and non-commercial media sector, as well as a more competitive and decentralized commercial sector" (11). Anti-media concentration struggles are global, too. In May 2011, Telmex—the Mexico-based telecommunication giant owned by the world's richest person, Carlos Slim—attempted to gain greater power over Mexico's media system by bundling Internet, telephone, and pay-TV services; Mexico's state communication and transport ministry rejected Telmex's convergence strategy (Reuters 2011). In 2008, Canada's CRTC announced new ownership regulations in response to sustained media democracy activism. In order to ensure a diversity of voices in Canada's media system, the rules stipulate that: 1) no company will be allowed to control more than two types of media in one local market (a company may own TV and newspaper in one city, or radio and TV, or newspaper and radio, but may not own all three simultaneously); 2) no company will be allowed to control more than 45 percent of the total TV audience; and, 3) deals between TV distributors, such as cable and satellite TV companies, will not be allowed if they result in one company or person controlling the delivery of the programming (CRTC 2008). In January 2011, Paulo Bernardo, Brazil's communications minister, proposed a ban on cross-media ownership in order to forbid one media company from owning a radio station, newspaper, and TV station in the same region (Magro 2011). In 2009, Argentina set limits upon what the Clarin Media conglomerate could own and compelled other media giants to shed some of their holdings as a way to diversify the public airwaves (Barrionuevo 2010). In 2011, the activist group Avaaz told Australia's media regulator that media ownership should be capped:

> We believe by instituting a strict 20 per cent limit on the amount of media any one person or company can own, we can ensure that no single person or company is able to stifle freedom of expression through commercial media. (AAP 2011)

States, therefore, do sometimes respond to public protests against media concentration.

Ownership: Domestic versus Foreign. States may use policy to enable or restrict a foreign media corporation from owning domestic telecommunications and broadcasting systems. Many states limit foreign ownership of their domestic media systems. In Russia, the state prohibits TNMCs from establishing TV channels capable of being received in and broadcast over a territory comprising more than 50 percent of the Russian population (MPAA 2010). The Malaysian state prohibits direct foreign investment in terrestrial broadcast networks and also imposes a 20 percent limit on foreign investment in cable and satellite operations. In the Philippines, TNMCs are barred from owning the broadcasting system (terrestrial and satellite). Thailand also bans foreign ownership of, or investment in, its broadcasting system. In the Ukraine, TNMCs are not allowed to own or establish TV stations. In South Africa, the Minister of

Communications allows TNMCs to own no more than 20 percent of the broadcasting system. In Canada, the state's Broadcasting Act demands that "the Canadian broadcasting system shall be effectively owned and controlled by Canadians." All media companies broadcasting entertainment in Canada must be effectively owned by the Canadian corporate class. In the US, the broadcasting industry is protected from foreign ownership.

Content Subsidies and Content Quotas

States use policy to directly and indirectly give financial assistance (or subsidies) to media firms. A direct subsidy is when the state transfers public wealth to a media corporation in the form of a grant (state allocation of a sum of money to a media firm) or tax credit (state refund on a portion of a media firm's production costs). An indirect subsidy is when the state encourages the production of certain kinds of entertainment commodities by establishing an environment that supports business (Cowen 2006). For more than twenty years, The European Union's MEDIA programme has subsidized European media companies to help them produce TV shows and films, increase their international market reach, and make Europe's regional media industry more competitive. Between 2001 and 2006, MEDIA allocated more than half a billion Euros to 8,000 media projects in over thirty states. The 2007–2013 MEDIA fund allocated €755 million to media production. The British Film Institute (BFI) provides lottery grants to domestic film companies to encourage British film production, while state tax relief programs offset production costs for those firms that commit to making "British" films (Doyle 2012: 11). In 2008, the Mexican government funded the Chapala Media Park, a multi-media production complex in Jalisco, in the hope of attracting globalizing production companies (Palfrey 2010). In 2009, the Canadian state established a $35 million Canadian Media Fund (CMF) to financially assist Canadian NMCs to produce "Canadian" TV shows and new media (Canadian Press 2009). In 2010, Singapore's Ministry of Information, Communication and the Arts awarded $2.7 million in grants to nurture creative talent as part of a creative industry development strategy (Government of Singapore 2010). In 2011, South Africa lured a British film production company to Cape Town to shoot *Dredd*—a 3-D science fiction action film—with a 25 percent South African tax rebate/subsidy (Perry 2011). The UK gives a 25 percent tax credit to any film production company that shoots there. This subsidy has caused India's finance minister to complain that Bollywood media moguls are running away to Britain (PTI 2010). The US Federal government and state-level governments use subsidies (in the form of tax credits) to support TV and film production. In 2010, US states collectively spent a whopping total of $1.4 billion on tax credits/subsidies to media corporations (*The Economist* 2011). Miller (2010) says that if a TV show or film is shot in the US, "the credits generally thank regional and municipal film commissions for subsidizing everything from hotels to hamburgers" (151).

In addition to subsidizing media firms, states employ content quotas to ensure that media firms make and screen national TV shows and films. TV content quotas are the state regulations which compel TV networks (including cable and satellite specialty channels) to schedule and broadcast a certain daily percentage of national TV content. The film or screen quota is "a governmental regulation that makes it compulsory for movie theaters to screen the feature films of national origin for a specified period of time" (Byoungkwan and Hyuhn-Suhck 2004: 164). TV content quotas try to ensure that national TV shows will be broadcast by networks for a certain period of time. Screen quotas ensure that national films will be shown in theaters for a certain number of days per year. Content quotas support the screening of national entertainment by TV networks and theater chains, while limiting the amount of non-national TV shows and films they can expose viewers to.

Around the world, states use content quotas to compel media firms to screen nations. The EU Directive on Broadcasting adopted on October 3, 1989 (previously referred to as the "Television Without Frontiers Directive," and now called the "Audiovisual Media Services Directive") established European content quotas for TV broadcasting. All European TV networks and video on-demand services must reserve at least 51 percent of broadcast prime time for European-made TV shows (Goldsmith et al. 2001). French quotas far exceed the requirements established by "Television Without Frontiers": in France, 40 percent of the total number of feature films screened and the total transmission time allocated to TV broadcasting must be made by France-based NMCs. The remaining 60 percent of films and TV shows must be of EU origin. In July 2009, Italy implemented the Broadcasting Law Act 44, which reserves 50 percent of monthly TV broadcasting time for EU TV shows. A further 10 percent of the prime time monthly transmission quota is reserved for EU entertainment products made within a five year period. Italy also requires all theaters of more than 100 seats to reserve 15–20 percent of their seats, in at least three cinemas, for the showing of Italian and EU-made films. In Poland, TV broadcasters must commit a minimum of 33 percent of their quarterly broadcasting time to TV shows and films originally produced in the Polish language. In Spain, TV broadcasters must invest a minimum of 5 percent of their annual revenues pre-buying European films, TV movies, documentaries, or pilot animation series (Hopewell 2007). All Spanish theaters must show one EU film in its original language or dubbed into one of Spain's languages for every three days that a non-EU country film (e.g., Hollywood film) is screened. In Australia, all TV networks must broadcast a minimum daily quota of 55 percent Australian TV content between 6am and midnight. In Canada, the Canadian Radio and Telecommunication Commission (CRTC) compels TV networks to fill 50–60 percent of their daily schedule with Canadian TV programs. In South Africa, all public TV broadcasters must commit 55 percent of their schedule time to South African content. In Vietnam, at least 50 percent of broadcast time must be Vietnamese content, and foreign TV shows cannot be aired during prime time. In Malaysia, TV broadcasters must commit 70–80 percent of the daily schedule to Malay content. In China, all TV broadcasters must commit 75–85 percent of the schedule to Chinese entertainment, and foreign TV shows are banned during prime time, (Jaffe 2011). No more than twenty foreign (mostly Hollywood) films can be imported into China each year. Until recently, Korean TV broadcasters committed 85 percent of broadcast time to Korean TV shows, while Korean movie theaters screened Korean films for a minimum of fourteen consecutive days at least seventy-three days a year.

In numerous countries—both Western and Eastern—states employ content quotas to ensure that the TNMCs and NMCs operating within their territories will produce and circulate nationalistic entertainment media. Content quotas are used by states to achieve both cultural and economic goals. Culturally, quotas ensure that a portion of broadcasting time and screen space is committed to the presentation of nationalistic content so as to secure banal nationalism from a foreign threat: "Quotas are designed to protect cultural diversity and social cohesion in the face of increased cultural imports (mostly from the USA) and potential loss of national identity" (Freedman 2008: 36). Economically, quotas support state-led industrial strategies for developing and protecting national media firms. Broadcasting and screen quotas establish a demand for national TV shows and films, giving national production companies a financial incentive to create them. Proponents of quotas say that if states did not impose quotas upon TV broadcasters and theaters, there would be a diminishment of non-US entertainment produced and distributed and, as a result, a significant reduction in the representation of national cultures on the world's screens. As an Australian quota advocate observes: "The simple truth is, were there no [quota] regulation, there would be very few Australian programs on free-to-air commercial networks" (Brown 2011). Morley (2006) says: "If policies of cultural protectionism and cultural subsidy are always problematic, nonetheless, there are circumstances in which they may be both necessary and wise" (38). Certainly, countries that do not have screen quotas annually exhibit very few national films. English Canada, for example, does not have a screen quota. Canadian films pull in an average of 1 percent of Canada's own box-office receipts (Takeuchi 2008). The Canadian box office is typically between 90 and 94 percent made in Hollywood (Takeuchi 2008). In 2010, US films made up 92.7 percent of Canada's box office revenue; 4.2 percent of the revenue went to other foreign films; 3.1 percent went to Canadian films. In 1994, Mexico signed the North American Free Trade Agreement (NAFTA); it subsequently reduced its screen quota from 30 percent to 10 percent. The Mexican screen industry, which produced 100 films per year in the 1980s, now produces only about thirty films or fewer per year. In 2001, Taiwan reduced its film-import restrictions when it joined the World Trade Organization; foreign films now make up 97 percent of Taiwan's domestic box office.

The US is one of the only countries in the world that does not have an official cultural-nationalist quota policy. The FCC does not regulate TV broadcasters to ensure that a proportion of the TV shows they broadcast represent the "American Way of Life." AMC Entertainment Inc., Regal Entertainment Group, and other giant theater chains are not compelled by force of law to screen American films. Official screen quotas are not needed in the US: the sheer size of the US entertainment market and the ingrained nationalism of US viewers ensure that many TV shows and films which represent "America" will be produced and screened.

Licensing

State media regulators also intervene in the media market by granting or denying TV broadcasters the right to use a frequency or portion of the electro-magnetic spectrum for a set period of time. The frequencies allocated to TV networks are, in the first instance, public goods. The airwaves, like the air we breathe, are common to us all, i.e., public goods. The process of licensing frequencies slices up society's electro-magnetic spectrum and gives pieces of it to individual TV networks. The state gives TV networks the right to use a part of the spectrum for a set period of time. The state does not charge TV networks for this right (though if there is competition for the same frequency, the state may hold a bidding war). To acquire the right to use a particular frequency, TV networks must submit a broadcast license application to a state regulatory agency. The regulator can then scrutinize the application to ensure that the TV network will abide by its existing media policy. It may then grant or refuse that TV network a license. For example, to qualify for a broadcast license in the US, the applicant must: 1) be a US citizen; 2) exhibit a good character (media owners should not have a criminal record); 3) demonstrate business savvy and access to capital; 4) possess the technology required to utilize the frequency; and 5) meet Federal Communication Commission TV program guidelines (Helewitz and Edwards 2004). Applications that meet these five conditions are most often approved by the FCC. However, before a broadcast license is actually granted to a TV network, the application is opened for a public hearing so that the voices of the citizens who may oppose the license can be heard. If the TV network at any time fails to heed the media policy, the state can impose fines, revoke the license, or refuse to renew the license at a later date.

Censorship

States may use media policy to censor TV shows and films, both those that are domestically produced and those imported from elsewhere. Censorship of the kinds of entertainment allowed to flourish in society at any given time is often associated with past and present-day authoritarian states (e.g., the Soviet Union, Nazi Germany, China, Iran, and North Korea), yet liberal democratic states censor entertainment too. Every state has a specific censorship regime comprised by both state (government agencies) and non-state actors (corporations). State agencies review, rate, edit, modify, and sometimes ban films and TV shows. They may edit entertainment to make it more agreeable or acceptable. To deter the circulation of disagreeable or unacceptable content, states may threaten media corporations with fines or the termination of their broadcasting licenses. Sometimes, states explicitly prohibit certain kinds of TV shows and films from being screened. State censorship regimes limit the consumption of entertainment that is deemed objectionable, harmful, offensive, or threatening to community standards ("national culture"). The meaning of objectionable, harmful, offensive, or threatening is defined in relation to the dominant political, religious, and moral notions of acceptable, agreeable, safe, or secure "national" standards.

Political censorship. States often censor entertainment because it is perceived to challenge the cultural authority of the state. By preventing the circulation of entertainment which might undermine dominant views of the nation and foment cultural rebellion or revolution, states use censorship as an instrument of social control. Since 2008, the Chinese State Administration of Film, Radio, and Television (SARFT) has forbidden all TV networks from broadcasting any foreign cartoons from 5pm to 9pm, and has compelled them to schedule Chinese cartoons produced by China's own animation factories. In 2010, SARFT forbade TV networks from airing TV shows which represent "time travel" in TV dramas because they encourage a "frivolous" view of history. SARFT also banned reality-TV dating shows which featured "fake participants, morally-provocative hosts and hostesses and sexual innuendo." Between May and July of 2011, SARFT banned all TV networks from broadcasting police and spy dramas, and encouraged them to schedule more wholesome TV shows instead (Hough 2011; No Author 2011a). The state justified these acts of censorship as a means of protecting traditional Chinese culture. In 2008, Burma (also known as Myanmar) censored *Rambo IV* (2008) because the film portrays Burmese soldiers ruthlessly attacking, raping, and killing members of the country's ethno-cultural and religious minority group, the Karen people. John Rambo, the US-Vietnam War veteran, is depicted as heroically intervening in Burma to help the Karen people and using black-ops tactics to kill evil Burmese soldiers (Bell 2008). The film was censored because of its negative—though, for the Karen people, accurate—representation of the Burmese state committing cultural genocide.

Political censorship can be performed for expedient and time-sensitive reasons too. So as to not upset China, India's state film censor ordered a Bollywood studio to cut a scene in *Rockstar* (2011) which showed a Free Tibet flag (Sapa 2011). The large Tibetan exile community in India protested, but were not listened to. The Indian state elite censored the Free Tibet flag so as to not upset a positive relationship with China. In 2011, Germany forbade the *Valley of Wolves: Palestine* (2011) from being screened. This Turkey-produced action film, about a Turkish commando team which tracks down the Israeli military commander responsible for the 2010 Gaza flotilla raid, was censored for its anti-American and anti-Israel content (JAP 2011). In July 2011, the British state censored an episode of *The Daily Show* because it presented Parliamentary footage in a comedic and satirical context: John Stewart had satirized parts of Rupert Murdoch's Parliamentary hearing over the *News of the World* phone hacking scandal (Stableford 2011). In 2008, the Discovery Channel did not air "On Thin Ice," the seventh episode of David Attenborough's "Frozen Planet" BBC TV series, in the US. The Discovery channel insists that this episode was dropped due to a "scheduling issue," but others claim that the Discovery Channel refused to air the TV show, fearing that its account of human-made climate change would offend those US consumers who deny global warming and the threat it poses. Sometimes, indirect corporate self-censorship can be just as threatening to the free flow of ideas as direct state censorship (Shackle 2008).

Religious censorship. States censor entertainment for religious reasons too. In authoritarian and theocratic states, TV shows and films that reject, defy, or challenge the dominant religion are censored. In 2008, Afghanistan's Ministry of Information and Culture censored prime-TV Indian soap operas about the lifestyles of the Hindu rich and powerful. According to Afghanistan's theocratic elite, these Bollywood-exported reality-TV shows promoted immorality (morality being defined by a strict interpretation of the Koran) (BBC 2008). In an episode of the American TV sitcom *Friends*, the word beef was removed from character dialogue because it was used in the context of cooking (the cow is India's sacred animal and not to be eaten) (Khurshid 2011). Bangladesh bans TV channels from broadcasting any "promotional" or "advertising" content relating to non-Muslim festivals such as Christmas, Purnima (Buddhist), and Puja (Hindu) rituals (Greenslade 2011). In Saudi Arabia, the Committee for the Promotion of Virtue and the Prevention of Vice's Anti-Witchcraft Unit censored

Harry Potter because the franchise's depiction of a young sorcerer affronted the dominant Wahhabi ideology (Miller 2011).

Moral Censorship. States also censor entertainment whose content they deem "obscene" or "indecent." For censors, obscene and indecent content refers to kinds of expression that strongly offends the prevailing morality or good taste of a community at a given time. Despite the popular image of the US as a marketplace of ideas, the US boasts a puritanical TV censorship regime. As Miller (2010) notes:

> In the US, the First Amendment to the Constitution supposedly guarantees freedom of speech against government censorship. But the hyper-religious sexual obsessions of the US population [. . .] give the FCC an incentive to stop people watching and listening to what they want. (130)

Since the Communications Act of 1934, the US state has prohibited "indecency" and "profanity" on the airwaves. The FCC defines "indecency" as "language or material that, in context, depicts or describes, in terms patently offensive as measured by contemporary community standards for the broadcast medium, sexual or excretory organs or activities" (FCC 2011). "Profanity" refers to "language so grossly offensive to members of the public who actually hear it as to amount to a nuisance" (FCC 2011). US TV networks often censor themselves so as not to offend the presumably good taste of their viewers and advertising clients. In 1952, the word "pregnancy" was not allowed to be spoken by characters in *I Love Lucy* (despite the fact that the show's star Lucille Ball was pregnant!). Between 1964 and 1966, Mary Ann from *Gilligan's Island* and Jeannie from *I Dream of Jeannie* were not allowed to show their belly buttons. In 2004, Janet Jackson's one-second nipple exposure during Super Bowl XXXVIII's half-time show resulted in a public uproar.

Other states censor content they deem indecent and profane too. In Canada, the CRTC and the Canadian Broadcast Standards Council (CBSC) collaboratively monitor the airwaves for provocative TV content, but TV shows featuring sex, nudity, coarse language, and violence are infrequently censored. Instead, Canadian TV networks issue "viewer discretion advisories" before a potentially offensive TV show begins. In 2006, Canada did forbid the broadcast of *Bumfights*: in this reality TV show, a fight promoter gives alcohol, drugs, and money to homeless people on the condition that they pummel each other for the camera. In 2008, Thailand's National Film Board banned *Zack and Miri Make a Porno* (2008), fearing that Thai teens would try to do the same. "The screening of this [American] film may encourage copycats here," said Thai Culture Ministry secretary Vira Rojpojchanarat (*The Nation* 2008). In 2009, Venezuela banned an episode of *Family Guy* in which Brian, the talking family dog, leads a protest movement to legalize marijuana. The show flouted regulations that prohibit the transmission of "messages that go against the whole education of boys, girls and adolescents" (BBC 2009; Pierce 2009). In 2010, South Korea forbade the screening of *Kick-Ass* (2010), the hyper-violent filmic adaptation of Matthew Vaughn's comic book, because of the eleven-year-old protagonist Hit-Girl's frequent use of the word "cunt" (Green 2010). Indecency and profanity are often politically contingent and culturally relative constructs, but states all over the world daily use these constructs to decide what people should and should not be watching.

After decades of sexual repression due to rampant hetero-normative homophobia, "lesbian, gay, bisexual, and transgender" (LGBT) people are increasingly visible in society and in entertainment. State and industry censors in many countries nonetheless try to screen LGBT people out of society by censoring the TV shows, films, music videos, and even advertisements that represent them.

Italy's state-owned television station, Rai2, censored out the gay love scene in *Brokeback Mountain* (2008) (Gilbey 2008). The Greek National Council for Radio and Television (GNCRT) encouraged MAD TV Greece and MTV Greece to blur out and censor music videos such as Katy Perry's "Firework" and Pink's "Raise Your Glass" because they feature gay men kissing in public. In Singapore, gay and lesbian sexual relationships are deemed by law to be "an act of gross indecency" and are punishable by a maximum of two years in jail (News Editor 2008); in 2008, Singapore's Media Development Authority (MDA) fined StarHub Cable Vision US $7,200 for showing a commercial for a pop song by Olivia Yan called "Silly Child," which depicted kissing women. The MDA said: "Within the commercial, romanticised scenes of two girls kissing were shown and it portrayed the relationship as acceptable. This is in breach of the TV advertising guidelines, which disallow advertisements that condone homosexuality." In 2011, Malaysia's AMP Radio Networks abided by Malay state restrictions against the circulation of music that violates "good taste or decency or [is] offensive to public feeling" by censoring Lady Gaga's electro-pop club hit, "Born This Way." AMP said that:

> the particular lyrics in Born This Way may be considered as offensive when viewed against Malaysia's social and religious observances [. . .] The issue of being gay, lesbian or [bisexual] is still considered as a taboo by general Malaysians. (Powers 2011)

In the US, the MPAA film rating system often determines the age suitability of films based on tacitly homophobic criteria. Films that depict sexual activity between members of the LGBT community are given a strict, usually "NC–17," rating. Films with heterosexual sex scenes are rated "R." The "NC–17" rating usually means that a LGBT film will not be mass-distributed or mass-marketed, and will not be exhibited by most movie theaters. Headed by the Republican Joan Graves, the MPAA rating board perhaps panders to the homophobic Evangelical Christians and social conservatives who currently dominate right-wing politics (Kirby 2011).

The LGBT community continues to struggle for recognition and representation by states and corporate actors in the US and worldwide. As the above examples show, state and corporate censorship regimes continue to criminalize, stigmatize, and repress the bodies, behaviors, and images of those who do not abide by compulsory hetero-normativity on and off screen.

In sum, states control a number of policy and regulatory tools for intervening in and influencing media markets. States maintain and enforce intellectual property rights, decide upon the form and extent of media ownership, subsidize firms, compel firms to schedule and screen a certain percentage of national content, grant or refuse broadcast licenses, and censor entertainment.

NEOLIBERAL MEDIA POLICY

NMCs and TNMCs exist in a world of states that use media policy to govern media corporations. NMCs and TNMCs want strong states to facilitate and legitimize their profit-interests in national and transnational contexts. They support policies that buttress their profit interests while challenging those that do not. Currently, NMCs and TNMCs want states whose ultimate policy and regulatory goal is to establish the optimal conditions for profit-making, worldwide. They seek to establish a transnational or global media policy order that is conducive to their global business operations. NMCs and TNMCs promote a media policy framework that frees them from "public interest" and "cultural-nationalist" obligations while maintaining state support and subsidization of their business operations. The new global policy regime sought by media firms is called *neoliberalism*.

Neoliberalism refers to "the set of national and international policies that call for business domination of all social affairs with minimal countervailing force" (McChesney 2002: 49). Neoliberalism is a code word for philosophical free-market fundamentalism (Bourdieu 1998; Couldry 2006; Harvey 2007; Schiller 2000; Hall 2011; Herman and McChesney 1997; McGuigan 2005). Neoliberal ideology posits that human wellbeing is best advanced by the maximization of corporate freedoms aided by governmental policies that support property rights, free markets, free trade, and the unrestricted cross-border flow of industrial and finance capitalism. Neoliberal ideology says that the state ought to be nothing more than a "night watchman" that concerns itself with building and administering policies that support market relations in all areas of life. This neoliberal night-watchman state must also set up a military, a police force, and a system of law that "secures" market relations. But beyond corporate security functions, the state should not do anything else (e.g., provision public goods including education, health care, culture, and so on). As a policy, neoliberalism advocates drastic reductions in state expenditure (on public goods), minimal taxation (on corporations and the rich), and the elimination of regulations on corporations (which might protect public interests). The global diffusion of neoliberal ideology has been an uneven process, with varied political effects (Harvey 2005a).

Neoliberalism has influenced the way citizens and consumers think and talk about the media policy frameworks of many nation-states (Flew 2002; Hamelink 2002; Hesmondhalgh 2005; McChesney 2006; McGuigan 2005; Mosco 2004). Chakravartty and Sarikakis (2006) claim that neoliberal ideology "has succeeded in defining the ways in which we debate the role of the state in communications policy" (18). Neoliberal ideology defines the relationship between states and media corporations as inherently antagonistic: states that attempt to intervene in or shape the conduct of media corporations are anti-freedom, while states that allow media corporations to conduct business in whatever way they like and which take a "hands off" approach to corporate conduct support "freedom." Lack of state intervention is what supposedly makes media corporations (and society) "free." Pickard (2010) argues that a neoliberal ideology elevates a "freedom from" (the freedom of media corporations from state regulation) over a "freedom to" (the public's freedom to a diverse, accessible, and informative media system) (171).

Neoliberal ideology represents NMCs and TNMCs, not governments, as best able to support freedom of expression, creativity, and innovation. The profit-motive drives competition between media corporations, encourages innovation, and leads to new, edgy, and innovative entertainment products. States are barriers to creativity and innovation. Neoliberal ideology portrays media corporations as a democratizing force that destabilizes state cultural elites by giving consumers what they want. It represents corporate manufactured entertainment as good (culturally diverse and inclusionary) and state-supported cultural products as bad (culturally monolithic and exclusionary). For neoliberals, media corporations give people what they want, not what state media mandarins think they need.

The above neoliberal talking points are hegemonic in many countries. They obscure how reliant NMCs and TNMCs are on state power, regulation and policy. In fact, neoliberalism proscribes three media policies for states: liberalization, de-regulation, and privatization.

Liberalization. Neoliberals believe that "cultural" free-trade is great. They advocate the free movement of media corporations between borders and promote the liberalization of cross-border trade in audio-visual goods. Liberalization is a policy that allows NMCs and TNMCs to act and transact wherever they want, whenever they want, without "protectionist" interference from states. Liberalization also eliminates "trade-distorting" media policies (such as protections, subsidies, ownership regulations, or quotas) that give advantages to NMCs at the expense of TNMCs. According to liberalizers, national barriers to the cross-border flow of entertainment media limit the consumer's ability to choose what they want to watch and undermine the rights of citizens to freely impart and receive information. To reduce such barriers, neoliberals promote audio-visual free trade between states, bilaterally through state-to-state free trade agreements and multilaterally through institutions such as the World Trade Organization (WTO). Neoliberal economists trumpet the benefits of audio-visual free trade for all, viewing it as a way to improve economic welfare, efficiency, and consumer choice. But not every country possesses the same competitive advantages as the US, whose free trade advocacy supports US audio visual trade dominance.

Deregulation. Neoliberals argue that corporations are the primary engines of all economic development in society. As such, they should be free to conduct their business as they like. Deregulation describes all attempts to reform, minimize, or eradicate state regulation of the affairs of NMCs and TNMCs. Deregulation is the revision or removal of all existing constraints on the capitalist "will to power." Neoliberals believe that deregulation leads to competitiveness, higher productivity, greater efficiency, and lower prices for consumers. If a state has a regulation in place which requires 60 percent of every NMC to be owned by national executives and shareholders, neoliberalism calls for the removal of this ownership restriction and the opening up of the system to foreign direct investment. If a state has a content quota regime that compels all TV networks to commit a proportion of their broadcast time to nationalistic entertainment, neoliberals call for the negation of this impediment to profit-maximization. If a state says one NMC can only own a certain number of TV stations, the neoliberal says let the NMC own as much as it wants. If a state has a regulation that says telecommunications should be a state-protected monopoly, the neoliberal demands it be subject to the forces of market competition. If a state stipulates that TV broadcasters may run ads for a maximum total of 18 minutes per hour, the neoliberal says let the broadcaster run as many ads for as long as they want. Using the slogan of "deregulation," neoliberals pressure states to abandon public interest regulations. The result of deregulation, however, is re-regulation of the media system on behalf of the private sector (McChesney 2004).

Privatization. Neoliberals believe that almost everything in society—from the media to water to healthcare to education—should be privatized, that is, privately owned, commoditized, and sold by profit-seeking corporations. Ure (2003) says that though privatization has several different meanings:

> at its most decisive it refers to the 100 per cent transfer of ownership through the sale of a state-owned enterprise (SOE) to private sector equity holders as a publicly listed company by means of a share issue privatization (SIP). (1)

For neoliberals, the state has no business in any industry. They argue that markets work more efficiently than states and advocate the transfer of state ownership rights to public telecommunication firms and TV broadcasters to profit-seeking NMCs or TNMCs. Privatization can happen in stages. Partial privatization occurs when some functions of a state-owned firm are outsourced to private-sector contractors. An example of partial privatization would be when a public broadcasting company outsources the development of entertainment content to NMCs. While the broadcaster remains publicly owned, it contracts a variety of jobs to profit-seeking firms, effectively transferring public expenditure to the private sector. Public-private partnerships reflect a "corporatist" relationship between states and NMCs. Since the 1980s, there has been a broad movement to privatize telecommunications and broadcasting systems across North America, Western and Eastern Europe, Latin America, Africa, the Middle East, and Asia.

From the 1980s to the present day, neoliberal policies of liberalization, deregulation, and privatization have been implemented by many different states. Hitherto state-owned telecommunications and public broadcasting systems have been liberalized, deregulated, and privatized (Chadha and Kavoori 2000; Freedman 2008).

GLOBAL MEDIA GOVERNANCE

In addition to being implemented by policy-makers at the level of nation-states, media policy is negotiated by a plurality of public and private actors at an emerging "global" level of media governance. While media policy is traditionally the task of states, policy-makers are increasingly influenced by and brokering deals through extra-territorial or "global levels" of governance. According to Raboy and Padovani (2010), "The global environment for the governance of media and communication" is "based on the interaction and interdependence of a wide array of actors and processes taking place in dispersed policy venues" (152). As result, there has "been a shift from vertical, top-down, and state-based modes of regulation to horizontal arrangements, while at the same time, governing processes have become more permeable to interventions from a plurality of players with stakes in media and communication" (152–153). A neoliberal policy framework that supports the profit interests of NMCs and TNMCs is being pushed by the US through global media governance institutions such as the World Trade Organization (WTO) (Comor 1997; Costanza-Chock 2005; Dizard 2001;

Hill 2002; Thussu 2000). The United Nations (UN), however, has long functioned as a space of protest against US-backed neoliberalism.

US STATE ADVOCACY FOR GLOBAL NEOLIBERAL MEDIA POLICY: THE FREE FLOW AT THE WTO

Not all states in the world system are equally responsible for the globalization of neoliberal policy; many states do not support it. As Morris and Waisbord (2001) say: "the US government wields more influence in shaping international communications policies than any other state; members of the European Union (some more than others) speak louder than the majority of Third World countries in global communications matters" (xvi). Indeed, neoliberalism originated in the US. From the early 1980s to the present day, the US state has struggled to universalize neoliberalism. While the US recognizes the media sovereignty of other states, it infrequently respects it unless such state media sovereignty aligns with a neoliberal world order. The US state has worked through a number of global governmental organizations in order to establish bilateral, multilateral, and global trade agreements that entrench and institutionalize neoliberal policy within many states (Flew 2002; Hamelink 2002; Hesmondhalgh 2005; McChesney 2006; McGuigan 2005; Mosco 2004).

A policy precursor to the full-blown neoliberal media policy of liberalization, deregulation, and privatization is the US's free flow of "information doctrine." According to Schiller (1976), this doctrine emerged following World War II and accompanied the US's general foreign policy to make the world safe for the freedom of enterprise to do business wherever it wants. Schiller (1976) referred to a 1946 memo by US Assistant Secretary of State William Benton, who stated that:

> The State Department plans to do everything within its power along political or diplomatic lines to help break down the artificial barriers to the expansion of private American news agencies, magazines, motion pictures, and other media of communications throughout the world. Freedom of the press—and freedom of exchange of information generally—is an integral part of our foreign policy. (28)

The free flow of information doctrine has long been a strategic priority for US foreign policy-makers. As an extension of liberal internationalist foreign policy, the doctrine represents the movement of information and media across borders as essential to building a free, democratic, and peaceful world order based on cultural exchange, economic interdependency, and pluralism (Rosenberg 1982: 215). Throughout the 1980s and 1990s, this free flow was made tantamount to free trade in audio-visual products (Comor 1994; 1997). Herman and McChesney (1997) say that the free flow of information doctrine is now "an aggressive trade position on behalf of US media interests. The core operational idea behind the principle was that trans-national media firms and advertisers should be permitted to operate globally, with minimal government intervention" (17). At present, the free-flow doctrine promotes the core tenets of neoliberal media policy. Fitzgerald (2012) says: "The US state has advanced US-based multinational communication and culture industry corporations by aggressively exporting its policies of privatization and deregulation [. . .] under the banner of 'free flow in information'" (150). Paradoxically, the US state cajoles other states into accepting the free flow of audio-visual products while simultaneously telling them to uphold a stringent US copyright regime that restricts and criminalizes the free exchange of non commodified TV shows and films.

On behalf of US TNMCs, the US state has battled unilaterally, bilaterally, and multi-laterally through a number of institutions to universalize its particular neoliberal media policy regime. For more than one hundred years, the International Telecommunications Union (ITU) viewed national telecommunication systems as state monopolies and public utilities, but in the 1980s and 1990s the ITU was brought into line with the US's neoliberal deregulation and privatization policy (Comor 1997; Hills 2002; Thussu 2000). The US has won consent to regional free-trade agreements such as the North American Free Trade Agreement (NAFTA) and bilateral audio-visual free trade agreements with many countries (Jin 2011). Since 2002, the US has bilaterally negotiated partial and full audio-visual free-trade agreements with Chile, Costa Rica, Guatemala, Honduras, El Salvador, Nicaragua, Singapore, the Dominican Republic, Australia, Morocco, and South Korea. Furthermore, the US state pressures the International Monetary Fund (IMF) and World Bank to compel developing countries to adopt neoliberal media policies as a condition of their receiving financial loans, aid, and technology transfers (Dizard 2001: 178). US intellectual property law is enshrined by the World Intellectual Property Organization (WIPO) as world law (Ryan 1998) and the US state, on behalf of the MPAA, demands that all countries uphold and enforce copyright (Bettig 1996).

The World Trade Organization (WTO) is the most powerful global promoter of neoliberal media policy (Comor 1997; Costanza-Chock 2005; Dizard 2001; Hills 2002; McDowell 1994; Thussu 2000). Established in 1995, the WTO is:

> the only global international organization dealing with the rules of trade between nations. At its heart are the WTO agreements, negotiated and signed by the bulk of the world's trading states. The WTO's goal is to help producers of goods and services, exporters, and importers conduct their business around the world. The WTO pushes for the liberalization, privatization and de-regulation of all media systems. (McDowell 1994: 110)

The most significant WTO trade agreements which affect the media policy of states are the General Agreement on Tariffs and Trade (GATT), the General Agreement on Trade in Services (GATS), and the Agreement on Trade-Related Aspects of Intellectual Property Rights (TRIPS) (Puppis 2008).

The General Agreement on Tariffs and Trade (GATT) deals with international trade in goods. Members of GATT include Organization for Economic Cooperation and Development (OECD) countries in the North and South. The basic principles of the trade agreement are non-discrimination and market access. Non-discrimination means that states cannot favor the profit-interests of a NMC at the expense of a TNMC. If a state grants certain benefits to a NMC, then it must also grant those same benefits to a TNMC. The GATT also encourages all states to lower trade barriers that impede the cross-border flow of audio-visual media. The GATT originally acknowledged the right of states to use screen quotas, but in the 1993 Uruguay round of GATT negotiations, the US called upon GATT members to give up their screen quota rights. Canada, France, and other EU countries refused to heed the US's request (Freedman 2008: 201). The General Agreement on Trade and Services (GATS) is a trade agreement that covers audio-visual services (film and TV) as well as services in telecommunications. Through GATS, the US strives to incorporate audio-visual media and culture into its global trade regime by defining them as services.

The Agreement on Trade-Related Aspects of Intellectual Property Rights (TRIPs) was integrated into the General Agreement on Tariffs and Trade (GATT) treaty at the end of the 1994 Uruguay Round negotiations. This was the result of intense lobbying by the US and a few other states, which sought to bring the promotion and protection of copyright under world trade regulation. To become a member of the WTO, states must ratify TRIPS. If WTO member states do not support TRIPS, they can be sanctioned by other states. "The ability to impose trade sanctions considerably strengthens the enforcement of copyrights, even in developing countries—which meets the interests of the big companies" (Puppis 2008: 409). Hesmondhalgh (2008), bringing the issue of copyright into the CI paradigm, says that TRIPS represents "a new nexus of state and financial power underpinned by neoliberalism [which] is now becoming increasingly tied to the global governance of symbol production and consumption" (97). TRIPS enshrines US copyright law as global copyright law. By reducing culture to the status of a commodity, TRIPS normalizes and legitimizes "a fundamentally 'Western' notion of culture across the world" (Hesmondhalgh 2008: 102).

Through the WTO, the US state and TNMCs have used GATT, GATS, and TRIPS as instruments for pushing neoliberal media policy upon states and media systems around the world. The biggest beneficiary of a global neoliberal media order is the US, which is home to the world's most powerful and profitable TNMCs. Contrary to reports of the demise of the state, the US state has "acted frequently, with initiative and decisiveness, to assure the promotion of the ever-expanding communication sector to its present status as a central pillar of the economy" (Schiller 2000: 49). The US state advances neoliberal media policy through national and transnational institutional regulatory structures on behalf of the powerful bloc of TNMCs that are based in the US territory.

Non-US national elites have both embraced and resisted the US neoliberal media policy regime. Neoliberalism is negotiated by state elites, who face top-down pressure from the US state and transnational capital, as well as bottom-up pressure from national blocs of corporate media elites. As Hall (1991) argues, "transnational capital attempts to rule through other local capitals, rule alongside and in partnership with other economic and political elites" (28). In these cases, US and non-US state and media elites often form contingent or long-term global-local alliances. According to Harindranath (2003), "a transnational, cosmopolitan elite [that is] impervious to national boundaries or nationalist sentiments" benefits from neoliberalism and support for TNMCs and NMCs. This means that in the current era "It is no longer accurate to think solely in terms of the West suppressing the Rest, but who gets co-opted into this exclusive club of international elite, and how, and who doesn't and what the consequences are" (Harindranath 2003: 156). Neoliberalizing states service "corporate elites, in media and other industries" and this "occur[s] on every continent, both in industrialized and developing countries" (Artz 2003: 5).

Despite US and global pressure to adopt neoliberal media policy, state elites continue to be relatively autonomous decision-makers. "National governments continue to be major, perhaps the main, players, both domestically and as advocates for their national interests in international fora" (Raboy 2007: 345). The US and US-based TNMCs do not always get what they want from other state media policy-makers. Though the US does struggle to persuade other states to adopt its neoliberal media policy prescriptions, the US neoliberal media policy has been embraced by state elites everywhere. The notion that a "global neoliberal media order" has been consolidated, and that there are no alternatives to it, is US and transnational corporate wish-fulfillment, not fact. For many years, US neoliberal media policy has been vehemently rejected by state elites on behalf of national media firms. As Freedman (2003) says, "apart from the USA, few countries are willing to seek commitments on audio-visual liberalization if this requires them to open up their own markets" (291). Over the past forty years or so, blocs of states have formed strategic alliances at the United Nations to criticize US global media dominance and, more recently, to reject US neoliberal media policy.

THE UNITED NATIONS, UNESCO, AND CULTURAL SOVEREIGNTY

The United Nations Educational, Scientific and Cultural Organization (UNESCO) is a specialized agency of the United Nations (UN) which has 196 member states. The purpose of UNESCO is to contribute to global peace and security by promoting international collaboration through education, science, and culture in order to further universal respect for justice, the rule of law, and human rights along with the UN Charter's fundamental freedoms.

At the highpoint of cultural imperialism criticism (the 1970s), UNESCO became a flashpoint for struggles against US global media dominance and the free flow of information doctrine. In protest against the media asymmetries and inequalities that divided the rich Western states from the poorer postcolonial Rest and the perpetuation of media dependency, in the 1970s intellectuals in the Non-Aligned Movement (NAM) proposed a New World Information and Communication Order (NWICO) (Taylor 1997: 47). The NWICO movement challenged the US's global media dominance and the free flow of information doctrine that supported it. The concept of cultural imperialism was used as a critical political resource by the NAM in its struggle for a NWICO (Boyd-Barrett 2003: 39; Taylor 1997: 47; Smith 1980: 32). By 1976, the NAM demanded that the US and other Western neo-colonial states respect their right to use the media as an instrument of national development (Thussu 2000: 41). The Tunisian Information Minister Mustapha Masmoudi (1979) summarized the NAM's criticisms of American and Western cultural imperialism as follows:

1. owing to the socio-technological imbalance, there was a one-way flow of information from the center to the periphery, which created a wide gap between the haves and the have-nots;
2. the information-rich were in a position to dictate the terms to the information-poor, thus creating a structure of dependency with widespread economic, political, and social ramifications for the poorer societies;
3. this vertical flow (as opposed to a desirable horizontal flow of global information) was dominated by Western-based transnational corporations;
4. information was treated by the transnational media as a commodity and subjected to the rules of the market;

5. the entire information and communication order was a part of, and in turn propped up by, international inequality that created and sustained mechanisms of neo-colonialism (cited in Thussu 2000: 44).

The International Commission for the Study of Communication Problems (or the Macbride Commission) was formed in response to NAM's grievances. At the UNESCO General Conference of 1978, the *Mass Media Declaration* was put forth in order to recognize the role of the media in national development. By 1980, and following the NAM's summits in Colombo (1976) and Havana (1979), a resolution was adopted at the Baghdad meeting of the Inter-Governmental Coordinating Council for Information of Non-Aligned Countries. There, NWICO principles were articulated within the context of international law regarding the cultural and communicational sovereignty of states (Boyd-Barrett 2003: 40; Smith 1980). The Macbride Commission's final report, *Many Voices, One World*, was issued in 1980.

NAM's struggle for a NWICO has been retrospectively criticized for lacking a class analysis, particularly an analysis of the local postcolonial elite's interest in building and profiting from their own national media industry. The Macbride Commission has also been criticized for overestimating "the mutual interest people have in each other's culture" (Hamelink 1997: 80), and perhaps for subscribing to a simplistic notion of cultural identity. The NAM's struggle for a NWICO at UNESCO should nonetheless be remembered. The NAM performed an ideology critique of the US free flow of information doctrine, revealing the un-democratic nature of a global corporate media system that consistently presented itself as the beacon of freedom and democracy. "NWICO was a *protest* whose proponents argued that the structure and operation of global communication had grossly inequitable consequences" (Boyd-Barrett 2003: 35). "What the NWICO provided was a moral platform", writes Thomas (1997), "a *raison d'être* for the restructuring of global communications systems in favour of a system whose control was proportionately distributed between North and South" (165). The NWICO turned the UN into a platform where criticisms of US cultural imperialism were taken seriously. The NWICO struggle at the UN provided a bridge between the anti-imperialist intellectuals of postcolonial peripheries and the radical political economists of communication in the metropolitan cores (Mosco 1996: 76). NWICO brought the critique of cultural imperialism to US academia, which was supported by the critical political-economy scholarship of Schiller and others.

The goals of the NWICO and the Macbride Commission, however, did not materialize (Hamelink 1997: 75). What emerged in the years following the NWICO proposal and the Macbride Commission was the opposite of what was intended: the further global growth of US-based TNMCs and the continuance of cultural imbalances. From its inception, the US state and US media corporations opposed NWICO. The US experienced an economic crisis during the 1970s, a crisis that the US's post-Fordist computer, information, and telecommunications economy was supposed to resolve (Roach 1997: 102). NWICO's principle of communication and cultural sovereignty was perceived as a threat to the profit interests of US media corporations. So neoconservative think-tanks such as the Heritage Foundation argued that NWICO supported state control of the media and would lead to replicas of the Soviet Union's totalitarian propaganda system

(Roach 1997; Thussu 2000). Fearing that NWICO would erect national barriers to the spread of democracy and accumulation of profits, the Inter-American press Council, The International Press Institute, the World Press Freedom Committee, and the US news media echoed ideological charges against NWICO (Boyd-Barrett 2003: 45; Schiller 1992: 23–25). The final blow to the NWICO came in 1985, when the Reagan Administration, followed by the like-minded Thatcher government, withdrew from UNESCO. This muzzled criticisms of cultural imperialism and nearly destroyed the NWICO ideal (Fraser 2003: 143; Taylor 1997: 49).

The NAM's struggle for NWICO at UNESCO failed, but since the early 1990s many postcolonial and neo-colonial state elites have joined forces at UNESCO to contest some components of the US neoliberal policy and the continued dominance of US-based TNMCs. While the US, TNMCs, and the WTO struggle to universalize neoliberal policies, many states have tried to exempt "culture"—films, TV shows, books, songs—from free trade agreements. The *l'exception culturelle* (cultural exception) effort was initiated by France at the 1993 General Agreement on Tariffs and Trade (GATT) negotiations. The goal of cultural exemption is to treat cultural goods differently than other traded goods and services because of the intrinsic differences of such goods (see Chapter 2). Many cultural policy-makers argue that cultural goods encompass values, identities, and meanings that go beyond their strict commercial value, and that states need to protect and promote their culture (and culture industries). At UNESCO, states take a "cultural exception" from the US and TNMC-backed neoliberal regime of audio-visual free trade.

In 2001, the UNESCO's General Assembly adopted the Universal Declaration on Cultural Diversity, which called cultural diversity "the common heritage of humanity." Perhaps sensing that UNESCO might once again pose a challenge to US audio-visual trade dominance, the US rejoined the organization in 2003. In the fall of 2005, delegates from over 180 nation-states (led by Canada and France) approved the final document of the *UNESCO Convention on the Protection and Promotion of Diversity of the Cultural Expressions* (CPPDCE). The US and Israel voted against this proposal. In the wake of the inability of many states to win acceptance to the "cultural exception" in WTO negotiations, the CPPDCE provided a moral, though not legally binding, justification for the exemption of culture from free trade. The CPPDCE came into force in March 2007. The CPPDCE claims that the "cultural aspects of development are as important as its economic aspects" (Article 6), and declares the sovereign right of nation-states to "maintain, adopt, and implement policies and measures that they deem appropriate for the protection and promotion of the diversity of cultural expressions in their territory" (Article 6). This grants states the right to support the production and distribution of national cultural goods, provide subsidies to NMCs, and implement measures "aimed at enhancing the diversity of the media, including through public service broadcasting" (cited in Puppis 2008: 417). In sum, the CPPDCE challenges the neoliberal media policy agenda pursued by the US. And the cultural exception to free trade it promotes is proving to be the global media policy rule.

US policy-makers, the MPAA, and TNMCs vehemently (and predictably) oppose the CPPDCE. I will briefly address and evaluate some of the claims they make against the CPPDCE.

First, the US claims that the CPPDCE is a means by which states protect their NMCs (not their "cultures") against the power of US-based TNMCs. The US state views the CPPDCE as an industrial policy that largely supports the profit goals of fledgling and powerful national media firms in other countries, rather than supporting cultural diversity. The MPAA, for example, says that "The Convention appears to be more about trade and commercial activities than about the promotion of cultural diversity" (MPAA 2005). This point has some merit. As Doyle (2012) notes, some states that say they want to protect and promote cultural diversity "are also keen to foster the circumstances in which their own indigenous television and film companies will become more commercially successful [at home] and more competitive in international markets" (12). The Canadian state, for example, demands that the US respect its sovereign right to protect and promote its cultural diversity while tolerating high levels of media concentration domestically by a few convergent media conglomerates that direct their TV and film production sectors to create entertainment media for export to foreign markets. The EU claims to defend its cultural diversity, while also supporting the development of powerful EU-based media firms to "compete more effectively against the strength of audio-visual suppliers from the US" (Doyle 2012: 12). The CPPDC may cover the profit-interests of a national media bourgeoisie, but in doing so it provides the resources for the cultural workers employed by that bourgeoisie to create and export TV shows and films that, in many instances, do contribute to greater global cultural diversity.

Second, US critics present the CPPDC's call for states to protect and promote their national cultures as a threat to cultural diversity. They argue that cultural diversity emerges through interactions and mixings between many cultures, not through state-sanctioned cultural protectionism. Appropriately, US state actors present the free flow of US TNMCs and entertainment media ("culture") between borders and the dismantling of all barriers to this flow as the fast route to cultural diversity. US State Department Ambassador Louise Oliver (2005), for example, says that the United States is the most culturally diverse country in the world, and that cultural diversity has been achieved "by our commitment to freedom and our openness to others, and by maintaining the utmost respect for the free flow of ideas, words, goods and services" (Oliver 2005). Greater cultural diversity ostensibly results from US TNMCs doing business wherever they like, however they like, and in the absence of non-US state attempts to promote and protect their own cultures/industries. A largely one-way flow of cultural products, from the US to the rest of the world, is paradoxically imagined by this neoliberal discourse to support "mixing" and greater cultural diversity. The CPPDCE, which enables other states to produce and export cultural goods to be mixed with the US and other countries, is framed as a barrier to such mixing and cultural diversity. The US position on the CPPDCE clouds the actuality of US global media dominance and the fact that mixing is infrequently a two-way street. Furthermore, it obscures how the CPPDCE explicitly claims support for the exchange of ideas, cultural mixing, and cultural diversity—"cultural diversity forms a common heritage of humanity and should be cherished and preserved for the benefit of all"—while also claiming that "cultural diversity is strengthened by the free flow of ideas, and that is nurtured by constant exchanges and interaction between cultures" (26).

Third, US opponents of the CPPDCE depict it as an instrument used by state elites to maintain their cultural control of their societies. They seem to view cultural protectionism as a way for state elites to monopolize the meaning of nation and close down minority opportunities for imagining the nation in a variety of ways. In response to the CPPDCE, US State Department Ambassador Louise Oliver (2005) claimed that "ambiguities in the text might be misused by a government as a justification for adopting policies and measures that would protect and promote the majority culture within its territory at the expense of minority cultures." Cultural protectionism can be abused by state elites, but so too can "free trade." Furthermore, all cultural protectionist policies do not necessarily lead to top-down state control of national culture at the expense of bottom-up imaginings of the nation by a range of people. Actually, cultural protectionist policies can support bottom-up public participation in national imaginings and "dialogic participation by all members of the cultural community" (Baker 2002: 250–251). But US state actors frame the CPPDCE's cultural protectionism as leading to the "worst case" cultural scenario, conveniently overlooking its potential cultural benefits. The CPPDCE is depicted as a tool of state oppression which forces the assimilation of minority groups into a majoritarian nationalist culture, as opposed to something which might enable the cultural voices of minority groups to flourish. As the CPPDCE says, "The protection and promotion of the diversity of cultural expressions presuppose the recognition of equal dignity and respect for all cultures, including the cultures of persons belonging to minorities and indigenous peoples" (26).

The many debates for and against the CPPDCE will likely continue. Whatever the outcome, the very existence of the CPPDCE suggests that pure neoliberal media policy is viewed by many states as a threat to their national cultures and culture industries and that the totally liberalized, deregulated, and privatized media landscape dreamed of by US-based TNMCs is not forthcoming. Cognizant that a hasty implementation of neoliberal media policy would result in a quick takeover of many NMCs by US-based TNMCs and a loss of a space for imagining their national cultures, states worldwide use (and sometimes abuse) media policy to protect and promote NMCs and a diversity of cultural products.

CONCLUSION: MEDIA POLICY, WITHOUT GUARANTEES

Sovereign states can and do play a significant role in governing the cross-border production, distribution, marketing, exhibition, and consumption of entertainment media. This challenges the notion that US cultural imperialism is triumphant; national economies, polities, and cultures curtail the total dominance of US-TNMCs. States devise ways to protect and promote domestic NMCs and their own "national" economies, polities, and cultures. US-based TNMCs want total control over global media markets; on behalf of these TNMCs, the US state strives to cultivate transnational consent to neoliberal media policy. But TNMCs and the US state are not able to able to waltz right into whatever state they want and do whatever they like, at least not without first negotiating with the national gatekeepers. US TNMCs and the US state struggle for world media hegemony; sometimes they get non-US media firms and states to do what they want, on other occasions they fail to win consent to their goals. At present, the interests of TNMCs and the US state are mediated by the interplay of national gatekeeper interests, including political elites, national media business owners, and citizens and social movements (Chadha and Kavoori 2000: 428). Chadha and Kavoori (2000) say that the "active sense of [national gatekeeping] engagement needs to be recognized and worked into existing theoretical constructs such as those related to media imperialism" (428). This chapter agrees with this assessment.

In the world system, the political and business elites of each state remain significant gatekeepers. These gatekeepers may use the discourse of national cultural protection and promotion to maintain political control or shore up the profit- interests of NMCs. Politicians who publicly represent themselves as national protagonists engaged in a struggle to defend the national culture from a threatening American Other may win votes, but such cultural nationalist posturing "risks cloaking the interests of emergent bourgeoisies seeking to advance their own market power under the sign of national cultural self-determination" (Miller, et al. 2005: 80–81). Media policy can be exploited by the owners of NMCs who claim to be interested in protecting or promoting national culture when, in actuality, they are only interested in protecting and promoting their own business operations. Fledgling NMCs seek state intervention (protection and promotion) when pitted against strong US TNMCs. When NMCs grow stronger, they link into an alliance with TNMCs. Media policy that seeks to protect or promote the nation from a threatening external Other is always problematic and open to abuse by state and business elites.

Yet, state media policies that protect and promote national culture and culture industries do not always or necessarily subscribe to backward, primordial, or static notions of the nation, pose ideological and legal impediments to cultural mixing and cultural diversity, or support state-corporate conspiracies to indoctrinate the public with a one-dimensional nation-ideology. When the market fails to support social equality, cultural diversity, and a vibrant democracy, state media policy can be used to build conditions that do so. On these grounds, state intervention can give crucial support to the public "right to communicate," "cultural diversity," and "civic media products." It can challenge the tendency of media corporations to concentrate and monopolize markets with anti-trust laws. It can support public broadcasting and public cultural initiatives. It can curb foreign control of national media systems, use subsidies to support small media firms and employ content quotas to ensure that national TV shows and films are screened.

In response to the dominance of US-TNMCs, state media policy can protect and promote national culture industries to enable more and more diverse media expressions to travel the world. This, in turn, may create "more potential for cultures to meet and share elements" (Morris 2002: 286). The goal of cross-cultural understanding remains a noble goal in the face of chauvinism, xenophobia, intolerance, and racism. When US-TNMCs and their NMC allies fail to support this non-economic goal and jointly diminish the quantity and quality of diverse cultural sources and expressions, states can intervene. State support for diverse media production and distribution sources that are geared toward increasing the quantity and quality of diverse media sources and content should be supported. The protection and promotion of national culture industries and national films and TV shows need not result in paternalistic or ideological content but, rather, can provide a space for negotiating nation-ness as economies, states, and cultures change.

Media policy can have both progressive and regressive effects. The kinds of cultural projects supported by media policy can be hegemonic or counter-hegemonic. Some may support elite interests, while others may represent oppositional and marginalized publics within the state. For example, three films that critique neoliberalism in the post-9/11 era were assisted by state media policy. *The Constant Gardner* (2005), a film critical of neo-colonialism in Africa, was supported by the now defunct UK Film Council. *The Corporation* (2004), an anti-capitalist documentary about the "psycho-pathic character" of the modern corporation, received funding from Canadian cultural policy agencies (TV ONTARIO, Canadian Television Fund, Telefilm Canada, British Columbia Film). *The Power of Nightmares* (2004), a three-part documentary about the eerie convergences between neo-conservativism and Islamic fundamentalism, was supported by the BBC. Clearly, media policy can and does support the production and distribution of diverse media content. The political and creative outcomes of media policies geared to promoting and protecting nations are "without cultural guarantees."

CHAPTER 4

Producing Entertainment in the New International Division of Cultural Labor (NICL)

INTRODUCTION: THE PRODUCTION CONTEXT OF GLOBAL ENTERTAINMENT

Global entertainment media appears to viewers through many screens—TV sets, laptop computers, and mobile devices—without a human history. TV shows and films are often experienced by viewers as autonomous entities—"things" set apart from the sphere of physically exhausting and intellectually challenging work. An action movie's spectacle or a good drama's narrative realism implore us to forget the conditions of their making. "Behind the scenes" outtakes included in DVD box-sets may offer some insight into how entertainment is produced, but more often they function to promote new TV shows or films. Whether by temporarily "escaping" from the big problems of the world, blissfully immersing ourselves in virtual communities built by fandom managers, or chatting about our favorite TV shows and films with fellow Facebook users, we are accustomed to overlooking the conditions of entertainment's production and the social relations between the people who make it. In 2009 Chinese film-goers expressed their fandom of *Transformers 2* by dressing up as Bumblebee (a yellow General Motors Camaro who transforms into a friendly Auto-bot) (Rigney 2009). They were probably unaware that director Michael Bay blamed the poor quality of the film on the 2007 Screen Actors Guild strike deadline, which rushed *Transformers 2*'s completion. Bat-fans of *The Dark Knight* (2009) enthusiastically discuss action scenes on interactive websites sanctioned by Warner Bros; the visual effects work of Conway Wickliffe, who died while filming *The Dark Knight*'s most intense car chase sequence, is given much less attention (Staff and Agencies 2008). Environmentally conscious viewers who identified with the anti-colonial "back to nature" allegory of *Avatar* (2009) (Chan 2010) likely didn't know that the film was manufactured by a polluting industry that sends "over 140,000 metric tons of ozone and diesel particles into the air each year" (Burns 2009). Viewers put on 3-D glasses to immerse themselves in *Tron: Legacy*'s (2010) virtual landscape, but many may not have understood why the film was shot at the Canadian Motion Picture Park studio in south Burnaby, British Columbia, instead of at a complex in Los Angeles, California (Falconer 2009).

The ways in which viewers interpret and use global entertainment media is an exciting site for ethnographic analysis and reception studies (as discussed in Chapter 6). But political-economists remind us that connected to and shaping entertainment's consumption is a production context of waged work. As Deuze (2007) says:

the current lives of people all over the world and most particularly in Western capitalist democracies cannot be understood without an understanding of media—albeit not so much through the content of the media, but through the way all elements of work are organized in media as an industry. (x)

Entertainment is produced by media corporations within and for the market. A division of labor and waged work shape entertainment in profound ways (Banks and Hesmondhalgh 2009; Deuze 2007; Garnham 1990, 2000; Hartley 2005; Hesmondhalgh 2007; Holt and Perren 2009; McGuigan 2010; Mayer, Banks and Caldwell 2009; Meehan 2007; Mosco 1996; Ross 2009; Wasko 2003). Media corporations combine technology and human labor power to manufacture films and TV shows as entertainment commodities that are offered to consumers for sale in a marketplace. No one TV show or film is manufactured by a solitary "author"; they are the product of thousands of cultural workers organized by a "division of labor." The process of entertainment production is divided into specific, routinized, and standardized tasks; these tasks are assigned to workers in specialized departments with specific skill sets. Media corporations need labor power to make entertainment. Many skilled hands and creative minds are hired to complete projects.

The waged work and division of labor integral to entertainment production in capitalism have gone global. So has Hollywood. "[T]he transformation of Hollywood from an exclusive and centralized base to a global network of production sites [. . .] alters in some fundamental ways the political economy of the commercial film industry (Elmer and Gasher 2005: 2). Critical studies of the "altered" political economy of Hollywood show how entertainment is manufactured by cultural workers within a

---

BOX 4.1

ALICE IN WONDERLAND'S (2010) DIVISION OF CULTURAL LABOR

More than eight-hundred cultural workers with a variety of specialized skills were hired to assemble Walt Disney Pictures' global blockbuster *Alice in Wonderland* (2010). Ten producers conceptualized and executed the film's artistic and economic "vision." A director (and nine assistant directors) guided the conduct of the actors and technical crew. A casting director auditioned and selected actors to play fictional characters. Over one hundred actors—and voice actors, extras, and stunt workers including fire jugglers and body doubles—performed. Textile artists, boot makers, dyers, and fitters, crafted the costumes. Set designers, construction workers, illustrators, prop-makers, painters, and model-makers built sets. Cinematographers, camera operators, rigging grips, dolly grips, lighting programmers, and technicians made images. A composer developed a score for the film and brought notation to ear with conductors, choir contractors, mixers, and boom operators. Special effects, visual effects, and animation specialists, as well as a number of image editors were hired for post-production work. Many more workers—including drivers for the star actors, actor assistants, stand-ins, secretaries, security guards, payroll accountants, location managers, studio teachers, horse grooms, title designers, and dialect coaches—also contributed to the project. The Disney "magic" of *Alice in Wonderland* was produced by many cultural workers whose skills were organized by a complex division of labor.

"New International Division of Cultural Labor" (NICL) (Miller et al. 2005). The NICL explains the "differentiation of cultural labour; the globalization of labour processes; the means by which Hollywood coordinates and defends its authority over cultural labour markets; and the role national governments play in collusion with TNMCs [transnational media corporations]" (Miller et al. 2005). In this chapter, I describe the general economic, political, and technological characteristics of the NICL, and then examine two important forms of entertainment production in the NICL: "runaway productions" and "international co-productions."

Which economic and political actors coordinate the NICL? Have historical relations between media centers and media peripheries been de-stabilized or re-consolidated? Why is entertainment production moving from Los Angeles, California, to cities around the world? Which factors shape the decision of LA-based studios to offshore production tasks? Do runaway productions and co-productions help or hinder the development of national media industries and place-specific representations? How do nation-states attract runaway productions and participate in co-productions? What are the benefits and costs of doing so? This chapter's answers to these and many more questions complicate the CI paradigm, which views "Hollywood" as a US-owned industry that is located within the territorial borders of US, staffed by a US workforce, and interested in exporting "American" TV shows and films to the world. But entertainment production is no longer contained in one US national box; it is coordinated across many "national" industries, territories, and cultures, triggering new social conflicts and political debates.

GLOBAL HOLLYWOOD AND THE NEW INTERNATIONAL DIVISION OF CULTURAL LABOR (NICL)

The 1960s Western film star John Wayne once said that "Hollywood is a place you can't geographically define. We don't know where it is" (cited in Bordwell et al. 1985: xiii). Contra Wayne, many people *do* think they know where Hollywood is. Hollywood is perceived as a metonym for "entertainment" and a symbol for an "American" place of origin (Braudy 2011). Hollywood itself is marked by a forty-foot tall and three-hundred by fifty-foot long sign perched above the Hollywood Hills of Los Angeles, California. For many international actors, "making it big" in Hollywood means moving to sunny LA, getting their name cemented in a star on the Hollywood Boulevard's Walk of Fame and buying a gated mansion in the Hills. When governments bemoan the negative influence of foreign entertainment on their national identities (and cultural industries), they often blame a US-specific "Hollywood." Hollywood—a specific place in Los Angeles, California, USA—is regularly imagined by US citizens and publics worldwide as the world's home of entertainment. But Hollywood is not just "America." The concept of "global Hollywood" views nationally-based media companies, states, and cultural workforces as significant producers of entertainment, but emphasizes that the production of entertainment itself in the NICL is not reducible to any one nationally specific industry, state, or class.

Transnational media conglomerates (TNMCs) run the NICL, and own the major and minor film and TV production studios clustered in and around Los Angeles, California ("Hollywood"). TNMCs, not distinctly "American" firms, are the parent companies of the world's most powerful studios. Warner Bros (Time Warner), Fox Entertainment Group (News Corporation), The Walt Disney Motion Pictures Group (The Walt Disney Company), Paramount Pictures (Viacom), Universal Studios (NBC-Universal), and Sony Pictures Entertainment (Sony Corporation) are the largest entertainment studios in the world. These mega-companies focus on profit-maximization by financing, producing, distributing, and marketing entertainment worldwide (see Chapter 2). "Within the context of intensifying globalization and complex economic imperatives from corporate conglomerates who run the industry from the outside," says Banks (2008), "very little of what constitutes Hollywood in our [national] cultural, economic and historical imaginary still exists under the sign of [an American] Hollywood" (63). Global Hollywood is ubiquitous, connecting together and integrating what were once imagined to be distinctive national cultural industries.

In the NICL, media corporations, nation-states, and cultural workers from many countries are productive parts of global Hollywood. The goal of completing specific entertainment projects links them together. Entertainment production often begins and ends with the TNMC-owned "Hollywood" major studios, but it does not only occur within the place of Hollywood itself. TNMCs are financial flagships, coordinating and controlling organizationally and territorially decentralized entertainment production networks (Coe and Johns 2004; Storper and Christopherson 1987, 1989). TNMCs have become highly centralized in terms of capital ownership, creative decision-making, and copyright control, yet flexible in terms of the companies they work with (Wayne 2003). To produce entertainment, TNMCs employ numerous in-house subsidiary firms and contract (or "outsource") independent production firms that complete specialized tasks. TNMCs also offshore entertainment production to smaller media firms in other countries, moving tasks from one centralized and often geographically contained division of labor to a number of specialized media firms in a de-centralized and territorially unbound division of labor. Auto-assemblage, electronics manufacture, and call-center services have been "outsourced" from the US to other countries. So too has entertainment production. In the NICL, tasks that were once undertaken by cultural workers employed by a media firm in one city (e.g., Los Angeles) are being outsourced to cultural workers employed by many media firms in many cities (e.g., Los Angeles, Toronto, London) (Elmer and Gasher 2005). US TNMCs contractually aggregate and disaggregate small media firms on a project-by-project basis when making TV shows and films in the NICL.

The NICL is coordinated by many nation states, not just one powerful US state that aggressively pushes the trade interests of its own media corporations in weaker countries. Though entertainment production is not embedded in any one national territory, it is facilitated and legitimized by the media and cultural policy agencies of nation-states, which are gatekeepers and stewards of transnational entertainment production. States have not "lost sovereignty" to TNMCs (Appadurai 1997), nor are they passive "victims" of foreign cultural infiltration. States competitively court entertainment production in an attempt to achieve economic and cultural "development" goals. TNMCs and the network of firms they hire "push" through the borders of states, while nation-states in turn invite and "pull" them across their borders. TNMCs travel the world in search of contractor firms to service them. States induce TNMCs to localize within their territories by providing them with economic incentives to do so. Eight film commissions from Sweden, Norway, Denmark, and Finland, for example, promote "Scandanavian Locations" to TNMCs as ideal sites for making entertainment (Rehlin 2010).

Most entertainment production happens in cities: "each city fosters its own ecology of [entertainment] production with parallel and often mutually dependent sets of industrial districts, distribution chains, and content creation hubs" (Mayer 2008: 72). Curtin (2003: 205) uses the term "media capital" to describe the growth of new city-centers of media finance, production, and distribution. Media capitals entail large "creative clusters" (Scott 1999). The World Intellectual Property Organization (WIPO) defines a "creative cluster" as "the geographic concentration of a creative industry (craft, film, music, publishing, interactive software, design, etc.) that pools together its resources in order to optimize the creation, production, dissemination and exploitation of creative works" (WIPO 2010). Media firms which are clustered together tend to perform better than isolated firms because they can efficiently service each other, mobilize knowledge from universities, and benefit from the "buzz" that surrounds their activities (Amin 1999; Storper and Venables 2004).

LA is the world's core media capital "bound up in a web of relations that exist at the local, regional and global levels, as well as the national level" (Curtin 2003: 204). But LA is not the only media capital. According to the "peripheral vision thesis" of Sinclair, Jacka, and Cunningham (1996), many country-specific and regional media capitals have emerged and established a strong presence in the cross-border entertainment trade. "Instead of a single market dominated by a single central production centre that ships programmes and meanings out to the periphery, there is now a series of different and overlapping markets" (Sparks 2007: 44). There are numerous media capitals. Hong Kong (China), Prague (Czech Republic), Seoul (South Korea), Cairo (Egypt), Lagos, Enugu, and Abuja (Nigeria), Gauteng (South Africa), Toronto, Montreal, and Vancouver (Canada), and Bombay (India) are home to media production, distribution and marketing activities, cultural resources, reputation, and talent. In these (and many other) city-centers, the capacity for financing, producing, and distributing entertainment is growing rapidly. Countries once traditionally viewed as weak or peripheral now exhibit strong media capitals (Reeves 1993; Straubhaar 1991; Tracy 1988). As result, the production of entertainment no longer happens in just one country, but in many countries, while the flow of entertainment is no longer one way, but two-way and multi-directional. Hong Kong's media products, for example, flow to Malaysia, mainland China, Japan, South Korea, the US, and states within the European Union (WTO 2010: 3).

Many cultural policy-makers, development consultants, and petite bourgeois urbanites believe that creative media capitals are engines of "development" for cities that are "transitioning" from industrial to post-industrial capitalism. The concepts of "creativity" and the "creative city" are very popular (Howkins 2007; Landry 2000; Florida 2004, 2005; Markuson 2006). Florida (2005) argues that development in post-industrial cities rests upon "the three Ts: Technology, Talent and Tolerance" (6). High-tech infrastructures, university-educated, entrepreneurial, and innovative workers and a multicultural milieu wherein diverse ethno-cultural identities, sexualities, and subcultures are recognized and mined for new innovations lead the way to urban regeneration, job growth, and trickle-down prosperity. TNMCs territorialize in creative cities to reap the Floridian benefits of "cool capitalism" (McGuigan 2009). But not all creative cities attract TNMCs. In fact, they are ranked according to how well they serve the entertainment production exigencies of TNMCs. In 2009, *Variety* asked hundreds of entertainment location managers, unit production managers, cinematographers, and directors to rate their favorite creative cities according to visual appeal, tax incentives, film-office support, production resources, and ability to double as another location. Los Angeles was rated the best location to shoot in North America; Morocco was ranked #1 internationally (Blair 2009).

The ranking of media capitals indicates that locational differences and uneven forms of media development exist in the NICL. The world in which entertainment is produced is not, as Friedman (2007) would have us believe, "flat." Contra utopian neoliberal ideology, the NICL is far from a level playing field. The NICL mirrors longstanding asymmetrical power relations between a hierarchy of nation-states, media industries, and cultural workers. History's most economically and culturally powerful states (the US, for example) are at the top of the NICL's hierarchy. Satellite states are "the lowest levels of an international hierarchy of media capitals" (Davis and Kaye 2010). Entertainment production is often not a two-way street. Much entertainment—in terms of ownership, copyright control, and creative influence—begins and ends in Los Angeles: the world's largest media capital. The NICL, however, does not represent a strict center-periphery model of the world system. Distinctly "American" media corporations based in a single "dominant" US center do not "dominate" peripheral media capitals by coercing them to become weak production dependencies. Rather, states, firms, audiences, and workers—center and satellite—exist in a dynamic relationship of "asymmetrical interdependence" (Strauhbhar 1991), not domination. In the world system, the US is a powerful media center and US-based TNMCs have extraordinary economic and cultural power to shape media production, distribution, marketing, and consumption of entertainment media in other nation-states. However, there is more going on in the NICL than media imperialism.

BOX 4.2

SEOUL AS A MEDIA CAPITAL: "KOREAN WAVE"

Los Angeles is the world's major media capital and US-based TNMCs rule world entertainment markets. Yet, non-US media capitals exist and play an increasingly important role in the world system.

In East and Southeast Asia (China, Hong Kong, Japan, Taiwan, and Vietnam), the South Korean metropolis of Seoul is an important "media capital" (Jin 2007). South Korean media corporations produce and export popular entertainment media throughout East and Southeast Asia. From the 1950s to the early 1990s, Korea's media industry was dominated by the US, but in the mid-1990s the Korean state established a nationalist media policy regime that significantly reduced US entertainment media imports and stimulated the growth of domestic production. The result was a "Korean Wave" of popular culture throughout the region consisting of TV shows (*Winter Sonata, A Tale of Autumn*, and *Lovers in Paris*), films (*Shiri, Joint Security Area, Old Boy, Chihwaseon, Taegugki*, and *Spring, Summer, Fall, Winter, and Spring*) pop music (K-pop, including *BoA* and *Girls Generation* or, *SNSD*), and video games (Shim 2006). In 2011, the exported Korean Wave was worth $4.2 billion (Oliver 2012). To become a strong media capital, South Korea developed a national TV and film production industry, which generated content for five large Korean TV networks (KBS1, KBS2, MBC, EBS, and SBS). Korean TV broadcasters then established co-production relationships with other countries as a way to get Korean TV shows and films circulating in foreign markets. TV networks in East and South Asia now license culturally proximate entertainment from Korean companies. Korean TV shows and films are more relevant to East and South Asian viewers than much US entertainment is; they contain stories that East and South East Asian viewers can relate to. Korean TV shows and films "typically deal with family issues, love and filial piety in an age of changing technology, and often reinforce traditional values of Confucianism" (Ryoo 2009: 140). The success of the Korean Wave is "closely related to the ability of South Korean media to translate Western or American culture to fit Asian tastes" (Ryoo 2009: 145).

South Korea's growth as a regionally powerful media capital has stoked Japanese nationalist fears of the Korean Wave as a form of "cultural imperialism." In 2003, Japanese TV networks spent $6.28 million purchasing the licensing rights to South Korean TV shows (Takaku 2011). In 2010, the Korean TV industry took in $81.62 million from Japan's TV networks. On August 7 and August 21, 2011, thousands of Japanese cultural nationalists marched outside the Fuji Television Network to protest against the Korean Wave engulfing Japan. Japanese protestors demanded the state place restrictions on the number of Korean TV shows imported and scheduled by Japanese TV networks (Takaku 2011). But Fuji TV Network was simply acting as a rational capitalist: Korean TV is cheaper to acquire and is popular with local Japanese viewers. Instead of investing in home-grown Japanese content, Fuji TV Network buys content from South Korea. "Rather than produce TV programs on our own, it is better to buy cheaper programs from foreign nations. South Korean dramas also attract fairly good ratings," said a Fuji TV Network spokesperson (Takaku 2011).

Korea is a powerful regional media capital, but one that is locked into an asymmetrical power relationship with US-based TNMCs. Jin (2007) argues that while Korea has become an "emerging market with its diverse product sourcing and growing exports" (766) in the East and South Asian region, "cultural imperialism has not disappeared from Korea" (762). US-TNMCs control much of Korea's media industry through foreign direct investment, joint ventures, and licensing agreements. The flow of entertainment between Korea and the US is not reciprocal. In 2003, US TV imports in Korea accounted for 77.8 percent of all imported TV shows, while Korean TV exports to the US accounted for only 0.4 percent of Korea's total exported TV shows—quite an imbalanced relationship (Jin 2007: 763). The audio-visual trade imbalance between Korea and the US will likely increase in the future due to a neoliberal free-trade agreement (FTA) between the two states, signed on June 30, 2007. The FTA stipulates a more open broadcast market for US entertainment products in Korea, ensures improved market access for US TNMCs, decreases Korean TV content quotas, and enables 100 percent US foreign direct investment in and ownership of Korean media and telecommunication firms. Korea is a powerful regional media capital, but in relation to the US, it is still a satellite.

The asymmetrical power relationship between media capitals in a hierarchical world system is mirrored by asymmetrical power relations between cultural workers in a hierarchical creative class system. Wasko (2003) uses the phrases "above-the-line" and "below-the-line" to describe the way cultural workers are segregated from one another based upon the tasks they are equipped to do and the amount they are paid by media firms to do them. Above-the-line workers tend to be high-earning and highly-skilled executive producers, deal-makers, directors, script writers, and star actors.

Below-the-line cultural workers earn lower wages and do more technical work. Grips, wardrobe stylists, drivers, make-up artists, engineers, lighting specialists, pre- and post-production editors, security guards, set painters, special effects technicians, camera operators, extras, and set-builders all fit into the category of "below-the-line" worker. From the TNMC base in Los Angeles, a largely US "above-the-line" creative class travels to satellite media capitals. There, they hire the labor of "below the line" cultural workers (Wasko 2003). Above-the-line cultural workers are more mobile than below-the-line workers and possess more economic power and cultural influence over entertainment production. The cultural workers of the NICL not united; they are divided by skill-sets, assigned tasks, location, and pay.

Though divided in material ways, cultural workers are brought together by their waged work on entertainment projects and their use of information and communication technologies (ICTs). Computers, the World Wide Web, the Internet, mobile devices, and satellites transfer flows of digitized information between two or more of the media capitals that are producing entertainment. "The ICT revolution has increased both the opportunities and the need for international expansion, as it enables [media] firms to disperse their resources and capabilities across national boundaries" (Flew 2007: 26). As Goldsmith and O'Regan (2003) note:

> advances in information and communication technologies have enabled elements of
> film and television production to be perhaps more widely dispersed than at any previous
> time in the history of the media. A single project's financing, pre-production, production,
> post-production and marketing each can and do take place in different parts of the
> world. (7)

Thompson (2007) concurs: "One important cause for the off-shore trend [. . .] is the fact that technological change now offers the possibility of making films entirely abroad, from planning to post-production." In the NICL, ICTs link up center and satellite media capitals for entertainment co-productions, putting workers separated by oceans, lakes, and land in real-time contact with one another. ICTs enable new forms of transnational collaboration. Entertainment production happens round the clock, all hours and all days. ICTs also extend production into people's private lives and places, blurring labor time and leisure space. For many, the "working day" does not have a clear beginning or end.

ICTs establish informational feedback loops between geographically separate but virtually close cultural workers. But cross-border entertainment production is not a seamless operation. The lack of face-to-face communication between workers sometimes leads to miscommunication. Finding a way to harmonize the production schedules of cultural workers located in different media capitals can also prove difficult. "Production problems" often arise from locally specific class conflicts and union struggles since cultural workers in different countries do not all share the same work ethic, wages, or union.

The general economic, political, and technological features of global Hollywood and the NICL have been discussed. The next section will examine in greater detail the political-economy of two forms of entertainment production in the NICL: the "runaway production" and the international co-production.

The "Runaway Production"

An important form of entertainment production in the NICL is the "runaway production." This "phrase [was] coined by the US film industry to describe the outsourcing of film work from Hollywood to cheaper foreign locales" (Johnson-Yale 2008: 114). A "runaway production" occurs when a Los Angeles-based studio outsources and offshores parts of the entertainment production process to below the line (and sometimes above the line) cultural workers clustered in media capitals throughout the NICL. Between 1998 and 2005, the proportion of total production spending in the US shifted from 71 percent to 47 percent, while that of the rest of the world rose (WTO 2010: 10). This was largely due to film and TV show productions "running away" from the US to Canada, the United Kingdom, Australia, New Zealand, and many other countries. What kinds of productions "run away"? It was once thought that high budget and high concept blockbuster films could *not* be off-shored because of the need for executive producers to oversee the production process from start to finish, while low budget productions, such as standardized and easy to assemble TV formats, could be offshored (Scott and Pope 2007). This no longer holds true. Shot in New Zealand, *The Lord of the Rings Trilogy* (2001, 2002, 2003) is a significant example of a high-budget, high-concept, and spectacular entertainment product that was offshored. Since 2003, New Zealand's Large Budget Screen Production Grant has attracted traveling studios with a 12.5 percent tax break on every NZ$50 million spent on production. New Zealand has a thriving film industry and was the chosen place for numerous global hits to be filmed, including: *The Last Samurai* (2003), *The Lion, The Witch and the Wardrobe* (2005), *King Kong* (2005), *10,000 BC* (2008), *Avatar* (2009), and *X-Men Origins: Wolverine* (2009).

Runaway productions tend to be classified as either "creative" or "economic." When a production company shoots a TV show or film "on-location at far-flung sites in the search for scenic and artistic effects deemed essential for the achievement of specific aesthetic goals," a "creative runaway" has occurred (Scott and Pope 2007: 1365). If a TV show or film script requires a setting like an iconic city landmark, beach, ocean, forest, or canyon, the production company will "runaway" to whatever NICL location provides the desired landscape. War films such as *Apocalypse Now* (1979) and *Platoon* (1986), for example, were shot in the Philippines because its lush environments could pass as Vietnam. *Rush Hour 3* (2007) was shot in Paris, France (around the Eiffel Tower), where some of the film's action is set. Parts of *The Pirates of the Caribbean* were shot in St. Vincent, Dominica, and the Bahamas. These locations provided a backdrop of beautiful beaches, tropical sites, and ocean vistas. For more than ten years, *Survivor*, the reality TV game show, has been shot on location at "exotic" sites in countries including Borneo, Australia, Thailand, Fiji, Brazil, and Nicaragua. *The Hurt Locker* (2008) was shot in Jordan within miles of Iraq because director Katherine Bigelow wanted to give the film an authentic war-zone look and feel (Dawson 2010). Creative runaways are primarily motivated by a production firm's imperative to shoot "authentic" (or "realistic") representations of territory, culture, or people.

Cost-savings and the bottom line, not "creativity" and the pursuit of aesthetic realism, motivate "economic runaways." An economic runaway is an "outsourcing" job driven by a TNMC's relentless search for lower production costs. All TNMCs search for ways to cut the cost of producing entertainment. To minimize risk and maximize profitability, media companies shoot TV shows or films "on-location" in non-US media capitals that reduce a project's budget. Which place-specific factors motivate economic runaways? How do media capitals "pull" production firms in? Entertainment production moves to media capitals based in nation-states that offer a low-waged but skilled workforce, subsidies and tax breaks, desirable locational features, and favorable currency exchange rates.

Entertainment production gravitates toward low-cost but highly skilled clusters of cultural workers. Many US cultural workers are unionized; due to years of collective bargaining with media moguls, they are the recipients of decent wages and good benefits. TNMCs, however, view the gains of US cultural workers as an impediment to profit-maximization. They overcome this territorial limit by offshoring work to countries where the unions are weaker (or non-existent) and the cost of cultural labor is therefore much cheaper. Non-US cultural workers get paid significantly less than cultural workers in the US for doing identical tasks. Economic runaway productions are therefore a corporate response to and "a reflection of the high labor costs in Hollywood compared with a number of alternative locations" (Scott and Pope 2007: 1366). The main reason why studios runaway from LA to Toronto, for example, is because production costs "can be reduced [by] 20 percent" (Vang and Chaminade 2007: 413). Toronto's cultural workers are no less skilled than LA cultural workers; they get hired by LA's travelling studios because they are compelled and willing to settle for less pay.

Entertainment production also moves from LA to other media capitals because state cultural ministries, heritage departments, and media commissions offer subsidies and tax breaks. States use a combination of direct subsidies and indirect tax rebates to attract entertainment production, often dispatching cultural attaches and business leaders to LA to promote the "added value" of their country to Hollywood's executives. A direct subsidy is a state's allocation of public money to a production company. An indirect subsidy is a state's minimization or rebate of a portion of the production company's costs or taxable revenue. State subsidies help production companies to significantly reduce the cost of making entertainment. There are many examples. The German Federal Film Board (FFA), its Federal Film Fund (DFFF), and regional funders like Medienboard Berlin-Brandenburg, Filmstiftung NRW in North Rhine-Westphalia, Bavaria's FilmFernsehFonds Bayern, and Normedia release millions of dollars in annual subsidies to regional film and TV productions (Meza 2009). Italy gives runaway productions a 25 percent tax deduction up to $7 million (Vivarelli 2010). France gives a tax rebate of 20 percent to media companies; this cost saving recently lured Martin Scorsese to Paris to shoot parts of *Hugo* (2011), a film adapted from Brian Selznick's fictional homage to turn-of-the-century French filmmaker Georges Méliès. The United Kingdom offers a giant tax rebate program, handing up to 25 percent cash-back for films budgeted at $31.8 million or less. Australia, Belgium, Brazil, Canada, Denmark, Fiji, Iceland, New Zealand, South Africa, Sweden, and many more states offer big bundles of subsidies and tax breaks to attract travelling studios as well.

Entertainment production is drawn to media capitals with specific locational features. Temperate climates attract year-round runaway productions. "Studio complexes" that cater to the needs of traveling firms by offering a range of services are a major "pull factor" (Goldsmith and O'Regan 2003, 2005, 2007; Scott and Pope 2007). Goldsmith and O'Regan (2003) state that:

There has been something of a recent vogue internationally for large-scale studio complexes comprising sound stages, construction workshops, production offices, perhaps a watertank and backlot, and a number of tenant or related service companies enabling considerable amounts of work on a project to be conducted on a single site. Studio complexes with multiple sound stages capable of meeting the production needs of high-budget and blockbuster production while simultaneously servicing telemovie, television series or advertising production are springing up or being talked up around the globe. Existing facilities are undergoing extensive and often extremely costly refurbishments to remain technologically competent and internationally competitive. (7)

Studio complex development is big business in the NICL. States and investors seem to believe that "if we build studio complexes, production companies will come." In Italy, Rome's Cinecitta Studios and LA-based Montana Artists Agency recently co-financed the establishment of Italo facilities. With thirty soundstages and a 300-acre back-lot, it is one of Europe's largest studio complexes (Vivarelli 2010). In Canada, Toronto-based Comweb Corp built a $20 million studio complex that "serves as a hub for [entertainment] production and related services" (Punter 2010). In cities across the United Kingdom, old military bases and industrial production zones are being renovated and converted into backdrops for spectacular action films. *Clash of the Titans* (2010) was shot at Longcross Studios, once a tank-testing site in southwest London. The Gotham City scenes of *The Dark Knight* (2008) were shot in an old warplane hangar based in a North of London village called Cardington. Though the production companies behind these films had to bring their own equipment, facilities, and services, the UK stages were approximately 80 percent cheaper to rent than those in LA (Dawtrey 2010). In the media capitals of Canada, Australia, New Zealand, Mexico, the Czech Republic, Romania, and South Africa, studio complexes are built to lure entertainment production contracts away from LA.

Entertainment production also runs away from LA to media capitals with favorable currency exchange rates. An exchange rate is the rate at which one national currency may be converted into another. States that have weak currencies relative to a strong US dollar attract production companies that are looking to get more bang for their buck. When the currency of a non-US state is at par with or worth more than the US dollar, the financial incentive to offshore is diminished. For example, when the Canadian dollar was worth three-quarters of the US dollar in the mid-1990s, US firms moved from LA to Vancouver, Toronto, and Montreal to produce TV shows and films. When the Canadian dollar rose to become worth approximately the same as the US dollar, runaway productions to Canadian cities slightly declined (CFTPA 2008). By the fall of 2007, "it was no longer economically advantageous based on currency exchange rates for US productions to film North of the border" (Weeks 2010: 94). Other countries have seen their status as a runaway location decline because of the flux of abstract global financial transactions and exchange rate fluidity. The rise of the Australian dollar against the US dollar, for example, "increased the costs of shooting on Australia's Gold Coast, making it a less attractive location for TV production" (Ward and O'Regan 2007: 178). In the NICL, the ability of local media capitals to attract travelling studios is at the mercy of ever-fluctuating finance capitalism.

BOX 4.3

TWILIGHT: NEW MOON (2009) AND *TWILIGHT: ECLIPSE* (2010)

AS "RUNAWAY PRODUCTIONS"

Twilight is a popular entertainment franchise adapted from Stephanie Meyer's super-natural romance fantasy novels. *Twilight* is not a distinctly "American" entertainment franchise: firms, states, and workers beyond the territorial borders of the US were drawn into *Twilight*'s manufacture. Summit Entertainment, *Twilight*'s production company, is headquartered in Santa Monica, California, but it also has offices in London. Summit is not owned by a distinctive US business class, but by transnational media entrepreneurs including Bernd Eich Rehovot (a German), Arnon Milchan (an Israeli), and Andrew G. Vagna (a Hungarian). *Twilight*'s lead male actor was not sourced from the US star system: actor Robert Pattinson was recruited from London to play the heartthrob vampire, Edward Cullen. *Twilight* (2008) was shot in the US, in Portland Oregon (the city was used as a "body double" for Forks, Washington, USA). But the first and second parts of *The Twilight Saga*—*New Moon* (2009) and *Eclipse* (2010)—were shot in Vancouver, one of the largest media capitals in North America (Gasher 2002; Tinic 2004, 2005). Nicknamed "Hollywood North," Vancouver's entertainment industry annually generates more than a billion dollars. Hundreds of feature films and TV shows have been shot in Vancouver, including *Tron: Legacy* (2010), *The A Team* (2010), *Night at the Museum 2* (2009), *The Day The Earth Stood Still* (2008), *Juno* (2007), *X-Men 3* (2006), *Fantastic Four* (2005), *Battlestar Galactica*, and *The L Word*. In 2010, $317,825,454 was spent on entertainment production; $277,366,474 of that total came from foreign production companies (British Columbia Film Commission 2011). Summit Entertainment produced *New Moon* and *Eclipse* in Vancouver because of state subsidies, currency rates, and locational features (climate, studios, and landscapes).

Summit Entertainment took advantage of generous British Columbia (BC) tax credits. The BC Film Commission offers a 33 percent tax credit to foreign companies which hire BC cultural workers, a 6 percent tax credit to companies that shoot scenes outside of BC's core production zone, a 17.5 percent tax credit to firms that hire BC digital animation or visual effects services, and a 16 percent tax credit for the total wages a company pays to Canadian workers. Summit Entertainment capitalized on a beneficial currency exchange rate as well. Vancouver was scouted as a possible shooting location for the first *Twilight* film (2008), but Portland, Oregon, was selected instead because of the high Canadian dollar value. When the Canadian dollar declined, Summit Entertainment re-located *New Moon* and *Eclipse* to Vancouver. "With the position the Canadian dollar is in right now, we've been able to have another kick at the can, and we've been successful. So here it is," enthused Joan Miller, commissioner of the Vancouver Island North Film Commission (cited in The Canadian News 2009). Summit Entertainment was also attracted to Vancouver's location-specific features. Vancouver is 1,072 miles from Los Angeles and shares the same time zone. This temporal and locational proximity made it easy for creative executives to coordinate and collaborate with workers in Vancouver. Additionally, *New Moon* and *Eclipse* were shot in Vancouver because of its advanced studio complexes including Vancouver Film Studios (VFS), Lions Gate Studios, Bridge Studios, and North Shore studios (Will 2009). Vancouver's mild climate, lush forests, cloudy skies, and mountains were also attractive to Summit Entertainment. Following the shooting of *New Moon*, Bill Bannerman, the film's co-producer, said: "The weather is perfect for us: rainy, dismal, in the sense of the visuals, the mist on the ocean, the cloudiness, the erratic wind activity [. . .] Everything is exactly what it should be" (cited in Netherby 2009). In sum, *New Moon* and *Eclipse* are examples of economic and runaway "runaway productions" from LA to "Hollywood North."

INTERNATIONAL CO-PRODUCTIONS

Another important kind of entertainment production in the NICL is the international co-production: a media policy and business arrangement between two or more states and media corporations committed to the production of a TV show or film that intends to circulate in two or more national markets. International co-productions occur when media corporations from two or more different states agree to "collaborate and pool goods, rights or services" in order to produce a film or TV show that "either of the co-producers alone would find difficult to achieve in any other way" (Enrich 2005: 2). A co-production is when two or more media corporations and their "home" states collaborate on the production of a single entertainment product that will be distributed and marketed in two or more national markets. In the world system, NMCs from different countries are partnering up with each other to make popular entertainment products. International entertainment co-productions are an increasingly popular media policy and business strategy. For example, *Snow Cake* (2006), an independent drama about the friendship between an autistic women and a man traumatized by a car accident, was a co-production by Toronto-based Rhombus Media and London-based Revolution Films. *Silent Hill* (2006) is Canadian-French-Japanese tripartite film co-production based on the survival horror video game released by Tokyo-based Konami. *Blindness* (2008), a film adapted from Portuguese author José Saramago's novel about a mass epidemic of blindness and total social breakdown, was co-produced by Canada (Rhombus Media Inc.), Japan (Bee Vine Pictures), and Brazil (02 Films). *The Bang Bang Club* (2010), a film about four photojournalists who document the transition from apartheid in South Africa, was co-produced by Canada (Foundry Films, The Harold Greenberg Fund), Germany (Instinctive Film), and South Africa (Out of Africa Entertainment). *Snow Flower and the Secret Fan* (2011), a film based on Chinese-American author Lisa See's novel by the same name, was co-produced by IDG China Media of Shanghai, News Corporation's Fox Searchlight, and LA-based Big Feet Productions, which is owned by Wendi Deng Murdoch (wife of Rupert Murdoch) and Florence Low Sloan. The tragic-comedy *Eternity Water* (2011) was co-produced by Germany's X-Filme Creative Pool, Russia's Studio FAF, and Israel's Evanstone Films. *Mongol: The Rise of Ghengis Khan* (2007), *The Last Station* (2009), *Another Saturday*, and *Baikonur* (2011) resulted from collaborations between German and Russian companies. The award-winning *Gangor* (2011) is a Bollywood-Italian co-production. US-based Columbia Pictures (owned by Japan-based Sony), co-produced the 2010 remake of *The Karate Kid* with the PRC's state-owned China Film Group Corporation. *Wonders of the Universe* is a series of science TV programs co-produced by the UK and the US. In sum, film and TV show production is coordinated by many media firms across many different countries.

Though entertainment co-productions have recently increased in popularity, they have been happening for at least sixty years. Lee (2007) notes that "the practice of co-productions among different national media industries has a long history both in the East and West" (6). Following World War II, France and Italy signed the first international co-production agreement as a means of rebuilding their national cinemas, which had been destroyed during the war. By the mid-1960s, many European states were co-producing films (Guback 1969). In the early 1970s, Hong Kong and Taiwan media firms started co-producing kung fu films with support from US capital. Nigeria and Ghana have been co-producing films with old imperial industries since the 1970s too (Diawara 1987). In 1980, India's National Film Development Corporation co-produced *Gandhi* (1982) with UK-based Goldcrest Films. There were more than sixty-six bi-lateral co-production treaties established between 1950 and 1994 (Taylor 1995) which supported thousands of co-productions (Kraidy 2005: 101). From the mid-1990s to the present day, industry trade journals and magazines report an increase in international film and TV co-productions. "TV co-ventures thriving as global economy dictates partnerships," declares one headline (Binning 2010). In 2007, co-productions made up over 30 percent of the films produced "in most European countries" (Morawetz et al. 2007: 422). Between one-third and one-half of all film productions by the major media capitals of the European Union are co-productions (WTO 2010). In 2006 and 2007, seven feature film co-production projects occurred between Canada and China (Canada China Business Council 2008). In 2008, 43 percent of films released by Morocco's screen industry resulted from international co-productions with Tunisia, Mali, Algeria, Chad, Egypt, Senegal, France, Germany, and Canada (Euromed 2008). In the first six months of 2011, Hollywood studio applications for equity co-production deals with the powerful China Film Co-Production Corporation rose by 30 percent (Coonan 2011).

There are two types of international co-productions: *equity co-productions* and *treaty co-productions*. Equity co-productions usually happen between US-based TNMCs and non-US based NMCs. Treaty co-productions happen between non-US states and NMCs under a treaty, or international legal agreement, which governs the relationship. "Equity co-productions constitute a strategic and temporary partnership between two or more companies, driven by the search for maximal profits and usually not eligible for treaty status" (Kraidy 2005: 101). They "do not directly involve issues of cultural policy and national identity" (Kraidy 2005: 101). Treaty co-productions are "formal partnerships concluded under the auspices of national governments" and bring together "artists, technicians, financiers" and "government officials from two or more countries" (Kraidy 2005: 102). They are "formal affairs that fall in the realm of international relations" and involve issues of cultural policy and national identity (Kraidy 2005: 102). The US is home to the largest TNMCs, but has no co-production treaties with other states. Many other states are home to NMCs and boast many of co-production treaties with other states (Pendakur 1990:221).

Although the US has no co-production treaties, TNMCs based there regularly finance the production of films and TV shows made elsewhere. Equity or venture co-productions occur when a US-based TNMC co-finances the production of a TV show or film by an NMC in another country, often in return for distribution rights to the finished entertainment product. Since making high-quality entertainment products is very expensive, non-US-based NMCs often look to US-based TNMCs for financing. In exchange for financing, the contributing TNMCs get the international distribution rights to the finished TV show or film (Gulder 2011). *Flashpoint*, for example, is an equity co-production by US-based CBS Corporation and Canada-based CTV. Other examples of equity TV co-productions between US-based TNMCs and Canadian NMCs include CBS/CTV's *The Bridge*, NBC/CTV's *The Listener*, and ABC/Global

TV's *Rookie Blue*. In 2011, Entertainment One, a Canadian production company, secured financing for *The Firm*, a TV series based on the John Grisham novel, from three sources: Canada-based Shaw Media, US-based NBC Universal, and US-based Sony International Networks. As a result of this collaboration, Entertainment One secured the financing to produce a high-quality TV drama. Shaw Media-owned Global TV got the Canadian distribution rights, NBC Universal got the US distribution rights, and Sony Entertainment's Axion got the distribution rights for 125 other countries (Krashinsky 2011). News Corp's Fox International provided the finance for AMC's zombie drama, *The Walking Dead*. In return, it got the international distribution rights to this globally popular TV show. Equity co-productions infuse cash into production companies so that they can produce TV shows with high production values; the financing entities then get distribution rights and content to disseminate via all of the media platforms they own.

Whereas equity co-productions usually involve amicable relations between US-based TNMCs and non-US NMCs, co-production treaties are used by non-US states and NMCs to economically and culturally counter the global dominance of US-based TNMCs. Treaty co-productions happen when two or more NMCs from two or more different states come together to collaboratively produce an entertainment product with financial assistance from host states. Many states share interdependent co-production treaties. Since 1986, Australia has co-produced 131 films and TV shows with treaty partners in the United Kingdom, Canada, Italy, New Zealand, Ireland, Germany, China, Singapore, and South Africa. The European Convention on Cinematographic Co-Production, ratified in 1992, paved the way for over fifty co-production treaties between European states. Canada has co-production treaties with more than fifty states too. South Africa has co-production treaties with Canada, Italy, Germany, the United Kingdom, France, Australia, and New Zealand. South Korea has co-production treaties with France and New Zealand. In 2011, India and New Zealand signed a co-production treaty. John Key, the New Zealand Prime Minister, said:

> India is a rapidly rising player in the region, and we want to build on our already strong cultural and economic ties [. . .] This Agreement will also offer greater certainty to investors looking to fund New Zealand-India film co-productions. (cited in Goundry 2011)

Since 2011, the Russian Cinema Fund (RCF)—a state subsidizer with an annual budget of $88.3 million—has been courting co-production treaties with many countries and, in 2012, it signed an agreement with Germany (Wiseman 2011).

Co-production treaties refer to official "agreements between two or more national governments to create rules for collaborative [entertainment] projects to qualify for subsidies and fulfill quota restrictions in each country" (Miller et al. 2005). A co-production treaty is basically a legal framework which establishes regulations for a co-production process and governs the creative and business conduct of all participating NMCs. While the specific details of co-production treaties vary, treaties intend to ensure that creative, financial, and technical contributions and benefits will be shared among participants. Co-production treaties are based on the notion of reciprocity. They encourage a balance or symmetrical exchange of financial and creative input between participants. The treaty covers aspects of entertainment production such as concept development (who will write the script?), financing (how much money will each state and NMC commit to the project?), production (where will the film or TV show be shot? Where will the soundtrack be composed? Where will post-production happen?), distribution (will both country-specific NMCs share the right to distribute the finished entertainment product? In which national markets?), division of labor (who will direct the film or TV show? Which national stars will be cast? How many cultural workers from each participating country will be hired?), filming locations (what local or national places or spaces will be shot? Which specific sites will be available as backdrops?), and language (which language will the TV show or film be in?). If the participating NMCs accept and meet the treaty co-production's terms of agreement, their production gains "national status." "National status" guarantees that the participating NMCs will be supported by each firm's home and host state. So long as the participating NMCs abide by the terms and conditions of the co-production treaty, they gain "national status" and access to state subsidies, tax credits, or tax breaks.

There are powerful economic motivations underlying the participation of NMCs in treaty co-productions (Hoskins and McFadyen 1993). First, co-production treaties allow two or more NMCs to pool their financial resources in an attempt to establish a production budget comparable to those wielded by TNMCs. NMCs are often unable to raise the necessary financing for the production of high-quality TV shows or films, putting them at a competitive disadvantage. The treaty co-production establishes a co-financing arrangement that allows both partners to benefit. Second, co-production treaties give participating NMCs access to financial support from at least two states, so long as their entertainment product counts as "national content" in each country. State subvention (direct and indirect subsidies) helps participating NMCs reduce production costs. Third, co-production treaties grant each participating NMC access to the other's market by establishing bi-national distribution linkages and cross-national under-standing of the local specificities of each country's home audience. Fourth, treaty co-productions may grant participating NMCs access to a "culturally proximate" third country market. Many European NMCs, for example, co-produce TV shows and films with Canada because they want to access the US market. Fifth, treaty co-productions represent a learning opportunity for the above the line and below the line workers involved. Creative, corporate, and technical knowledge is often shared or transferred through co-production initiatives. Sixth, treaty co-productions are an important risk reduction strategy for NMCs. They spread the financial risk of making entertainment between a number of states and firms. Seventh, treaty co-productions may provide one participating NMC with access to cheap labor in the country in which the partnering NMC is headquartered. Eighth, treaty co-production deals may give NMCs access to attractive filming locations.

While NMCs exploit the economic opportunities associated with treaty co-productions, states support treaties to achieve economic and media policy goals (Jaeckel 2001). Selznick (2008) argues that states perceive treaty co-productions as a way to "enhance a national media industry (by allowing the country to identify itself with a larger budget production) and national culture" (6). Policy-makers fixated on GDP say that treaty co-productions benefit the national culture industry and help it develop into an international competitor. In this respect, international co-productions

Canada is one of the world's international co-production leaders. Canada's first co-production treaty was signed with France in 1963. Today, Canada boasts media co-production treaties with more than fifty countries. Over the past ten years, Canada has co-produced nearly 800 films and TV shows with fifty countries such as the United Kingdom, France, Germany, Australia, Venezuela, Mexico, Ireland, Denmark, Poland, India, China, Greece, and South Africa. In 2008, forty-four television co-production projects and fourteen theatrical film co-production projects were undertaken by Canada. Recent examples of co-productions include: *Barney's Version* (a Canadian-Italian co-production based on the novel of the same title by Canadian literary star Mordecai Richler), *Splice* (a Canadian-French co-production about human-animal DNA mixing), *Silent Hill* (a Canadian-Japanese-French co-production based on the Japanese video game), and *The Tudors* (Canadian-Irish co-production, based on the life and romances of King Henry VIII, during his reign in England).

Telefilm Canada, of the Canadian Department of Heritage, administers the co-production application process and the terms and conditions of co-production agreements. Telefilm Canada's rationale for audio-visual co-production is as follows:

> Co-production agreements enable Canadian and foreign producers to pool their creative, artistic, technical, and financial resources in order to co-produce films and television programs which are granted domestic status in their respective countries. These agreements provide producers increased access to funding and markets, therefore reducing the risks associated with the increasingly high costs of audiovisual productions. These bilateral agreements also help strengthen the audiovisual industries in each country, reinforce international alliances in the cultural sector, and promote Canadian culture abroad.

Canadian international co-production activities generate economic activity valued at close to an average of $535 million a year; the Canadian state views co-productions as a national economic development strategy, a way to represent Canadian culture to Canadians, and a means of promoting Canadian national culture-commodities worldwide.

are used by states to develop their media capitals (Jaeckel 2001:155). Co-productions attract foreign direct investment (FDI), spread the financial risk of entertainment assemblage between NMCs, create jobs for cultural workers, attract tourists, stimulate creative clusters, and give participating NMCs access to distribution networks in international markets. Policy-makers concerned with protecting or promoting local or national culture perceive treaty co-productions as a way to induce national culture industries to make high-quality films and TV shows which represent local or national cultures.

Treaty co-productions involve economic, political, and cultural negotiations between all stakeholders. Making a single TV show or film that will travel well between at least two countries is challenging. Treaty co-productions compel NMCs to make entertainment products that will resonate with the presumed tastes and preferences of viewers in two or more countries. Coordinating cultural workers from two or more different states also poses challenges for NMCs. At the same time, the finished entertainment product must be fit for broadcast or screening in two or more countries, which means that it must support each participating state's media policy regime. But this can be difficult, as no two states have identical media policy frameworks (see Chapter 3). Some states support hyper-commercial branded film content; others ban product placements. Some states forbid the presentation of nudity in prime-time television; others welcome it. All NMCs that co-produce entertainment try to create a product that will fulfill the particular media policy stipulations of the participating states. For these reasons, and many more, international entertainment production under a co-production treaty is difficult.

BOX 4.5

INTERNATIONALLY CO-PRODUCED FILMS: *BABEL* (2006), *CHANDNI CHOWK TO CHINA* (2009), AND *DISTRICT 9* (2009)

Lee (2007) says "The changes from a national to a transnational production mode in media industries reconfigure their industrial operations, as well as transform the textual qualities of the final products." (6–7). How are the texts of entertainment being transformed by co-productions? What kinds of texts do international co-productions create?

Some co-productions lead to texts that express a post-national, cosmopolitanist, and hybrid culture which mixes cultural referents, styles, and images from several different countries. Lee (2007) says "co-productions resemble and best reflect the mode of larger inter-national and interpersonal interactions of the world that we live in" and drive "us to think beyond the boundaries that we draw, the space that we occupy, and the ideas or ideologies that we hold on to" by "connecting the entire globe as one imaginary mega-community" (7). Furthermore, co-produced films and TV shows "offer cultural amalgams where we witness the encounter of universality and the particularities of human experiences and the coexistence of history and contemporaneity" (Lee 2007: 7). At best, co-produced films and TV shows represent interstitial spaces and links between the global and local, foreign and domestic, and national and international spheres to encourage a deeper understanding of self and other.

Babel (2006), directed by Alejandro González Iñárritu and written by Guillermo Arriaga, is exemplary. *Babel* is an international equity co-production between companies from many countries: Paramount Pictures, Paramount Vantage, Anonymous Content and Media Rights Capital (US-based), Zeta Film (Mexico-based), and Central Films (France-based). Below the line workers in Japan, Morocco, Mexico, and elsewhere contributed to the film. *Babel* was shot on location in numerous cities: Tokyo, Ibaragi, and Tochigi (Japan), Casablanca and Ouarzazate (Morocco), Sonora, Tazarine, Tijuana, and Tecate (Mexico), and San Diego and San Ysidro (California, US). The film conveys many languages: English, Arabic, Spanish, Japanese, Japanese sign language, Berber, and Russian. It stars an ensemble multi-national cast: Brad Pitt (US), Cate Blanchett (Australia), Peter Wright and Harriet Walter (United Kingdom), Claudine Acs and Driss Roukhe (Morocco), Adriana Barraza and Gael García Bernal (Mexico), and Rinko Kikuchi, Kōji Yakusho, and Satoshi Nikaido (Japan). *Babel* is a multi-narrative drama which unfolds across different places, time zones, and experiences. It attempts to balance representations of the particular and the universal by emphasizing the similarities and differences, connections and disconnections between many people living in an increasingly interdependent yet fundamentally unequal world system (Smith 2010). Critically acclaimed, *Babel* (2006) conveys the complex connectivity in and between worlds, both concrete and imagined. The most interesting co-produced entertainment media conveys bi-national, tri-national, and multi-national experiences and aesthetics which destabilize the presumed naturalness of nation-ness and showcase the complex connections and cultural disjuncts appropriate to the contemporary world.

At worst, co-productions result in texts that appeal to "the lowest common denominator of cultured interest with little hope for broad social or political resonance" (Halle 2002: 33). In the European context, co-produced entertainment is pejoratively called "Europudding" (Selznick 2008: 23–24). The mixing and melding of directors, actors, places, styles, and cultural elements raises fears that local or national particularity, uniqueness, and genuine difference are being eroded (Betz' 2001; Laborde and Perrot 2000: 106). Tinic (2003) claims that co-productions sometimes lead to texts which express a "hodgepodge type of production" that attempts to "characterize cultural elements of all nations and thereby reflect none" (183). By fusing too many different cultural references together, these texts try to please everyone, but ultimately resonate with no one. The result is indecipherability (Halle 2002). Pudding, hodgepodge, and hybrid TV shows and films represent a postmodern global pastiche of vulgar cultural stereotypes.

Chandni Chowk to China (2009) is an example of co-produced cultural pudding text that failed to please investors and viewers. This action-comedy-adventure-drama-fantasy-musical was touted as a Hollywood-Bollywood co-production. It was co-financed and co-produced by US-based Warner Brothers Pictures and India-based R.S. Entertainment, People Tree Films, and Onion Films. It was shot in Thailand, India, and China. It was directed by Bollywood's Nikhil Advani and stars Indian martial arts actor Akshay Kumar, Denmark-born but Indian super-model Deepika Padukone, and Chinese action star Chia Hui Liu. Hindi, Cantonese, and English languages are spoken in the film. *Chandni Chowk to China*'s production budget was $12 million. Worldwide, it grossed about $13.5 million, paying its owners back about $1.5 million. The film was panned by critics and viewers. Internet Movie Database (IMDb) awarded it 4.2 out of 10. Rotten Tomatoes rated it 44 percent. The *Hindustan Times* reviewer Khalid Mohamed (2009) said the film was a case of "too many Bros spoiling the broth." Nkhat Kazmi, of *The Times of India*, said "The Film is low on both IQ and EQU [. . .] the story rambles incoherently [. . .] and there is no emotional connect with any of the characters." Steven Rea (2009) of *The Philadelphia Inquirer* stated that "Chandni Chowk is entertainingly goofy for about 30 minutes. And then, for the next two hours-plus, it's agony." Negative reviews portray *Chandni Chowk to China* as unpopular cultural hybridity.

The most commercially successful co-produced texts avoid explicit references to national cultures. Too often, the cultural value of co-produced entertainment is judged according to realist aesthetic criteria which privileges the representation of particular and universal experiences and/or national and transnational identities. NMCs, however, know that co-produced entertainment that too boldly asserts a cultural identity or entails a hodgepodge of two or more identities will minimize their product's transnational profit potential and appeal. To avoid the cultural discount and the cultural pudding effect, NMCs co-produce entertainment media that intentionally avoids the realist representation of national and hybrid cultures. They manufacture TV shows and films that viewers, regardless of their specific national location or identity, can identify with or enjoy. In this context, science fiction and fantasy genre TV shows and films are ideal for co-productions because they are not "closely tied to the social, political and linguistic experiences of a particular country" (Tinic 2010: 100). Science fiction and fantasy genre stories lend themselves to international co-production treaties (Cornea 2007; Selznick 2008: 35; Shimpach 2005).

District 9 (2009) is a great example of an internationally co-produced science fiction film. *District 9* was co-produced by NMCs in Canada, New Zealand, and South Africa. It was made by above the line and below-the-line cultural workers in the US, Canada, New Zealand, and South Africa. The film was directed, written, edited, and scored by Neill

BOX 4.5 (Continued)

Blomkamp (born in South Africa, but a Canadian citizen), Terri Tatchell, Julian Clarke, and Clinton Shorter. *District 9* was produced by the New Zealand-based global Hollywood icon Peter Jackson. The special effects were designed by Weta Workshop (New Zealand) and Image Engine (Canada). The film was shot on location in Chiawelo-Soweto, South Africa, an impoverished slum, an "uneven landscape [. . .] dotted with rubble, cesspools, and ramshackle buildings of concrete or tin" (Smith 2009). Like *Slumdog Millionaire*, a film whose production company hired impoverished children to play themselves, *District 9* cast some of the slum's residents as extras. Deprived of a basic income and access to theaters, they will likely never see their own performances. The film featured many South African actors too. *District 9*'s distributor is TriStar Pictures (Los Angeles, California). TriStar Pictures is owned by Columbia Pictures, a subdivision of the Columbia TriStar Motion Picture Group, which is controlled by Sony Entertainment, a subsidiary of Japan-based Sony. *District 9* is a co-produced entertainment commodity that expresses the new international division of cultural labor and complicates nationalist classification.

District 9 is about the landing (or hovering) of an alien ship in Johannesburg, South Africa. Unlike the plots of many blockbuster science fiction films (*War of the Worlds, Independence Day, Battle: LA*), the invading aliens do not wish to annihilate the human race, destroy every major city, or colonize earth. They are peaceful and initially welcomed by humans. The state, however, fails to establish a way of communicating with the aliens and integrating them into society as equals. The state subordinates the aliens to the status of animal-like second-class citizens ("Prawns") and segregates them into a ghetto slum called "District 9." There, they feed on garbage and live in abject poverty. Brutalized and harassed, these Prawns are the source of media moral panic, xenophobia, and mass resentment. Eventually, the state contracts a munitions corporation (Multinational United) to force the Prawns off of the land and relocate them to "District 10." The state wants to convert District 9 into a space of capital accumulation. The oppressed aliens befriend a human, who tries to help them. *District 9* can be read as a national allegory of South African apartheid and a contemporary or future-oriented allegory of the consequences of neoliberal capitalism: a planet of slums, race-class segregation in sprawling ghettoes, and hundreds of thousands of people reduced to desperate and humiliating subsistence rituals. As director Neil Blomkamp says, "I actually think Johannesburg [as portrayed in *District 9*] represents the future. What I think the world is going to become looks like Johannesburg" (cited in Smith 2009). As an internationally co-produced science fiction film, *District 9* is able to convey a nationally and globally resonant story without suffering the "cultural discount."

RUNAWAY AND INTERNATIONAL EQUITY CO-PRODUCTIONS: CRITICAL VIEWS

Do runaway and international equity co-productions between US-based TNMCs and non-US NMCs benefit or harm a country's national entertainment industry, cultural workers, and "culture"? Tinic (2004) argues that these cross-border productions entail "a contradictory process that at times limits the labor and resources invested in indigenous production but also provides the requisite capital and experience otherwise unavailable for domestic productions" (52). The proponents of runaway and international co-productions highlight a mutually beneficial power relationship between TNMCs and the host media capital. They say these productions break down national barriers between workers by enabling global-local creative collaborations, build economically sovereign entertainment industries, give expression to national culture, and contribute to the post-Fordist service economy. Critics of these productions emphasize an asymmetrical, imbalanced, and inequitable power relationship between TNMCs and local media capitals. They say that entertainment production in the NICL supports the profit interests of TNMCs at the expense of all national media capitals by transforming them into service-dependencies, watering down or wiping out the textual representation of place-specific cultural identities, disciplining and punishing unionized workers by encouraging a "race to the bottom," and transferring public wealth to private hands.

At best, a media capital's capture of a runaway production from LA upgrades and professionalizes the cluster's capacities, networks, and skills. "Service production helps local crews learn to produce according to industry-leading craft standards" (Davis and Kay 2010). By working with and learning from TNMCs, smaller media capitals may eventually grow large enough to compete with them and over time, gain independence from them. Recounting this optimistic argument, Klein (2004) states:

> perhaps we should see outsourcing and runaway productions as signs that foreign film industries are finally finding a way to make global Hollywood work for them. Instead of being merely consumers of Hollywood movies and unremunerated suppliers of Hollywood talent, these industries are becoming paid manufacturers of Hollywood movies. Hosting Hollywood productions may strengthen local film industries, as they build sound stages, invest in the latest camera and sound technology and develop the sophisticated digital post-production facilities that Hollywood movies require. These investments could provide local film industries with the infrastructural resources they need to make movies with both Hollywood-style production values and distinctive local content. (3)

Hopes of gradually building a strong and sovereign national entertainment industry through the strategic capture of runaway productions from LA are often dashed by those with more sober views. Johnson-Yale (2008), for example, notes an "embedded contradiction" (128) in a state's attempt to develop a strong and nationalistic entertainment industry that is independent of global Hollywood's major studios through temporary integration with them. Does the capture of runaway productions strengthen or weaken national cultural industries? Around the world, answers to this question are varied, and often contentious.

Media capitals prosper by producing, controlling, and exploiting copyrighted entertainment. Runaway and equity co-productions often integrate media capitals into global Hollywood as service providers, not as owners of copyrighted entertainment (Davis and Kaye 2010). Media capitals supply TNMCs with labor-power, but they do not reap long-term symbolic or financial benefits from what is produced. Intellectual property law ensures that TNMCs are recognized as the authors and owners of entertainment. Instead of focusing "inward" on the production of national entertainment, media capitals focus "outward" on competitions with others for production contracts. The resulting relation of service dependency with TNMCs deters domestic entertainment production "by absorbing resources that might otherwise have been devoted to it" (Davis and Kaye 2010). Media capitals co-produce what appears to be US entertainment for screens worldwide. They infrequently produce high-quality indigenous entertainment for local screens (Elmer 2002; Gasher 2002; Tinic 2005). Runaway productions may build up local production capacity, but they do not always lead to local copyright control. Toronto, Canada, and the Gold Coast of Australia, for example, capture many runaway productions, but these cities do not produce, own, or distribute much indigenous entertainment (Davis and Kaye 2010; Vang and Chaminade 2007; Ward and O'Regan 2007). *My Big Fat Greek Wedding* (2002), for example, was a Canadian equity co-production with the US. It was written by a Canadian and starred a Canadian actor, but it is not owned by a Canadian firm. HBO, Gold Circle Films, and MPH Entertainment control the film's copyright.

Media capitals co-produce a lot of entertainment with global TNMCs. Much of that entertainment does not represent the local or national specificity of the places in which it is shot. In fact, runaway productions and co-productions transform local and national places into US cities. Elmer (2002) describes this as the "body-double" effect: "As competition increases in the television and film industry, we can only assume that the use of landscape 'body-doubles'—cheaper locations used to stand in for more expensive spaces—will also increase" (431). Non-US cities are often cast as a "faceless, underpaid, 'stand-in' actor for American landscapes" (Elmer 2002: 431). These cities actively promote themselves to TNMCs as backdrops for stories about US places and cultures and designed for US viewers (Gasher 2002). In the NICL, cities compete for runaway productions by emphasizing their lack of distinctiveness. Cities promote themselves as a "Placeless" space (Lukinbeal 2004). Cities that do not closely resemble any specific place in the world and which can be easily shot as any place—most often the US—are attractive to TNMCs. Non-identity has become a locational selling point. As Scott and Pope (2007) argue:

> Foreign location production practically guarantees locational anonymity, thereby preventing the production location from communicating a place-specific look and feel, considered to be a hallmark of preeminent cultural cities such as Los Angeles, Paris or New York.

Tinic (2005) also argues that co-productions with the US do not lead to greater place-specific or national media representation. They build up the service sectors of a national culture industry and are fully supported by state cultural policy regimes, but paradoxically they make TV shows and films which tell stories about other places and people, or which tell stories with no places or people at all. Cultural policies built to contain the so-called threat of Americanization actually foster textual Americanization. Cross-border productions with US-based TNMCs often result in entertainment that represents America. Through co-production policies, "other nations' screen industries, which are mostly built on policy responses to external domination, may now, ironically, be enabling that domination" (Miller et al. 2004: 139). Many entertainment co-productions between US-TNMCs and non-US NMCs do not represent local or national cultural places, people, or themes.

Is the transformation of national media capitals into entertaining images of US cities a symptom of US cultural imperialism? The body double phenomenon represents the exceptional ability of TNMCs to territorialize in, appropriate, and re-make the landscapes of other countries in the US's image. Yet, "strong" US-based TNMCs do not *impose* body doubling to deliberately screen out and dominate "weak" non-US cultures (though this may be the ultimate effect). Yes, body doubling obliterates place-based cultural specificity, but a coercive political power relationship between the US and the rest does not lurk behind this industrial practice. State executives, business leaders, and workers in non-US media capitals consent to make-over their places into US cities for strategic economic reasons. They seems to care more about cash than the integrity of their locational cultures. Furthermore, US cities are body doubles too. Corporate executives believe that entertainment can be manufactured anywhere in the world. "Any place in the world"—including US cities—can be made-over to look like someplace else. TNMCs not only transform places outside of the US into fictional landscapes within the US, but also convert US domestic landscapes into foreign ones. In *The Kingdom* (2007), the Maricopa County Courthouse in Phoenix, Mesa, the Polytechnic campus of Arizona State University, and the Arizona desert are converted into Saudi Arabia, the US' oil-rich authoritarian ally.

In the NICL, all countries are becoming body doubles for other countries. Body doubling is fast becoming a generalized industrial practice. This worries cultural nationalists who believe that place-specific national symbolism is being watered down or wiped out. Cultural policy solutions are offered. Tinic (2005), for example, argues that

---

BOX 4.6

TORONTO AS A PLACELESS BODY DOUBLE

Toronto (Ontario, Canada) is a "body double" city. Toronto usually does not appear as Toronto in the entertainment commodities resulting from LA runaway productions. Toronto plays Chicago in *Our America* (2001), *Chicago* (2002), *The Grid* (2004), *Man of the Year* (2005), *Stir of Echoes: The Dead Spark* (2006), *A Raisin in the Sun* (2006), and *The Time Traveller's Wife* (2007). In *The Pentagon Papers* (2002) and *True Confessions of a Hollywood Starlet* (2007), Toronto stands in for Los Angeles; it plays San Francisco in *Monk: The Series* (2002). *Hairspray* (2006) was set in Baltimore, Maryland, but filmed in Toronto. In *Assault on Precinct 13* (2004) and *Four Brothers* (2005), Toronto is a body-double for Detroit. Toronto is made over into Philadelphia in *History of Violence* (2004) and *Diary of the Dead* (2006); it is Pittsburgh in *Land of the Dead* (2004). In *Death to Smoochy* (2001), *Harold & Kumar Go to White Castle* (2003), *Dark Water* (2004), *Get Rich or Die Trying* (2005), *The Path to 9/11* (2005), *Jumper* (2006), *The Echo* (2007), *The Incredible Hulk* (2007), and *Grey Gardens* (2007), Toronto is a simulacrum of New York City. In more than six-hundred entertainment productions that were offshored to Toronto between 1999 and 2006, Toronto appeared "as itself" in only about 5 percent of them. In the other 95 percent, Toronto was transformed into place-specific locations in thirty-four other jurisdictions, mainly in the US (Davis and Kaye 2010). Between 2001 and 2007, Toronto housed more than two-hundred TV shows and film shoots by US production companies; a mere twenty of those two-hundred entertainment products represent Toronto as Toronto. Only *Degrassi: The Next Generation* (2001–2006) is well known, and it was an international co-production, not an offshoring job. Toronto's identity as a placeless body double, however is fully endorsed by the Toronto Film & Television Office, whose website offers "Diverse locations to suit your script; Toronto has doubled for New York, Boston, Washington, Chicago and other US locales."

Canadian content regulations are needed to "stipulate that stories [emerging through runaway TV productions] must draw on the sociocultural specificities of places within the nation. In brief, 'place' must be acknowledged rather than erased for content to qualify as 'national' " (161–162). Weeks (2010) believes runaway productions to cities in Canada and elsewhere not only deprive Canadian and transnational viewers of entertainment featuring familiar and place-specific imagery, but also distort the "authenticity" of America:

> Hollywood is reshaping what America looks like through how it chooses to represent American cities, towns and rural areas on film. As a result, the American seen on the big and small screens is not necessarily authentically American, leading to confusion or even disillusionment with the product. (100)

For Weeks (2010), body doubling is bad for everyone: "[W]hen these culturally important visual products no longer accurately represent the places in which Americans and Canadians live, both societies are critically harmed" (101).

By saying body doubled entertainment harms society, critics such as Weeks (2010) presume that entertainment which conveys "accurate" and "authentic" representations of specific national places is "beneficial" to society. "National culture" is a problematic concept (as discussed in Chapter 3). Do viewers expect and want entertainment to provide "accurate" and "authentic" representations of national places? And how exactly will they benefit by seeing these representations? Media studies 101 teaches students that entertainment does not "reflect" reality but, rather, entails partial and selective constructions of reality. Critics of body-doubling seem to believe that entertainment could provide "accurate" and "authentic" representations of national places. Furthermore, they suggest that global entertainment *should* transmit "accurate" and "authentic" representations of nation-places to viewers. A value-judgment about the quality of entertainment is made: territorial realism is the moral criteria. A tacit claim about the purpose of entertainment follows: nationalist imagining. Accordingly, TV shows like *Law & Order*, which are set in New York City and shot in New York City, are "good." They help US citizens see themselves and the real life of their cities. TV shows about New York City but which are not shot there are "bad." They confuse US citizens and debilitate authentic nationalist imagining. "Good" TV shows do not puzzle viewers with unfamiliar sites; "bad" TV shows do.

Let's extend the argument. Marvel Entertainment Studios' action flick *The Incredible Hulk* (2007) is set in New York City, but this film was a runaway production to Toronto. Many Toronto locations—the University of Toronto, residential neighborhoods, and Yonge Street—were dressed up as New York City. An epic fight scene between The Hulk and The Abomination occurs in Manhattan, but this scene was shot on Yonge Street. Sam the Record Man, the Big Slice pizza store, and The Zanzibar strip-club—all seedy-chic Yonge Street landmarks—appear in the final cut. Torontonians would not be fooled by this makeover. New Yorkers would probably know that the backdrop of the climactic fight is not Manhattan. But critics of body-doubling would attack the "inauthenticity" of the scene, viewing it as causing "harm" to viewers in Toronto and NYC (and their respective national societies). Following this logic, *The Incredible Hulk* (2007) is a bad film because it does not accurately represent Manhattan, yet claims to do so. However, Canadian and US viewers of *The Incredible Hulk* (2007) were likely *not* attracted to the film because it claimed to feature Manhattan action scenes, but because they are fans of the comic book and TV ads stoked their desire to see gigantic computer-generated monsters smashing cities to rubble.

Nevertheless, critics of body doubling make an important point about the possible negative effects of the misrepresentation of distinct cultures and places. Co-productions between two or more non-US states also put distinctive local and national cultures and places under erasure too (Davis and Nadler 2009; Tinic 2005). By attempting to make a film or TV show that will travel well internationally. The co-producing media firms often neglect the representation of the two participating countries, and efface each participating state's distinctive geography and culture. The crime thriller *Eastern Promises* (2007), for example, is a Canada-UK co-production which received critical acclaim. Supported by Telefilm Canada and was directed by Canadian David Cronenberg, it is a story of Russian gangsters set in London; it contains no "distinctly" Canadian referents. *Splice* (2009) is Canada-France co-produced science fiction-horror film about a young scientist couple (Adrien Brody and Sarah Polley) who splice human DNA with animal genes to create a monster. Telefilm Canada subsidized this film and it was shot in Toronto and Hamilton (Canadian cities), but these cities are rendered placeless by the film. In 2005, Canada co-financed Thinkfilm's production of *American Soldiers*, a low-budget co-production shared by Canada and the UK's Alliance Atlantis film production arm, Momentum Pictures. The film is about US soldiers fighting "terrorist insurgents" in Iraq after an attack in 2004. The film was shot in Hamilton, in Ontario, Canada. Areas in Hamilton, a post-industrial city, were made over into a war-torn Iraq. In this co-produced film, Canada was used as a fictional stage for a controversial US-invasion of another country! These examples highlight a "central tension" between the cultural and economic priorities of co-production treaties: an entertainment product that is too local, regional, or national will not travel well, while an entertainment product that tries too hard to break out into the US and transnational market does so at the expense of regional and national specificity. Economic interests are regularly privileged over cultural goals in co-productions (Tinic 2005).

Discussions about the cultural politics of place-based representation in entertainment are important, but they are likely not as pressing to the workers employed to produce representations of national places. Getting a job probably matters more to cultural workers than a film's territorial realism or capacity to enable nationalist identification. While runaway productions may not contribute to a strong entertainment industry or result in "authentic" national imagery, they do create jobs for workers in host countries. Jobs lost by workers in the US due to offshoring are gained by workers with similar skills elsewhere. The generation of "new" creative jobs is argued to be a good thing. In these hard economic times, cultural workers want jobs, don't they? Runaway productions may also lead to a "halo effect" that benefits local economies by generating buzz about the media capital and jobs in hotels, restaurants, and other service sectors. Runaway productions do create jobs, but quantitative increases in cultural industry and service jobs tell us nothing about the quality of the jobs created. The idealized "creative class" employed by runaway productions may actually be a super-exploited "precariat" class (Ross 2008).

Due to neoliberal governance, the disorganization of unions, and the new managerial tactics that accompanied the shift from Fordist to post-Fordist regimes of accumulation, cultural industry jobs have become notoriously flexibilized, casualized, and precarious (Gill and Pratt 2008; Huws 2003, 2007; Miller 2010; Neff, Wissinger and Zukin 2005; Ross 2004, 2008, 2009; Ursell 2000). Runaway jobs from LA are no different; they do not provide cultural workers with long-term, secure, and lucrative careers. Runaway productions rely on temporary and contract-based work. When a runaway production arrives in a media capital, cultural workers might get hired. After these workers finish the job, their contracts often expire. Moving from one employment contract to the next may empower some workers with a sense of self-reliance and self-management but, over the long term, contractual work can be objectively disempowering. Young cultural workers "gift" their labor power to media firms as interns in hopes of securing a full-time job that rarely materializes. Minimum-waged jobs incoffee shops and retail stores are taken on by cultural workers who wait patiently for a cool and subjectively fulfilling creative contract to appear somewhere. When these idealized contracts fail to materialize, cultural workers find themselves systematically underemployed and needing to rely on credit cards and financial support from family members. Feelings of insecurity become normative. In response to these exploitative conditions, cultural workers may seek unionization. But runaway productions are no friend to unionized and militant cultural workers. In fact, in order to attract runaway productions, cultural workers are expected to disorganize themselves (by rejecting unionization and collective bargaining) and become more competitive (by accepting lower wages and becoming more flexible for employers). At the same time, and as result of their control of financing and distribution, the TNMCs that offshore work to production companies compel them to reduce the cost of production. This intensifies the exploitation of workers (they do more, in less time, and for less pay). Administered by TNMCs, runaway productions create part-time and often low-paying jobs, not lifelong and high-paying careers in the culture industry.

Runaway productions do not necessarily build a strong national entertainment industry or create good jobs. This has led many to question the net benefit of state subsidies to global Hollywood. Marxists might argue that state subsidies to global Hollywood are an act of "accumulation by dispossession," whereby public wealth is privatized (Harvey 2005). Neoliberal states accumulate public wealth through collective taxation and then dispossess citizens of this wealth by efficiently transferring it to the individual TNMCs which produce entertainment. Citizens partially co-finance runaway entertainment productions, but get no share of the control or the profit. Public wealth could "trickle down" to a democratically organized or publically owned media system, but instead it "trickles up" to TNMCs. In the era of austerity policies which promote deficit-cutting, lower state expenditures, and public service reductions, fiscal conservatives might view runaway subsidies as a waste of money. In many countries, citizens, businesses, workers, and policy-makers are debating future subsidies to global Hollywood. New Zealand's subsidization of blockbusters such as *The Lord of the Rings* trilogy (2001–2003) and *The Hobbit* (2012), for example, caused political controversy. Some argue that subsidizing these Peter Jackson films was essential for the development of New Zealand's cultural industry. Others say that the hundreds of millions of dollars in subsidies allocated to these big-budget films bankrupted the country (Chai 2010).

As global Hollywood integrates more media capitals, further political debates about the value of subsidies will likely occur. Citizens ought to participate in public debates about the allocation of resources (especially to TNMCs). At present, states subsidize TNMCs, not because a democratic consensus forged through the deliberative dialogue of citizens gives them the legitimacy to do so, but because they fear the consequences of not doing so. Many states view integration with global Hollywood's circuits of entertainment financing, production, and distribution as the prerequisite for competition with other states; "de-linking" is viewed as a recipe for economic calamity. The unintended consequence of integration with global Hollywood is a competitive "race to the bottom" between states, even the world's most economically and culturally "powerful" states. Here is the pattern: a media capital emerges in the NICL and offers lower wages and higher subsidies to TNMCs than LA does (Toronto and Vancouver, for example). Seeking a discount, the TNMC temporarily travels to that media capital to shoot TV shows and films, efficiently exploiting workers and absorbing the subsidies. A few more media capitals emerge and attempt to exceed the first one's attractiveness to TNMCs by providing even cheaper labor and ever-greater subsidies (the Gold Coast and London, for example). The TNMC moves once again, on to the newest "value-added" location. More media capitals emerge; they "up the ante," offering even lower waged workers and higher subsidies (cities in the Netherlands, New Zealand, Hungary, and South Africa, for example). Diminishing tax revenue and mounting job losses leads the State of California to offer production companies wages and subsidies comparable to those of the states that "drained" LA of Hollywood capital. This pattern repeats itself, over and over again, until every media capital in the NICL is integrated into global Hollywood, each under the thumb of TNMCs.

This "race to the bottom" is being universalized. Nation-states try to out-compete other nation-states, cities gear themselves to rival other cities, and municipalities attempt to undercut neighboring municipalities. Ruling parties—conservative or liberal—have internalized "common sense" assumptions about "competitiveness." Nation-states increasingly gear their regulatory agencies and cultural ministries to the maintenance of a "competitive" value-added place. Because TNMCs "invest" in the states that are most compliant with their profit-interests (i.e., "competitive"), states sweeten deals for them at the expense of worker rights and democracy. TNMCs "discipline both labor and the state, such that the latter is reluctant to impose new taxes, constraints or pro-worker policies in the face of possible declining investment" (Miller et al. 2005: 52). Clearly, runaway productions have served the profit-interests of TNMCs well. In the NICL, inter and intra-state competitions for runaway productions allow TNMCs to "reduce costs, increase flexibility, enter new markets and shift [financial] risk onto less powerful players without loss of control over the key creative, financial, distribution and marketing decisions, which remain in Hollywood" (Davis and Kaye 2010). While the "big" decisions—financing, marketing distribution, casting, and so forth—often do remain in LA, the TNMCs that shape these decisions are no longer tied to LA's territory or workers.

BOX 4.7
PRAGUE'S RACE TO THE BOTTOM

Following the 1989 Velvet Revolution and the collapse of the Soviet Union, the Czech Republic privatized its publicly owned Barrandov Studios and opened the domestic media market to foreign direct investment. A Prague-centered media elite established alliances with global Hollywood production companies. Prague captured numerous "runaway productions," including *Mission: Impossible* (1996), *The Bourne Identity* (2002), *The League of Extraordinary Gentlemen* (2003), *Alien vs. Predator* (2004), *Hellboy* (2004), *The Illusionist* (2005), *Casino Royale* (2006), *Babylon A.D.* (2008), *Chronicles of Narnia: The Lion, The Witch and the Wardrobe* (2009), *Wanted* (2009), and *G.I. Joe: The Rise of Cobra* (2009).

TNMCs shot these films in Prague for a number of reasons. Production companies minimized production costs by capitalizing on Prague's non-unionized and low-paid workforce (Davidson 2007). Prague set-builders are paid half as much as US set-builders. Czech extras are paid about $30 a day, while US extras get paid $100–150 a day. Production firms used Prague's studio complexes, including Barrandov Studios, Milk and Honey Films, and Stilking Films. They also rented out parts of Prague's beautiful geographical landscape (ancient castles and architecture) from the municipal government as "naturalistic" set pieces (Green 2003). The currency exchange rate was also attractive to US runaway production firms. For a short period, Prague's cultural industry grew by capturing runaway productions. Some journalists even described Prague as "Hollywood of the East" (Toumarkine 2004).

By 2008, this "Hollywood of the East" was facing intense competition from numerous other Eastern European states and nearly every state in the West. "Business in Prague has cooled down," said Ludmila Claussova of the Czech Film Commission. "2008 was quite bad in terms of the foreign films shot here—perhaps the worst year in a long time" (cited in Holdsworth 2009). The Czech Culture Ministry reported that, overall, runaway productions from LA to Prague had fallen between 2004 and 2010 (Tizard 2010). Why? The Czech Republic offered global Hollywood cheap labor, studio complexes, beautiful environments, and decent exchange rates. But this was not enough. TNMCs wanted subsidies too, which were not being provisioned. Thus, production companies started flying over Prague and landing in other countries such as Hungary, which offered greater subsidies. Fearing the economic downturn and following the advice of the "Prague industryites" who had "advocated a cash-back [to global Hollywood] policy for over a decade," the Czech state started offering a "20 percent refund on investment to producers of films that qualify, using cultural criteria and other factors" (Tizard 2010). In 2011, the Czech Republic Film Commission traveled to Los Angeles with a Czech government delegation led by Czech Minister for Foreign Affairs, Karel Schwarzenberg. There, Schwarzenberg met with TNMC executives to promote the new tax rebate. With more and more states offering "competitive" subsidies, Prague's star as the "Hollywood of the East" may be beginning to fade.

POLITICAL AND DISCURSIVE STRATEGIES FOR MAKING GLOBAL HOLLYWOOD A US "HOME"

Do runaway productions threaten Hollywood's economic dominance? The answer received depends upon the person asked and the definition of Hollywood they offer. When defined as a handful of TNMCs, "Hollywood" is stronger than ever. Between

2001 and 2008, global Hollywood's major studios accumulated unprecedented profits. In 2007, Hollywood's domestic box office was $9.63 billion; worldwide box office totals in that same year reached an all-time high of $26.72 billion (Theatrical Market Statistics 2007: 2). Wayne (2003) notes that "In virtually every country around the world Hollywood has increased the percentage of its films imported by foreign markets over the past 25 years" (90). Runaway productions profit the shareholders and CEOs of global Hollywood handsomely; their dominance is not in decline. When defined as a media capital clustered in LA and around Southern California, Hollywood continues to be a concentrated power "center for most entertainment financing, deal-making, marketing, and pre and post-production work" (Curtin 2003; Pope and Scott 2007; Scott 2004a; Ward and O'Regan 2007). Entertainment production tasks are being offshored, but this does not herald the end of LA as the largest and most powerful media capital. Most of the above-the-line managerial-administrative control of entertainment production remains in LA, the headquarters of global Hollywood.

LA-based cultural workers tell a different story. They face hard economic times due to the offshoring of entertainment production tasks to far-flung media capitals. US media unions, business groups, and local state officials worry that runaway productions are eroding Hollywood's industrial base. Numerous reports describe the decline, hollowing out, and eventual fall of an LA-based global Hollywood. A 2002 Center for Entertainment Industry Data and Research (CEIDR) report entitled "The Migration of Feature Film production from the US to Canada and Beyond Year 2011" claims that the US is "in imminent danger of suffering permanent, irreversible damage to its world renowned film industry." The report demands that the Department of Commerce take action through the World Trade Organization (WTO) against "anti-competitive" state subsidies. A 2010 Milken Institute study entitled "Film Flight: Lost Production and Its Economic Impact on California" similarly reports that runaway productions from LA to foreign media capitals have caused California to "lose" 10,600 entertainment industry jobs, more than 25,500 related jobs, $2.4 billion in wages, and $4.2 billion in total economic output since 1997. Entertainment that is either wholly or partially filmed in California has fallen sharply, from 272 productions in 2000 to 160 productions in 2008, as has California's share of North American employment in the entertainment industry, declining from 40 percent in 1997 to 37.4 percent in 2008 (McNary 2010). The Milken Institute's solution to the problem of runaway production is to *increase* subsidies and tax benefits to TNMCs in hopes of keeping them in Hollywood (McNary 2010). The recently formed "Bring Hollywood Home Foundation" even proposes to curb runaway productions from LA to other media capitals by adding cash to an existing five-year $500 million tax credit program and substantially lowering taxes for TNMCs (Carinacas 2010). Hollywood is now apparently competing with itself.

The CEIDR and Milken Institute reports address real material problems. Runaway productions do reduce the number of jobs available to LA-based below-the-line cultural workers. Runaway productions do pressure US cultural workers to become more competitive, which in this context, means working harder for less pay, lowering their expectations, and making "flexible" concessions to their employers, just as many of the non-unionized cultural workers in other countries do. Each report's proposed policy solution to the problem of runaway production, however, entails an incredibly limited but typically neoliberal understanding of the world. The CEIDR report calls upon the US government to dismantle "anti-competitive" and "trade distorting" foreign state subsidy systems by enforcing "free trade" laws. This strategy seeks to deprive non-US nation-states of the sovereign right to protect and promote their cultural industries and would ultimately open them up to further TNMC control. The Milken Institute Report calls upon the US government to build up a system of subsidies and tax breaks for TNMCs that rivals those of the other nation-states "competing" for runaways in the NICL. This strategy basically calls for the US to join the "race to the bottom" by beating other nation-states at their own game. Both policy recommendations lead to a similar outcome, TNMCs gaining more power over states and workers in the NICL. The proposed solutions to the problem of runaway productions are not solutions at all. They perpetuate the problem by serving the powerful interests of TNMCs.

In foreign affairs, the US government still promotes "free-trade" in audio-visual markets. Domestically, the US government has joined the "race to the bottom." As of 2011, almost every state in the US gives subsidies and tax breaks to TNMCs in the hope of keeping Hollywood in the US and making sure it stays there. In 2006, only Louisiana and New Mexico offered subsidies. Since then, other states—red and blue—have competitively followed. State-administered economic incentives established in order to capture Hollywood productions are not disinterested acts. They represent the power of TNMCs to maximize profits at the expense of US and non-US based cultural workers alike. They are the outcome of unequal social class power relations in the NICL. Instead of focusing on how TNMCs structure the NICL to favor their short-term profit-interests at the expense of the long-term material needs of cultural workers everywhere, the discourse of "runaway production" foments residual myths of national particularity in a period when the jet-setting CEOs who run global Hollywood really do not care about "nation." Class conflict between TNMCs and cultural workers is re-packaged as a vulgar nationalist contest for supremacy between territorially-bound states, industries, and workers.

Transnational class conflict is infrequently discussed by the many unionists, lobbyists, and journalistic critics of runaway productions. But that is exactly what is at stake in public disucissions about runaway productions. US cultural workers (and cultural workers elsewhere) face hard times because of the profit-maximization goals of TNMCs. From the mid-1980s to the present day, "production companies and the networks initiated a series of cost-cutting strategies that translated into an attack on labor, mainly on below-the-line workers such as technicians, extras and engineers" (Christopherson 2011). In addition to downsizing their operations, blaming unionized cultural workers for their financial woes, hiring precarious, self-employed and temporary cultural workers, and intensifying worker exploitation in the US over the past thirty years, TNMCs have wielded outsourcing as tool of class power. But instead of naming class power as a threat to the material wellbeing of workers, many commentators cultivate moral panic about the consequences of entertainment media outsourcing for "America" as a whole, pitting the US state against all other states and US cultural workers against workers elsewhere. Instead of challenging the class power of transnational media owners, commentators blame workers in Canada, Australia, or New Zealand for the precarious lives of US cultural workers. This predictably leads to a protectionist nationalist argument, not a transnational form of cultural class solidarity.

Protectionist arguments about the "natural" territorial home of Hollywood production being Los Angeles, California, are regularly parroted. Johnson-Yale (2010) insightfully argues that "[T]he discourse of runaway production has functioned as a regime of truth" (21). As it currently operates, the discourse represents and reinforces "a particular ideological worldview that constructs Hollywood as the best and most authentic producer of media and all other locations, both home and abroad, as criminal interlopers" (31). In fact, the history of entertainment production has been defined by mobility, not stasis. From the early twentieth century to the present day, production has moved from New York City to LA, to numerous US cities, and outward into the global arena. The discourse of runway production centers LA as the natural territorial home of Hollywood entertainment, defines entertainment production and products in national terms, supports counter-productive policy measures, mystifies the NICL's power relations, and establishes a nationalist containment strategy for deterring transnational class solidarity between cultural workers in the US media capital and those hired by TNMCs elsewhere.

For all of the above reasons, the very concept of "runaway production" should perhaps be abandoned. Newer concepts, such as "cross-border cultural production," which encompass "the expansion of production away from traditional centers, whether to other countries or to other locations within the same country" (Wasko and Erikson 2009: 1), may provide a more adequate view of the NICL because they deprive entertainment "production" of a natural territorial home to "runaway" from. That being said, the cross-border cultural production concept must tussle with the political and economic actors who make and re-make Hollywood a "home" in the US. For example, the Motion Picture Association of America (MPAA)—the lobby group that promotes the financial interests of TNMCS in the NICL—describes its goal of "Advancing a Unique American Industry":

> When people think of US film and television production, they tend to think of "Hollywood," New York and other leading American filmmaking communities. But increasingly today, film and television production is a nationwide growth engine that is bringing new jobs and economic opportunities to communities across the country. From Pontiac, Michigan, to Albuquerque, New Mexico, to Chicago, Illinois, to New Orleans, Louisiana, film and television production is lifting communities in all 50 states in our union today. We are a national community of 2.5 million creative professionals—costume designers to make-up artists, stuntmen to set builders, writers to actors—who work in all 50 states of our union. (MPAA 2011)

For the MPAA, the home of Hollywood entertainment production is every subsidizing state in the US, not just California or New York. The MPAA's discursive re-making of the US nation-state as the authentic home of entertainment production ignores the hundreds of emerging media capitals and thousands of cultural workers that contribute subsidies, studios, locations, and labor-power to global Hollywood's entertainment factory. Until powerful actors within and outside US borders stop politically and discursively defining Hollywood's home as "America," the "runaway production" concept will likely continue to have legs.

CHAPTER 5

Designing Global Entertainment Media

Blockbuster Films, TV Formats, and Glocalized Lifestyle Brands

INTRODUCTION: WHAT MAKES ENTERTAINMENT MEDIA GLOBALLY POPULAR?

What makes some TV shows and films more territorially mobile and transnationally attractive than others? Political-economists will likely answer this question by emphasizing the economic power of horizontally and vertically integrated US-based TNMCs to push their entertainment media into markets everywhere. Neoliberal proponents of "consumer sovereignty" (see Chapter 6) may say that entertainment media with "global legs" responds to and reflects what viewers in every country want. Political-economic and neoliberal explanations of the global popularity of certain media products privilege corporate control or sovereign consumer choice over a more nuanced analysis of how the textual form and content of entertainment media might be *designed* to be consumed in many countries. Undoubtedly, the control of production and distribution by TNMCs supports the global reach of certain TV shows and films. Viewer tastes and preferences matter, too. Between the "push" of TNMCs into media markets and the "pull" of nationally grounded consumers are "texts" which are designed to travel well between anything from ten to one hundred markets or more. What, then, makes a specific entertainment text globally popular?

Some scholars explain the global popularity of certain TV shows and films with reference to their distinctly "American" texts. Globally popular TV shows and films are said to reflect the unique qualities of US culture which inspire identifications from viewers in many different countries. Olson (1999), for example, argues that US entertainment media is globally popular because of "the capability of certain texts to seem familiar regardless of their origin, to seem a part of one's own culture, even though they have been crafted elsewhere" (18). Olson (2000) also says that US TV shows and films are globally popular because their texts transparently reflect the qualities of a universalistic American multi-culture, which can be easily identified with by viewers everywhere. "[B]y virtue of their ethnic diversity, the United States [. . .] produces media programming that is differentiated within and anticipatory of global market tastes" (11). The US is "particularly successful in exporting film and television" because it is a "microcosm of international audience taste" (6), which gives the US a "competitive advantage" (Olson 1999: 28). While Olson is correct to say that the global popularity of certain entertainment products can be partially explained with reference to texts, this argument is problematic. The claim that globally popular US TV shows and films reflect the multi-cultural life of the US nation relies upon a flawed mimetic theory of entertainment. US entertainment products may entail partial and selective *representations* (not reflections) of the nation, but most products are not realistic or deeply diverse.

In fact, the most globally popular US TV shows and films are fantasies. In 2009, the most globally popular prime-time US TV shows were *Heroes* (a science fiction TV show about people with supernatural powers), *Lost* (a mystery, science fiction drama about the survivors of a plane crash on an unknown island), *Prison Break* (an action crime prison drama about two brothers trying to escape prison), *Dexter* (a black comedy crime drama about a police murder analyst who is also a serial killer), *House* (a medical dramedy about a misanthropic doctor), *24* (a geopolitical action-thriller-drama about the national security state versus terrorism), *Desperate Housewives* (a comedy-drama about the domestic lives of suburban women), *Terminator: The Sarah Conner Chronicles* (a science fiction TV show based on *The Terminator* film trilogy), *Grey's Anatomy* (US medical drama), and *True Blood* (a horror, fantasy, erotic thriller about vampires and humans) (ADMIN 2009). The top ten highest-grossing global Hollywood films in 2010 were *Toy Story 3, Alice in Wonderland, Harry Potter and the Deathly Hallows Part 1, Shrek Forever After, The Twilight Saga: Eclipse, Iron Man 2, Tangled, Despicable Me*, and *How to Train Your Dragon* (Box Office Mojo 2011). These films are about talking Mattel toys, bored little girls chasing rabbits down holes, magical wizards with British accents, goofy green ogres, human vampire lust, comic book heroes, long-haired princesses, super-villains, and Viking children befriending dragons. These globally popular films are not based on realism or US multiculturalism.

Acland (2003) states that a "vital project for contemporary cultural theory" is understanding how the globally popular narrative is read (38–39). This chapter seeks to understand how TV shows and films are *written* by TNMCs to be transnationally popular in advance and in anticipation of specific viewers. Fu (2006) encourages scholars to extend political-economic explanations of the global presence of US entertainment media by examining "whether the content of productions from a major exporter like the United States is becoming increasingly multifaceted or globally textured [as opposed to one-dimensional and nationalistic]" (831). To this end, this chapter focuses on the business, textual encoding, and viewer-targeting strategies of TNMCs. TNMCs design entertainment commodities that are intended to travel well between national markets. This chapter examines three kinds of entertainment media texts that TNMCs design to be popular in two or more national markets: 1) global blockbuster event films; 2) global-national TV formats; and, 3) glocalized lifestyle brands. TNMCs profit-maximize by textually encoding or designing entertainment media to circulate in global, national, and transnational markets. This chapter links the popularity and profitability of entertainment products to the business, textual, and audience targeting strategies of TNMCs. It also examines the business and textual design strategies used by non-US NMCs to get their entertainment distributed within the US market.

Two important concepts employed in this chapter are the cultural discount and cultural proximity. The *cultural discount* refers to how an entertainment product "rooted in one culture and thus attractive in that environment, will have diminished appeal elsewhere as viewers find it difficult to identify with the styles, values, beliefs, institutions and behavioral patterns of the material in question" (Hoskins, McFayden, and Finn 1994: 367). Culturally discounted entertainment media is valued less by foreign viewers, who lack the cultural background needed to understand the product. When TV shows and films present cultural references that may only be easily understood by viewers in one country, this product will have a hard time crossing borders and appealing to many different viewers in many countries (Hoskins and Mirus 1988: 500). Culturally discounted TV shows and films may generate revenue for a firm in one national market, but will likely not do so in many national markets. For TNMCs, the cultural discount is an obstacle to transnational profitability. In order to overcome the cultural discount, TNMCs design specific types of entertainment media that are intended to travel well between many different national markets. *Cultural proximity* accounts for how viewers tend to prefer TV shows and films that are intended for people with similar cultural backgrounds, tastes, and preferences to their own (Straubhaar 1991). The "culturally proximate" audience is not defined by geographical or territorial proximity, but by similarities in language, history, culture, lifestyle, and taste. TNMCs presume that people may prefer entertainment media that represents their own culture or a similar one, and therefore they design culturally proximate entertainment to target a variety of culturally proximate audiences.

GLOBALLY POPULAR ENTERTAINMENT MEDIA:
THE BLOCKBUSTER EVENT FILM

The phrase "global popular entertainment" is derived from three words: "global," "popular," and "entertainment." According to the Oxford English Dictionary, "global" means "of or relating to the whole world"; "popular" refers to something "liked, admired, or enjoyed by many people or by a particular person or group" or cultural products "intended for or suited to the taste, understanding, or means of the general public rather than specialists or intellectuals"; "entertainment" refers to "an event, performance or activity designed to entertain others" or something that intends to provide "amusement or enjoyment" to others. Blockbuster films are the world's most genuinely globally popular entertainment media. They are designed to relate to the whole world, are liked, admired or enjoyed by many people in many countries, and are produced to suit the tastes and preferences of viewers with the goal of providing them with amusement and media corporations with profit. In what follows, the economic and textual characteristics of the blockbuster film are discussed.

The Economic Characteristics of the Blockbuster Film

The "blockbuster" is a film that boasts a huge budget, transnational audience, global marketing campaign, and massive return at the global box office. During World War II, the term "blockbuster" referred to the large bombs dropped by the US military on Germany and Japan. Today, "blockbuster" refers to spectacular entertainment dropped by TNMCs upon the world. The blockbuster film emerged in the 1950s when Hollywood studios were experiencing financial difficulties due to the Paramount Decree (1948). The state compelled studios to sell off their exhibition chains, ending an early form of horizontal integration. Hollywood's production-exhibition monopoly was challenged, while urban theater profits declined due to competition with network TV's captivation of suburbanites who found comfort in being entertained without having to leave their own homes. In response to financial difficulties, Hollywood studios explored a new business strategy in order to lure suburban TV viewers back to the theaters. They started producing fewer films, but much more expensive and spectacular films (White 1990). These "blockbuster" films helped Hollywood studios "differentiate the[ir] product from the supply of competing media such as television and helped revive the theater as a privileged place for the film experience and, more generally, high-quality entertainment" (Cucco 2009: 216).

Throughout the 1960s and early 1970s, old Hollywood produced many blockbuster films such as *Cleopatra* (1963), *Hello, Dolly!* (1969), and *Tora! Tora! Tora!* (1970). But Steven Spielberg's *Jaws* (1975) heralded new Hollywood's first major blockbuster marketing and windowing strategy. As Cucco (2009) says:

> For the first time, television was used massively to promote a movie (the film industry occupied most of the advertising space during prime-time) and for the first time a movie was released in all major theatres on the opening weekend (464 theatres, a record for that period), setting in motion a strategy that is widely used nowadays. (216)

George Lucas's *Star Wars* (1977) was the next mass-marketed and mass-released blockbuster film. *Jaws* and *Star Wars* heralded a new Hollywood blockbuster strategy that emphasized the exchange-value of high-concept, mass-marketed, mass-released, and mass audience-targeted films, complimented by synergistic merchandising. In the decades that followed, Hollywood produced a number of blockbuster films that decreased the representation of the US nation and increased the production of fantastical and imagined worlds.

The top-grossing blockbusters of the 1980s were: *E.T.: The Extra-Terrestrial* (1982), *Star Wars: Episode VI: Return of the Jedi* (1983), *Star Wars: Episode V: The Empire Strikes Back* (1980), *Batman* (1989), *Raiders of the Lost Ark* (1981), *Ghostbusters* (1984), *Back to the Future* (1985), *Indiana Jones and the Last Crusade* (1989), and *Indiana Jones and the Temple of Doom* (1984). The top grossing blockbusters of the 1990s were: *Titanic* (1997), *Star Wars: Episode I: The Phantom Menace* (1999), *Jurassic Park* (1993), *The Lion King* (1994), *Aladdin* (1992), *Independence Day* (1996), *The Sixth Sense* (1999), *Terminator 2: Judgment Day* (1991), *Toy Story* (1995), *Men in Black* (1997), and *Toy Story 2* (1999). The top ten films of the twenty-first century's first decade were: *Avatar* (2009), *The Dark Knight* (2008), *Shrek 2* (2004), *Pirates of the Caribbean: Dead Man's Chest* (2006), *Spider-Man* (2002), *Transformers: Revenge of the Fallen* (2009), *Star Wars: Episode III Revenge of the Sith* (2005), *The Lord of the Rings: The Return of the King* (2003), and *Spider-Man 2* (2004). Many of these and most blockbuster films designed for a transnational as opposed to national audience, exhibit the following economic characteristics: big budgets, big marketing campaigns, big and near-simultaneous release to theaters worldwide, synergistic and cross-promotional features, and a global as opposed to national audience (Balio 1998; King 2002; Maltby 2003; Wyatt 1994).

Big budgets. Blockbuster films have huge budgets; their cost differentiates them from low to average budget films. The cost of a Hollywood motion picture usually exceeds $100 million. In 2010, the average cost of a blockbuster film was between $200 and $300 million. The most expensive films of all time (not adjusted for inflation) are *Pirates of the Caribbean: At World's End* ($300 million), *Tangled* ($260 million), *Spider-Man 3* ($258 million), *Harry Potter and the Half-Blood Prince* ($250 million), *Avatar* ($237 million), *Pirates of the Caribbean: Dead Man's Chest* ($225 million), *X-Men: The Last Stand* ($210 million), *Superman Returns* ($209 million), and *King Kong* ($207 million) ("Most Expensive Films of All Time" 2012). These films were all produced in the first decade of the twenty-first century, which highlights the dominance of the high-budget strategy.

Big marketing. Blockbuster films are marketed globally as "high-concept" and "must see" events by TNMCs using all mediums of communication: interactive websites, in-theater previews, TV commercials, talk-shows, newspaper and magazine ads, and billboards and posters (Jockel and Dobler 2009: 85). As Acland (2003) says, "The extension of film marketing is also a function of the widening life cycle of film texts, drumming up audiences as works pass from one territory to another, from one medium to another" (77). Media conglomerates spend a lot of money drumming up audiences for blockbuster films. Marketing intends to get people to interactively engage with and participate in the flow of promotions accompanying blockbuster films, making them a transnational cultural event. More than one-quarter of a blockbuster film's budget is spent on mass marketing. In 2004, the average marketing cost for a blockbuster movie was about $34.4 million. Since then, costs have increased: the average cost of marketing a blockbuster film in 2008 was approximately $36 million (Friedman 2008). During the 2009 Super Bowl (a global media event), Hollywood studios spent as much as $3 million for each 30-second advertising spot for ten movies including *Monsters vs. Aliens* (2009), *G.I. Joe* (2009), *Star Trek* (2009), and *Transformers 2* (2009) (Eller 2009). In that same year, the MPAA stopped announcing the marketing costs of films (Barnes 2009). Media conglomerates market their films and TV shows through all of the exhibition windows they own and in as many countries as possible. Sony's worldwide marketing and distribution chief, Jeff Blake, notes that "The Internet is a rising medium for selling movies but it doesn't yet have the reach of TV. No single Internet space reaches consumers as effectively as TV" (cited in Eller 2009). Hollywood majors consistently outspend rivals when marketing their films.

Big release. Blockbuster films are mass-released to as many markets and as many cinemas as in as many countries as possible within a short period of time. The release gap between the US market and the international market is usually no longer than one month (Jockel and Dobler 2009). In order to generate as much revenue as possible in the shortest amount of time, TNMC-owned Hollywood studio-distributors launch "one universally appealing product [. . .] at the same time in almost all important markets to receive revenues as quickly as possible" (Jockel and Dobler 2009: 86).

Big synergy. Blockbuster films are designed to generate as much revenue as possible, not only by collecting box office receipts, but also by spinning off a number of ancillary commodities. As the hub of synergistic entertainment media franchises (see Chapter 2), a blockbuster is "a movie that that spawns additional revenue streams beyond what it earns from its various forms of distribution, primarily theatrical, video and television" (Thompson 2007: 4). Film content merchandise (action figures, video games, coffee mugs, T-shirts), licensing deals with TV networks and pay-per-view digital content providers (Apple TV, Netflix), home entertainment (DVD box-sets, blue-ray discs), and "enhanced" spin-off versions (digitally re-mastered, 3-D, director's cut + bonus material edition) all generate additional revenue for the blockbuster's owners (Jockel and Dobler 2009). TNMC-owned studios refer to blockbuster films as "tent-pole" films: they may hold up or support the weaker economy of an entire studio and compensate for financial losses incurred by a studio's production/distribution of less lucrative films, or "flops."

Big audience. Blockbuster films target a global as opposed to national audience. Nationalistic films are designed for national or bi-national viewers. Blockbuster films are designed to travel everywhere. Between World War II and up until the early 1990s, Hollywood's preferred audience was located in the US. A middle-class, largely Anglo-Saxon audience was targeted due to its sheer size as a single, English-language market. Throughout the 1990s, Hollywood stopped privileging "a special relationship with the national American audience" and began explicitly targeting the transnational audience (Wasser 1995: 423). By the late 1990s, approximately half of global Hollywood's total box-office receipts came from the US, and nearly 50 percent of global Hollywood's profits came from the global box office (Scott 2004b: 54). Hollywood's domestic profits had grown a mere 39 percent between 1985 and 1990, but profits from foreign markets exploded by 124 percent during the same period (Wagneleitner 1999: 482). By 2006, the US box office accounted for 37 percent of total profit, while the transnational box office accounted for 63 percent (Puente 2008). "Decades ago, a movie's foreign box office barely registered with studio executives. Now, foreign ticket sales represent nearly 68 percent of the roughly $32 billion global film market" (Schuker 2010). The Asia Pacific box office—China and Japan specifically—is the fastest growing for Hollywood (Dobuzinskis 2010). As a result, "Movies are no longer made for [only] an American audience; they are made for a global audience and produced with the intention of attracting the widest possible demographic" (Berardi 2006).

The Textual Characteristics of the Blockbuster Film

TNMCs design blockbuster films to be watched by many people from many different countries. As TNMCs geared their operations toward the reaping of maximum returns from the global box office, Hollywood studios began creating films scrubbed of cultural specificity so as to tap a transnational, as opposed to distinctly national, audience (Gitlin 1983). Waxman (1990) observes that "The worldwide hunger for US-made entertainment helps steer our own [American] culture, by encouraging projects that will sell overseas and discouraging those that foreign audiences are thought to spurn." TNMCs sanction the production of films that are designed to amuse a world audience and view explicitly US nationalist films (i.e., films about the specificities and peculiarities of the "American Way of Life") as impediments to global profit. TNMCs understand that films which are too nationalistic, too local in their storytelling, and too sensitive to particularity do not have "global legs." They invest in films with global appeal. Rob Moore, vice chairman of Paramount Pictures, says: "We need to make movies that have the ability to break out internationally" (cited in Schuker 2010). Mark Zoradi, former president of Walt Disney Corp's Motion Pictures Group, agrees: "no studio head is going to make a big expensive movie that costs $150 million or $200 million unless it has worldwide appeal" (cited in Schuker 2010).

TNMCs manufacture "globally popular" films that will maximize profit by appealing to youthful and family filmgoers within the US audience and in many other countries simultaneously (Acland 2003: 36). Global blockbuster films are designed to be financially successful worldwide, last a relatively long time at theaters, and travel easily from one national media market to the next due to being appreciated by people everywhere, regardless of their national cultural sensibilities (Cucco 2009). Global blockbuster film texts are designed to be polysemic (Fiske 1988). They are intended to be "open" to identifications and interpretations from many people located in many different countries. What are the specific textual characteristics of global blockbuster films? TNMCs design blockbuster films to resonate with a transnational audience using global stars, international casts, pre-sold properties, genre hybridity (often fantasy and science fiction), classical narrative structure, universal themes, and visual spectacle.

Global stars. Blockbuster films often feature globally recognizable stars. The star is an essential design feature of a film's global popularity. Worldwide, there is a surplus supply of starving actors, aggressively competing for roles. The star is an intertextual persona: it is shaped by an actor's qualities and relationships with fans, the fictional characters actors are hired to play, and the publicity machine surrounding them (King 2002: 150). A star may decrease or increase a film's overall attractiveness to viewers. A film studio's choice of star actor plays a central role in pre-selling the film, especially since some viewers choose to consume certain films based on star power. As an image-commodity, star personas "often perform a more important part than any other single factor in the selling of Hollywood movies" (King 2002: 152). Many global blockbuster films star predominantly US and white actors: "[W]hat do *Harry Potter, Spider-Man, Twilight, Pirates of the Caribbean, Lord of the Rings*, and Christopher Nolan's *Batman* series have in common?" asks Franich (2011). The answer: "White people, white people everywhere!"

Hegemonic whiteness may still be dominant in Hollywood casting agencies, but studios are experimenting with an emergent mixed-race and multicultural casting strategy that better represents US and transnational audiences. While Hollywood once cast mixed race actors as tragic or villainous mulatto antagonists pitted against white protagonists, mixed race actors—such as Halle Berry, Jessica Biel, Keanu Reeves, and Vin Diesel—are now cast in positive roles. Beltran and Fojas (2008) note that "Not only has multi-raciality, or, in today's vernacular, being 'mixed', taken on new meaning in US popular culture, but biracial and multiracial models, actors, and film and television characters seem to be everywhere" (1). Mixed race stars are cast in order to connect with a young and culturally diverse transnational audience. Carter (2008) calls this casting strategy "mixploitation": mixed race actors are used to pre-sell films to diverse transnational viewers. With the exception of Western Europe, "most of the world's media markets are populated by a majority of people who share the ethnicity of US minorities and immigrant groups" says Kraidy (2004). "It is probable that African, Asian, and Latin American viewers would be drawn to films and television programs that feature actors who share their ethnicity" (82). Films starring mixed race actors are globally resonant because they enable transnational identifications. *Fast Five* (2011), a film that grossed more transnationally than in the US market (33.5 percent of its gross came from the US, while 66.5 percent of its gross came from the rest of the world), stars a number of mixed and multicultural actors such as Vin Diesel, Jordana Brewster, Michelle Rodriguez, Rick Yune, and Ja Rule. The globally popular *X-Men* franchise also has a multicultural cast. These films champion liberal multicultural ideology and a politics of cultural recognition (Schrodt 2011).

International actors. Blockbuster films also cast internationally recognizable actors. Throughout the 1980s and 1990s, Hollywood films tended to cast international actors as villains and marginal characters (Holson 2004), but as TNMCs began to depend on the world box office, casting international actors in positive roles became "A passport to profitability" (Holson 2004). "Hiring international talent is a movie-making law," claims Stephen Moore, president of international film and home entertainment for Twentieth Century Fox. "It makes a great difference to us and certainly helps our ability to promote a movie" (cited in Holson 2004). Some of the most renowned actors featured in Hollywood films are not US citizens. Los Angeles attracts actors from around the world. Sean Connery, Anthony Hopkins, Emma Thompson, Catherine Zeta-Jones, Gerard Butler, Ewan McGregor, Ben Kingsley, Michael Caine, Jeremy Irons, Ralph Fiennes, Daniel Day-Lewis, Daniel Craig, Hugh Grant, Colin Firth, Kate Winslet, Jude Law, Orlando Bloom, and Keira Knightley are British. Keanu Reeves, Jim Carrey, Mike Myers, Kiefer Sutherland, Neve Campbell, and Rachel McAdams are Canadian. Peter O'Toole, Pierce Brosnan, Liam Neeson, Gabriel Byrne, and Colin Farrell are Irish. Mel Gibson, Nicole Kidman, Eric Bana, Cate Blanchett, Heath Ledger, and Sam Worthington are from Australia. Rink Kikucho, Tadanobu Asano, Masayori Oka, and Ken Watanabe are Japanese. Jackie Chan, Chow Yun Fat, Jet Li, and Russell Wong are from China. Mads Mikkelsen is Danish. Vincent Cassel and Audrey Tautou are from France. Benicio Del Toro is Puerto Rican. Gael García Bernal is Mexican, Peter Stormare is Swedish, Charlize Theron is South African, Penelope Cruz and Javier Bardem are Spanish, and Frida Pinto is from India. "The scale of Hollywood's appetite, its unrivalled power to vacuum up ambition and artistry from around the world, is part of its legend and grandeur" (Scott 2011). By casting international actors, global block-busters solicit the identification of viewers from multiple countries with their locally familiar home-grown stars.

Pre-sold properties. The scripts of many blockbuster films are derived from pre-existing works: best-selling novels, fairy tales, TV shows, comic books, or computer games that already have a large audience following and whose stories and characters are already widely recognized by many people. "Even before a high-concept film is going to be released, its basic ideas are already present all over the world" (Jockel and Dobler 2009: 85). *The Lord of the Rings*, for example, was adapted from Tolkien's novels, which already had a vast transnational fan following prior to its film release. The *Spider-Man* and *X-Men* franchises are based on Marvel comic books that had traveled the world for many years before the films were made. *The Harry Potter* film franchise is based upon J.K. Rowling's famous book series. Works of previous eras such as *Godzilla (1998)*, *War of the Worlds* (2005), *A Nightmare on Elm Street* (2010), *The Karate Kid* (2010), and *The Clash of the Titans* (2010) are recycled and remade (Pomerantz 2010). These "pre-selling" strategies attempt to minimize financial risk by maximizing the potential of viewers who are already familiar with films before they are released (Sood and Dreze 2006). Blockbuster films are based on "pre-sold" identities. TNMCs adapt and remake "stories or characters that the public already know" (Cucco 2009: 220) to try and ensure an audience for the film and establish an impetus for sequels, prequels, and more remakes.

Genre hybrids. Blockbuster films tend to be "genre hybrids." Genre is a way to classify types of film texts according to their common codes and conventions (e.g., horror, war, western, drama, thriller, action, adventure, science fiction). Film genres do not exist in isolation, but in relation to other texts. It is often difficult to make clear-cut distinctions between one film genre and another because many films are "inter-textual": they communicate meaning to viewers through reference to other existing texts derived from society and culture. No film genre is stable, but combines and recombines elements of pre-existing genres, sometimes resulting in new genres (Altman 1999). TNMCs employ genres to establish audience expectations and to attract specific viewers with presumably distinct viewing tastes and preferences for specific films (King 2002: 122). They manufacture blockbuster films as hybrid genres to "appeal to a range of potential audience constituencies" (King 2002: 137). Many blockbuster films entail hybrid inter-texts of many pre-existing texts, codes, and conventions. The mix and mash "some-thing for everybody approach" taken by studios is intended to attract as many different viewers as possible to one particular film. Using pastiche (the cobbling together of many existing works into one specific film text) and bricolage (the construction of a film text through the appropriation and repurposing of a range of available material), studios try to attract and appeal to as many viewers as possible.

Fantasy. Blockbuster films regularly mix together fantasy and science-fiction genres. Thompson (2003) notes that "Fantasy films feature prominently in the list of the top worldwide grossing films of recent years" (60). Many blockbusters do not try to represent reality but, rather, construct a new fantastical reality. With the exception of *Beverly Hills Cop* (1984) and *Titanic* (1997), the world's most profitable block-busters blend fantasy and science-fiction genre codes and conventions. This fantasy-sci fi combo: 1) appeals most to teens and young adults, which is global Hollywood's target transnational demographic (young people have disposable incomes and tend to spend much of their leisure time being entertained); 2) lends itself to a broad range of merchandising and cross-licensing endeavors (fantasy characters are turned into action toys, plots become video games, fast-food tie-ins); 3) attracts repeat viewings (people tend to want to buy their own DVD copy of the film and watch it again and again); and, 4) fosters an "esoteric knowledge" among the core audience (fans and hardcore viewers want to know everything about the fictional world so they collaborate together online and off, imagining, researching, and providing free publicity to the franchised film) (Thompson 2003). Most importantly, fantastical or hyper-real stories and characters do not suffer the "cultural discount." They do not reference specific "national" cultures or recognizable landscapes; they are more "open" to transnational viewer identifications than realist films about national places and people. Most global blockbusters represent an entirely new world, a new planet, an earth set in an imagined past or far-off future.

Narrative structure. The blockbuster's aesthetic and story structure tend to be conservative. "Formal experimentation and potentially radical content are generally avoided" (King 2002: 79). Unfamiliar shots, strange lighting techniques or experimental camera angles, alienating plot lines, un-relatable scenarios, and unlikable main characters do not appear in blockbusters. Blockbuster films are standardized and predictable:

> To avoid risks at the box office, the blockbuster has to appear to the public with a simple,
> immediate, easily recognizable identity [. . .] a high concept film [. . .] that can be
> summarized in just one sentence or image, making its marketing easier. (Cucco 2009: 219)

Most blockbusters have protagonist-centered and linear narrative structures. The blockbuster's storytelling form is transnationally, perhaps even universally, familiar. It has a clear beginning, middle, and end. The action proceeds in a linear sequence, from start to finish. In the beginning, a situation of normalcy or equilibrium is disrupted by a conflict or crisis of some kind. The conflict or crisis propels a protagonist or group of protagonists into action; the protagonist struggles, overcomes certain obstacles and challenges, and finally, resolves the conflict or crisis. At the finale of the blockbuster, the world is returned to "normal" or changed, for better or worse. Blockbuster films represent conflicts and crises of world-historic proportions. They stage threats and challenges that tap into or resonate with the hopes and fears of the whole world. In the science-fiction dystopia film *2012* (2009), for example, the human race needs to survive and rebuild the world after it is destroyed. In *Independence Day* (1996) and *Transformers* (2007), humans need to unite and save earth from invading alien machines. In *Lord of the Rings* (2001), the various species of Middle Earth need to unite as a force of good to stop the spread of evil. In *Jurassic Park,* (1993) humans square off against genetically engineered dinosaurs. Many blockbuster films tend to hail viewers as part of a world community by eschewing fine-grained national cultural observation for universally recognizable conflicts that attempt to appeal to anyone, anywhere, anytime (Olson 2000).

Spectacle. Blockbuster event films emphasize the visual, but not necessarily at the expense of narrative cohesion. Many mix visual spectacle with classic narrative techniques (King 2000). "Spectacular imagery, often utilizing the latest in special effects and other technologies, has remained a key ingredient of the big-budget attractions around which the fortunes of the studios revolve" (King 2002: 178). Previews present spectacle in order to lure viewers into theaters. The production of spectacular films to be viewed on the big screen (and in 3-D) is a way of distinguishing Hollywood blockbusters from small screen B-grade films and TV shows. As Cucco (2009) says:

> the bigger the screen on which they are shown, the better they are. Special effects, in fact,
> yield their performance better if screened on a big screen, underlining the difference
> between the enjoyment of the movie at the theatre or at home on television. (217)

The blockbuster film promises its viewers spectacle, moments of awe, wonder, and amazement. They are designed to establish a "must-see it on the big screen" attitude among viewers. Blockbusters are designed to create what Jenkins (2006) calls the "Wow Climax": the visual and emotional highpoint of a film, a peak spectacle that leads to sensorial overload. Visually rich—as opposed to dialogue-intense—films save Hollywood distributors in terms of the costs associated with international language dubbing and are easily comprehensible to transnational audiences that do not speak English. Visual eye-candy and wordless action sequences of violent aggression, including prolonged fight-scenes, gigantic battles, disasters, and death-defying stunts, attract transnational viewers (Acland 2003: 35). In *Independence Day* (1996), a giant UFO obliterates the White House and Capitol Building. In *Twister* (1996), killer tornadoes obliterate the built environment. In *Armageddon* (1998), giant meteors destroy New York City. In *The Sum of All Fears* (2002), a nuclear bomb annihilates Baltimore. In *The Day After Tomorrow* (2004), global warming unleashes deadly hurricanes, earthquakes, floods, and tidal waves upon the world. In *2012* (2009), France's Eiffel Tower collapses, Rio de Janeiro's Christ the Redeemer statue falls, India is submerged by a giant tsunami, St Peter's Basilica and the Sistine Chapel crumble, cruise ships are overturned, planes crash, and forests burn. As each studio tries to create bigger and bolder spectacles, viewers may become desensitized and bored. The global blockbuster may lead to spectacle fatigue.

BOX 5.1

PIRATES OF THE CARIBBEAN: AT WORLD'S END (2007) AS A BLOCKBUSTER FILM

Pirates of the Caribbean: At World's End is a global blockbuster film. IMDb ranks *Pirates* as the twelfth highest revenue-generating film worldwide. Its worldwide box office was $958,404,152 (32.1 percent came from the US box office and 67.9 percent from the global box office). *Pirates* represents the economic features of a standard global blockbuster event film. *Pirates* had a huge production budget of $300 million (Coyle 2009), making it the most expensive film of all time. It was mass-marketed through every medium available. In the weeks leading up to the film's global release week of May 19–25, 2007, *Pirates* TV advertisements, billboards, and web banners were released. To promote and cross-promote this film to viewers worldwide in advance of its release, numerous firms released *Pirates* action figures, board games, sculptures, t-shirts, fast food tie-ins, soundtracks, and Xbox 360, PS3, Wii, PSP, PS2, and Nintendo DS video games. *Pirates* stars actors from Australia, England, Hong Kong, US, Sweden, and elsewhere, including multi-nationally recognizable stars such as Johnny Depp, Naomie Harris, and Chow Yun-Fat. *Pirates* is a pre-sold property based on the famous Walt Disney theme park ride (Pirates of the Caribbean). It is aesthetically conservative and employs a typical Hollywood form: a relatively standard protagonist-centered and linear realist narrative that moves from beginning to middle to end. However, as part of a franchise, it draws upon characters, dramatic conflicts, and events from previous films. *Pirates* is a genre hybrid as well. It combines fantasy, history, comedy, horror, and action codes and conventions. *Pirates* is loaded with visual spectacle, and filled with intense and over-the-top action sequences and special effects.

The text of *Pirates* conveys globally appealing themes of friends versus enemies, humanity versus the supernatural, and good versus evil that are familiar to many people, regardless of gender, ethnicity, language, age, or national location. It was also inspired by

BOX 5.1 (Continued)

mythical and historic pirate tales and characters. *Pirates* is loosely based on the historic activities of a pirate coalition called the Brethren of the Coast and some of its conflicts with the British Empire's infamous British East India Company. *Pirates* draws upon legends about the Kraken and the Flying Dutchman too. By deriving stories and characters from well-known and transnationally circulating stories, *Pirates* was able to avoid the cultural discount. The film deals with multinational (as opposed to national) conflict. The Brethren of the Coast (consisting of different pirate lords representing people from many cultures and regions) conflict with Lord Cutler Beckett of the East India Trading Company (the world's premier multinational corporation). The rebellious pirates symbolize local autonomy, alternative economies, and diversity, while the East India Trading Company symbolizes British imperialism, capitalist industrialization, and cultural homogenization. In order to fight and resist British Empire, the Brethren must temporarily resolve their conflicts and unite. *Pirates* references historic struggles against Western colonialism and, perhaps, resonates with contemporary struggles against neo-imperialism. The space of action represented by *Pirates* is global, not national. *Pirates* was shot in the NICL (Palos Verdes, Saint Vincent and the Grenadines, Dominica, The Bahamas, and on sets constructed at Walt Disney Studios) in order to represent and recreate scenes and places from all over the world, not just in the US.

CULTURALLY PROXIMATE ENTERTAINMENT MEDIA: GLOBAL-NATIONAL TV FORMATS

While TNMCs design blockbuster films that travel well around the world and avoid the cultural discount, they are also sensitive to locational differences and the persistence of culturally proximate national audiences. Many citizen-consumers (with the exception of non-Francophone Canadians) prefer to watch TV shows and films produced in their own nations and which represent their own language, culture, history, values, and humor. As Straubhaar (1991) says: "audiences will tend to prefer programming which is closest or most proximate to their own culture: national programming if it can be supported by the local economy" (4). "[L]ocal products owe their competitive edge over foreign ones to their cultural proximity, the audience's familiarity with the language and the cultural context that they carry" (Straubhaar 1991). TNMCs design global TV formats that can be flexibly adjusted to culturally proximate audiences in nation-states.

What is a TV format? A TV format is "a template or set of invariable elements in a programme out of which the variable elements of individual episodes are produced" (Moran 2004: 5). TV formats are "program concepts that can be re-packaged to suit particular [national] markets and tastes" (Freedman 2003: 33). TV formats are not finished TV shows, but TV show concepts or "programming ideas that are adapted and produced [by national TV networks] domestically" (Waisbord 2004: 359). Worldwide, audiences are watching nationally adapted versions of global TV formats. *So You Think You Can Dance* is licensed to more than twenty-three national TV networks, from the US to Israel. *The Weakest Link* is licensed to TV networks in more than forty countries such as Chile, Greece, and Singapore. *Top Model* is licensed to over 120 national TV networks. For some scholars, the cross-border flow of TV formats—reality shows, game shows, talent competitions—signals the "triumph of media globalization even while asserting the continued importance of local or domestic programming" (Moran 2009: 116). The TV format was established in the early 1950s by the US, and with help from British TV broadcasters (Chalaby 2012). A US-British TV relationship developed the TV format as "a licensed adaptation based on the intangible property rights attached to a show that a broadcaster acquires and produces when the show's track record demonstrates that it is a ratings winner" (Chalaby 2012: 37). In the twenty-first century, the trade in TV formats is transnational, even though most globalizing TV formats have British, US, and Western European origins (Moran and Keane 2006: 80–81) and "Africa, parts of the Middle East, most of the former Soviet territories, and various parts of South and Southeast Asia are all sparsely represented at the international TV format fairs" (Moran 2009: 123). British, US, Netherlands, and Japanese media corporations rule the global TV format trade (*The Economist* 2011c).

British-based ITV, BBC Entertainment, and Freemantle Media Ltd (owned by RTL Group, one of Europe's largest media corporations) own at least forty-three TV formats such as *Who Wants to be a Millionaire?*, *What's My Line?*, *The Price Is Right*, *Family Feud*, *Idol*, *Got Talent*, and *Let's Make a Deal*. The US is home to many media entrepreneurs who claim proprietary rights to at least twenty-two TV formats. Supermodel Tyra Banks created *Top Model*; Ashton Kutcher, Jason Goldberg, and Nick Santora created *Beauty and the Geek*; Mark Burnett created TV formats such as *Survivor*, *Are You Smarter Than a 5th Grader?*, and *The Apprentice*. The Netherlands is home to Endemol (owned by Italy's Mediaset), which operates in twenty-three countries and owns TV formats including *Big Brother* (adapted in more than seventy countries), *Deal or No Deal* (nationalized in over one hundred countries), and *Fear Factor* (modified by over eighty countries). Endemol USA, based in Los Angeles, California, produces popular TV formats such as *Extreme Makeover: Home Edition* and *Show Me the Money* for ABC, *Exposed* for MTV, *Big Brother* and *Kid Nation* for CBS, and *Midnight Money Madness* for TBS. Japanese companies such as TV Asahi Corp own and license bizarre TV formats such as *Celebrity Thrift Challenge*, *Women Rate Each Other*, *Takeshi's Castle*, and *Love Aprons* to TV networks in the US, Britain, and elsewhere (Brook 2010; Ryall 2008). All of the above media corporations design TV formats "that contain 'attributes' that render, or at least endeavor to render, a finished creative product accessible to audiences in more than one national market" (Keane and Moran 2008: 157).

TV formats involve a cross-border business relationship between TV production companies that produce TV shows and sell temporary broadcast rights to them (a licensor) and national TV networks which consume the rights to broadcast the show (licensee) (Waisbord 2004). The trade in TV formats is relatively new. For much of TV's history, TV production companies based in one country produced TV shows for their own national market and then exported those TV shows to another country, in a dubbed form. During the first four decades of TV, this mode of transnational TV production-distribution was the norm (Waisbord 2004). US TV production companies licensed dubbed versions of popular American TV show such as *I Dream of Jeannie*, *The Beverly Hillbillies*, *Dallas*, *The Cosby Show*, *Miami Vice*, *The Simpsons*, and *Baywatch* to TV networks in other countries. For example, in 1994 NBC, in conjunction with TV studios Stuffed Dog Company and Quincy Jones Productions, produced *The Fresh Prince of Bel Air* and broadcast this hit TV show on NBC to US viewers. Soon after, Warner Bros Television acquired the syndication rights to the show, dubbed it, and licensed it to many different national TV networks. This cross-border production-distribution logic of licensing dubbed versions of US TV shows to non-US TV networks persists, but is coupled with the more flexible strategy of TV formatting.

In the global TV format trade, national TV networks purchase a license to make a domestic version of a foreign TV format from another company. The TV format trade involves a collaborative global-local business relationship between many different national media corporations, based in many different countries. The licensor (the TV format company) has "extensive knowledge of the format and its inception in other places; they understand the pitfalls and difficulties as well as the potential triumphs and successes" (Moran 2009: 118–119). The licensees (national TV networks) have "a more intimate sense of the home audience culture, a greater intuitive sense of what will be suitable for viewers" (Moran 2009: 119). The relationship between the licensor and licensee is most often collaborative, not conflicted. Sometimes the licensor will demand that the licensee make an exact copy of the TV show; in other instances, the licensor allows the licensee to make slight adjustments or creative adaptations. The TV format adaptation process may be "closed" or "open" (Moran 2009).

Closed adaptations occur when a licensor makes a licensee adapt the TV format in a standardized way. No adjustments or changes can be made to the form, content, or style of the TV format. Gordon (2009) refers to this as "programme modeling":

> the replication of the design, form, and content of a programme originating from elsewhere without any adjustments to fit the cultural, social, and economic context within which such a programme will be commercially disseminated by a state or network and viewed by a local audience. (313)

A closed adaptation reproduces the original TV format. According to Moran (2009), the goal of the closed adaptation:

> is to produce a "literal' approximation of the original version of the format program. This lookalike, equivalent translation process emphasizes a high degree of fidelity to the original, even if the new version makes little concession to the interests and taste of a new audience. (119)

For example, BBC Entertainment (licensor) demands that *Who Wants to Be a Millionaire?* be adapted in a standardized way by TV networks (licensees) everywhere. Open adaptations occur when a licensor is more tolerant of a licensee's adaptation of the TV format to fit with national audience tastes and preferences. In these cases, "the creative sovereignty of the local production team is greatly enhanced in the process of adaptation and production (Moran 2009: 119).

Why are TV formats so globally popular? Why are TV formats so in demand by TV networks? Why do so many national TV networks buy and adapt formats? There are economic, political, and cultural reasons for the popularity of global TV formats. Motivated by the profit-imperative, commercial TV networks are always on the look-out for ways to minimize production costs and risk while maximizing audience share and advertising revenue. They seek to acquire TV shows which do not cost much to make but which nonetheless are capable of drawing and delivering a large audience to their advertising clients. Worldwide, national TV networks acquire TV formats for the following reasons: they are cheap and easy to make, they are low risk, they can be flexibly adjusted to suit national audience preferences, they meet state media policy conditions, and they generate extra revenue as branded entertainment. These aspects of TV formats are discussed below.

TV networks buy TV formats because they are cheaper to produce than an original fictional TV show. TV formats relieve TV networks of the financial burden of having to hire and pay decent wages to professional directors, scriptwriters, and actors. "Buying formats, then, is a cost saving strategy that eliminates some of the highest fixed costs that fiction programming demands" (Waisbord 2004: 365). Also, TV formats enable TV production to be standardized and more "efficient." They help TV networks avoid "creative wastage" and under-utilized labor power. TV formats are like IKEA furniture. They come with "How to Make" booklets, and these instructional manuals outline "one best way" to make a TV show. The Taylorization of the TV format enables TV crews to quickly come to an understanding about the show they are working on and establish a predictable timeline for completing it. Low-cost production and production efficiency, not creativity, are what TV formats offer TV networks, and perhaps, why they are in demand.

TV networks also purchase TV formats because they help them to minimize financial risk. Many TV network executives assume that viewers will gravitate toward familiar TV formulas, not radically new, novel, or aesthetically edgy TV shows. Executives are attracted to TV formats because they have a proven track record in the international TV market and have already been backed by the global advertising industry. Instead of innovating new TV shows, TV network executives tend to follow the global TV format leaders. The acquisition and scheduling of TV formats by TV networks worldwide represents a "low-risk strategy in an industry [. . .] that is averse to risk-taking" (Keane and Moran 2008: 157). The globalization of TV formats reflects the fact that it is easier "to copy someone else's success than to take a risk on a new untested idea" (Keane and Moran 2008: 168). TV formats provide national TV networks with insurance against ratings failure. TV formats "are the ultimate risk minimizing programming strategy" (Waisbord 2004: 365).

Another reason why TV networks license TV formats is to meet state media policy requirements, such as content quotas. Many states compel national TV networks to schedule a specific amount of "national" media content each day of the week (see Chapter 3). A global TV format's copyright may be owned by a foreign media firm, but when this TV format is domestically produced by a national TV network, it will sometimes qualify as a "national" TV show. Hence, in order to appease state regulators and fulfill content quotas without producing an original TV show, TV networks acquire and nationalize global TV formats: "Format programming, then, is part of a business strategy to bypass local programming quotas. If stations broadcast domestic versions of foreign shows, those versions help satisfy quota requirements; if they buy canned foreign shows, they do not" (Waisbord 2004: 363).

Additionally, TV networks acquire TV formats because they are easily adaptable to the tastes and preferences of national audiences. TV formats are "a kind of unspecific, universal or de-nationalized program template or recipe" which "can be customized and domesticated for reception and consumption by specific audiences in local or national contexts" (Moran 2009: 116). TV formats rely on a "pie and crust model—whereby the format is the crust and the various localizations are the pie" (Keane 2002: 7). The TV format "crust" is filled up with culturally and linguistically familiar performers, participants, themes, and symbols in order to appease viewer demand for a nationally inflected product. Waisbord (2004) states that TV formats provide "opportunities for audiences to recognize themselves as members of national communities" (72). By doing so, TV formats may deter viewers from complaining that their national TV networks contribute to Americanization. TV formats allow national TV networks to appear as though they are supporting the production of "original" national entertainment media. According to Hans Schiff, the vice-president of the William Morris Agency, "The key element to formats is that you get the basic template of an idea and apply it to your domestic marketplace so when people turn on their television they assume it's a domestic show" (quoted in Freedman 2003: 36). TV networks schedule TV formats in order to foster the illusion that viewers are watching national TV shows when, in fact, they are watching a global TV format whose content has been nationally adapted.

Last but not least, TV networks and advertisers support TV formats because of the opportunities for product placement and branding they provide. TV formats can be flexibly adapted to suit the needs of any advertising client and are the most in-demand form of branded entertainment. According to a 2011 Nielsen report, US TV formats feature the most product placements or "exposures": *American Idol* (577 product placements and exposures for goods including Coca-Cola, Ford, AT&T, Chevrolet, Apple), *The Biggest Loser* (533 placements and exposures of brands including Subway, 24 Hour Fitness, Extra Sugar Free Gum, Ziploc, Muir Glen Organic Canned Tomatoes), *The Celebrity Apprentice* (391 product exposures), *Dancing With the Stars* (390 exposures), *The X Factor* (312 exposures), *Extreme Makeover: Home Edition* (224 Exposures), *America's Got Talent* (220 exposures), *America's Next Top Model* (178 exposures), *The Amazing Race: Unfinished Business* (161 exposures).

In sum, TV formats allow national TV networks to maximize profitability (ad dollars exchanged for big audiences) with a cheap to produce, standardized, flexible, and hyper-commercial media form.

Are globalizing TV formats a force of cultural homogenization or cultural diversification? Gordon (2009) argues that, in Jamaica, TV formats are agents of cultural homogenization. In the 1990s, the Jamaican state implemented neoliberal media policy to convert state-owned TV broadcasters into a variety of commercial TV networks. The goal was to restrict the state monopoly of information, establish profitable Jamaican NMCs, and enable diverse media expressions of Jamaica to flourish. The first and second objectives were achieved; the third was not. Profitable TV networks emerged, but they did not produce high-quality indigenous programming and largely functioned as "distribution systems for imported [foreign] Western programming" (311). Soon after Jamaica's neoliberal media turn, the three national TV networks—Television Jamaica (TVJ), CVM Television (CVMTV), and Love Television (LOVETV)—scheduled 61 percent US TV shows, 4 percent non-US international TV shows, and 34 percent "made in Jamaica" TV shows (Gordon 2009). Many of the national TV shows created by Jamaica's TV networks are indistinguishable from TV formats originating in the US and elsewhere. Gordon (2009) says "[E]ven as Jamaicans prefer to watch programmes that are reflective of their cultural or local orientation, what passes for local production is merely a localized version of American popular culture" (309). Programme modeling by Jamaican TV networks stunted the growth of high-quality indigenous TV shows, exacerbated a largely one-way media flow from the US to Jamaica, and deepened the integration of Jamaica's media system with US TNMCs. Gordon (2009) says TV formats are agents of cultural assimilation, not adaptation or hybridity. "The difference between the two is significant, as adaptation implies some sort of mutuality or harmony [. . .] while assimilation entails absorption to the point where things become identical" (323).

Yet, global TV formats may *not* be forces of global cultural assimilation or sameness:

> The TV format industry's maturation [. . .] seems to point *not* to a strengthening of the global and the local at the expense of the national but to a reconfiguration of the national that may be to the detriment of those other two levels. [. . .] TV formats are intimately dependent on the national. (Moran 2009: 123)

TV formats reproduce and refract banal nationalism (Billig 1995). "[N]ationhood continues to be suggested in the interstices of format adaptations—in a detail of color, a quiz question, an outdoor setting, a story situation, an accent, a theme song, and so on" (Moran 2009: 123). The "nation" represented by national TV-network-adapted global TV formats, however, is empty: it is abstracted from deep national experience, the politics of place, and history. While TV formats reflect "the persistence of national cultures in a networked world" (Waisbord 2004: 368), they do so by packaging hackneyed consumerist visions of nationhood that are out of touch with local realities. High-quality national TV shows that might be capable of representing the diversity of experiences—economic, political, and cultural—within a state are relegated to the margins by TV formats. As Freedman (2003) says, TV formats are "designed to maximize corporate profit rather than stimulate programme diversity or enhance local identities" (26).

BOX 5.2

TOP MODEL AS A GLOBAL-NATIONAL TV FORMAT

Top Model is a global TV format that has been adapted by national TV networks worldwide. *Top Model* was created by Tyra Banks, and produced by 10x10 Entertainment and Bankable Productions. It originally aired on US-based UPN in its first season but has since moved on to be aired on the CW. *Top Model* is a reality show which centers around a modeling competition between a bunch of female contestants. Each week, the aspiring models compete in modeling challenges and are then judged on their photos from a photo shoot. One woman is eliminated each week until the final episode when the *Top Model* winner is chosen and rewarded with a number of prizes, including a position with a prestigious modeling agency, a contract with Cover Girl cosmetics, and a cash prize. *America's Next Top Model* was originally made for the US, but has since been re-broadcast in 170 other countries. The *Top Model* format has also been nationally adapted in forty-six countries. *Top Model* format rights are sold internationally by CBS Television Distribution to national TV networks, which adapt, and broadcast nationalized versions of the show to their viewers.

BOX 5.2 (Continued)

Top Model is a closed adaptation. Each TV network which nationally adapts the global TV format does so in a highly standardized way. All adaptations are based on the original *America's Next Top Model* format. Each episode closely follows each contestant's day-to-day experience. A season has between nine and thirteen episodes and begins with between ten and twenty contestants. Each episode is filmed over the span of about a week. Makeovers are given to each of the contestants near the beginning of the cycle, around the second to fourth episode. Each episode is based on the work of modeling (dieting, fitness, runway walking, press interviews, staring at cameras, promoting a branded product, dealing with potential employers). Also, near the end of each season, the contestants are sent on trips to cities such as Paris, Milan, Tokyo, London, Cape Town, Bangkok, London, Sydney, Barcelona, Rome, Amsterdam, Sao Paulo, and Venice, where they train to participate in the global fashion circuit. Each episode follows the same narrative structure: modeling challenge, photo shoot, judgment, elimination. Each episode begins with a challenge which the models train to complete. The models then compete with each other to win that challenge. A prize is awarded to the victor. A photo-shoot then happens (e.g., close-ups, nude, lingerie, swimsuits, posing with male models and animals). In the judgment segment, the model's personality, performance, and photos are harshly scrutinized. After the commercial sign value of each model has been assessed and evaluated, the judges decide who will be eliminated. The host reveals the women who are safe from elimination, one by one, by giving them their photo. The final two models, who do not receive their photos, are told why their behavior and image is not fit for the industry. One is given her photo. The other is not. The eliminated model departs. Although the *Top Model* format is the same everywhere, each national TV network scripts localized model challenges, casts aspiring models from its country of origin and hires nationally recognized fashion icons as judges. Nationally adapted versions of *Top Model* allow contestants and viewers to explore other nation-specific fashion industries too. *Top Model* simultaneously affirms banal nationalism and consumer cosmopolitanism.

BOX 5.3

IDOL AS A GLOBAL-NATIONAL TV FORMAT

Idol is a reality-TV talent show format with global legs. Created by British TV producer Simon Fuller, managed by Los Angeles-based 19 Entertainment, and owned and distributed by Freemantle Media, the London-based but German-owned content and production division of Bertelsmann's RTL Group, *Idol* is a transnationally mobile TV format that has been adapted worldwide.

Pop Idol originally debuted on the British TV network ITV in 2001, was adapted by US-based Fox Broadcasting Company in 2002, and then spread around the world. The show has been licensed, locally adapted, and renamed by TV networks in nearly one hundred countries. Lebanon-based Future Television broadcasts *Super Star* (سوبر ستار) to the so-called "Arab world." The Brazil-based TV network Sistema Brasileiro de Televisão schedules *Ídolos Brazil*. *Thần tượng âm nhạc: Vietnam Idol* is broadcast by the state-run Vietnam Television. The Bulgarian TV network bTV broadcasts *Music Idol*, while people in France (and other French-speaking communities) watch *Nouvelle Star*, produced by M6, or Metropole Television. East Africans watch *Idols East Africa*, while Malaysians watch *Malaysian Idol*. In India, viewers watch *Indian Idol*, on Sony Entertainment TV (or SET), a Hindi-language entertainment channel. Worldwide, state and commercial TV broadcasters are united by their shared scheduling of one standardized and universalizing *Idol* TV format.

At the same time, viewers are consuming nationally specific versions of *Idol* that employ homegrown national talent (judges and singers), are broadcast in national languages, and are customized to suit national cultural preferences. Each *Idol* TV show is generically similar, but nationally particular. Each *Idol* maintains a specific look in set design, lighting and camera angles, colors, and logo (ovals with the TV show's name centered in custom lettering, written horizontally). Each *Idol* has a similar sounding theme song. Each *Idol* features hosts that play the same roles. Each *Idol* contracts people aspiring to media fame and fortune—Sreeram Chandra from Hyderabad (winner of *Indian Idol 5*) or Ho Chi Minh City born Trần Nguyễn Uyên Linh (winner of *Vietnam Idol 3*)—to compete with each other by singing hit songs derived from global and locally popular albums. Each *Idol* features a panel of national music industry experts, who judge the quality of each singer's performance. Each *Idol* has a predictable sequence of events. The singing competition proceeds through a series of stages: the auditions, theater rounds, semi-final, and grand finale. As the competition proceeds, performers are eliminated by the TV audience. Each *Idol* facilitates the interactivity of the audience; it encourages people to vote for their favorite contestant with a paid telephone call, text-message, or online web forum vote. In sum, *Idol* is an ideal-type global-national TV format and commodity form.

GLOCALIZED LIFESTYLE BRANDS IN THE AGE OF TRANSNATIONAL SATELLITE TV

Blockbuster films and global-national TV formats are two significant types of entertainment media. A third type of transnational entertainment media is not designed by TNMCs to have a genuinely global appeal (the blockbuster) or a lowest common denominator national appeal (the global TV format), but instead, designed to connect with viewers that share a similar "lifestyle" within and between many countries. In addition to targeting transnational viewers with global blockbusters and nation-specific viewers with TV formats, TNMCs target viewers with branded products that have been customized to connect with transnational cultural lifestyle differences. In order to capitalize upon differences, TNMCs started developing lifestyle media brands to unify select groups of people as members of branded media communities. To accomplish this goal, they pay attention to specific cultural identities and demographic details. Corporate management books such as Marilyn Halter's *Shopping for Identity: The Marketing of Ethnicity* (2000), Alfred Schreiber's *Multicultural Marketing* (2000), and Janeen Costa's *Marketing in a Multicultural World: Ethnicity, Nationalism, and Cultural Identity* (2000) represent the attentiveness of TNMCs to cultural difference and the integration of cultural difference into profit maximization strategies.

The emergence of branded media content coincides with the rapid growth of many commercialized and transnationalized satellite TV networks and channels (Chalaby 2002, 2005; Chan 2005b; Curtin 2005; Thussu 2006). In an earlier period, few public TV broadcasters operated within national territories and were inwardly focused on national markets. While TV broadcasting is by no means a post-public or post-national phenomenon (Morris and Waisbord 2001), TV broadcasters in many countries have become more plentiful, commercial, and transnational. Worldwide, there is a growing shift from public, free-to-air analogue broadcasting to privatized cable, digital, and satellite TV outfits. In 1989, there were a mere forty-seven licensed TV channels in the whole of the European Union; by 2010, there were nearly 10,000 licensed TV channels (Doyle 2012: 6). The "rise of transnational television lies at the heart of the current regional and global reshaping of media industries and cultures" says Chalaby (2005: 1). Sky TV and National Geographic (owned by News Corporation), CNN and Turner Classic Movies (owned by Time Warner) and MTV, Nickelodeon, and VH1 (owned by Viacom) are examples of trans-border satellite TV. Chalaby (2003) says transnational TV channels are a form of "de-territorialized broadcasting" that is distinct from national TV channels:

> Their audiences are multinational, their coverage is spread across boundaries and their schedules are designed to cross time zones. They are adapting to the global age by tearing apart the old relationship between place and TV that has traditionally prevailed in broadcasting history. (462)

While transnational satellite TV may be reconfiguring relations between territory, culture, and media, it is always grounded by locational forces that are materially and culturally specific to nation-states and the populations which reside within them (Curtin 2005). The TNMCs that own satellite TV networks and channels negotiate with and adapt themselves to national geographical, political, and cultural particulars.

The exhibition of lifestyle media brands through transnational satellite TV networks and channels is intertwined with a relatively recent corporate strategy called "glocalization," or "thinking globally and acting locally." Glocalization derives from the Japanese word *dochakuka*, which originally meant the adaptation of farming techniques to local conditions (Robertson 1995:28). McDonald's, for example, has gone global by localizing. Burke (2009) notes that McDonald's menu items have been adapted to the local tastes of the regions they do business in: "[T]he company sells McHuevo in Uruguay, McBurrito in Mexico, and the Maharaja Mac in India (replacing beef with lamb)" (53). While McDonald's is a symbol of the US, it does not seek to openly Americanize cultures. McDonald's globalizes by localizing and cooking its products with local and nationalist spices. They produce the same profit through the appearance of difference culture.

TNMCs express this dialectic when designing "glocalized lifestyle brands." In the media industry, glocalization refers to how TNMCs:

> maintain economies of scale while responding flexibly to cultural preferences.
> Customization can be applied at the level of product design, brand name, or packaging or simply of marketing and advertising in those cases where the product works fine as a global brand. (Averill 1996: 219)

TNMCs produce and distribute glocalized lifestyle brands that are customized to appeal to and resonate with national, regional, and demographic sensibilities (Aysha 2004: 249; Averill 1996: 219; Chang 2003). Sinclair, Jacka, and Cunningham (1996) note that TNMCs adapt media entertainment for particular geo-linguistic and cultural markets: "The resulting situation is not the passive homogenization of world television which cultural imperialism theorists feared, but rather its heterogenization" (13). The glocalization strategy is not undertaken to protect or promote cultures but, rather, to exploit them for commercial gain: "corporations are engaging in an emergent corporate strategy to penetrate resistant foreign markets by playing to a thin or superficial version of cultural differences as a means of establishing globally uniform habits of consumption" (Averill 1996: 203).

Viacom-owned MTV is a paramount example of a transnational TV network that profit-maximizes by glocalizing (Chalaby 2003; Cullity 2002; Fung 2006; Sowards 2003). According to Chalaby (2003), MTV began business operations in 1981 in the US, expanded into Europe in 1987, then Latin American in the early 1990s, and into Asia in the mid-1990s. MTV is now the world's largest transnational TV network. "MTV is a global brand which thinks and acts locally," says David Flack, Senior Vice President of MTV Asia's Creative and Content Division:

> Despite MTV being a global brand, we are local in approach. We reflect the taste and demands of our viewers and this differs in each market. Thus the need to create specific channels (in each country) that meet the needs of our target audience. (cited in Santana 2003)

In 1987, Viacom launched MTV Networks International. Broadcast by satellite to 164 countries through sixty-four local network affiliates in more than eighteen different languages, MTV Networks International reaches at least one billion young people daily with a global-local hybrid fusion of popular music, fast-talking video jockeys, rapid editing, and advertising messages (MTV Networks International 2006). MTV glocalizes in many national markets by establishing joint business ventures with local corporations (some state owned), complying with the cultural nationalist policy regimes of states, customizing programming in local or indigenous languages, employing local cultural workers and Video Jockeys (VJs), and scheduling a mix of US pop music and locally popular music acts (Chalaby 2006). In 2007, Viacom launched the MTV Arabia and Nickelodeon Arabia satellite broadcasting services (Arango 2008). By glocalizing in Europe, Africa, Latin America, and the Middle East, MTV develops hybridized entertainment products which express a synthesis of cultural themes and elements from two or more countries. MTV creates hybridity in its TV programming, a media mix of US pop culture and local culture. Chalaby (2006) documents how glocalization is key to the profit-maximization strategy of MTV: Viacom is gaining hold of cable pay-TV markets worldwide precisely because of its "mastery of adaptation and hybridization techniques" (46).

TNMCs also design lifestyle entertainment brands to capitalize on cultural particulars. These brands include paid and specialty TV channels that target members of communities across borders and cultural-linguistic divides. Lifestyle entertainment brands recognize and express the cultural tastes and preferences of segmented "lifestyle" groups defined "by age, race, income, gender and location" (Becker 2006) within and between states. They appeal to people on the basis of their particular lifestyle, not their national identities. Within this approach, the audience is not lumped into one humungous national box, but is segmented and divided into smaller and smaller demographic boxes. When developing lifestyle brands, TNMCs hire marketing researchers, cool hunters, and ethno-demographic specialists to identify, monitor and assess the qualities of diverse groups. They recognize the members of these groups as consumers and then try to represent their lifestyle in TV shows, a corporate strategy that reflects how difference sells (and pays). Difference sells (Frank 1997; Heath and Potter 2004). Lifestyle entertainment represents how TNMCs are heeding and capitalizing upon demands for cultural recognition and more diverse media representations of identities. In pursuit of profit, TNMCs recognize and represent diverse identities and lifestyles through the TV networks, channels, and shows they own. While there "is nothing new about the capitalist media's willingness to devour and reinvent itself in the search for the new, about its tendency to fragment, diversify, and explore alternative cultures" (Curtin and Streeter 2001: 229), TNMCs are now doing this all over the world. TV shows and films previously considered risky, edgy, or subversive are now mainstream fare (Curtin 1999).

Viacom, for example, owns many lifestyle entertainment brands that target a number of different communities as brand-loyal lifestyle groups. To affluent members of the transnational LGBT community, Viacom offers Logo ("With news, series and specials, more than twenty original shows, documentaries, films, music and information on popular destinations around the world, Logo features cutting-edge, relevant entertainment for LGBT audiences, and anyone else who enjoys this kind of programming"); for guys that identify as stereotypical "men", it offers Spike ("SPIKE celebrates men and all their aspirations. The brand speaks to the bold, adventurous side of men: to climb higher, work harder, be stronger, and of course, to be entertained along the entire journey"); to people that identify as "black," it sells "Black Entertainment Television" (BET) ("the leading provider of entertainment content for African Americans and consumers of Black culture worldwide. The primary BET channel reaches more than 90 million households in the United States, the United Kingdom, Canada, Middle East, Africa and the Caribbean"); to the parents of preschoolers it sells Noggin ("NOGGIN's mission is to be like preschool on TV—a place on-air and online where kids can gain key curricular knowledge in a curated and organized environment"); and to older children it distributes Nickelodeon. Viacom's premium TV brands target translocally situated viewers defined by cultural lifestyle, not by universal qualities or by a strict vision of "national culture."

A recurring worry among media democracy activists and cultural nationalists is that the rise of concentrated global media giants such as Viacom reduces source diversity and, as a result, reduces the diversity of representations circulating at any given time (Baker 2007; Noam 2009). Neoliberals, however, argue that transnational corporate concentration has not lead to a scarcity of diverse sources or media products but, instead, has created an abundance of media (Compaine 2005; Thierer and Eskelsen 2008). US and transnational media consumers have a greater and much wider range of TV and film content available to them than in any previous era. TNMCs like Viacom produce and distribute TV shows and films containing a plurality of diverse themes and stories. The ever-increasing number of entertainment selections (lots of customized films, TV shows, cable channels, stations, and websites that niche consumers may select from), however, masks ever-shrinking source diversity (few centralized and concentrated TNMCs) (Meehan 2010). However, the result may not be cultural homogenization as was feared by the CI paradigm, but cultural fragmentation.

TNMCs target national viewers and translocally differentiated groups with glocalized and lifestyle entertainment forms that give the appearance of a diverse global culture. TNMCs "seek less to homogenize [global] popular culture than to organize and exploit diverse forms of creativity toward profitable ends" (Curtin 1990: 60). This TNMC strategy is an exemplar of what Kraidy (2004) refers to as "corporate transculturalism": "a profit-driven strategy that actively and systematically seeks to capitalize on cultural fusion and fluid identities" (90). TNMCs based in the US do not necessarily have a financial interest in manufacturing entertainment content that promotes US "national culture." They recognize and represent everything and everyone, so long as they can be commoditized and sold on world markets.

Glocalized and lifestyle brands signal not the weakening of US-based TNMCs, but their dynamism. While these entertainment forms depart from the "Americanist" texts and culturally monolithic commodity representations of previous periods, they also highlight a transnational corporate strategy set on overturning the remaining barriers to capitalist accumulation posed by territorial expressions of cultural nationalism and translocal cultural particularisms. They respond to local fears of cultural Americanization from without (cultural domination by outsiders) and exclusionary cultural-nationalist homogenization from within (assimilation by insiders). However, while the global cultural superstructure is changing, the economic base may not be. The contradiction between the culturally diverse and heterogeneous commodity appearances and unified and monolithic TNMC ownership structures, the disconnect between the upwardly mobile, cosmopolitan, and elite consumers of such entertainment and the world's territorialized working majority, and the void separating commercial images of global cultural diversity from the often brutal material realities of classism, racism, and sexism all over the world represent ongoing sites of tension and conflict in the global cultural economy.

REVERSE ENTERTAINMENT FLOW: FROM THE REST TO THE US

US TNMCs use a number of business and textual strategies to produce blockbuster films, global-national TV formats, and glocalized and lifestyle-targeted transnational TV channels to export globally. Non-US NMCs devise savvy business and textual strategies to enter the US market with reverse entertainment flows (Keane 2006). Entertainment does not only flow from the US to the Rest, but also from the Rest into the US. What challenges do non-US NMCs face when trying to break into the US? What global-local business practices and textual encoding, production, and distribution strategies do non-US NMCs use to get their entertainment into the US market? Non-US NMCs face great obstacles and barriers when trying to enter the US market; in order to overcome them, they employ three "reverse flow" strategies: 1) targeting audiences in diaspora with culturally proximate media; 2) licensing re-makes; and, 3) "transculturating" foreign-ness.

Non-US NMCs that wish to circulate a film or TV show in the US market face a number of barriers to entry. Since the 1960s, the percentage of non-US films released in the US has declined. In the 1960s, imported films accounted for 10 percent of the US box office; in the 1980s, it was 7 percent; in the 2000s, it declined to less than 1 percent (Christopherson 2011). The US is not a closed cultural regime, but its media market is difficult to enter (Kaufman 2006). Why do non-US NMCs have such a difficult time breaking into the US market? First, although the US is a land of diasporic diversity, many US viewers—like culturally proximate viewers elsewhere—have parochial media tastes and preferences. Scott (2011) notes that "As fashion, gaming, pop music, social media and just about everything else have combined to shrink the world and bridge gaps of culture and taste, American movie audiences seem to cling to a cautious, isolationist approach to entertainment." Subtitled, dubbed, and often aesthetically innovative "foreign" TV shows and films tend not to attract a large English-speaking US audience. Non-US entertainment is regularly framed as boring or difficult to watch, assessed according to US entertainment norms, and relegated to some exclusive "art house" niche. Second, vertically and horizontally integrated US-based TNMCs are gatekeepers to the entertainment flowing into the US from elsewhere. They assume that the US audience will not watch non-US entertainment, and for this reason they do not acquire the licensing rights to many non-US TV shows and films. The oligopolistic market power of TNMCs is strengthened when they block non-US entertainment and leverage their distribution firms to only carry entertainment produced by the studios they own. Third, non-US NMCs do not produce TV series and films in accordance with the MPAA's ratings system. An "R" or "NC-17" rating may turn off mainstream US viewers, distributors, and TV networks. Yet despite these barriers, non-US NMCs have had some success in getting their media to viewers in the US by using strategies which are discussed below.

Targeting Diaspora. Non-US NMCs often break into the US market by targeting viewers in diaspora in the US. A diaspora is a community of people who share language and culture, and who have moved from one state to many others. Some people choose to move from their home state in search of better opportunities (e.g., a higher wage than corporations in their homeland pay; a higher standard of living). Many people are forcibly pushed out of their home states by natural disasters (tsunamis, earthquakes, famine) or state coercion (genocide, ethnic cleansing, war). The US is a "land of immigrants," accepting more legal immigrants as permanent residents than any other state. From 2000 to 2010, nearly 14 million people migrated to the US. In 2010, the US's legal and illegal immigrant population totaled 40 million. The US immigrant population has doubled since 1990, tripled since 1980, and quadrupled since 1970 (Camarota 2011). The leading states of origin for the majority of immigrants to the US are Mexico, India, the Philippines, and China (James and Rytina 2009). Immigrants to the US hold memories of their national homeland and a commitment or will to imagine a future in the US. Millions of people live in between cultures. After landing in the US, migrants maintain contact with family members and friends in their country of origin. They also maintain a connection to the internal political affairs and happenings of their homeland. Often, new immigrants to the US are isolated, marginalized, and under-represented by the dominant national framework and national media system. They look for ways to reconnect with their country of origin, to affirm a sense of identity and belonging. Non-US NMCs capitalize on the migrant's longing for home. They target viewers in diaspora, in the US state, with culturally proximate news and entertainment media. Members of migrant communities have longed used print and electronic media to keep in touch with their homeland (Thussu 2006: 188). Non-US NMCs produce and distribute culturally and linguistically proximate TV channels, TV shows, and films that are intended to resonate with and be consumed by immigrant communities in the US (or the US-based firms that target them).

BOX 5.4

SPANISH-LANGUAGE TV, THE LATINA/OS DIASPORA AND YO SOY BETTY, LA FEA

NMCs headquartered in Latin American states target the cultural-linguistically proximate Latino population in the US. The "differences between Cuban émigrés in Miami, Mexican illegal immigrants in California, and the urban populations of Latin American states are secondary to a sense of a Latin-American community that finds itself in international Spanish-language television programming" (Sparks 2007: 143). Mexico's Televisa and TV Azteca, Venezuela's Venevision, Brazil's O Globo, and Colombia's RCN and Caracol target the US-Latino population and the US-based TV networks that target this demographic, such as Univision (owned by US private equity firms TPG Capital and Thomas H. Lee Partners) and Telemundo (owned by NBC-Universal). Latin American-based NMCs regularly engage in joint ventures, equity alliances, co-production deals, and licensing agreements with US-based Latino-targeting networks. Spanish language entertainment flows to the US from South to North, and from the US down the continent, from North to South, signaling a two-way and multi-directional flow. Latin American NMCs target their home market, culturally proximate markets, and the US market too. They target the Spanish-speaking US audience through licensing agreements with US Spanish-language TV broadcasters. They target the English-speaking US audience through a licensing agreement with an English-language TV broadcaster. Also, they may license a TV show's makeover rights to TV networks in the US, which then interpret and locally adapt it (Miller 2010).

The most frequent kind of South-to-North entertainment flow is the telenovela, the most popular kind of TV show in Latin American countries. Telenovelas originated in Latin America. The Cuban radio-novela format morphed into the Cuban telenovela in the 1950s. After the Cuban revolution, many telenovela writers and producers fled, landing in various Latin American states to establish a telenovela industry. Though telenovelas originated in Latin America, they are now a globally popular TV form, watched all over the world on almost every continent, from Africa to Asia to Europe. Telenovelas are defined by humor (serious issues, often dealt with humorously), romance (hetero-normative love stories and heartbreaks), improbable events (fantastical rags-to-riches storylines), and melodrama (universal themes, exaggerated plots, and archetypal characters). Telenovelas have a different narrative pattern to US soap operas. US soap operas have open narratives (they can go on forever); telenovelas have closed narratives (usually only 75–150 episodes are produced). The dramatic conflicts of US soap operas often never get resolved, while telenovelas narrative conflicts do. The soap opera is designed to be watched forever; telenovelas are designed to be watched ritualistically, over a short period of time.

Yo Soy Betty, la fea, a story of a physically unattractive but highly intelligent economist working as a secretary in a fashion corporation, is an example of a telenovela that entered the US market (in its original, dubbed, and adapted form). The Colombian TV network Radio Cadena Nacional (RCN) developed *Yo soy Betty, la fea* between 1999 and 2001. Between 2001 and 2010, this Colombian TV show was exported, licensed, dubbed, and adapted worldwide. In India, *Yo Soy Betty, la fea* is called *Jassi Jaissi Koi Nahin* (*There is No One Like Jassi*); in Turkey, *Sensiz Olmuyor* (*Won't Work Without You*); in Russia it is *Не родись красивой* (*Be Not Born Beautiful*); in Germany, it is *Verliebt in Berlin* (*In Love in Berlin*); in Mexico, it is *La fea más bella* (*The Most Beautiful Ugly Girl*); in

Croatia/Serbia, it is *Ne daj se, Nina* (*Don't Give Up, Nina*); in Vietnam, it is *Cô gái xấu xí* (*Ugly Girl*); in the Philippines, it is *I Love Betty La Fea* (*I Love Ugly Betty*); in Poland, it is *BrzydUla* (*Ugly Ula*); in Brazil, it is *Bela, a Feia* (*Beauty, the Ugly*); and in the US and Anglo-Americanized markets of Canada, the UK, and Australia, it is the ABC-TV adapted *Ugly Betty*. As Miller (2010) says, "Betty, the original character in Colombian telenovela *Betty la Fea*, has traveled around the world and back again in a variety of guises, speaking a vast assortment of tongues" (198).

Licensing Remakes. Non-US NMCs can also get their films and TV shows into the US audio-visual market as remakes. While non-US NMCs target migrants, exiles, and expatriates in the US, they also tempt US-based TNMCs with remake rights to films and TV shows. Non-US NMCs market and sell the English-language remake rights to TV series and films they own to US-based TNMCs. US film and TV production companies have long been in the business of licensing and adapting non-US TV shows and films. *Three's Company* (1977–1984) was based on the UK's *Man About the House; All in the Family* (1971–1979) was based on the UK's *Till Death Do Us Part*. In 1987, Walt Disney adapted the French comedy, *Three Men and A Cradle* as *Three Men and a Baby*. Licensed remakes of non-US films from East Asia are common too (Keane 2006). East Asian NMCs have eagerly sold remake rights to films such as *The Ring* (2002) and *Dark Water* (2004) (Japan); *My Sassy Girl* (2001) and *My Wife is a Gangster* (2001) (Korea); and *Infernal Affairs* (2001) and *The Eye* (2003) (Hong Kong). In 2010, US-based Liberty Media released *Let Me In*, an adapted version of the Swedish drama-fantasy-horror film, *Let the Right One In* (2008). The Swedish film *Män som hatar kvinnor* or *Men Who Hate Women* (2009) was adapted as *The Girl with the Dragon Tattoo* (2011) by Sony-owned Columbia Pictures (King 2011).

US TNMCs remake foreign films and TV shows when they believe that their stories will appeal to the US audience. Levy (2010) says the top ten most significant and well-received Hollywood remakes of foreign films are *Let Me In* (2010) / *Let The Right One In* (2008) (Sweden), *Some Like It Hot* (1959) / *Fanfaren der Liebe* (1952) (West Germany), *12 Monkeys* (1996) / *La Jetée* (1962) (France), *The Magnificent Seven* (1960) / *The Seven Samurai* (1954) (Japan), *Scent of a Woman* (1992) / *Profumo di Donna* (1974) (Italy), *Solaris* (2002) / *Solyaris* (1972) (Soviet Union), *The Departed* (2006) / *Infernal Affairs* (2002) (Hong Kong), *A Fistful of Dollars* (1964) / *Yojimbo* (1961) (Japan), *The Birdcage* (1996) / *La Cage aux Folles* (1978) (France-Italy), and *Funny Games* (2007) / *Funny Games* (1997) (Austria). Critics charge that these remakes reflect the inability of US production companies to develop novel ideas. They also say that remakes Americanize foreign TV shows and films, emptying non-US works of their cultural and aesthetic specificity in order to appeal to a lowest common denominator audience. TNMCs counter this argument. They say they want to make a non-US TV show or film better than the original, market it to a larger audience than the original was able to reach, and make an important story more nationally and transnationally accessible by overcoming its cultural discount. While non-US NMCs get a version of their entertainment into the US by selling English-language remake rights, the US TNMCs usually benefit most:

Although there are short term benefits [of selling English-language remake rights], each film sold to Hollywood cedes further ground to the studios' dominance of the international marketplace, while simultaneously eroding the non-US film industry's ability to exhibit outside its own borders. (Goldman 1993)

US-based TNMCs, however, are not the only firms that remake entertainment media originally made elsewhere. Non-US NMCs regularly pillage Hollywood's intellectual property archives in order to make their own versions of US entertainment media (Prigge 2010). Turkey adapted Steven Spielberg's classic *E.T.: The Extra-Terrestrial* (1982) as *Badi* (1983) and integrated footage from *Star Wars* (1977) into *The Man Who Saves the World* (1982) without Spielberg's consent; Italy adapted *Groundhog Day* (1983) as *Stork Day* (2004). Bollywood remade films such as *Fight Club* (1999) as *Fight Club: Members Only* (2006) and *Mrs. Doubtfire* (1993) as *Chachi 420* (1998); Russia turned *Twelve Angry Men* (1957) into *12* (2007). Japan remade *Sideways* (2004) as *Sideways* (2009). US TNMCs and non-US NMCs adapt, modify, and remake each other's stories, resulting in often strange and interesting hybrid texts.

Transculturation. Non-US NMCs try to get their entertainment products circulated in the US market by taking stories derived from local and national traditions and "transculturating" them to suit US tastes and preferences. Wu and Chan (2007) define "transculturation" as the process by which non-US NMCs transform a local or national story in a way that makes it travel well in the US and wider global markets by incorporating "globalized norms and concepts in the production of local cultural products" to enhance "their acceptability around the world" (198). Hong Kong-based NMCs, for example, produced US and globally popular films such as *Crouching Tiger, Hidden Dragon* (2000), *Hero* (2002), and *The House of Flying Daggers* (2004) by reviving ancient Chinese stories and turning them into action-packed spectacular blockbuster films. They did so with financial and distribution support from US-based TNMCs. Non-US NMCs often align with US-based TNMCs in order to cash in on US and Western viewer interest in and fantasies of other cultures. They try to make entertainment that appeals to US and Western viewers while maintaining a sense of cultural distinctiveness and tradition (Wu and Chan 2007: 211).

BOX 5.5

TRANSCULTURATING *CROUCHING TIGER, HIDDEN DRAGON*

Crouching Tiger, Hidden Dragon (CTHD) is the first foreign-language movie that made more than US $100 million at the US box office. *CTHD* was recognized at the Academy Awards in 2000 and 2001 and received ten Oscar nominations. Wu and Chan (2007) state that *CTHD* is a Chinese film that was able to break into the US and wider world markets due to a combination of local-global business and textual strategies. To get *CTHD* into the US, Chinese NMCs (Asia Union Film & Entertainment, China Film Co-Production Corporation, EDKO Film, and United China Vision) formed strategic local-global financing and production/distribution partnerships with production studios and distribution firms owned by US-based TNMCs (Sony Pictures Classics, Good Machine, Columbia Film Production Asia, Warner Brothers, Columbia Tristar, and Sony Pictures Classic). *CTHD* was an equity China-US co-production. This local-global business alliance was crucial to *CTHD*'s circulation outside of China. To design *CTHD* to appeal to a US audience, Chinese and US firms

BOX 5.5 (Continued)
"transculturated" the film text. Following the logic of the "cultural discount," the production companies downplayed overly particularistic cultural references to China that could be seen as too different, distant, and unappealing to a US audience. Many particular Chinese cultural references—wuxia stories, iconic settings, use of Chinese custom, period costumes, music, architecture, the Mandarin language—are seen and heard in *CTHD*, but these local cultural references are mixed with more universally appealing themes about individual struggles for freedom, love, constraining social norms, and ideals of honor and selfless duty. By encoding *CTHD* with these local-global themes, the production companies hoped to appeal to Chinese, US, and transnational audiences (210). The East-West entertainment flow is imbalanced and not reciprocal. Nevertheless, the global-local production of *CTHD* shows that reverse entertainment flows from the East to the West are possible.

CONCLUSION: BEYOND US IMPERIAL MEDIA CONTENT?

This chapter has examined the business and textual strategies employed by US-based TNMCs in order to go global. TNMCs design global blockbusters, global-national TV formats, and glocalized lifestyle brands that are intended to travel well in many markets, not just the US market. US-based TNMCs are the world system's most economically powerful actors. However, they are not always agents of cultural "Americanization." This flies in the face of the CI paradigm, which argues that the global encroachment of US TNMCs is Americanizing global culture and diminishing diverse media content. The findings of this chapter suggest that the CI paradigm's account of the media content produced and distributed by US-based TNMCs rests upon a number of problematic assumptions.

First, cultural imperialism critics rely upon a Fordist-era monopoly media model that has not got to grips with new post-Fordist accumulation logics. As Curtin (1999) observes: "assumptions about the homogenizing power of huge media conglomerates [. . .] fosters a mis-recognition of the actual forces at work in the contemporary culture industries" (2). A complete shift from Fordist-era monopoly media capitalism (concentrated and centralized media ownership, mass production of entertainment commodities for a single mass or uniform audience) to post-Fordist flexible specialization (de-conglomerated, disintegrated, and de-centralized firms, customized production of entertainment commodities for a plurality of micro or niche audiences) has not completely transpired (Christopherson and Storper 1986, 1989; Storper 1989, 1993). But there are significant changes that need to be addressed. While media ownership remains concentrated and centralized, US-based TNMCs are at the core of de-centralized cross-border production networks that make a wide variety of specialized and customized TV shows and films for a plurality of viewer niches. One concentrated media conglomerate (Walt Disney, for example) controls and contracts a multiplicity of differentiated TV and film production firms in order to flexibly customize branded media products for a variety of audience groupings: global, national and trans-local. US-based TNMCs produce and sell a wide variety of entertainment commodities—blockbuster films, TV formats, lifestyle brands—which sometimes represent the US, but which also portray many other cultures.

Second, critics of cultural imperialism tacitly assume a cause-effect relationship between media source shrinkage and media content uniformity. Certainly, US-TNMCs are the primary source of many of the TV shows and films circulating around the world. Their TV shows and films are a dominant presence in many countries, but the TV shows and films TNMCs license to and co-produce with NMCs carry a range of diverse cultural representations, not all of which are "American." Furthermore, there is no guarantee that an increase of non-US corporate media sources would lead to an abundance of TV shows and films that are deeply diverse. In fact, many non-US NMCs produce standardized entertainment media. Tunstall (2007) notes that "in the last two decades, most national TV systems have been making their own cheap but popular programming—including soaps, game shows, quizzes and reality programming" (322). A few TNMCs may be better able to create diverse media products than many small media firms because of the capital resources they control. The shrinkage of global media source diversity due to the global growth of US-based TNMCs does not necessarily lead to culturally homogeneous entertainment content. US TNMCs rule world audio-visual markets, but not all of the TV shows and films they make are agents of cultural Americanization.

Cultural imperialism scholars are correct in their view that the overarching goal of TNMCs is market domination, but the kinds of media content they develop in pursuit of this goal have changed. TNMCs know that the manufacture and export of overtly "Americanized" films and TV shows to countries around the world is not a solid business strategy. As *The Economist* (2002) puts it: "Think Local: Cultural Imperialism doesn't sell." Certainly, many TV shows and films still do represent the US and the "American Way of Life," but US-TNMCs are de-Americanizing the content of TV shows and films so that they may more easily capture and control global, national, and trans-local lifestyle markets. In order to expand their profit margins, TNMCs are designing entertainment media that intends to connect with transnational, national, and sub-national audience groupings, not just the US audience. In sum, the residual commodity forms of cultural imperialism—US nationalist films and TV shows that promote one-dimensional or homogeneous images of "the American Way of Life" to the US and to the wider world—co-exist with emergent global, transnational, and sub-national commodity forms. The corporate executives and above-the-line creative workers of TNMCs take the concepts of the cultural discount and cultural proximity seriously. They attempt to minimize the perceived threat of "Americanization" by designing global blockbusters, global-national TV formats, and lifestyle brands.

CHAPTER 6

Global Entertainment Media, Local Audiences

INTRODUCTION: FIGURES OF THE AUDIENCE

To whom do scholars refer when talking about "the audience"? What is implied about the audience when it is talked about? Whether active or passive, resistant or controlled, sovereign or dominated, "the audience" is often nothing more than the "subject-effect" of institutional discourses on the audience. Scholars, journalists, and policy-makers have much to write and say about the audience. The audience of global entertainment media is often a blank screen that policy-makers, scholars, and others project their own image of an audience upon. The actual audience—the millions of people that watch, consume, and live with and through entertainment media—rarely gets to speak. It is spoken of and spoken for. The "audience"—what it is, who it refers to, what its relationship to entertainment media is—is fluid and objectified (Butsch 2003; Livingston 2004). An audience is constructed through discourses—ways of talking about and representing—about "the audience." When we talk about the audience, we construct "figures of the audience" (Allor 1996: 209) or ideal type models of relations between global entertainment media and local audiences. Miller et al. (2005) say that the "audience is artificial, a creature of the industry, the state and academia, which proceed to act upon their creation" (32).

This chapter examines how the discourses of TNMCs, governments, and academies construct the audiences for global entertainment media. This chapter analyzes "five figures" of global entertainment media's local audience: 1) neoliberalism's figure of the audience as a sovereign consumer; 2) political-economy's figure of the audience as a commodity; 3) the CI paradigm and cultivation and effects researcher's figure of the audience as a victim of Americanization and capitalist-consumer ideology; 4) cultural studies figure of the audience as an active meaning-maker; and, 5) new media studies' figure of the audience as an interactive user.

NEOLIBERALISM: THE AUDIENCE AS MARKET/SOVEREIGN CONSUMER

Neoliberalism is a dominant way of representing global entertainment media's local audience. Neoliberal doctrine depicts people as "sovereign consumers." The notion of consumer sovereignty is derived from the work of neo-classical economists such as Adam Smith (2012) and Friedrech von Hayek (2007). Proponents of consumer sovereignty argue that: 1) people are private, rational, and self-interested individuals that have sovereignty over and are determining of their own needs and wants; and, 2) people's individual needs and wants are expressed through the marketplace, which is the most efficient and most effective mechanism for responding to needs and wants (the market matches consumer demand with producer supply). Tucker (2004) summarizes this thus:

> Consumer sovereignty is the freedom of consumers to cast their dollar votes to buy, at prices determined in competitive markets. As a result, consumer spending determines what goods and services firms produce. In a capitalist system, most allocative decisions are coordinated by consumers and producers interacting through markets. (443)

Neoliberals represent the audience as "consumer markets" for products. Mass and niche consumers ("markets") are depicted as having the power to determine what type of films and TV shows TNMCs produce and distribute in society. Consumers are the kings of entertainment markets, reigning over serf-like TNMCs. "The media and entertainment industry is striving to meet the 'anywhere, anytime' content demands of today's consumer," says John Nendick of the market research firm Ernst & Young Global Media & Entertainment Leader (Staff Writer 2006). US-based TNMCs and the commercial entertainment they sell flow around the world because they give the transnational audience what it wants (Cowen 2002). Neoliberals say that sovereign consumers drive the global production and distribution of Hollywood TV shows and films. Economies of scale make it very easy for US-based TNMCs to globally distribute their products and very difficult for non-US NMCs to compete (Scott 2004b; Segrave 1997). TNMCs maintain large production budgets, produce high-quality entertainment products, and control international distribution networks. However, neoliberals say that when given a choice between globalizing US entertainment or locally produced entertainment, sovereign consumers demand films and TV shows that have ostensibly been made in the US. The global popularity of US entertainment is seen as a reflection of global consumer demand (Balko 2003; Olson 1999). The world's sovereign consumers demand high-quality entertainment. US-based TNMCs effectively meet that demand by producing entertainment for them.

There is something to neoliberalism's figure of the sovereign consumer. TNMCs have the power to produce and distribute whatever entertainment products they choose, but if these commodities fail to satisfy consumer tastes and preferences, they will not travel very far and will not generate much revenue. If consumers reject a film or TV show, TNMCs do not make money, and so in an attempt to profit-maximize, TNMCs produce entertainment that responds to and reflects perceived and calculated consumer tastes and preferences. TNMCs spend a tremendous amount of money, time, and energy trying to understand what consumers want. But, ultimately, it is the sovereign consumers who decide the box office success of a film or the popularity of a TV show. Consumers, not TNMCs, decide the market success or failure of entertainment. Consumption drives entertainment production. Neoliberals say the growth and collapse, rise and fall, profitability or bankruptcy of TNMCs rests upon their ability to efficiently and effectively satisfy sovereign consumers.

Neoliberalism's figure of the sovereign consumer is perpetuated by the CEOs and managers of US-based TNMCs in order to challenge the CI paradigm, denigrate cultural protectionism, and make a moral case for the global primacy of US entertainment. For example, in a speech entitled "Good-bye to Hollywood" given at a California Town Hall in 1990, former co-Chairman and Co-CEO of Time Warner J. Richard Munro warned about "very influential people who want America to stop exporting so many media and entertainment products." Munro claimed that Hollywood does not force states to open their markets:

> no soldier or representative of our government is in the business of being an enforcer of Hollywood. We require no nation, province or individual to buy our magazines, watch our TV programs, attend our movies, or listen to our records.

Munro says sovereign consumers are responsible for the global dominance of US entertainment: "When people buy 'Hollywood' [. . .] they do so freely, out of their own volition [. . .] because they want the best value for the best price." Sovereign consumers freely choose US TV shows and films because they "are as good or better than those produced by any other country." They are attracted to US entertainment because it symbolizes:

> the right to listen to Madonna as well as Mozart; The freedom to go into a store and buy clothes in the color or style you want, or to turn on a television and have choices other than what the Ministry of Culture thinks you should have.

Munro rejects the notion that the globalization of US entertainment media flattens cultures, insisting that it reflects global cultural diversity. US entertainment media is depicted as offering globally transparent texts that are "open to the widest expression of viewpoints and tastes," and this is because the US has "more of this diversity than any other nation on Earth." Munro concludes that US entertainment media reflects the global village and calls upon the US state and his "colleagues at Time Warner [. . .] to reverse the tide of economic-cultural protectionism through negotiation and common sense." By explaining the global dominance of US entertainment media with reference to markets and sovereign consumer choice, Monroe overlooks the many ways in which the US government promotes and protects the global profit interests of US-based TNMCs.

However, neoliberal arguments such as Munroe's face many criticisms. First, neoliberalism removes entertainment from the sphere of public deliberation (where it is treated as a public good and something that shapes ways of life) and places it in the sphere of the market (where it is treated as a commodity, something that is exchanged for money). In order to challenge those who believe TNMC conduct should be guided by state-supported non-market goals such as the public interest, citizenship, or national culture, neoliberals present a good society as a fundamentally market society. Neoliberals say that the flow of entertainment worldwide should be "left to market forces" and that the choice to produce and distribute entertainment in society is best enabled by markets. They depict state intervention in entertainment markets as unwanted and unwarranted. Neoliberals argue that freedom of consumer choice has the greatest value in society. If Chinese consumers want to watch more than fourteen US blockbuster films a year (the current PRC quota), then they should be able to do so. If "Gen Y" US youth wish to fill their daily media diet with reality TV show re-runs instead of civically-valuable news content, then they have a right to do so. The Chinese consumption of more US blockbuster films may dilute the PRC's official national culture; "Gen Y"

Americans may grow up knowing more about the latest *Idol* winner than the First Amendment. But no worries! The consumers know what is best. By placing consumer choice above all other values in society, neoliberals overlook the negative cultural externalities of entertainment markets. Neoliberals promote optimal consumer choice as an index of a good society, regardless of the consequences—economic, political or cultural—of such choice. By only depicting entertainment media as a commodity and audiences as markets of sovereign consumers, neoliberals downplay how entertainment media is a powerful and influential communicational medium.

Second, neoliberals equate freedom of choice in the marketplace with political freedom. They condemn state attempts to regulate entertainment markets, viewing state intervention as a threat to freedom. Appiah (2006), for example, argues that people everywhere ought to be able to freely choose whatever entertainment they like. Pellerin (2006) says that "The US supports expanding cultural liberty around the world, but not at the price of limiting people's choices to consume whatever cultural products they want." Here, the consumer's choice to consume globalizing entertainment media is depicted as an act of freedom. Yet, the choice to consume is infrequently "free." Consumers select goods that have been chosen by others—financers, executives, advertisers, cultural workers. In the age of corporate concentration and oligopolistic markets, the free market is a myth, peddled by corporate-financed think tanks. Furthermore, there is no "free lunch" in the marketplace. To enjoy entertainment, people must first pay for it (with their attention or hard earned wages). The market includes and excludes people based upon their ability to pay. Wealthy consumers in rich and poor states alike are much freer and much more able to consume globalizing entertainment media than the millions of poor people that live on less than $2 a day. Not every person can pay to participate in branded entertainment communities. Millions of people worldwide are systematically excluded by and under-represented in the markets of TNMCs because they do not possess the money to pay for entertainment media (and the goods and services featured in advertisements). Because TNMCs are most interested in meeting the demands of those consumers that have money to pay for entertainment, they regularly privilege the tastes and preferences of already affluent socio-economic groups as free and equal consumers, thereby reproducing the marginalization and exclusion of under-privileged groups and entire populations. Worldwide, and due to socio-economic inequality, entertainment markets regularly fail to be a source of free choice. Additionally, and as proven by China, political freedoms do not always follow consumer freedoms.

Third, neoliberals claim that the supply of US entertainment products in the global marketplace reflects sovereign consumer demand. The consumer is constructed as a rational actor and chooser. But critics of neoliberalism's notion of consumer sovereignty pose the following question: do consumer wants spontaneously arise from consumers themselves (i.e., internally defined), or might such wants and needs be socially constructed by others (i.e., externally defined)? Neoliberals represent "sovereign consumers" as independent decision makers. But what if consumer decisions are heavily influenced by community norms (established political or religious ideology) or by aggressive advertising campaigns? TNMCs annually spend hundreds of millions of dollars on multi-media marketing campaigns that are intended to convince consumers that their specific wants can and will be met by entertainment. TNMCs define cultural wants and needs: they use advertising to shape the cultural meaning of "want" and the wants of consumers for the TV shows and films they sell. As Galbraith (1998) said in his critique of the sovereign consumer idea:

> Consumer wants can have bizarre, frivolous, and even immoral origins, and an admirable case can be made for a society that seeks to satisfy them. But the case cannot stand if it is the process of satisfying wants that creates the wants. (125)

That advertising exists to influence consumer decision-making problematizes neoliberalism's figure of the sovereign consumer as king of the global marketplace.

Fourth, neoliberals imagine media corporations (sellers) supplying paying consumers (buyers) with the TV shows and films they want, when and where they want them, as if consumer choice is the primary cause of a TV show or film's social existence. They perceive the tastes and preferences of consumers as ultimately determining which TV shows and films corporate sellers manufacture, distribute, and exhibit. Yet, entertainment media commodities do not circulate in markets as result of consumer choice alone. In fact, an individual consumer's desire to watch this or that TV show or film plays a relatively small role in shaping the overall industrial process through which entertainment media commodities are chosen to be brought into the world. All of the TV shows and films which consumers think they want and need in any country have been chosen by a number of industry stakeholders far in advance (and in anticipation) of individual consumer choice. The notion that individual consumers themselves determine the TV shows and films available on the market at any given time and place is incredibly simplistic. Consumers do *select* which TV shows and films they want to watch (from thousands upon thousands of available selections provisioned by exhibitors such as theater chains and TV networks), but the choice to produce a TV show or film and distribute, market, and exhibit it is made primarily by the corporate actors who control the capital resources to do so (see Chapter 2). Neoliberal discourse on magical markets and sovereign consumers conceals the human origins of TV shows and films. The commonplace notion that the availability of a TV show or film on any market—regional, national, or global—is created entirely by the wishes of individual buyers (i.e., sovereign consumers) abstracts TV shows and films from the human origins of their production: waged labor. Media commodities are reified and rendered as autonomous objects whose existence is determined by consumers who, sorcerer-like, summon them into the market. Neoliberals are thus guilty of "commodity fetishism" (Jhally 1987).

Fifth, neoliberals depict the entertainment market as a democratizing force because it gives consumers what they think they want. Neoliberalism conflates market transactions in the economic sphere with democratic processes in the political sphere. Business historian Thomas Frank (2000) calls this conflation, "market populism." Promoted by neoliberal think-tanks, politicians, and industry elites, market populism represents markets as "a far more democratic forum of organization than democratically elected governments" and says that markets, "in addition to being mediums of exchange," are "mediums of consent" (xiv). Market populists view global entertainment media as a model for democracy. A *New York Times* piece entitled "Democracy Rules, and Pop Culture Depends on It" presents interactive reality-TV formats as models of democracy: "inspired by Fox's *American Idol* and the open culture of the Internet, voter-based competitions are proliferating in every corner of the entertainment world" (Leeds 2007). Reality TV formats give the every-person the ability to speak, be recognized, and be responded to. Political liberty is rendered tantamount to consumer interactivity and public deliberation in a representative democracy is reduced to consumer voting practices. Pay-per-voting for one's favorite *Idol*, the next top model, or the most engaging Super Bowl advertisement supposedly expresses the popular will of ordinary people more efficiently and meaningfully than elections! Yet, markets are not necessarily democratic (Klein 2007), and most TV shows and films do not simulate a model for grassroots democracy. In a liberal democratic state, every citizen has a political right to vote. TNMCs only include people as free and equal choosers of TV shows and films if they have the capacity to pay.

POLITICAL ECONOMY: THE AUDIENCE AS COMMODITY

Political economists further criticize neoliberalism's figure of the sovereign consumer and complicate the view that TNMCs reflect what the marketized audience wants. Murdock and Golding (2005) say that "while mainstream economics focuses on sovereign [consumer] individuals, critical political economy starts with sets of social relations and the play of power" (62). Political economists argue that TNMCs use entertainment to commercialize the audience (or more precisely, audience attention) and sell the resulting commodity audience to advertising corporations (Smythe 2001; Meehan 2005, 2007). Political economists represent global entertainment media's audience as a commodity, produced by TNMCs, valuated by ratings firms, and sold to advertising companies.

In capitalism, all corporations sell things and convince people to buy what they sell. Commodity production on a world scale requires mass consumption. No consumption means no realization of profit which means no reproduction of the circuit of capital. If commodities are not sold, corporations cannot profit. As Sturken and Cartwright (2001) note: "A capitalist society produces more goods than are necessary for it to function, hence the need to consume goods is an important part of its ideology" (192). Financial, industrial, and service corporations annually spend a tremendous amount of money on transnational sales efforts, not only to persuade people to consume, but also to teach millions of people worldwide to perceive themselves as consumers. Corporations hire advertising corporations, which develop and place ads for products everywhere they can. The advertising industry is concentrated, centralized, and controlled by a few large conglomerates. Advertising corporations perform a crucial consumer-demand creation function on behalf of other corporations, which must daily offload large quantities of commodities to realize profit. Advertisers manufacture consumer demand by placing advertisements for commodities on billboards, in magazines and newspapers, before, during, and in-between films and TV shows, and on websites. They help corporations which sell commodities with similar use-values to differentiate the brand image or sign-value of such commodities from those offered by rival firms (Klein 2000). For some critics, advertising is "the most powerful and sustained system of propaganda in human history" (Jhally 2000: 27). Advertising promotes an environmentally calamitous and emotionally turbulent global consumerist culture that socializes people to assess their status, self-worth, and quality of life through, and in relation to, commodities.

BOX 6.1

TOP SIX GLOBAL ADVERTISING COMPANIES, 2011

COMPANY	HEADQUARTERED	MARKET VALUE
WPP Grey, Burson-Marsteller Hill & Knowlton JWT, Ogilvy Group TNS and Young & Rubicam	United Kingdom and Ireland	15.8 Billion
Omnicom Group BBDODDB Worldwide TBWA Worldwide Diversified Agency Services (DAS) Omnicom Media Group (OMG)	United States	14 Billion
Publicis Groupe Leo Burnett Worldwide Publicis Worldwide Saatchi & Saatchi	France	10.2 Billion
Dentsu	Japan	8.7 Billion
Interpublic Group McCann Worldgroup Draft fcb Lowe and Partners Worldwide	United States	6.2 Billion
Hakuhodo	Japan	2.4 Billion

Source: Forbes Global 2000

Political-economists argue that media corporations serve the advertising exigencies of the system. The NMCs and TNMCs that control the means of producing and distributing entertainment media are the main channels of advertising. Through them, advertising corporations promote messages about and brand images of commodities in an attempt to manufacture trans-local demand. TNMCs, NMCs, and globalizing entertainment media is thus at the center of the transnational promotion of "the culture-ideology of consumerism that drives the capitalist system, giving the whole a meaning and, in a real sense, providing a universal substitute for moral and spiritual values" (Sklair 2001: 85). As Schiller (1979) said: "The apparent saturation through every medium of the advertising message has been to create audiences whose loyalties are tied to brand named products and whose understanding of social relations is mediated through a scale of commodity satisfaction" (23). According to Herman and McChesney (1997), entertainment media supports an informational and ideological environmental that helps sustain the political, economic, and moral basis for marketing goods and legitimizes a profit-driven social order (10). Warf (2007) says that media giants "facilitate the advertising that makes possible mass consumption and participation in the world economy. This process does much more than sell goods—it shapes audiences' perceptions, aspirations, outlooks, and lifestyles" (104).

Worldwide, advertising markets continue to grow. After a recessionary slump in 2008 and 2009, "2010 was the year of recovery for the advertising industry" (Nielsen 2011b). In 2010, all regions and all mediums—TV, radio, newspapers, magazines, the Web—recorded growth in ad sales. The biggest increases in ad spending occurred in the Middle East, Africa, and Latin America (Airlie 2011). In 2010, worldwide ad spending for entertainment and media was $1.4 trillion. In that same year, US ad spending was $443 billion (Elliot 2011). A large amount of the ad revenue annually collected by NMCs and TNMCs is generated by selling time and space (or "spots") to advertising corporations. Advertising dollars support the production and distribution of entertainment media by NMCs and TNMCs which, in turn, support the needs of advertising corporations to cultivate consumers. Entertainment franchises rise and fall based upon their ability to serve the needs of advertising corporations. This is because media corporations are not only in the business of producing and selling entertainment to consumers, but are also in the business of producing and selling audiences to advertisers (Napoli 2009: 163). They operate in "dual markets": they produce content to attract an audience and an audience to attract advertisers. Entertainment media—TV shows and films—are used by corporations to attract, commodify, and deliver audience attention to advertising corporations (Smythe 2001).

TV Advertising. The TV industry is a dual commodity or two-sided market. Two kinds of commodities are bought and sold: TV shows and audiences. TV shows are scheduled by TV broadcasters to lure viewers into a steady flow of advertisements. TV broadcasters then sell the attention of these viewers to advertising companies, which are the main source of revenue for TV networks. Large corporations pay TV networks to schedule advertisements for their goods and services. TV networks schedule TV shows between the ads, organizing their transmission to viewers into units of time over the course of a day, a week or an entire season. Viewers who watch TV without time-shifting devices or digital video recorders (DVRs) are bound by the TV network's schedule: to see show X, the viewer must turn on the TV and tune in at time Y. TV networks use schedules to attract, capture, sort, and deliver an audience to the ad firms that pay to advertise between TV shows, making the TV schedule the site where viewer demand for TV shows and advertising demand for viewer attention converge. Advertisers want an audience to be exposed to an ad for a particular kind of product, so a particular kind of TV show is scheduled by the TV network in order to meet that demand. In this way, advertising firms shape what TV shows get conceptualized, produced, licensed, exhibited, and watched. TV schedules are a dominant part of the mediascape, and are relied upon by the generations of viewers who grew up with and found comfort in their regularity and predictability.

Advertising corporations use TV networks to reach millions of people with commercial messages. TV networks, in turn, treat their audiences as commodities (things that are bought and sold). Smythe (2001) argues that the principal commodity produced and exchanged by TV networks is the "audience," and that by watching TV shows, viewers inadvertently "worked" for TV networks:

> I suggest that what [advertisers] buy [from television networks] are the services of audiences with predictable specifications who will pay attention in predictable numbers and at particular times to particular means of communication. As collectivities these audiences are commodities. (270)

Since Smythe's time, TV broadcasting, TV advertising, and audience commodification have gone global. Globally, total broadcast TV advertising is expected to rise to $221.9 billion by 2015. Although North America is the largest TV advertising market, the world market for audience commodities delivered by TV networks continues to grow (Global Entertainment Media Outlook 2011). The trade in audience commodities reportedly accounts for almost 50 percent of the global TV industry's revenues (Doyle 2012: 4).

The flow of ad dollars into media corporations depends on ratings. TV networks must convince advertising corporations that an "audience" (a certain number of people with specific demographic characteristics) will be watching the entertainment they schedule. They do so by paying for audience ratings: information about the number of people that watch entertainment at a specific point in time. Ratings firms emerged in response to the need of media corporations and advertisers for a supposedly neutral research mechanism that could generate "objective" information about the audience they exchanged. Media corporations buy ratings from Nielsen Worldwide, a firm that measures who is watching, what is being watched, and for how long. Media corporations use the information they purchase from Nielsen to set and justify the price of the space and time they sell to advertising firms. Based in the US, but with business operations in more than 100 countries, Nielsen is the global leader in audience measuring. Advertising firms use Nielsen ratings to determine when and where to place their ads and give them—and their larger industrial clients—some assurance that the ads they place will reach an audience. At the core of the business transaction between media corporations and advertisers is the belief that Nielsen provides a relatively accurate picture of the audience. But this is questionable.

Ratings firms use diaries, surveys, people-meters, and other measurement technologies to determine who is watching what entertainment and when. But they do not count everyone (Meehan 1990). The only viewers who count in ratings are those counted by ratings firms. Ratings firms extrapolate the "audience" from the small audience sample group they choose to measure; the audience is made synonymous with the few hundred or thousand viewers selected for measurement. Millions of viewers are resultantly not counted. Ratings firms, therefore, do not reflect the total "audience." They manufacture a partial and selective image of the audience to serve the business needs of media corporations and advertisers. Ratings firms assemble an audience and deliver it to TV networks and advertisers as a commodity. Ratings tell us very little about the lives of the actual viewers who watch TV. There is a huge void separating the audience objectified by ratings and the actual viewers that watch specific films and TV shows. The advertising industry is most interested in reaching viewers with disposable income to spend on goods, which leads TV networks to only compete for the consciousness of people everywhere who have the ability to spend. As result, millions of people all over the world are never rated by ratings firms or targeted by TV networks with TV shows. Because advertising firms do not pay for the attention of poor people, TV networks will not order and schedule TV shows or films with poor people in mind.

In-Cinema Advertising. TV networks capture the largest audience and draw the most ad revenue, but advertisers are devising new ways to broaden their reach. The cinema has subsequently become a major site for delivering viewers to ads. Using a strategy called "in-cinema advertising" (Nielsen 2008), theater chains profit from the sale of audience attention to their advertising clients. In-cinema advertising is "any advertising, on or off-screen, in a movie theatre" (Nielsen 2008). *On-screen* cinema advertising refers to TV-style commercials that are shown for anywhere between fifteen and thirty minutes, prior to the start of a movie in the opening reel. Off-screen cinema advertising refers to advertisements placed in the theater's lobby, concession stand, and auditorium. Marketing and publicity uses the promise of filmic spectacle and excitement to lure desirable demographics of viewers into theater complexes. But in-cinema advertising defers, disrupts, and delays the movie experience. Before and after a film is screened, viewers are exposed to advertisements—not just preview trailers for other films, but for a variety of other commodities too: cars, cell phones, soft drinks and more. Since 2005, global in-cinema advertising has grown, and by 2009, it was a $500 million business in the US and a $2.11 billion business globally (Cinema Advertising Council 2010). In-cinema advertising is desirable to global advertisers because it guarantees them a captive and attentive audience (Nielsenwire 2008). In the theater, audiences are literally "captive": changing the channel or skipping ads with personal video recorders is not an option. And while TV viewers tend to talk while watching, movie audiences are deterred from doing so. In-cinema advertising compels captured and captive viewers to focus on the advertisements projected before their eyes and gives them few opportunities to subvert the intentions of the sponsors.

Product Placement and Branded Entertainment. Media corporations work with advertising corporations to place and expose viewers to branded commodities within scripted TV shows and films. Product placement occurs when branded products and services are placed within the fictional content of entertainment media. TV networks and film studios work with advertising firms to place products within scripts (Hesmondhalgh 2007: 196). There were more than 200,000 product placements in US TV shows between January and June of 2008 (Harris 2009). Annual advertising expenditure on filmic product placement is approximately $1.2 billion (Kivijarv 2005). While products have been tied to film scripts since the 1920s (Newell, Salmon and Chang 2006), the 1982 release of *E.T. the Extra-Terrestrial* marked global Hollywood's scripting of a product into a plot line. In that film, a cute alien with a glowing finger follows a trail of Hershey's Reese's Pieces to a suburban American home where it is befriended by a sad little boy. Since *E.T.*'s time, product placement has become institutionalized. Faced with a fragmenting audience due to new competition from satellite and cable TV firms, home video and DVD rental services, the Internet and new media, major film studios increased their production budgets to create even more spectacular blockbuster films (Grainge 2008: 14–15). As film studios were incorporated into media conglomerates, the blockbuster film became a powerful means of advertising products. As Wasko (2003) observes: "film now represents not only a commodity in itself, but also serves as an advertising medium for other commodities and increasingly generates additional commodities" (170). Film commodities circulate between theaters of the world and home and mobile entertainment spaces, capturing and delivering audience attention to brand imagery associated with thousands of carefully placed products.

The fusion of marketing tactics with fictional storytelling expressed by product placements obliterates the boundary between entertainment and advertisement, resulting in "branded entertainment" forms (Donaton 2005). Branded entertainment weaves a branded commodity or service into the storyline of a branded TV show or film. Brands are now integral parts of TV and film narratives and often gain additional meaning by interacting with the values, style, and action of on-screen protagonists (McChesney 2004: 148). What is the difference between product placement and branded entertainment? Traditional product placement inserts branded products into scenes after the script is written. Brands are not meaningfully integrated within the story, but feature mainly as set-dressing and props. Branded entertainment attempts to write specific branded products into the script. In some instances, branded products become the precondition for a script and shape story concepts. In sum, media conglomerates and global advertising corporations expose people all over the world to images of the latest goods and services in advertisements disguised as filmic ad TV entertainment.

BOX 6.2

xXx AS BRANDED ENTERTAINMENT

---

xXx (2002), starring multicultural action star Vin Diesel (as Xander Cage), is an example of branded entertainment. Branded commodities are part of Cage's subcultural style. Cage sports a Joe Rocket Phoenix leather jacket, Billabong beach-wear, and Vans shoes. "Kids know when you're trying to fake them out," claims Jay Wilson, Vans' vice president of marketing. "We really try to connect emotionally with the kids and find new ways of doing things. We're getting more public relations on this thing than we ever imagined" (cited in Pinsker 2002). Throughout *xXx*, Cage kicks, jumps, and climbs his way through a number of high-intensity action sequences, feet supported by Vans. Throughout *xXx*'s narrative, Cage downs Red-Bull energy drinks to maintain his stamina; his burly Russian foes drink J&B whiskey. Cage uses new media technology such as Motorola video cell phones, Kodak equipment, Sony Playstation 2 game consoles, IBM computers, and Microsoft products. Cage also wears a Swiss Army Hunter watch. Revolution Studios expressed "an interest in the Hunter watch for Diesel to wear in the movie," said Cheri McKenzie, Swiss Army's vice president of marketing. The characteristics of the Swiss Army brand identity were appropriately fitted to those of Cage. "The Hunter really suits his character. There's something about the distinctive look and feel of the watch that matches his character." Indicative of the power of brand managers to shape film scripts, McKenzie adds:

We always review the storylines of all TV and film scripts before we agree to place product on any character. We look at storyline and content to make sure the usage doesn't do anything to compromise our brand image. I think the Hunter is strong, it looks tough but sleek, and it's contemporary and highly technological, which fits in very well with the look and style of the movie. (cited in Strandberg 2002)

xXx also stars automobile brands including Corvette and Jeep. A '67 Pontiac GTO, otherwise known as "The Goat," is driven by Cage in a number of action sequences. The car is equipped with tires supplied by BFGoodrich, another sponsor. Pontiac decided to encode a preview for the GTO 2004 model into *xXx*'s DVD version; this US auto-maker also invested in *xXx*'s sequel (Brand Channel 2004).

CULTIVATION THEORY/IDEOLOGY STUDIES: THE AUDIENCE AS INFLUENCED

CI theorists, cultivation scholars, and media effects researchers sometimes represent global entertainment media's local audience as a victim of ideological influence by TNMCs. Cultivation scholars claim that repeated exposure to the representations of the world communicated by entertainment media influences how people perceive themselves and the world in which they live (Gerbner 1998; Gerbner et al. 1994). The more a person or group of people is exposed to a similar representation of reality, the more they may come to believe that the representation of reality is valid, normal, or legitimate. If a person or a group of people are exposed to a partial and selective media representation of the world over a long period of time, they may develop a perception of reality that is similar to or based upon that media representation. The concern is that entertainment media's representation of reality is never value-neutral and that TV shows and films represent local and global realities that are ideological. An "ideology" is a system of ideas characteristic of a dominant class or group in society, or illusory, false, or distorted ideas that may be contrasted with true or objective knowledge (Williams 1977). TV shows and films may influence people's perception of the world and their behavior by exposing them to ideologies which support powerful corporate class interests or distort the actual conditions of their lives.

Do globalizing TV shows and films have an effect upon the views, beliefs, and behaviors of people? In some contexts, entertainment media may be an instrument of social and political influence which is used by powerful groups in society (corporations, governments, the ruling class) to get less powerful groups (viewers, subordinate and marginalized people, the working class, young people) to think and act in a way that is contrary to their best interests. For some CI scholars and radical Marxist critics, globalizing entertainment media serves the interests of the few at the expense of the many. It is a means of transnationally spreading and imposing upon viewers dominant ideologies of American nationalism and capitalist-consumerism. These ideologies, carried around the world by entertainment media, threaten established traditions, truths, and identities. The exchange relationship between TNMCs and audiences is asymmetrical, not reciprocal. The global circulation of entertainment media enables TNMCs to get something from the audience (attention, money, consent) and results in the audience losing something (knowledge, time, identity). This figure of global entertainment media's local audience is a victim that suffers the negative ideological and cultural effects of "Americanization" and capitalist-consumer indoctrination.

Exporting the Ideology of the American Way of Life. Critics of cultural imperialism as a form of Americanization have long argued that globalizing entertainment media is a means of carrying an American nationalist ideology around the world. In 1901, British journalist W. T. Stead's *The Americanization of the World* was published. Stead observed how US industrial production models, consumerism, and US cultural values were going global, and that the Americanization of the world was happening (Rydell and Kroess 2005: 9). Following World War II, fears of "Americanization" were expressed in many countries. In *The Uses of Literacy*, Richard Hoggart (1957) bemoaned the saturation of Britain with US commercial culture. Hoggart linked the "aesthetic breakdown" of traditional British working class communities to imported teenage milk-bars, drape-suits, picture ties, record players, and juke-boxes (203) and argued that youth were being assimilated into "a [media] myth world compounded of a few simple elements which they took to be those of American life" (204). From World War II to the UNESCO debates of the 1970s to present-day disputes about the cultural exception, scholars, activists, and cultural policy-makers continue to argue that globalizing US entertainment media is Americanizing the local beliefs and behaviors of viewers. In this discourse, TV shows and films represent America and elicit local viewer consent to dominant US values, identity, and foreign policy at the expense of local—namely ethno-nationalist—cultural identities. Ghana's Minister of Chieftaincy and Culture S. K. Boafo says "Foreign, particularly American, films and music, fashions, fads and language, have all served to dilute Ghanaian culture" (cited in *The Statesman* 2007). Chairperson of the Council of Canadians Maude Barlow (2001) claims that "US and Western values and lifestyles, driven by a consumer-based, free-market ideology and carried through the massive US entertainment-industrial complex" are infiltrating "every corner of the Earth" and "destroying local tradition, knowledge, skills, artisans and values."

Llosa (2001) summarizes the view held by many critics who view globalization as "Americanization":

> The disappearance of national borders and the establishment of a world interconnected by
> markets will deal a deathblow to regional and national cultures and to the traditions,
> customs, myths and mores that determine each country or region's cultural identity. Since
> most of the world is incapable of resisting the invasion of cultural products from
> developed countries—or, more to the point, from the superpower, the United States—that
> inevitably trails the great transnational corporation, North American culture will
> ultimately impose itself, standardizing the world and annihilating its rich flora of diverse
> cultures. In this manner, all other peoples, and not just the small and weak ones will
> become no more than 21st century colonies—zombies or caricatures modeled after the
> cultural norms of a new [US] imperialism [. . .] that will impose on others its language
> and its ways of thinking, believing, enjoying and dreaming.

For critics of Americanization, globalizing US TV shows and films dominate and destroy local cultures. They are agents of foreign infiltration that impose messages about and images of America upon helpless local viewers. Global entertainment media turns non-US citizens against and away from their own ways of life and encourages them to think and dream about being, or one day becoming, "American." As such, globalizing entertainment media threatens a "territorially-based national culture or [the] cultural identities deriving from membership in a political state, a stateless nation, or an ethnic group" (Morris 2002: 279). In this discourse, something foreign (global entertainment media) pollutes, corrupts, or tarnishes something domestic (national identity).

While some non-US cultural policymakers, businesses, and viewers worry about the Americanization of their local and national cultures, US foreign-policymakers are concerned that the globalization of entertainment media will fall short in building transnational consent to the American Way of Life. US strategists debate whether or not US-based TNMCs help or harm the image and influence of the US state in world affairs. What representations of America do globalizing TV shows and films expose local viewers to? How do globalizing entertainment texts represent US values, national identity, and foreign policy? Do globalizing TV shows and films cultivate pro or anti-American sentiment? Do media representations of America help or hinder US geopolitical interests? Does entertainment attract people to the US or cause them to hate it? Liberal and conservative scholars present different answers to these questions about the geopolitics of global pop media.

Liberals say that globalizing Hollywood entertainment is an agent of US "soft power." Nye (2008) describes soft power as "the ability to obtain what you want through co-option and attraction, not coercion or bribery" (95). For Nye and others, globalizing entertainment media is a potent instrument of US soft power that attracts people to US values, identity, and foreign policy. Fraser (2003), for example, says "American soft power—movies, pop music, television, fast food, fashions, theme parks—spreads, validates, and reinforces common [American] norms, values, beliefs, and lifestyles." "Make no mistake," says Fraser, "America's global domination is based mainly on the superiority of US hard power. But the influence, prestige, and legitimacy of the emerging American Empire will depend on the effectiveness of its soft power" (13). Liberals, like Nye and Fraser, say that globalizing entertainment media cultivates transnational ascent to US leadership by communicating an attractive image of "America" as a land of multiculturalism, democracy, liberty, capitalism, consumerism, upward mobility, and technological progress. They promote the state's use of entertainment to achieve soft power objectives and establish pro-American worldviews.

Conservatives, however, claim that global Hollywood entertainment causes anti-Americanism (Gentzkow and Shapiro 2004; Graber 2009; Wellemeyer 2006). A 2003 report by The Council on Foreign Relations says that anti-Americanism is partly caused by "the broad sweep of American culture. Hollywood movies, television, advertising, business practices and fast-food chains from the United States are provoking a backlash" (24). In this right-wing revision of the CI paradigm, globalizing entertainment media impresses upon cognitively lacking and culturally traditional viewers a negative view, whereby US global TV shows and films foster a "false consciousness" about the US by representing it as a land of sex, smut and violence, stupid teenagers, vapid consumerism, and political corruption (Defleur and Defleur 2003). Kuhner (2009) says:

[T]he greatest source of global anti-American hatred is our decadent popular culture [. . .] The overwhelming majority of people in the world—whether it be the Middle East, Africa, Latin America, Asia or Eastern Europe—are traditionalist. They deeply believe in God and family, hearth and home. [. . .] America's MTV morality is not only superficial and profoundly anti-human, but doomed. It cannot sustain or inspire a civilization of any meaningful consequence.

Richard Kimball and Joshua Muravchick, resident "scholars" at the American Enterprise Institute for Public Policy Research, say that Hollywood films vilify the US and foment left-wing internationalist angst (Wellemeyer 2006). Jim Phillips, a Heritage Foundation researcher, claims that Hollywood is the ultimate source of conspiracy theories about the US and that its films encourage global paranoia about US foreign policy (Wellemeyer 2006). In sum, conservatives portray globalizing US entertainment media as the emissary of anti-Americanism abroad. They criticize entertainment's representation of America because it does not correspond with their own conservative view of "America." TV shows and films that do not represent rigid Christian values, happy nuclear-patriarchal families, veneration of the military, hyper-nationalism, and the sexual chastity/repression of youth are "un-American," and thus responsible for anti-Americanism abroad.

Debates between liberals and conservatives about the utility of global entertainment media to US soft power or hegemony are riddled with problematic claims and hidden assumptions. First, liberals and conservatives hold a simplistic notion of what "America" is and a problematic notion of the relationship between "America" and entertainment media. "America" is not one thing. The meaning of America is in flux and is regularly fought over by US and non-US citizens. America is not a monolith reducible to blood or soil, but a terrain of struggle over naturalized and normalized meanings. Different political groups in the US—neo-Nazis and communists, Christian fundamentalists and atheists, conservatives and liberals, right-wingers and left-wingers—struggle daily to define what America is and means. All proponents and detractors of "Americanization" should specify what they mean by "America" before celebrating or lamenting its cultural effects.

Second, global entertainment media does not reflect "America," but represents many partial and selective images of America. Entertainment media represents hegemonic and counter-hegemonic struggles over the meaning of America as they unfold within the US and wider world. As Gray (2007) says: "there exist numerous competing Americas in the American global media, some of them satirically looking back at and attacking other Americas as presented in the more happy, glowing, and affirmative of American media products" (131). Gray (2007) encourages global media studies scholars to "stop conceiving of the meanings of media flows leaving America and Hollywood as so unitary, standardized and predictable" (146). The notion that all TV shows and films exported from the US to the world represent America in the same way "is as ludicrous as to assume that all American people share the same image of the nation" (Gray 2007: 146). Globalizing US entertainment media provides the world with competing images of America, liberal and conservative, utopian and dystopian, attractive and repulsive. "[W]e must study more of them if we are to understand how the world engages in imagining America" (Gray 2007: 146).

Finally, conservatives and liberals presume that the representation of America by globalizing entertainment media is the primary source of anti- or pro-American feeling, but this risks exaggerating the power of entertainment to shape political beliefs and actions. In some countries it is true that the importation of US entertainment media may strengthen local and national identities or instigate a cultural backlash against the perceived threat of American influence (Kang and Morgan 1988). Traditional identities are being revived and re-imagined in numerous countries in response to fears about Americanization. These backlashing and reactionary identities "build trenches of resistance on behalf of God, nation, ethnicity, family, or locality" (Castells 1997: 356). Dr. Jassim Asfour, General Secretary of Egypt's Cultural Council, for example, says that Americanization must be fought in order to "protect our national identity and revive our Arabic and Islamic culture" (cited in Za'za 2002). Appearing on Saudi Arabia's government-run Saudi TV on September 14, 2008, Sheik Saleh al-Lihedan of Saudi Arabia's Supreme Judiciary Council issued a fatwa against Western satellite TV shows (Abu-Nasr 2008). In instances such as these, globalizing entertainment media connects with or exacerbates an anti-American cultural backlash but does not directly cause it. The root of anti-American feeling is most often high politics, not *Transformers* or *Shrek the Third*.

Yet the globalization of US entertainment media may have *no effect* on people's political judgment of the US. People may dislike US foreign policy, yet enjoy consuming US entertainment. People may hate American TV shows, but identify with or support US foreign policy. Positive and negative attitudes toward the US are most frequently expressed by publics in response to US foreign policy decisions and conduct, not the content of US entertainment. Between 2001 and 2008, US-based TNMCs made record profits. In 2009, the export of US films around the world earned US-based TNMCs $29.9 billion (MPAA 2009). However, in that same period, anti-Americanism boiled over border after border due to the unilateral and militaristic foreign policy of the US state. In this period, globalizing films and TV shows did not cause anti-Americanism. US foreign policy did. Between 2001 and 2006, anti-American sentiment grew in Turkey. In 2006, a hit movie at the Turkish box office for a few weeks was *Garfield: A Tale of Two Kitties* (Bronk 2006). Was *Garfield* to blame for anti-Americanism in Turkey? Probably not. But "rather than face the tough realities of war and international diplomacy, the blame-Hollywood-first crowd argues that our unpopularity in Turkey is the result of an animated cat" (Bronk 2006). Globalizing entertainment media might contribute to or reinforce existing anti-American sentiment within countries that have had a negative experience with US foreign policy, but TV shows and films do not directly cause anti-Americanism. When entertainment media glamorizes unpopular US foreign policies frames other people, places and cultures in negative ways or attempts to build ideological consent to contentious US state conduct, anti-American sentiment may be induced. As Miller (2005) observes: "In the final instance, the links between popular culture and US government aims and policies are key to anti-Americanism, *not the content of popular culture*" itself (27).

Exporting the Ideology of Capitalist-Consumerism. Marxists claim that global entertainment media communicates a capitalist-consumer ideology (Artz 2003). As capitalism goes global, it requires a system of ideas and beliefs to legitimize and naturalize it. Entertainment products carry capitalist-consumer "ideology" around the world, integrating people into capitalism as compliant workers and consumers. As Herman and McChesney (1997) say:

> the power of international corporations is not only economic and political but extends to basic assumptions and modes of thought [. . .] To no small extent the stability of the system rests upon the widespread acceptance of a global corporate ideology. (35)

According to Marxists, global capitalism is a system based on inequality. The root conflict in society is between owners and workers, the rich and the poor. Ideology represents the world from the point of view of the rich while claiming to reflect everyone's point of view. Carried by entertainment media, capitalist ideology represents rugged individualism, extreme self-interest, and competition as good for everyone; private property as sacrosanct; the myth that capitalism creates a vast, upwardly mobile, and everexpanding middle-class society; rich people as innately better than poor people; and, the interests of corporations as being the same as those of society ("What's good for global business is good for everyone").

Global entertainment media is a carrier of consumerist ideology too. Supported by advertising, it promotes the belief that over-consumption, the individualistic pursuit to possess more and more commodities, and the expression of personal identity through commodities is normal and ideal. Consumerist ideology ties the pursuit and expression of identity to the consumption and use of commodities. In countries undergoing a capitalist-consumer transformation, advertisements and entertainment media encourage viewers to model themselves and their behavior on the fictional and hyper-real consumer types and lifestyles portrayed (Wei and Pan 1999). At the same time, entertainment media may be the ever-expanding capitalist system's way of symbolically compensating millions of people for the alienating, exploitative, and routinized waged work they endure each day (Jameson 1979). The consumer market offers targeted yet fleeting gratifications and pleasures to people in exchange for their acquiescence to unfreedom in the sphere of production (Horkheimer and Adorno 1972). In sum, Marxists claim that globalizing entertainment media carries capitalistconsumer ideology and cultivates transnational ascent to it. It is a function and effect of the global capitalist system.

BOX 6.3

GLOBALIZING THE AMERICAN BEAUTY IDEAL

Does the globalization of US and Western beauty ideals influence and encourage changes in how women in non-Western cultures perceive themselves and their bodies? Advertising corporations rely on commercialized images of "beautiful" and "attractive" women to sell their products. Beauty products are framed as magical solutions to media-generated anxieties. Advertising pushes a false perception that a single set of qualities represent ideal beauty, and this makes millions of women around the world feel as though they are ugly or lacking in some way (Wolf 1992). Although "beauty" is culturally contingent—there is no universal agreement about what beautiful is—the Western beauty ideal of white skin, blonde hair, youthful, slim, virginal, and upper class is becoming globally hegemonic

BOX 6.3 (Continued)

(Patton 2006). This beauty ideal is communicated and normalized by ads, TV shows and films, which "teach" people what beautiful means. So many media products tell women to define themselves through the possession and display of external objects (commodities) instead of by cultivating their internal qualities (character). In the US and elsewhere, beauty is marketed as something to be bought at the mall. Identity is something to be tried on, worn, and thrown away. Young women are constantly pressured by advertising to buy into, and remake themselves in the image of, idealistic media-generated beauty types, which sometimes leads to self-loathing, self-mutilation, and eating disorders. Global media images of beauty have many negative and embodied effects.

The partial and selective US and Western beauty ideal is being exported to the world by ads and ad-supported TV shows and films. Globalizing entertainment media spreads the US and Western beauty ideal around the world, encouraging transformations in the way women perceive themselves and their bodies. Globalizing TV images of US and Western beauty ideals are being used in both creative and highly self-destructive ways by adolescent and teenage girls worldwide. The South Korean beauty ideal, for example, was once connected to being average or overweight in size. But that image of beauty has changed (Jung and Lee 2006): South Korean women now pursue thinness through obsessive dieting and pay for cosmetic surgery on their eyelids in order to appear more "Western" in the hope of getting a good job or appearing sexually desirable to men, both Eastern and Western (Rainwater-McClure, Reed and Kramer 2003). According to Bissell and Chung (2009), the global TV show *Sex and the City* is now a lifestyle template for the shopping rituals of young South Korean females (233).

In Fiji, globalizing US entertainment media has cultivated a new perception of beauty in young Fijian women too (Becker 2004). Before American TV shows were imported by Fijian TV broadcasters, Fijian men and women viewed "fat" bodies as beautiful bodies. Large bodies were not only aesthetically pleasing to Fijian men, but were also a sign of a woman's capacity for hard work and maternal care. Eating disorders were non-existent; skinny was not cool. Fijian women were not traditionally motivated to reshape and remake their bodies through intensive dieting, exercise routines, or shopping. But after being introduced to the US beauty ideal by imported TV shows, many Fijian women started trying to emulate the look and lifestyle of the fictional characters. They believed that by looking more like the TV characters, they would be able to achieve their local dreams of getting a good job, gaining social status and being adored by men. Fijian women emulated TV characters in order to position themselves competitively vis-à-vis their peers in an emerging Fijian capitalist economy. Sadly, they developed psychological and physical afflictions in the process. To be like the TV images of American women, Fijian women dieted intensively, exercised, and developed eating disorders. They began to repudiate their traditional body type and perceive it as a sign of poverty, cultural backwardness, and laziness.

Becker (2004) argues that "behavioural modelling on Western appearance and customs [derived from imported TV] appears to have undercut traditional cultural resources for identity-making" (552). In Fiji, many Fijian schoolgirls now believe being beautiful means looking like the TV images of skinny, white, and consumerist American women. Young Fijian women have joined the unhappy ranks of millions of North American women who daily and desperately model themselves on a hyper-real beauty ideal. As Becker (2004) says:

> disordered eating may also be a symbolic embodiment of the anxiety and conflict the youth experience on the threshold of rapid social change in Fiji and during their personal and collective navigation through it [. . .] Vulnerable girls and women across diverse populations who feel marginalized from the locally dominant culture's sources of prestige and status may anchor their identities in widely recognized cultural symbols of prestige popularized by media-imported ideas, values and images. (555)

CULTURAL RECEPTION STUDIES/ETHNOGRAPHY:
THE AUDIENCE AS ACTIVE MEANING-MAKER

While CI scholars and Marxists view global entertainment media as an instrument of Americanization, ideological influence and cultural change, cultural studies scholars examine globalizing entertainment media as a form of "popular culture." Williams (1976) says that the word "popular" has four meanings: "well liked by many people"; "inferior kinds of work"; "work deliberately setting out to win favour with the people"; "culture actually made by the people for themselves" (198–199). Global entertainment media is liked by many people; some entertainment products are considered aesthetically inferior by cultural critics who make value-judgments (or cultural distinctions) about good entertainment and bad entertainment in order to legitimize their own tastes; almost all entertainment is designed to resonate with a specific audience demographic that has been targeted by advertisers; entertainment is not made by viewers, but viewers do actively interpret it. Cultural studies scholars are interested in why certain entertainment products "win favour with the people" and become popular among audiences. For cultural studies scholars, global entertainment media's local audience is not a victim of Americanization or ideological dupe, but an active meaning-maker who adapts, responds to, and indigenizes imported texts.

Cultural studies scholars say that part of the popularity of entertainment is rooted in the pleasures of the polysemic text. Polysemic texts do not convey one single meaning but, rather, are open to many interpretations. Fiske (1988) argues that the US TV show *Dallas* holds different meanings in different national reception contexts: "*Dallas* is a different text in the USA, in North America, and in Australia, indeed, it is many different texts in the USA alone" (14). For Fiske, global entertainment texts do not entail singular messages that serve singular ideological agendas; they can be progressive and regressive, liberal and conservative, critical and affirmative. Cultural studies scholars also claim that viewers are active meaning-makers. They seek to understand what goes on in the reception context by studying how viewers actively interpret, use, and make meaningful films and TV shows (Ang 1985; Appadurai 1997; Buell 1994; Fiske 1988; Gillespie 1995; Classen and Howes 1996; Liebes and Katz 1990; La Pastina 2003; Morley 1992; Strelitz 2003). Do all local viewers uncritically internalize global TV show images in predictable ways? Do the messages carried around the world by Hollywood films mean the same thing to everyone, everywhere? Does the global flow of entertainment media necessarily have negative local effects, or can pop consumption be empowering? How do viewers use entertainment media? What do TV shows and films "mean" to the people that watch them?

Cultural studies scholars present many interesting answers to these questions which complicate some accounts of cultural imperialism, especially those that inflate the ideological power of media firms.

Cultural studies scholars say the CI paradigm's emphasis on the economic power of TNMCs downplays the agency of viewers. "Cultural imperialism theory assumes that television audiences are passive receptors of foreign television messages" argues Fraser (2003). But "television viewers actually tend to be active negotiators of meaning when they watch foreign television programs" (167). Morley (2006) contends "that audiences are active in various ways, as they select from and re-interpret, for their own purposes, the media materials they consume" (39). To move beyond the CI paradigm, cultural studies posit a much more dynamic and interactive power relationship between TNMCs, the global entertainment media they produce and distribute, and local audiences.

Hall's (2000) "Encoding/Decoding" model of communication played an important role in this turn toward studies of the meaning-making activities of global entertainment's local viewers. Hall says communication is part of "a structure produced and sustained through the articulation of linked but distinctive moments—production, circulation, distribution/consumption, reproduction" (167). Hall claims that communication—the movement of a message from a Sender to a Receiver—is part of the circuit of capital accumulation. Media corporations (Senders) "encode" TV shows and films (with "preferred" messages), distribute these products (and the messages they are encoded with) to viewers (Receivers) who interpret ("decode") the messages in a variety of ways. The effects of this process are without guarantees because "each of the moments [. . .] is necessary to the circuit as a whole, [but] no one moment can fully guarantee the next moment with which it is articulated" (Hall 2000: 167). In the moment of production, media corporations (encoders) make entertainment media. But in the moment of consumption, viewers (decoders) interpret, reformulate, criticize, and even re-constitute the messages.

Hall (2000) posits three types of hypothetical viewer decodings: 1) a *dominant hegemonic decoding* (viewers passively and uncritically accept the preferred meaning of a TV show or film); 2) a *negotiated decoding* (viewers understand the preferred meaning, but slightly dissent from it); 3) an *oppositional decoding* (viewers understand the dominant or preferred meaning of the film or TV show message but reformulate, criticize, and re-constitute it in a different, and possibly politically subversive, way). Though the production context places limits upon meaning-making in the consumption context (viewers cannot make whatever meanings they like without reference to the encoded text), the production context does not guarantee or determine what happens in the consumption context. Hall (2000) says that encoding "will have the effect of constructing some of the limits and parameters within which decoding operates. If there were no limits, audiences could simply read whatever they liked into any message" (173). The production and consumption of global entertainment media are part of the same circuit of capitalist accumulation, but they are not identical processes. In the production contexts, media corporations frame meanings, set agendas, and make messages that intend to inform, persuade, or simply entertain. In the consumption context, viewers struggle over the connotative meaning of texts, which are polysemic, multi-accentual, and open to recoding.

Extending Hall's model of communication, cultural studies scholars employ reception studies and ethnographic methodologies to examine how local viewers decode the texts of global TV shows and films. Reception studies scholars document how different viewers decode the meanings of entertainment media (Murphy 2005) and how the meaning of entertainment is not just "in the text," but emerges through a relationship between viewers, texts, and reception contexts. They examine who watches specific TV shows and films, what people think and feel while watching, where people watch, why people watch, and how people actually decode the TV shows or films they watch.

Ethnographic researchers examine what entertainment media *means* to specific groups of viewers and how people experience and use entertainment media in conjunction with their everyday lives. "Ethnographers immerse themselves in a culture often different from their own, to retell the lives of a particular people, to narrate their rites and traditions, and to understand and explain their cultural practices" (La Pastina 2003: 125). Ethnographers want to understand the entertainment reception/consumption practices of a group of people in the same way in which that group of people does. Using participant observation, informal conversations, and in-depth interviews and questions, cultural ethnographers explore the lived relationship between global entertainment media and local viewers.

Ang's (1984) cultural studies ethnography focused on how and why transnational viewers watched the US TV soap opera, *Dallas*. In *Watching Dallas*, Ang (1985) criticized France's cultural minister Jack Lang, the late US New York critic Susan Sontag, and Michele Mattelart for claiming that *Dallas*—an open serial TV soap about a wealthy US family made rich by oil extraction and sales—was a "symbol of American cultural imperialism" (2). Ang said the perception that *Dallas* was cultural imperialism does not help scholars understand why so many people watch the TV show. While the "ivory towers of the policy-makers and other guardians of the national culture" (3) worry about cultural imperialism:

> in the millions of living rooms where the TV set is switched on to *Dallas*, the issue is rather one of pleasure. For we must accept one thing: *Dallas* is popular because a lot of people somehow enjoy watching it. (Ang 1984: 3–4)

To prove that watching *Dallas* gives people pleasure, Ang developed a study built around her own identity and experience watching the show "as an intellectual and a feminist" (12). Ang confronted the capitalist-consumer ideology of the TV show while negotiating with its narrative, content, and themes in a pleasurable way. Ang also conducted some loose ethnographic audience research on how women in the Netherlands derived pleasure from *Dallas*. Ang placed an advertisement in a Dutch women's magazine (*Viva*) asking middle-class Dutch women to talk about why they liked or disliked the TV show *Dallas*. The survey responses indicated that women derived pleasure from watching *Dallas* for a variety of reasons.

Liebes and Katz's (1990) book on *Dallas* examines how Israeli Arabs, new Israeli immigrants from Russia and Morocco, and Los Angeles-based viewers locally decode *Dallas* in different ways depending on their social networks, their ethno-cultural backgrounds, their political views, and their location. In their thesis statement, the authors challenge the CI paradigm:

> Critical studies of the diffusion of American television programs overseas have labeled this process 'cultural imperialism' as if there were no question but that the hegemonic message the analyst discerns in the text is transferred to the defenseless minds of viewers the world over for the self-serving interests of the economy and ideology of the exporting country. Perhaps so. But labeling something imperialistic is not the same as proving it is. To prove that *Dallas* is an imperialistic imposition, one would have to show (1) that there is a message incorporated in the program that is designed to profit American interests overseas,

(2) that the message is decoded by the receiver in the way it was encoded by the sender, and
(3) that it is accepted uncritically by the viewers and allowed to seep into their culture. (4)

Liebes and Katz attempt to debunk the CI paradigm's claims by combining ethnographic and textual methods to study "the actual interaction between the TV program and its viewers" (4). Liebes and Katz attribute some of *Dallas*'s popularity to US mass marketing, economies of scale, and control of distribution ("the sheer availability of American programs in a marketplace where national producers—however jealous— cannot fill more than a fraction of the hours they feel they must provide"). But their main claim is that *Dallas* is popular among different ethno-cultural groups in Israel and the US due to the TV show's universalistic text. "[T]he universality, or primordiality, of some of its themes and formulae [. . .] makes [American] programs psychologically accessible," as do "the polyvalent or open potential of many of the stories, and thus their value as projective mechanisms and as a material for negotiation and play in the families of man" (4).

Cultural studies scholars have also examined the local "uses and gratifications" of globalizing entertainment media (Jiang and Leung 2012). Why do people choose some entertainment products over others? How do people use TV shows and films in their everyday lives? Instead of asking "How does global entertainment media change people's minds and behaviors?" the uses and gratifications researcher asks "What is the role of global entertainment media in people's local lives?" What do people do with the entertainment media they consume? How do specific TV shows and films satisfy the viewer's wants? There is no one single list of entertainment media uses and gratifications, but many possibilities. People may use global TV shows and films to get a sense of fashion trends, consumer lifestyles, and "what's hot and what's not" in cosmopolitan media capitals. Viewers may turn to (and tune into) global entertainment media to keep up with and attempt to emulate ways of life associated with other parts of the world. In this respect, entertainment media may be used as a means of cultural distinction by middle-class consumers. While much globalizing entertainment media is dubbed into local languages, some English-language TV shows and films may be used by viewers to learn or practice English, the global lingua franca and the main means of developing and expressing a cosmopolitan identity (Parameswaran 1999). Globalizing entertainment media may also be used by local viewers to imaginatively escape their day-to-day material woes through rituals of relaxation, stimulation, or emotional release. It may also provide local viewers with a virtual tourist trip to distance places and locales. Meyrowitz (1986) says that globalizing electronic media severs the link between geography and community; viewers may thus consume global entertainment texts as a way to develop "para-social relationships" with faraway fictional characters and the place-based communities in which they live (Livingstone 1990). Finally, viewers may use media to learn about societies, cultures and lifestyles that are different from their own.

Cultural studies scholars make an important contribution to the analysis of the relationship between global entertainment media and local identity formation and self-expression. Ang (1996) says that "the practices of active meaning-making in the process of media consumption—as part of creating a lifestyle for oneself—need to be understood" (12). The meanings and uses viewers make through contact with globalizing entertainment media is often contingent upon racialized, classed, sexualized, gendered, locational, and religious identities and identifications (Ang 1996). Identity is a "point of temporary attachment" to subject positions, constructed through a variety of discursive practices (Hall 1996: 5–6). Particular viewers—female audiences (Ang 1985), children (Buckingham 1993), and ethnic groups (Gillespie 1995; Naficy 1993)—consume entertainment media in ways that are shaped by and shaping of their identities. Global entertainment media is often used as a source of local identity construction by viewers who "playfully identify with characters, sharing their roles. Subsequently, sometimes changed, they return to life to act perhaps in different ways" (Wilson 2001: 91). In short, the choice to consume global entertainment media is not only influenced by identity, but may also enable local viewers to construct and assert new identities (Strelitz 2002). Watching entertainment media is a way for viewers to identify with fictional roles and to construct and perform their own identities based upon the fictional material they expose themselves to. Viewers may identify or disidentify with the behaviors and lifestyles of the scripted and non-scripted characters they see (Breakwell 1992; McQuail 1997; Seiter 1996; Wilson 2001). Globalizing TV shows and films are used by viewers to model identities.

Wilson's (2001) ethnographic study of Malaysian viewer responses to the globalizing US talk show *Oprah Winfrey* highlights four different types of local identification with globalizing entertainment media: open identification; privatized identification; selective identification; and critical distancing (98). *Open identification* is when viewers identify or empathize with the behavior and lifestyles of the people and characters they see on screen. Cultural proximity between local viewer and global media content is achieved in the absence of geographical proximity. Local viewers feel comfortable or "at home" with the ways of being and acting portrayed by foreign entertainment media. They recognize themselves or their own experiences in foreign content, which is relatable and easily accommodated to their own lives. "Identifying with both particular subjects on screen and the roles they inhabit, viewers unpack a story for others and themselves" (Wilson 2001: 100). *Privatized identification* occurs when viewers use the content of globalizing entertainment media to talk about and make public their private lives. By publicly discussing the identities and experiences of foreign fictional characters or non-fictional screened lives from afar, local viewers engage in an indirect form of communal therapy. Through talk about global TV shows, viewers bring private issues that concern and conflict them—unhappy marriages, abusive husbands, anxiety about appearances, sexual gratification—into the public domain for discussion as a way to share and make sense of their lives (Gillespie 2002). "Privatized identification is a form of maintaining 'face', the social necessities of politeness, while unobtrusively recognizing that life is otherwise" (Wilson 2001: 102). *Selective identification* occurs when local viewers selectively adjust their own behavior to accord with a foreign social role that is represented to them by entertainment. Here, viewers are more suspicious, more cautious, and more discerning of cultural difference than when openly identifying with globalizing texts, but they may still use the material selectively. *Critical distancing* occurs when local viewers distinguish and affirm their own social and cultural differences from the lifestyles presented by global entertainment media. In these instances, local viewers take the foreign way of life, as presented by global entertainment media, as evidence of an unbridgeable chasm between themselves and distant others. Thus, viewers dis-identify with global entertainment media, and reinforce notions of here and there, us and them, we and they, self and other.

In addition to exploring the nexus of global media and local identification, cultural studies scholars examine the reception, use, and effects of entertainment within youth cultures. TNMCs seek to align their products with the music, fashion, and images that appeal to young people as "cutting-edge" or "cool" (Moore 2007). Using subcultural marketing research and trans-local "cool-hunting" strategies, TNMCs mine the style, ethos, and music of transnational youth to design TV shows and films which resonate with "an army of teen clones marching—in 'uniform' as the marketers say—into the global mall" (Klein 2000: 129). Connected by ICTs (satellite television, the Internet, and mobile media), young people in many countries now share a common referent system of brand logos, entertainment images, and styles of dress (Heaven and Tubridy 2003; Havens 2001; Kellner and Kahn 2003; Lemish et al. 1998; McMillin and Fisherkeller 2009). Havens (2001) notes that "young people in the current media-saturated societies pick up on, rework and re-circulate the cultural material available in mass-mediated texts to express individual and collective dreams, worries, experiences, and identities" (61). Global entertainment media is a resource of youthful self-making and remaking. Global TV shows and films may encourage young people to turn away from their local histories, cultures, and traditions and embrace a future which resembles hyper-real images of US capitalist-consumer society (or some modified version of Western capitalist-consumer modernity). This can be an empowering experience for young people. By exposing themselves to images of fictional foreign people and places, youth may temporarily and imaginatively escape from the geographical and material borders and boundaries of the actual. Thompson (1995) points out that part of the attraction of global (American) entertainment media for local viewers is that they provide meanings which enable "the accentuation of symbolic distancing from the spatial-temporal contexts of everyday life" (175). US modernization theorists argue that youth in postcolonial countries may use global entertainment media to imagine a way of living that is different from (and possibly "better" than) their own "traditional" way (Pye 1963; Rogers 1965; Schramm 1963). Globalizing entertainment media introduces young people to the "worlds of outside" (Gillespie 1995).

Yet, exposure to the "worlds of outside" can lead youth to feel profoundly disappointed in themselves and their circumstances due to structural barriers to their emancipation (classism, racism, and sexism). Much ad-driven globalizing entertainment media represents the world as a global shopping mall that is filled with happy young consumers who have the power to buy and own anything they want. Yet, millions of young people—especially young subaltern women—remain concretely disenfranchised, under-employed, marginalized, and impoverished. Meyorowitz and Maguire (1993) say that global TV shows "have enhanced our awareness of all the people we cannot be, the places we cannot go, the things we cannot possess," so that "for many segments of our society" entertainment media "has raised expectations but provided few new opportunities" (43). Globalizing TV shows and films may encourage youth to dream of attaining a standard of living they will never attain and encourage them to try to become what they will never be. As Baudrillard (1997) put it, it is US entertainment culture "which, the world over, fascinates those very people who suffer most at its hands, and it does so through the deep insane conviction that it has made all their dreams come true" (77).

BOX 6.4

GLOBAL ENTERTAINMENT MEDIA AND YOUTH IN MALTA

In the mid-1990s, Malta embraced neoliberal media policy (liberalization, de-regulation, and privatization), and Malta's commercial TV networks began scheduling a mix of local and foreign TV shows. Maltese cable TV network schedules are now full of British and American TV programs. In an important ethnographic study, Grixti (2006) documents how globalizing media entertainment has influenced and been taken up by Maltese youth. Grixti (2006) says the import of Anglo-American TV shows into Malta's mediascape led to "greater awareness among the young about the options and choices available to them— not simply in terms of consumer products but more importantly in terms of new ideas encountered through greater contact with a range of different lifestyles and belief systems" (110). How did global TV shows influence and get taken up by Maltese youth? In what follows, Grixti's findings are summarized.

First, Maltese youth started distancing themselves from "traditional" Maltese culture (as defined by the Roman Catholic Church) in order to embrace "Western society" (as defined by global media entertainment) as their own. The cultural identities available to Maltese youth at the present time are a hybrid mix of local and global, national and transnational, and are shaped by the intermingling of global media and local tradition. Second, Maltese youth watch more non-Maltese entertainment media than their parents do. Though locally-made and culturally proximate TV shows are available, middle-class young people prefer to consume global entertainment media. When they do watch Maltese TV, they mock its poor quality. Third, middle-upper-class young people are more receptive to globalizing entertainment media than working-class youth, who prefer to watch culturally proximate TV shows. The middle-upper-class Maltese youth "frequently associate being young, forward-looking, modern, technologically advanced and enlightened with being in tune with what comes from overseas—or, more specifically, with what comes from Western Europe, Britain and the United States, particularly through the media" (Grixti 2006: 111). They view traditional and indigenous Maltese culture as other, inferior, and backwards. "These young people appear to be choosing to nurture cultural (and in some cases linguistic) discontinuity with their own inherited environment in favor of commonality with the foreign" (Grixti 2006: 113). Fourth, many Maltese youth are ceasing to speak their native language. The Maltese language is a traditional marker of inclusion in Maltese culture and a means of distinguishing Maltese people from foreigners (who tend to speak English). Yet, many young Maltese now speak the English language and believe it to be "superior" to their own language. They use the English language as way to convey their modern-ness. As Grixti (2006) notes:

> for one prominent section of the Maltese population, the deliberate choice of English as the only language of communication has become a means of distancing themselves from local insularity, and of aligning themselves with (and appropriating the attributes of) the outsider/foreigner. (114)

Fifth, by consuming globalizing entertainment media, the Maltese youth feel themselves to be connected to and belonging to a larger global community that is highly materialistic. "[T]hey are driven by consumerism and are constantly looking for something new, but without really knowing what they want" (117). Grixti nonetheless says the effect of global TV in Malta is hybridity.

Hybrid Identities and Indigenized Consumption

Postcolonial scholars argue that globalizing entertainment media may not erode local and national cultures, but may, in fact, mix with them and result in new de-territorialized ethnicities and hybrid combinations. Sreberny-Mohammadi (1996) points out that the CI paradigm's simple image of American cultural domination obscures the reciprocal nature of interaction between cultures over centuries. Hannerz (1997) uses the term creolization "to describe the ongoing, historically cumulative cultural interrelatedness between center and periphery" (126). Cultural mixing is increasing the result of cross-border flows of entertainment media. The contact between globalizing entertainment media and local audiences enables cultures to change, and to change with each other. When TV shows and films move from one place to another, they create hybridity effects due to the ability of local viewers to adapt, indigenize, and re-contextualize texts in accordance with their own ways of life. Classen and Howes (1996) say that "the process of re-contextualization whereby foreign goods are assigned meanings and uses by the culture of reception may be termed hybridization" (6). Darling-Wolf (2000) agrees: "When a text is exported into a different cultural environment composed of a different pool of cultural resources, it might not produce the expected interpretations" (137). Cultural hybridity effects thus describe the mixings which result from contact between globalizing entertainment media and local viewers. Cowen (2007) notes that cultural hybridity effects complicate the CI paradigm:

> the funk of James Brown helped shape the music of West Africa; Indian authors draw upon Charles Dickens; and Arabic pop is centered in France and Belgium [. . .] in the broad sweep of history, many different [cultural] traditions have grown together and flourished [. . .] the greater reach of one culture does not necessarily mean diminished stature for others.

Whenever globalizing entertainment media touches down within a local reception context, meanings and identities are mixed up. According to some proponents of cultural hybridity, the globalization of entertainment media is resulting in a transnational "superculture [that] is based on the premise that the hybrid is the essence of contemporary cultural activity" (Lull 2001: 157). This superculture "is based on the central idea that culture is symbolic and synthetic, and that contemporary syntheses can be constructed from symbolic and material resources that originate almost anywhere on Earth" (137).

GLOBAL ENTERTAINMENT MEDIA RECEPTION STUDIES 2.0:
THE AUDIENCE AS INTERACTIVE PROSUMER

New media studies scholars claim that the shift from Web 1.0 to Web 2.0 and the diffusion of new media technologies have transformed the old power relationships between media conglomerates and media viewers and have given rise to a new audience figure, the "prosumer."

Web 1.0 and Web 2.0 are terms that periodize the user's experience of the World Wide Web. Web 1.0 generally refers to the period between 1993 and 2001 or so. During this time, users supposedly played a passive role in relation to Web-based firms. Some people participated in Web-based chat rooms and posted on *Star Wars* and *Buffy* fan websites, but many Web users simply read news websites, browsed for pre-posted content, checked email, shopped, and watched porn. Using Web 1.0, media corporations largely used the Web to transfer media content to their consumers. Web 2.0 is different because websites are now designed to facilitate a much more interactive user experience.

In Web 2.0, people are not only consumers of media content, but are also active producers of media content. In the Web 2.0 model, the once passive media consumer (the "coach potato" stereotype) becomes an interactive media producer, or what some scholars call a "prosumer." In *The Third Wave*, Toffler (1984) coined the term "prosumer" when he predicted that the role of producers and consumers would one day merge. The era of the prosumer has arrived; media content is now regularly produced by the same people that consume and use it. Anyone reading a TV show blog can start a blog about a TV show nearly instantly. Every person that creates and distributes a personalized video about what they like or dislike about *Prometheus* (2012) using YouTube.com can also watch fan videos on Youtube.com, uploaded by people from all over the world. On film and TV show websites, fans read reviews from other users and post their own. Web 2.0 enables users to interact with media content, produce media content, and share and collaborate with other users in virtual communities.

Prosumer interactivity relies on a technological infrastructure (hardware and software). Millions of people have become prosumers as result of the diffusion of personal computers, the Internet, and access to the means for producing and distributing media content. Personal computers and the hardware and software for capturing, creating, and manipulating sounds, texts, and images are much more affordable than they were in the past. People hitherto excluded from the means of producing and distributing media content now have near professional media content production capacities at their fingertips. Websites, chat-boards, email messaging services, and list-serves combine with Web 2.0 social media platforms such as Facebook, YouTube, MySpace, Twitter, and blogs give users a means of disseminating their own media content far and wide.

Technological optimists celebrate Web 2.0's interactive prosumers, and some talk of a fundamental transformation of the old power relationships between media conglomerates and media audiences (Shirky 2008). We once lived in a world system where a few giant media conglomerates controlled the means of producing, distributing, and exhibiting all media content. But Web 2.0 and a reduction in the cost of personal computers, software, and hardware have lowered the barriers to entering the global media marketplace. Web 2.0 creates a sense that people are becoming micromedia corporations, producers, distributors, and exhibitors of their own user-generated media content, which can be viewed by people all over the world. Ordinary people—not just media corporations—are sources of media content. Web 2.0 has fostered a plurality of diverse expressions and enabled the transnational production, distribution, and exhibition of more self-made media content than ever before. As more and more people utilize the new means of expressing themselves by creating content, posting videos, blogging, texting, and messaging to larger and larger groups, the world system will not only boast more sources of media content, but more media content in general. Using Web 2.0 technology, people are making the most private details of their everyday lives public, for all to read, hear, and see. Personalized public expressions and forms of amateur creativity proliferate. The private lives, feelings, and expressions of people from many countries are now a new kind of global entertainment media.

In response to the growth of prosumer interactivity and do-it-yourself media production, new media studies scholars are less interested in what global TV shows and films are doing to the local audience (meeting their demand, exposing them to ads, brainwashing them, destroying their culture, or enabling hybrid identities) and much more interested in what prosumers are interactively doing, saying, and expressing in relation to entertainment media. For proponents of a new—and increasingly global—"convergence culture" (Jenkins 2004), there are important changes in the way people watch TV shows and films, the temporal parameters of watching, and the space of watching. Due to convergence, people now use all kinds of technological devices to watch TV shows and films. People can watch TV shows and films on high-definition flat screen TV sets, personal computers, and mobile devices including iPods, smart-phones, and tablets. People's entertainment viewing time was once determined by TV networks and theater chains, but in convergence culture, viewers increasingly make their own schedules. Using on-demand and pay-per-view services, people watch whatever TV shows and films shows they want, at whatever time they like. By downloading TV shows and films from the Web (legally or illegally), people create personalized libraries of audio-visual content, retrieving and sharing media content with peers and knowledge communities. Digital video-recorder technologies (DVR) enable viewers to miss regularly scheduled TV shows and films, record them, and watch them at a later date. While TV shows and films were once watched exclusively within the household or at the theater, they now regularly leave the home and the theater. Stored on notebook computers, PSPs, and other mobile devices, they enter a number of different places and spaces of viewing: the bar, the mall, the city street, the subway, the automobile, the airplane, the bus, and so on.

The globalization of convergence culture represents a number of salient transformations in the ways in which people experience entertainment media, in the US and in many other countries. Using the Web, many people from many countries interact with each other on websites like IMDb.com to chat about their favorite films and TV shows. People create and maintain daily blogs about the characters, plots, and themes of TV shows and films. They participate in cross-national fan networks or "knowledge communities" to share information about entertainment media, interactively appropriate, poach, and repurpose content derived their favorite TV shows and films, and engage in new forms of collaboration (Jenkins 1992, 2006, 2008). These are undoubtedly meaningful user experiences. But are they as "revolutionary" as some technological optimists say (Shirky 2008)? Do the new forms of "interactivity" and "participation" enabled by this globalizing yet "grassroots convergence culture" (Jenkins 2004) undermine asymmetrical power relations between media corporations and consumers? Not entirely. Political-economists draw attention to how media corporations authorize, enable, and sanction prosumer interactivity in order to profit-maximize. Media conglomerates are using Web 2.0 and the energy of prosumers for their own economic gain (Andrejevic 2007; Fuchs 2011) by developing interactive Web sites that: 1) cultivate brand-loyal consumers; 2) crowd-source forms of unpaid cultural work; and, 3) collect and commodify user-generated content.

Media conglomerates develop Websites which aim to cultivate and maintain the goodwill and affective investments of "brand-loyal" consumers. Media corporations strive to get ordinary viewers to forge their identities and communities through copyrighted TV shows and films (Jenkins 2008: 70). They want viewers to develop a life-long relationship with a TV show or film brand, and to talk and walk, eat and sleep, extend and imagine the fictional world of TV shows or films. This is because a consumer's long-term good feeling toward a TV show or film is a significant—though difficult-to-quantify—source of profit. Positive feelings toward an entertainment franchise often contribute to "brand equity" or "brand value." A media firm that owns a TV series or blockbuster film franchise which many people like can generate more revenue by selling licenses to these products than a media firm that owns less appreciated content can. A distribution company can charge an exhibition company more for the licensing rights to a TV series or film that is widely liked than they can for products that are not. The exchange-value, here, hinges not on any tangible thing, but on the perceived or actual positive feelings of a large number of consumers toward the media property.

To generate brand equity for their TV shows and films, media firms go to great lengths to cultivate brand-loyal viewers. Web sites that interactively engage viewers and immerse them in the fictional worlds of TV shows and films represent one strategy for doing so. Brooker (2001) says that interactive Web structures "enable an immersive, participatory engagement" with media content "that crosses multiple media platforms and invites active contribution; not only from fans, who after all have been engaged in participatory culture around their favored texts for decades, but also, as part of the regular 'mainstream' viewing experience" (Brooker 2001: 470). *The Amazing Spider-Man* (2012) website structure, for example, allows users to interactively learn about the film, view pictures, watch trailers and videos, download Web wallpapers, Twitter skins, Avatars, Facebook covers, and animated gifts, acquire an "augmented reality" application for their smartphone, play a Spider-Man game, and listen to The Amazing Spider-Man soundtrack. It invites users to actively follow Spider-man on Facebook, Twitter, YouTube, Pinterest, and blogs. *The Amazing Spider-Man* website is designed to engage and immerse people as brand-loyal prosumers in the fictional world of Spider-Man, which "over-flows" (Brooker 2001) into their everyday lives. Corporate Webs like these are interactively spun to enhance and increase consumer affect, brand equity, and the amount of money media firms can charge for their TV shows and films.

Media conglomerates also design Web sites that get prosumers to perform tasks once exclusively assigned to waged cultural workers. Howe (2006) calls this "crowd-sourcing." Media corporations develop websites that invite fans to share their creative ideas with production companies (Shefrin 2004). Fan websites solicit demographic data about viewer tastes and preferences to aid marketing research (Andrejevic 2007). Media firms also harness prosumer interactivity as a source of unpaid promotion. Fan chatter on corporate-sanctioned chat boards creates buzz about TV shows and films. While fan fiction, blogs, and YouTube mash-ups posted to TV show and film websites contribute to the intangible value of brands. In these instances, the prosumer is not a "cultural dope" or "resistant" meaning-maker, but an unwaged cultural worker. Web 2.0 enables media firms to exploit crowds of prosumers as content generators, demographic researchers, and data inputters (Andrejevic 2007). In this interactive corporate convergence culture, the spheres of production (waged work) and media consumption (leisure) are blurring together, while hitherto unproductive places and time periods are transformed into spaces of value creation.

Additionally, media firms use interactive Web sites to collect user data, which users themselves create and submit. Web 2.0 companies such as Google, MySpace, YouTube, and Facebook are data surveillance companies. They all depend on user interactivity and user content creation. They collect content generated by their users and assemble it into an approximation of a person, a data self. The data self is a kind of personal profile—a picture of a user's tastes and preferences. New media firms combine user generated content from multiple sources—website ad clicks, searches, customer loyalty cards, virtual shopping carts—to create a data profile of an individual. They then sell the data profile as a commodity to advertising firms, which use these profiles to customize ads. Data profiles help advertising firms make inferences about what kinds of people we are and what kinds of products we might want. From there, they customize their ad message to targeted groups with the hope that this campaign will entice them to buy. The data surveillance process—from collection of user content, to sorting and segmenting this content into data profiles, to selling data profiles as commodities to ad clients, to advertising firms developing targeted campaigns—transforms prosumers into digital serfs (Fuchs 2011). They work for new media corporations, but not in exchange for a wage.

Although the globalization of convergence culture is bringing about important changes in the way people experience and interact with entertainment media, the commercial functions of globalizing TV shows and films persist. The structures of political-economic power that have historically governed global entertainment media's existence have not been revolutionized by Web 2.0. Furthermore, US media conglomerates are the most significant owners of global convergence culture. And the global "digital divide"—the uneven distribution of ICTs and imbalances in ICT access—prevents much of the world population from interacting in convergence culture. No more than 30 percent of the total world population uses the Internet, but nearly 80 percent of US citizens are online. In 2010, a total of 2 billion people used the Internet, about 10 times the number of users in 1998. But 70 percent of the world population is without Internet access (Winseck 2011: 36). At present, globalizing convergence culture mainly includes media-literate, tech-savvy, middle-upper class people in rich and poor countries. Exported to the world primarily by US media firms, convergence culture is an "emergent" phenomenon in many countries and experienced only by the most privileged, the most educated and the most socio-economically well off. Yet, as the digital divide shrinks due to the diffusion of ICTs and media literacy, more people from more countries will likely be "included" in global convergence culture. As convergence culture globally spreads, media firms will tap more interactive prosumers as unpaid contributors to their profits.

CONCLUSION: RESISTING WHAT?

This chapter discussed five different figures of global entertainment media's local audience. Neoliberalism's figure of the sovereign consumer is dominant, but highly problematic. Political-economy's account of the audience as a commodity continues to provide a way of understanding how TNMCs and NMCs trade in audience attention. CI scholars, cultivation theorists, and Marxists highlight the possibly negative psychological and behavioral effects of global entertainment media. Using a mix of reception and ethnographic methods, cultural studies try to get down to earth with actual viewers to learn how they live with and live through global TV shows and films. New media studies scholars represent the audience as an interactive prosumer. The movement of media imagery and messages between national borders almost always involves local interpretation, translation, and adaptation by a range of viewers. In many countries, local viewer exposure to global entertainment media has complex effects that are not always reducible to Americanization.

The consumption of globalizing entertainment media by viewers is a culturally complex and sometimes contradictory process. But the interpretive agency of viewers should always be contextualized with reference to the broader political-economic determinations of the entertainment media they consume and the power relations they are part of:

> Scholars must balance an acceptance that audiences are in certain respects active in their choice, consumption and interpretation of media texts, with a recognition of how that activity is framed and limited, in its different modalities and varieties, by the dynamics of cultural power. (Morley and Robins 1995: 127)

Boyd-Barrett (2006) says that too much emphasis on viewer interpretation and the diversity of readings "stretches the significance of cultural products beyond the indications deductible from content analysis, but offers little insight into the processes determining which cultural significations are magnified for mass dissemination, and which are lost" (22). Scholars should not over-state the resistant politics (or political efficacy) of active media consumption and interpretation. This is especially true in the age of convergence, when media corporations consciously enable and exploit prosumer interactivity in order to profit-maximize. I am not suggesting that "resistance" to transnational corporate power is not possible or desirable; however, when deploying words like "resistance," it is very important to clarify in what material and discursive context "resistance" functions, and also to distinguish between different kinds of "resistances" and their practical limitations.

CONCLUSION

Global Media Studies Between Cultural Imperialism and Cultural Globalization

I would like to conclude this book by making a few claims that mediate between the CI and CG paradigms in global media studies. A paradigm that contemplates the continued dominance of US-based TNMCs vis-à-vis NMCs, the asymmetries and inequities in cross-border audio-visual trade, the linkages and relations between US and non-US media capitals, the spread of commercialism, and the consequences of these processes is vital for a proper investigation of the economic, geopolitical, and cultural power relations that shape the cross-border production, distribution, exhibition, and consumption of TV shows and films. A middle-ground paradigm will retain the CI paradigm's critical focus on capitalism, imperialism, and power while learning from the CG paradigm's insights. The most salient facets of the CI and critical CG paradigms can be synthesized to establish a critical yet non-reductive paradigm for studying global entertainment media.

The present structure of the world system is the outcome of the history of capitalism and the Westphalian state system. The world system has long comprised unevenly developed nation-states in a structural hierarchy of asymmetrical and unequal power relations, both coercive and persuasive. This is not likely to change any time soon. There is no global government that currently presents an alternative to the sovereign power of territorial states, and though global, capitalism still is coordinated by a system of territorial states. Following the end of the Cold War, all states in the world system—core, semi-periphery, and periphery—became more integrated and interdependent as result of the globalization of capitalism, the diffusion of information and communication technology, and the universalization of neoliberal policies. But capitalism is still governed in different ways as result of different state regulatory and policy regimes. The US continues to be the imperial superpower or hegemon of the world system, economically, militarily, and culturally (Agnew 2003; Ahmad 2004; Anderson 2002; Arrighi 2003; Bacevich 2002; Harvey 2003, 2004; Panitch and Gindin 2004). The US is also the world's center of entertainment media financing, production, distribution, exhibiting, and marketing, and US-based TNMCs are at the top of the world media hierarchy.

In the world system, all states are motivated by "national interests"; corporations, by profit. Though states and corporations are legally separate, their interests often converge. States—and not just the US imperial state—facilitate and legitimize the national and transnational profit-interests of media corporations. In turn, media corporations contribute to state-defined national, cultural, and economic goals. Not every state media policy is a direct reflection of corporate media interests. Not every trans-territorial act of profit-making is intrinsically tied to the state's "national interest." But states frequently do facilitate and legitimize the profit-interests of media corporations. And media corporations regularly do represent themselves as bearers of national interests. More comparative research on the synergistic power relationships between states and media corporations—territorial political logics and de-territorializing capitalist logics—is needed in global media studies.

We live in a world system of many media capitals, but the most powerful media capital continues to be located in the US: Los Angeles, California. In every country, US-based TNMCs have increased their economic presence and cultural power. The single most globally powerful and popular exporter of entertainment media is the US. Media flows in many directions, but the flows between the US and other countries are still not reciprocal. Nonetheless, many countries—neocolonial and postcolonial alike—have developed NMCs that control networks of media production, distribution, and exhibition. Though people all over the world consume a lot of entertainment media made by US-based TNMCs, non-US NMCs compete to control regional markets and strive to break into the gigantic US market. US-based TNMCs compete and collaborate with non-US NMCs through global-local alliances. In the NICL, they co-produce TV shows and films that are intended to travel well within and between many markets. National TV broadcasters load their schedules with a mix of domestic and foreign (often "American") TV shows and films in order to attract viewers and ad revenue. Although US-based TNMCs continue to be the most genuinely global producers, distributors, marketers, and exhibitors of TV shows and films, non-US NMCs, TV shows and films have not disappeared.

On behalf of the profit interests of US-based TNMCs, the US state and the MPAA struggle to universalize a "made-in-America" neoliberal media policy regime through a number of bilateral, multi-lateral, and global institutions and trade agreements. The entrenchment of some components of US neoliberal media policy by sovereign states has made it easier for US-based TNMCs to conduct business wherever they want, whenever they like. But the US's neoliberal media policy prescriptions for culture have been only partially embraced by the political and economic "gatekeepers" of other states. That being said, many neoliberal policy-makers have subscribed to the idea that the market is the best regulator. The mantra of "liberalize, de-regulate, and privatize" is embraced by many states and business elites. The US-originated commercial media model is globally dominant. While, public and state-run media systems face budgetary cut-backs and legitimacy problems. The supplanting of public by commercial media models was the result of politics, not inexorable market or technological forces.

State-managed capitalist integration with the US core, not isolationism, enabled non-US media capitals to emerge in many hitherto peripheral and semi-peripheral countries (Keane 2006). The result of integration is not economic stagnation or total cultural dependency, but the stifling of alternative and perhaps more egalitarian and democratic developmental paths. The adoption of the US commercial media model in many countries, the integration of many media capitals with the US media core, and the consolidation of the NICL have had mixed effects: not all negative, and not all positive. Integration with the US media core opened countries to flows of US foreign direct investment (FDI), liberal democratic ideology, notions of media professionalism, training, and skills transfers for cultural workers, the ideal of consumer sovereignty, and the circulation of more TV shows and films than were previously available (Thussu 2006: 182). But integration with the US core may also have eroded distinctive national media industries, spread consumer-capitalist ideology, damaged the public sphere, crushed public broadcasting, intensified the exploitation of cultural workers, diminished the value of citizenship, and fettered TV networks and screens around the world to US entertainment media.

The cultural consequences of the integration process are sometimes, but not always, tantamount to "Americanization." US TV shows and film products are part of the "second culture" of many countries (Gitlin 2001). Although transnational capitalist integration under the stewardship of the US state and US-TNMCs has occurred in many countries—and is still occurring—the dream of Americanizing the world is currently the exception to a national media policy rule: the protection and promotion of national cultures. Sovereign state attempts to protect and promote their "national cultures" and culture/creative industries can sometimes challenge the dominance of US TNMCs and buffer the effects of a perceptibly "Americanizing" media-culture. State media policies build up non-US NMCs and media capitals. Concerns about the uses and abuses of nationalist rhetoric by state policy-makers and fears that state-sanctioned national culture is exclusionary are valid, but the state and the nation are terrains of struggle. Citizens should not abandon either. Nation-state media policy regimes may be "captured" by ruling blocs of media capital, but they are not always already biased to those interests. They can be captured and used by progressive social forces to achieve goals that run against the grain of global capital.

Some globally popular films and TV shows are encoded with signs, themes, and stories derived from US society. But a lot of entertainment media that is popular beyond US borders does not represent the US nation. TNMC-owned TV shows and films are not globally popular due to their US "national" texts. Nor do they circulate as a result of sovereign consumer demand for all things "American." McChesney (2005) says that media corporations "will respect no tradition or custom, on balance, if it stands in the way of profits" (95). Yet, media corporations are pitching their entertainment media to global, national, and local customs in order to profit-maximize. Globalizing entertainment texts—blockbuster films, TV formats, glocalized lifestyle brands—are increasingly designed to be polysemic and open to a range of global, national, and local interpretations. Entertainment media conveys a wide variety of stories, narratives, characters, and themes. Some products affirm the nationalist and transnationalist status quo, while others are edgy and oppositional. Also, there are many TV shows and films being produced and exported by non-US media capitals. All globalizing entertainment texts should be studied in their specificity. There is much work to be done on excavating the histories, economic conditions, and popular characteristics of entertainment texts that travel well across borders.

The relationship between global entertainment media and the audience is complex (discursively and practically). Lauding the agency of sovereign media consumers to actively resist imported messages is no less ideological than bemoaning the media's domination of youthful viewers. The relationships between globalizing US entertainment and non-US viewers, and non-US entertainment and US viewers, are a fruitful site for reception studies. Significant research questions for local reception studies of global entertainment media include:

> Who is appropriating what cultural materials/texts/items and from where do these cultural products come? Also, who is appropriating more of what and from where? And, who is appropriating less of what from where? [. . .] When cultural resistance occurs, exactly what/who is being resisted? How does resistance manifest itself, i.e., what forms is it assuming. Finally, and perhaps most importantly, at what level is resistance manifesting itself? (Demont-Heinrich 2011: 671)

Entertainment media is not culture, though it does play a role in shaping cultures and societies. TV shows and films are powerful sources of identification and identity formation, but they are not the only sources. Cultures are not pure, essential, or fixed, but are hybrid mixes of elements from many different sources. That being said, cultural mixing is unequal, asymmetrical, and infrequently a two-way street. The US state and US-TNMCs have historically had (and continue to have) more material and symbolic resources, and hence more capacity to construct a stable cultural identity and impart it around the world without reciprocation of influence by non-US states and non-US media firms. Hall (1990) says hybridity tends to happen in "contact zones" between an imperialist state and other subordinate ones. The US state and US-based TNMCs have more structural power than others to package and promote the cultural ingredients that get mixed with others.

US TNMCs and entertainment media cross borders, but borders—material and symbolic—still matter. The spread of ICTs and electronic media creates the sense that we are living in a "global village." Yet, while ICTs and electronic media cultivate a structure of feeling that "we are one," they have not transcended concrete and place-based divisions rooted in national chauvinism, classism, racism, sexism, ethno-centrism, and forms of religious zealotry. Lule (2011) says the globalization of the media has established global village-like conditions, but this village is far from utopian. This is "a village characterized not by understanding or unity, but a village torn by avarice, strife and suffering" (10). ICTs and convergent media enable post-national, diasporic, and global identifications and imaginings, but they also remain instruments for the diffusion of hateful ideas. Cosmopolitan identifications with distant others happens alongside (but perhaps less frequently) than do superficial or deep attachments to locale and nation-ness. We do not live in a world system that is particularly amenable to genuine internationalist solidarity.

The world system we live in does, however, support transnational (though not exclusively US) corporate power. As Herbert Schiller (1992) observed:

> American cultural imperialism is not dead, but it no longer adequately describes the global cultural condition. Today it is more useful to view transnational corporate culture as the

central force, with a continuing heavy flavor of US media know-how, derived from long experience with marketing and entertainment skills and practices. (14–15)

Cultural imperialism may be a fact in some contexts, but it is not the only way to describe the transnational production, distribution, exhibition, and consumption of information and entertainment media by the US and others. Cultural imperialism's historic structures and effects nevertheless continue to haunt the present world system, but with significant differences. In the early twenty-first century, the political economies and cultures that influence and are influenced by the cross-border production, distribution, exhibition and consumption of TV shows and films continue to be important areas of theory, research and practice. My goal in this book has been to provide a helpful introduction to them and to support further research, discussion and debate. I conclude with a few questions:

Does global entertainment media help or hinder the democratic life of nations? Does it support or sideline issues of social justice, equality, and human rights? Does it contribute to the cultivation of informed citizens capable of deliberatively participating in a public sphere, or does it pacify and "dumb down" consumers? Does it nourish and inspire or crush and alienate the creative lives of the world's cultural workers? Does it initiate greater cross-cultural understanding and empathy between people separated by geography or does it tear them further apart? Does this transnational corporate culture, which so many people in so many countries believe they want, give them what they need to understand the reasons for war, cultural oppression, the ever-growing divide between rich and poor, and the worldwide environmental crisis? Does the new transnational cultural imperialism—or "cultural globalization"—help or hinder the transnational social activists that struggle to build a future that is better than the present? These are serious questions connected with global problems that I hope will inspire more cultural materialist studies of global entertainment media.

AAP. (2011, November 18). Inquiry hears calls for media ownership caps. Retrieved from http://www.sbs.com.au/news/article/1606083/inquiry-hears-calls-for-media-ownership-caps

Abramson, B. D. (2001). Media policy after regulation? *International Journal of Cultural Studies*, 4(3), 301–326.

Abu-Nasr, D. (2008, September 15). Saudi Fatwa pans 'immoral' TV. Retrieved from http://www.thestar.com/news/world/article/499265–saudi-fatwa-pans-immoral-tv

Acland, C. R. (2003). *Screen Traffic: Movies, Multiplexes and Global Culture*. Durham and London: Duke University Press.

Adegoke, Y. (2011, May 3). Satellite TV provider Dish Network Corp has been sued by Walt Disney and Starz Entertainment for giving away popular movies, including Disney's "Toy Story 3" and "Alice in Wonderland." Retrieved from http://www.reuters.com/article/2011/05/03/us-dish-disney-idUSTRE7425MC20110503

Adegoke, Y. and Levine, D. (2011, June 29). Comcast completes NBC Universal merger. Retrieved from http://www.reuters.com/article/2011/01/29/us-comcast-nbc-idUSTRE70S2WZ20110129

Adler, T. (2010). *House* set to be most popular U.S. TV export to Europe for 2nd year. Retrieved from http://www.deadline.com/2010/01/house-set-to-be-most-popular-u-s-tv-export-to-europe-for–2nd-year-running/

ADMIN. (2010, January 9). 10 Most popular TV shows on the International Primetime in 2009. Retrieved from http://www.cinemarealm.com/2010/01/09/10-most-popular-tv-shows-internationally–2009/

AFP. (2006, March 24). George Lucas attacks US cultural imperialism. Retrieved from http://www.smh.com.au/news/film/george-lucas-attacks-us-cultural-imperialism/2006/03/24/1143083953256.html

Agrell, S. (2010, January 13). Earthlings take issue with Avatar. *The Globe and Mail*, A13.

Ahmad, A. (1992). *In Theory: Classes, Nations, Literatures*. New York: Verso.

——. (2004). Imperialism of Our Time. In L. Panitch and C. Leys (Eds), *The New Imperial Challenge: Socialist Register 2004* (pp. 43–63). London: Merlin Press.

Ahn, H. and Litman, B. R. (1997). Vertical integration and consumer welfare in the cable industry. *Journal of Broadcasting and Electronic Media*, 41(1), 453–477.

Airlie, C. (2011, April 4). Global advertising spending rose in 2010, Nielsen says. Retrieved from http://www.bloomberg.com/news/2011–04–03/global-ad-spending-in–2010-rose–11-on-soccer-s-world-cup-neilsen-says.html

Albarran, A. B. (1996). *Media Economics: Understanding Markets, Industries and Concepts*. Ames: Iowa State University Press.

——. (2010). *The Media Economy*. New York: Routledge.

Allor, M. (1996). The Politics of Producing Audiences. In J. Hay, L. Grossberg, and E. Wartella (Eds), *The Audience and its Landscape* (pp. 209–219). Boulder, CO: Westview.

Altman, R. (1999). *Film/Genre*. London: British Film Institute.

Amin, A. (1999). An institutionalist perspective on regional development. *International Journal of Urban and Regional Research*. 2(1), 365–378.

Anderson, B. (1991). *Imagined Communities*. New York, NY: Verso.

Anderson, P. (2002). Editorial: Force and Consent. *New Left Review* (17)(Sept-Oct), 5–29.

Andrejevic, M. (2007). *iSpy: Surveillance and Power in the Interactive Era*. Kansas: University Press of Kansas.

——. (2008). Watching Television Without Pity: The productivity of online fans. *Television & New Media*, 9(1), 24–46.

Ang, I. (1985). *Watching Dallas: Soap Opera and the Melodramatic Imagination*. London: Methuen.

——. (1990). Culture and communication: towards an ethnographic critique of media consumption in the transnational media system. *European Journal of Communication*, 5(1), 239–260.

——. (1996a). In the realm of uncertainty: the global village and capitalist postmodernity. In H. Mackay and T. O'Sullivan, (Eds), *The Media Reader: Continuity and Transformation* (pp. 366–384). Thousand Oaks: Sage.

——. (1996b). *Living Room Wars: Rethinking Media Audiences for a Postmodern World*. London: Routledge.

Appadurai, A. (1997). *Modernity at Large*. Minneapolis: University of Minnesota Press.

Appiah, K. A. (2006, January 1). The case for contamination. Retrieved from http://www.nytimes.com/2006/01/01/magazine/01cosmopolitan.html?pagewanted=all

Arango, T. (2008, December 1). World falls for American media, even as it sours on America. Retrieved from http://www.nytimes.com/2008/12/01/business/media/01soft.html

Aronowitz, S. and Bratsis, P. (Eds). (2002). *Paradigm Lost: State Theory Reconsidered* Minneapolis: University of Minnesota Press.

Arsenault, A. (2011). The structure and dynamics of global networks in the media, telecoms, gaming and computing industries. In D. R. Winseck and D. Y. Jin (Eds), *The Political Economies of Media: The Transformation of the Global Media Industries*. New York: Bloomsbury Academic. Retrieved from http://www.bloomsburyacademic.com/view/PoliticalEconomiesMedia_9781849664264/chapter-ba–9781849664264-chapter–003.xml?print

Arsenault, A. and Castells, M. (2008). The structure and dynamics of global multi-media business networks. *International Journal of Communication*, 2, 707–748.

Artz, L. (2003). Globalization, media hegemony and social class. In L. Artz and Y. R. Kamalipour (Eds), *The Globalization of Corporation Media Hegemony* (pp. 3–32). Albany: State University of New York Press.

——. (2007). The corporate model from national to transnational. In C. J. Hamelink, L. Artz, and Y. R. Kamalipour (Eds), *The Media Globe: Trends In International Mass Media*. (pp. 141–162). Plymouth: Rowman & Littlefield

Artz, L. and Kamalipour, Y. R. (2003). *The Globalization of Corporate Media Hegemony*. New York, NY: State University of New York Press.

Associated Press. (2002, June 5). Disney sues over bears similar to Pooh. Retrieved from http://articles.latimes.com/2002/jun/05/business/fi-rup5.9

Averill, G. (1996). Global imaginings. In R. Ohman (Ed.), *Making and Selling Culture* (pp. 203–33). Hanover: New England UP.

Avery, H. (2006, October). Hedge funds and film finance: Show me the money. Retrieved from http://www.euromoney.com/Article/1079895/Title.html

Aysha, E. (2004). The limits and contradictions of Americanization. In L. Panitch and C. Leys (Eds), *The New Imperial Challenge: Socialist Register 2004* (pp. 245–61). London: Merlin Press.

Babe, R. (2009). *Cultural Studies and Political Economy: Toward a New Integration*. Lanham, MD: Lexington Books.

Bacevich, A. (2002). *American Empire: The Consequences and Realities of U.S. Diplomacy*. Cambridge: Harvard UP.

Bagdikian, B. (1997). *The Media Monopoly*. Boston, MA: Beacon Press.
——. (2004). *The New Media Monopoly*. Boston, MA: Beacon Press.
Bah, U. (2008). Daniel Lerner, Cold War propaganda and US development communication research: an historical critique. *Journal of Third World Studies*, 25(1), 183–198.
Baker, C. E. (2002). *Media, Markets and Democracy*. Cambridge: Cambridge University Press.
——. (2007). *Media Concentration and Democracy: Why Ownership Matters*. Cambridge: Cambridge University Press.
Balio, T. (1998). A major presence in all world's important markets: The globalization of Hollywood in the 1990s. In S. Neale and M. Smith (Eds), *Contemporary Hollywood Cinema* (pp. 58–73). New York: Routledge.
Balko, R. (2003). Globalization and culture: Americanization or cultural diversity? Retrieved from http://globalpolicy.org/globaliz/cultural/2003/03american.htm
Banerjee, I. and Seneviratne, K (Eds). (2006). *Public service broadcasting in the age of globalization*. Asian Media Information Centre.
Banks, M. (2008). Company town: production communities and the myth of a unified Hollywood. *Velvet Light Trap*, 62, (Fall), 62–64.
Banks, M. and Hesmondhalgh, D. (2009). Looking for work in creative industries policy. *International Journal of Cultural Policy*, 15(4), 415–430.
Banks, M. and O'Conner, J. (2009). Introduction: after the creative industries. *International Journal of Cultural Policy*, 15(4), 365–373.
Baran, P. (1957). *The Political Economy of Growth*. New York: Monthly Review Press.
Barber, B. (2008). Shrunken sovereign: consumerism, globalization, and American emptiness. Retrieved from http://www.worldaffairsjournal.org/article/shrunken-sovereign-consumerism-globalization-and-american-emptiness
Barlow, M. (2001). The global monoculture: "free trade" versus culture and democracy. *Earth Island Journal*. Autumn, 2001.
Barnes, B. (2009, March 31). MPAA decides it's too hard to measure film production and marketing costs. Retrieved from http://carpetbagger.blogs.nytimes.com/2009/03/31/showest-report-mpaa-decides-its-too-difficult-to-measure-film-production-and-marketing-costs/
Barrionuevo, A. (2009, October 10). Argentina enacts law on broadcasters. Retrieved from http://www.nytimes.com/2009/10/11/world/americas/11argentina.html
Barrionuevo, A. (2010, April 10). Tribes of Amazon find an ally out of 'Avatar.' Retrieved from http://www.nytimes.com/2010/04/11/world/americas/11brazil.htm
Basu, I. (2010, February 10). Hollywood finds a piggy bank in Bollywood. Retrieved from http://www.atimes.com/atimes/South_Asia/LB10Df01.html
Baudrillard, J. (1997). *America*. New York: Verso.
Baxter, M. (2011, October 17). Local programs no longer need quotas to survive. Retrieved from http://www.theaustralian.com.au/media/opinion/local-programs-no-longer-need-quotas-to-survive/story-e6frg99o-1226168014370
BBC. (2008, April 3). Indian soaps face Afghanistan ban. Retrieved from http://news.bbc.co.uk/2/hi/7328485.stm
—— (2009, September 27). Venezuela Bans Family Guy Cartoon. Retrieved from http://news.bbc.co.uk/2/hi/8277129.stm
BBC News UK. (2011, April 30). Royal Wedding: In Numbers. Retrieved from http://www.bbc.co.uk/news/uk-13248642>
Becker, A. E (2004). Television, disordered eating, and young women in Fiji: negotiating body image and identity during rapid social change. *Culture, Medicine and Psychiatry*, 28(4), 533–559.
Becker, R. (2006). *Gay TV and Straight America*. Piscataway, NJ: Rutgers University Press.
Bell, T. (2008, February 18). Banned Rambo film hot property in Burma. Retrieved from http://www.telegraph.co.uk/news/uknews/1579082/Banned-Rambo-film-hot-property-in-Burma.html

Beltran, L. R. (1978). Communication and cultural domination: USA-Latin America case. *Media Asia*, 5, 183–192.

Beltrán, M., and Fojas, C. (Eds) (2008). *Mixed Race Hollywood*. New York: New York University Press.

Berardi, D.M. (2006, May 15). Chaotic: globalization, the media and American popular culture. Retrieved from http://www.associatedcontent.com/article/32308/chaotic_globalization_the_media_and_pg3.html

Bettig, R.V. (1996). *Copyrighting Culture: The Political Economy of Intellectual Property*. Boulder, CO: Westview Press.

Betz, M. (2001). The name above the (sub)title: internationalism, co-production, and polyglot European art cinema. *Camera Obscura*, 46, 16(1), 1–44.

Bielby, D. D. and Harrington, C. L. (2008). *Global TV: Exporting Television and Culture in the World Market*. New York: New York University Press.

Billig, M. (1995). *Banal Nationalism*. London: Sage.

Binning, C. (2010, March 22). TV co-ventures thriving as global economy dictates partnerships. Retrieved from http://playbackonline.ca/2010/03/22/coventures–20100322/

Bissel, K. L. and Chung, J. Y. (2009). Americanized beauty? Predictors of perceived attractiveness from U.S. and South Korean participants based on media exposure, ethnicity and socio-cultural attitudes toward ideal beauty. *Asian Journal of Communication*, 19 (2), 227–247.

Blair, I. (2009, October 23). World's greatest film locations. Retrieved from http://www.variety.com/article/VR1118010354?refCatId=3782

Block, A. B. (2011, November 2). Copyright industries provided $931 billion to US economy in 2010, according to study. Retrieved from http://www.hollywoodreporter.com/news/copyright-industries-provided–931-billion-economy–256778

Bloomberg (2011, October 21). Top ten News Corp voting shareholders.Retrieved from http://www.telegraph.co.uk/finance/newsbysector/mediatechnologyandtelecoms/media/8841452/Top-ten-News-Corp-voting-shareholders.html

Blum, W. (2004). *Killing Hope: U.S. Military and CIA Interventions Since World War II*. Monroe, Maine: Common Courage Press.

Bodo, B. (2011, March 7). Media piracy in emerging economies. Retrieved from http://cyberlaw.stanford.edu/blog/2011/03/media-piracy-emerging-economies

Bonné, J. (11 July 2003). Simpsons evolves as an industry: Fox's much-loved TV show is a guaranteed cash cow. Retrieved from http://today.msnbc.msn.com/id/3403870/t/simpsons-evolves-industry/#.UJBe2sXA98E

Bordwell, D., Staiger, J., and Thompson, K. (1985). *The Classical Hollywood Cinema: Film styles and Mode of Production to 1960*. New York: Routledge.

Bourdieu, P. (1998). The essence of neoliberalism: utopia of endless exploitation. Retrieved from http://mondediplo.com/1998/12/08bourdieu

Bowles, S. and Edwards, R. (1985). *Understanding capitalism: Competition, command and change in the U.S. economy*. New York: Harper & Row.

Box Office Mojo. (2011). *Toy Story*. Retrieved from http://boxofficemojo.com/movies/?page=intl&id=toystory3.htm Box Office Mojo (2011).

——. (2012). *Avatar*. Retrieved from http://boxofficemojo.com/movies/?id=avatar.htm

Boyd, D. A. (1984). The Janus effect? imported television entertainment programming in developing countries. *Critical Studies in Mass Communication,* 1(2), 379–391.

Boyd-Barrett, O. (1977). Media imperialism: towards an international framework for the analysis of media systems. In J. Curran, M. Gurevitch, and J. Woolacott, (Eds) *Mass Communication and Society*, (pp. 116–135). London: Arnold.

——. (1997). International communication and globalization: contradictions and directions. In A. Mohammadi (Ed.), *International Communication and Globalization: A Critical Introduction* (pp. 11–26). London: Sage.

——. (1998). Media imperialism reformulated. In D. K. Thussu (Ed.), *Electronic Empires: Global Media and Local Resistance* (pp. 156–176). New York: Arnold.

——. (2003). Global communication orders. In B. Mody (Ed.), *International and Development Communication: A 21st-century Perspective* (pp. 35–52). Thousand Oaks, CA: Sage.

——. (2006). Cyberspace, globalization and empire. *Global Media and Communication*, 2(1), 21–41.

Bratich, J. Z., Packer, J., and McCarthy C. (Eds). (2003). *Foucault, Cultural Studies, and Governmentality*. New York: State University of New York Press.

Braudy, L. (2011). *The Hollywood Sign: Fantasy and Reality of an American Icon*. New Haven, Connecticut: Yale University Press.

Breakwell, G. M. (Ed.). (1992). *Social Psychology of Identity and the Self Concept*. London: Surrey University Press.

British Columbia Film Commission. (2011). British Columbia Film Commission Production Statistics 2010. Retrieved from http://www.bcfilmcommission.com/database/rte/files/2010FinalStats%20Package.pdf

Bronk, R. (December 11, 2006). Hollywood has not fueled anti-americanism abroad. Retrieved from http://abcnews.go.com/International/story?id=2717175

Brook, S. (2010, April 5). Britain leads the way in selling global TV formats. Retrieved from http://www.guardian.co.uk/media/2010/apr/05/britain-tv-formats-sales/print

Brooker, W. (2001). Living on Dawson's Creek: teen viewers, cultural convergence and television overflow. *International Journal of Cultural Studies*, 4(4), 456–472.

Brooks, D. (2008, May 2). The Cognitive Age. Retrieved from http://www.nytimes.com/2008/05/02/opinion/02brooks.html?em&ex=1209960000&en=1628bc39165590dc&ei=5087%0A

Brown, G. (14 Nov. 2011). Unless forced to, networks won't show local content. Retrieved from http://www.theaustralian.com.au/media/opinion/unless-forced-to-networks-wont-show-local-content/story-e6frg99o-1226193924090

Buckingham, D. (1993). *Children Talking Television: The Making of Television Literacy*. London: Falmer Press.

Buell, F. (1994). *National Culture and the New Global System*. Baltimore and London: Johns Hopkins.

Burke, P. (2009). *Cultural Hybridity*. Cambridge, UK: Polity Press.

Burns, D. D. (2009, October 9). Hollywood air pollution heading to Miami. Retrieved from http://www.examiner.com/film-industry-in-miami/hollywood-air-pollution-heading-to-miami

Butsch, R. (2003). Popular communication audiences: A historical research agenda. *Popular Communication*, 1(1), 15–21.

Byoungkwan, L. and Hyuhn-Suhck, B. (2003). The effect of screen quotas on the self-sufficiency ration in recent domestic film markets, *Journal of Media Economics*, 17(3), 163–176.

Cabral, A. (1973). *Return to the Source: Selected Speeches of Amilcar Cabral*. New York, NY: Monthly Review Press.

Camarota, S. (2011). Immigrant population at record 40 million 2010. Retrieved from http://www.prnewswire.com/news-releases/immigrant-population-at-record–40-million-in–2010–131205954.html

Canada China Business Council (2008). *Cultural Industries. Market Overview*. Retrieved from http://www.ccbc.com/research-reports/sector-research/cultural-industries

Canadian Heritage. (2009). Minister Moore announces Canada media fund to give viewers what they want, when they want it. Retrieved from www.pch.gc.ca/eng/1294862439605

Caranicas, P. (2010, March 15). Hollywood stems outflow. Retrieved from http://www.variety.com/article/VR1118016502

Cardoso, F. and Faletto, E. (1979). *Dependency and Development in Latin America*. Berkeley: University of California Press.

Carter, G. T. (2008). From blaxploitation to mixploitation: male leads and changing mixed race identities. In M. Beltrán and C. Fojas (Eds), *Mixed Race Hollywood* (pp. 203–222). New York: New York University Press.

Castells, M. (1997). *The Power of Identity*. Oxford, UK: Blackwell Publishing.

CBC Arts. (2006, November 14). Hollywood's leading role: air polluter. Retrieved from http://www.cbc.ca/news/arts/film/story/2006/11/14/hollywood-pollution.html

CBC News. (2010, 14 October). Chilean mine rescue watched by millions online. Retrieved from http://www.cbc.ca/news/technology/story/2010/10/14/tech-chile-miner-video-stream.html

CFO Staff. (2005, September 1). *Hollywood hits up Wall Street*. Retrieved from http://www.cfo.com/article.cfm/4334616/c_4334841?f=insidecfo

CFTPA/APFTQ. (2009). 09 Profile: An Economic Report on the Canadian Film and Television Production Industry. Retrieved from www.cftpa.ca/newsroom/pdf/profile/profile2009.en.pdf

Chadha, K. and Kavoori, A. (2000). Media imperialism revisited: some findings from the Asian case. *Media, Culture & Society*, 22(1), 415–32.

Chai, P. (2010, June 15). Minister defends Kiwi film subsidies: Treasury report charged Hollywood films of bankrupting state. Retrieved from http://www.variety.com/article/VR1118020691

Chakravartty, P. and Sarikakis, K. (2006). *Media Policy and Globalization*. Edinburgh: Edinburgh University Press.

Chalaby, J. K. (2002). Transnational television in Europe: The role of pan-European channels. *European Journal of Communication*, 17(2), 190–215.

——. (2003). Television for a new global order: transnational television networks and the formation of global system. *Gazette: The International Journal for Communication Studies*, 65(6), 457–472.

——. (2005). *Transnational Television Worldwide: Towards a New Media Order*. London: IB Tauris.

——. (2006). American Cultural primacy in a new media order: a European perspective. *The International Communication Gazette*, 68(1), 33–51.

——. (2012). At the origin of a global industry: The TV format trade as an Anglo-American invention. *Media, Culture & Society*, 34(1), 36–52.

Chan, J. M. (2005a). Global media and the dialectics of the global. *Global Media and Communication*, 1(1), 24–28.

——. (2005b). Trans-border broadcasters and TV regionalization in Greater China: processes and strategies. In J. K. Chalaby (Ed.), *Transnational Television Worldwide* (pp. 173–105). New York: I. B. Tuarus.

Chan, K. (2010, March 8). Will Avatar's environmental message change us? Retrieved from http://www.metronews.ca/vancouver/comment/article/471316–will-avatar-senvironmental-message-change-us\

Chan-Olmsted, S. M. (2005). *Competitive strategy for media firms: Strategic and brand management in changing media markets*. Mahwah, NJ: Lawrence Erlbaum Associates.

China Daily. (2011, March 23). Writer sues Disney/Pixar alleging stolen 'Cars'. Retrieved from http://www.china.org.cn/arts/2011–03/23/content_22204590.htm

Chmielewski, D. C. (2001, October 27). Broadcast version of Disney Channel to launch in Russia. Retrieved from http://latimesblogs.latimes.com/entertainmentnewsbuzz/2011/10/disney-channel-russia-launch.html

Chrisman, L. (2004). Nationalism and Postcolonial Studies. In N. Lazarus (Ed.), *Postcolonial Literary Studies* (pp. 183–198). Cambridge: Cambridge University Press.

Christian, O. (2012, February 10). South Korea's K-pop takes off in the west. Retrieved from http://www.ft.com/cms/s/ddf11662–53c7–11e1–9eac–00144feabdc0,Authorised=false.html?_i_location=http%3A%2F%2Fwww.ft.com%2Fcms%2Fs%2F0%2Fddf11662–53c7–11e1–9eac–00144feabdc0.html&_i_referer=http%3A%2F%2Fen.wikipedia.org%2Fwiki%2FKorean_Wave#axzz1mQZCA2ah

Christopherson, S. (1996). Flexibility and adaptation in industrial relations: the exceptional case of the US media entertainment industries, In L.S. Gray and R.L. Seeber. (Eds), *Under the Stars: Essays on Labor Relations in Arts and Entertainment* (pp. 86–112). Ithaca and London: Cornell University Press.

——. (2008). Beyond the self-expressive creative worker: an industry perspective on entertainment media. *Theory, Culture & Society*, 25(7–8), 73–95.

——. (2011). Hard jobs in Hollywood: how concentration in distribution affects the production side of the media entertainment industry. In D. R. Winseck and D. Y. Jin (Eds), *The Political Economies of Media: The Transformation of the Global Media Industries*. New York: Bloomsbury Academic. Retrieved from http://www.bloomsburyacademic.com/view/PoliticalEconomiesMedia_9781849664264/chapter-ba–9781849664264-chapter–006.xml?print

Christopherson, S. and Storper, M. (1980). The effects of flexible specialization on industrial politics and the labour market: the motion picture industry. *Industrial and Labour Relations Review*, 42(3), 331–347.

Christopherson, S., Garretsen, H., and Martin, R. (2008). The world is not flat: putting globalization in its place. *Cambridge Journal of Regions, Economy and Society*, 1, 343–349.

Cieply, M. (2009, November 9). A movie's budget pops from the screen. http://www.nytimes.com/2009/11/09/business/media/09avatar.html?pagewanted=all

——. (2012, February 6). China fund to support film projects worldwide. Retrieved from http://www.nytimes.com/2012/02/06/business/media/800-million-chinese-fund-to-back-film-projects.html

Cinema Advertising Council (CAC). (2010). Cinema advertising continues strong growth. Retrieved from http://www.cinemaadcouncil.org/docs/press/9g5olhw4vzthr59z.pdf

Classen, C. and Howes, D. (1996). Epilogue: the dynamics and ethics of cross cultural consumption. In D. Howes, (Ed.), *Cross-Cultural Consumption* (pp. i–xi). New York: Routledge.

Clover, J. (2010, August 17). Viasat secures Universal movie exclusivity. Retrieved from http://www.broadbandtvnews.com/2010/08/17/viasat-secures-universal-movie-exclusivity/

CME. (2009, March 23). Time Warner Inc. to acquire 31% interest in central European media enterprises, a leading central and Eastern European media company. Retrieved from http://www.cetv-net.com/en/press-center/news/115.shtml

Coe, N. and Johns, J. (2004). Beyond production clusters. Towards a critical political economy of networks in the film and television industries. In D. Power and A. J. Scott (Eds), *Cultural Industries and the Production of Culture*. (pp. 188–204). New York: Routledge.

Comor, E. (1994). *The Global Political Economy of Communication*. New York: St. Martin's Press.

——. (1997). The Re-Tooling of American Hegemony: U.S. Foreign Communication Policy from Free Flow to Free Trade. In A. Sreberny-Mohammadi et al. (Eds.) *Media in a global context: A reader* (pp. 194–206). London: Arnold.

Compaine, B. (2003). The media monopoly myth: how new competition is expanding our sources of information and entertainment. New Millenium Research Council. Retrieved from http://newmillenniumresearch.org/archive/Final_Compaine_Paper_050205.pdf

——. (2005). Global media. In E. P. Bucy (Ed.), *Living in the information age: A new media reader* (pp. 97–101). Belmont: Wadsworth Thomson Learning.

Conference Board of Canada. (2008, 26 August) Arts and cultural industries add billions of dollars to Canadian economy. Retrieved from http://www.conferenceboard.ca/press/2008/valuing-culture.asp

Coonan, C. (2011, June 21). Chinese international co-productions rise. Retrieved from http://www.variety.com/article/VR1118038882?refCatId=19

Cooper-Martin, E. (1991). Consumers and movies: some findings on experiential products. *Advances in Consumer Research*, 18(1), 756–761).

Costa, J. and Bamossy, G. J. (1995). *Marketing in a Multicultural World: Ethnicity, Nationalism and Cultural Identity*. London: Sage

Costanza-Chock, S. (2005). The globalization of media policy. In R. McChesney, R. Newman, B. Scott and B. Meyers (Eds), *The Future of the Media: Resistance and Reform in the 21st century*. pp. 259–274. New York: Seven Stories Press.

Couldry, N., Hepp, A., and Krotz, F. (Eds). (2009). *Media Events in a Global Age*. New York: Routledge.

Cowan, T. (1998). *In Praise of Commercial Culture*. Cambridge, MA: Harvard University Press.

Cowen, T. (2002). *Creative Destruction: How Globalization is Changing World Cultures*. Princetown, NJ: Princeton University Press.

——. (2006). *Good and Plenty: The Creative Successes of American Arts Funding*. Princeton, NJ: Princeton University Press.

——. (2007, February 22). Some countries remain resistant to American cultural exports. Retrieved from www.nytimes/2007/02/22/business/22scene.html?_r=D.

Cox, M. (2001). Whatever happened to American decline? International relations and the new United States hegemony. *New Political Economy*, 1(6), 311–340.

Coyle, J. (2009, December 14). From "Cleopatra" to "Lord of the Rings," "Avatar" joins tradition of the Hollywood colossus. Retrieved from http://www.startribune.com/templates/Print_This_Story?sid=79210367

Crispin Miller, M. (2001 December 20). What's wrong with this picture? Retrieved from http://www.thenation.com/article/whats-wrong-picture–0#

CRTC. (2008, January 15). CRTC establishes new approach to media ownership. Retrieved from http://www.crtc.gc.ca/eng/com100/2008/r080115.htm

Cucco, M. (2009). The promise is great: the blockbuster and the Hollywood economy. *Media, Culture & Society*, 31(2), 215–230.

Cullity, J. (2002). The global desi: Cultural nationalism on MTV India. *Journal of Communication Inquiry*, 26(4), 408–425.

Cunningham, S. (2009). Trojan Horse or Rorschach Blot? Creative industries discourse around the world. *International Journal of Cultural Policy* 15(4), 375–386.

Curran, J. and Park, M. J. (Eds), *De-Westernizing Media Studies*. New York: Routledge.

Curtin, M. (1993). Beyond the vast wasteland: the policy discourse of global television and the politics of American empire. *Journal of Broadcasting and Electronic Media*, 37(2), 127–145.

——. (1997). Dynasty in drag: imagining global tv. In L. Spigel and M. Curtin (Eds), *The Revolution Wasn't Televised* (pp. 244–262). New York: Routledge.

——. (1999). Feminine desire in the age of satellite television. *Journal of Communication*, 49(2), 55–70.

——. (2003). Media capitals: towards the study of spatial flows. *International Journal of Cultural Studies* 6(2), 202–228.

——. (2005). Murdoch's dilemma, or 'what's the price of TV in China?' *Media, Culture and Society*, 27(2), 155–175.

——. (2007). *Playing to the World's Biggest Audience: The Globalization of Chinese Film and TV*. Berkeley and Los Angeles: University of California Press.

Curtin, M. and Streeter, T. (2001). Media In R. Maxwell (Ed.), *Culture Works: The Political Economy of Culture* (pp. 225–250). University of Minnesota Press: Minneapolis.

Dadush, U. and Wyne, Z. (2011, November 10). Don't be afraid of the service sector. *International Economic Bulletin*. Retrieved from http://carnegieendowment.org/2011/11/10/rise-of-services-sector/8mtf

Dakroury, A., Eid M., and Kamalipour, Y. (Eds). (2009). *The right to communicate: historical hopes, global debates, and future premises*. Dubuque, IA: Kendall Hunt.

Darling-Wolf, F. (2000). Texts in context: intertextuality, hybridity and the negotiation of cultural identity in Japan. *Journal of Communication Inquiry*, 24(2), 134–155.

Davis, C. and Kay, J. (2010). International production outsourcing and the development of indigenous film and television capabilities: the case of Canada. In G. Elmer, C. Davis, J. McCullough, and J. Marchessault (Eds). *Locating Migrating Media*. (pp. 57–78). New York: Rowman & Littlefield.

Davis, M. (2006). *Planet of Slums*. New York: Verso.

Davidson, S. (2007). A chronology of Hollywood in post-'89 Prague. Retrieved from http://prague.tv/articles/cinema/a-chronology-of-hollywood-in-post–89-prague

Dawson, N. (2010, March 5). Time's up: Kathryn Bigelow's The Hurt Locker. Retrieved from http://www.filmmakermagazine.com/news/2010/03/times-up-kathryn-bigelows-the-hurt-locker-by-nick-dawson/

Dawtrey, A. (2009, April 14). Michigan nabs $146M movie studio: Unity Studios to build complex in Detroit suburb. Retrieved from http://www.variety.com/article/VR1118002418

——. (2010, April 9). The new Brit backlots: Hollywood finds stages in old warehouses, military bases. Retrieved from http://www.variety.com/article/VR1118017349

Dean, J. and Fong, M. (2008, September 8). Opening ceremonies aim to illustrate rise to global power. Retrieved from online.wsj.com/article/SB121819051298123857.html

Debord, G. (1983). *Society of the spectacle*. Detroit: Black and Red Press.

Defleur, M. L. and Defleur, M. H. (2003). *Learning to Hate Americans: How U.S. Media Shape Negative Attitudes Among Teenagers in Twelve Countries*. Spokane: WA: Marquette.

de Mesa, A. (2007, 23 July). True colors of nation branding. Retrieved from http://www.brandchannel.com/features_effect.asp?pf_id=377

Demont-Heinrich, C. (2011). Cultural imperialism versus globalization of culture: riding the structure_agency dialectic in global communication and media studies. *Sociology Compass*, 5(8), 666–678.

Denning, M. (2004). *Culture in the Age of Three Worlds*. New York: Verso.

Deuze, M. (2007). *Media Work*. New York: Polity.

Diawara, M. (1987). Sub-Saharan African film production: technological paternalism. *Jump Cut: A Review of Contemporary Media*, 32, 61–65.

Dick, K. (2011). The MPAA vs. Gay Sexuality. Retrieved from http://www.thewrap.com/blog-post/mpaa-vs-gay-sexuality–3114?page=0,0

Dizard, W. (2004). *Inventing Public Diplomacy: The Story of the U.S. Information Agency*. Boulder: Lynn Rienner Publishers.

Dobuzinskis, A. (2010, March 10). Global movie box office nears $30 billion in 2009. Retrieved from http://www.reuters.com/article/2010/03/10/boxoffice-idUSN1013895820100310

Domhoff, W. G. (2009). *Who Rules America? Challenges to Corporate and Class Dominance*. New York: McGraw-Hill.

Donaton, S. (2005). *Madison and Vine: Why the Entertainment and Advertising Industries Must Converge to Survive*. New York: McGraw-Hill.

Dore, S. (2010, June 24). Bollywood flies to Santa Fe for Kites. Retrieved from: http://www.variety.com/article/VR1118021011

Dorfman, A. and Mattelart, A. (1975). *How to Read Donald Duck: Imperialist Ideology in the Disney Comic*. New York: International General Editions.

Dorman, V. (2011, May 16). Building a market for creativity. Retrieved from http://rbth.ru/articles/2011/05/16/building_a_market_for_creativity_12867.html

Kellner D. and Kahn R. (2003). Global youth culture. Retrieved from http://www.gseis.ucla.edu/faculty/kellner/essays/globyouthcult.pdf

Doyle, G. (2010). From television to multi-platform: More for less or less from more? *Convergence*, 16(4), 1–19.

——. (2012). *Audio-visual services: international trade and cultural policy*. ABDI Working Paper 355. Tokyo: Asian Development Bank Institute.Retrieved from http://www.abdi.org/working-paper/2012/04/17/5049.audiovisual.srvc.intl/trade.cultural.policy/

Drache, D. (1995). (Ed.), *Staples, Markets, Change: Harold A. Innis, Selected Essays*. McGill-Queen's UP: Montreal and Kingston.

During, S. (1997). Popular culture on a global scale: a challenge for cultural studies? *Critical Inquiry*, 23(2), 808–26.

Eagleton, T. (2000). *The Idea of Culture*. Oxford: Blackwell Publishers.

Economic Bulletin. *Don't be afraid of the service sector*. Retrieved from http://carnegieendowment.org/2011/11/10/rise-of-services-sector/8mtf

Egan, J. (2009, September 11). Canada at war over tax incentives. Retrieved from http://www.variety.com/article/VR1118008490

Eligon, J. (2008, September 9). Judge rules for Rowling against writer of lexicon. Retrieved from www.nytimes.com/2008/09/09/nyregion/09potter.html?ref=media.

Eller, C. (2009, April 20). Studios struggle to rein in movie marketing costs. Retrieved from http://articles.latimes.com/2009/apr/20/business/fi-ct-movies20

Elliot, S. (2011, June 14). Study finds rebound in entertainment and media spending. Retrieved from http://mediadecoder.blogs.nytimes.com/2011/06/14/study-finds-rebound-in-entertainment-and-media-spending/?ref=media

Elmer, G. (2002). The trouble with the Canadian 'body double': runaway productions and foreign location shooting. *Screen, 43*(4) 423–431.

Elmer, G. and Gasher, M. (2005). *Contracting out Hollywood: Runaway Production and Foreign Location Shooting*. Latham, MD: Rowman & Littlefield.

Enrich, E. (2005). Legal aspects of international film co-production. Retrieved from http://www.obs.coe.int/online_publication/expert/coproduccion_aspectos-juridicos.pdf.en

Epstein, E. J. (2005, April 25). How to Finance a Hollywood Blockbuster. Retrieved from www.slate.com/articles/arts/the_hollywood_economist/2005/04/how_to_finance_a_hollywood_blockbuster.html

Euromed. (2008, July 15). Interview with Abdelhak Sakhi, Head of Production at the Moroccan Cinema Centre (CCM). Retrieved from http://www.euromedcafe.org/newsdetail.asp?lang=ing&documentID=12727

European Commission. (2010a). Commission launches public consultation on future of cultural and creative industries. Retrieved from http://www.organzanetwork.eu/news/commission-launches-public-consultation-future-cultural-and-creative-industries

——. (2010b). Green Paper: Unlocking the potential of cultural and creative industries. Retrieved from http://ec.europa.eu/culture/our-policy-development/doc/GreenPaper_creative_industries_en.pdf

European Federation of Journalists. (2005). Media power in Europe: the big picture of ownership. Belgium: Aidan White. Retrieved from http://www.ifj.org/assets/docs/245/202/08737f5-ec283ca.pdf

Falconer, R. (2009, April 8). First location shot from 'Tron 2.0. Retrieved from http://www.cinemaspy.com/movie-news/first-location-shot-from-tron–2–0–2213/

Fanon, F. (1963). *The Wretched of the Earth*. New York, NY: Grove Press.

FCC. (2011). Obscenity, indecency and profanity. Retrieved from http://www.fcc.gov/guides/obscenity-indecency-and-profanity

Feigenbaum, H. B. (1996). *Why Hollywood is like Japan—only better*. Business in the Contemporary World, 8(1), 36–42.

——. (2003). Digital entertainment jumps the border. *Scientific American*, 56–57.

——. (2009). The paradox of television privatization: when more is less. *Policy and Society*, (27), 229–237.

Fejes, F. (1981). Media imperialism: an assessment. *Media, Culture and Society*, 3(1), 281–92.

Fernandes, R. (26, May 2012). Legal actions pushing down Bittorrent popularity in the U.S. Retrieved from http://tech2.in.com/news/general/legal-actions-pushing-down-bittorrent-popularity-in-the-us/310542

Film and Television Action Committee (FTAC). (2002). *Send a letter to congress*. Retrieved from http://www.ftac.net/index.html

Fiske, J. (1988). *Television Culture*. New York: Routledge.

Fitzgerald, S. W. (2012). *Corporations and Cultural Industries: Time Warner, Bertelsmann, and News Corporation*. Lanham, Maryland: Rowman & Littlefield Books.

Flew, T. (2002). Broadcasting and the social contract. In M. Raboy (Ed). *Global Media Policy in the New Millennium* (pp. 113–129) Luton: University of Luton Press.

——. (2007b). *Understanding Global Media*. New York, NY: Palgrave Macmillan.

——. (2011). Media as creative industries. In D. Winseck and D.Y. Jin (Eds), *The Political Economies of the Media: The Transformation of the Global Media*. New York: Bloomsbury Academic.

——. (2012, May 24). Resurrecting media imperialism. Retrieved from http://terryflew. com/2012/05/resurrecting-media-imperialism.html

Florida, R. (2004). *The Rise of the Creative Class*. New York: Basic Books.

——. (2005). *Cities and the Creative Class*. New York: Routledge.

Forbes Profile: Rupert Murdoch. Retrieved from http://www.forbes.com/profile/rupert-murdoch/

Foreign Policy. (2009). The world's most popular TV shows. Retrieved from http://www.foreignpolicy.com/articles/2009/10/19/the_worlds_most_popular_tv_shows

Foster, J.B. (2000). Monopoly capital at the turn of the millennium. *Monthly Review*, 51(11). Retrived from http://monthlyreview.org/2000/04/01/monopoly-capital-at-the-turn-of-the-millennium

Foster, J.B., McChesney, R. W., and Jonna, R. J. (2011). Monopoly and Competition in Twenty First Century Capitalism, *Monthly Review* 62 (11), 1–23.

Fourie, P.J. (Ed.). (2010). *Media Studies: Policy, Management and Media Representation*. Juta Academic.

Francia, R. (2007, November 23). 5 Hollywood studios sue Chinese website for copyright infringements. Retrieved from http://tech.blorge.com/Structure:%20/2007/11/23/5-hollywood-studios-sue-chinese-website-for-copyright-infringements/

Franich, D. (2011, 26 April). *The Fast and the Furious*: Five reasons this franchise has lasted a freakin' decade. Retrieved from http://popwatch.ew.com/2011/04/26/the-fast-and-the-furious-five-reasons-this-franchise-has-lasted-a-freakin-decade/

Frank, A. G. (1966). *The Development of Underdevelopment*. New York: Monthly Review Press.

——. (1969). *Latin America: Underdevelopment or Revolution*. New York: Monthly Review Press.

——. (1975). *On Capitalist Underdevelopment*. Bombay: Oxford University Press.

——. (1972). *Lumpenbourgeoisie: Lumpenproletariat. Dependency, Class and Politics in Latin America*. New York, NY: Monthly Review Press.

Fraser, M. (2003). *Weapons of Mass Distraction: American Empire and Soft Power*. Toronto: Key Porter Books.

Freedman, D. (2003a). Cultural policy-making in the free trade era: an evaluation of the impact of current World Trade Organization negotiations on audio-visual industries. *International Journal of Cultural Policy*, 9(3), 285–298.

——. (2003b). Who Wants to be a Millionaire? the politics of television exports. *Information, Communication & Society*, 6(1), 24–41.

——. (2006). Dynamics of power in contemporary media policy-making. *Media, Culture and Society*, 28(6), 907–23.

——. (2008). *The Politics of Media Policy*. Cambridge: Polity Press.

French, P. (2010, March 14). Avatar was the year's real milestone, never mind the results. Retrieved from http://www.guardian.co.uk/film/2010/mar/14/avatar-kathryn-bigelow-hollywood-history

Freund, C. P. (2003). We aren't the world: American culture is not dominating the globe. Retrieved from http://www.reason.com/0303/cr.cf.we.shtml

Friedman, J. (2008, March 6). Movie ticket sales hit record. Retrieved from http://articles.latimes.com/2008/mar/06/business/fi-boxoffice6

Friedman, T. (2000). *The Lexus and the Olive Tree: Understanding Globalization*. New York, NY: Anchor Books.

——. (2007). *The World is Flat 3.0: a Brief History of the Twenty First Century*. New York, NY: Farrar, Straus and Giroux.

——. (2010). Globalization. Retrieved from http://2010.newsweek.com/top–10/most-overblown-fears/globalization.html

Fu, W. W. (2006). Concentration and homogenization of international movie sources: examining foreign film import profiles. *Journal of Communication*, 56(1), 813–835.

——. (2009). Screen survival of movies at competitive theaters: vertical and horizontal integration in a spatially differentiated market. *Journal of Media Economics*, 22(2), 59–80.

Fu, W. W. and Govindaraju, A. (2010). Explaining global box-office tastes in Hollywood Films: homogenization of national audiences' movie selections. *Communication Research*, 37(2), 215–238.

Fuchs, C. (2010). New imperialism: information and media imperialism? *Global Media and Communication*, 6(1), 33–60.

——. (2011). Web 2.0, prosumption, and surveillance. *Surveillance & Society*, 8(3), 288–309

Fung, A. (2006). Think globally, act locally: China's rendezvous with MTV. *Global Media and Communication*, 2(1), 71–88.

Furtado, C. (1964). *Development and Underdevelopment*. Berkeley: University of California Press.

Galbraith, J. K. (1998). *The Affluent Society*. New York: Mariner Books.

——. (2007). *The New Industrial State*. Princeton, N. J.: Princeton University Press.

Gara, T. and Hagey, K. (2010, March 10). Unleash your creativity, Murdoch tells Arab world. Retrieved from http://www.thenational.ae/news/uae-news/unleash-your-creativity-murdoch-tells-arab-world

García-Canclini, N. (1997). Hybrid cultures and communicative strategies. *Media Development*, 44(1), 22–29.

——. (2005). *Hybrid Cultures: Strategies for Entering and Leaving Modernity*. Minneapolis: University of Minnesota Press.

Gardels, N. and Medavoy, M. (2009). *American Idol After Iraq: Competing for Hearts and Minds in the Global Media Age*. Malden, MA: Wiley-Blackwell.

Gardiner, N. (2009, December 25). Avatar: the most expensive piece of anti-American propaganda ever made. Retrieved from http://blogs.telegraph.co.uk/news/nilegardiner/100020721/avatar-the-most-expensive-piece-of-anti-american-propaganda-ever-made/

Garnham, N. (1990). *Capitalism and Communication: Global Culture and the Economics of Information*. London: Sage Publications.

——. (1998). Policy. In A. Briggs and P. Cobley (Eds), *The Media: An Introduction*. (pp. 210–23) London: Longman.

——. (2000). *Emancipation, the Media and Modernity: Arguments about the Media and Social Theory*. Oxford: Oxford University Press.

——. (2005). From cultural to creative industries: an analysis of the creative industries approach to arts and media policy making in the United Kingdom. *International Journal of Cultural Policy*, 11(1), 15–29.

Gasher, M. (2002). *Hollywood North: The Feature Film Industry in British Columbia*. Vancouver: University of British Columbia Press.

Gentzkow, M. A. and Shapiro, J. M. (2004). Media, education and anti-Americanism in the Muslim world. *Journal of Economic Perspectives*, 18(3), 117–133.

Gerbner, G. (1977). Comparative cultural indicators. In G. Gerbner (Ed.), *Mass Media Policies In Changing Cultures* (pp. 199–205). New York, NY: John Wiley & Sons.

——. (1998). Telling stories, or how do we know what we know? The story of cultural indicators and the cultural environment movement. *Wide Angle*, 20, 116–131.

Gerbner, G., Gross, L., Morgan, M., and Signorielli, N. (1986). Perspectives on media effects. In J. Bryant and D. Zillmann (Eds), *Living with Television*. Hillsdale: Erlbaum.

——. (1994). Growing up with television: the cultivation perspective. In J. Bryant and D. Zillman (Eds), *Media Effects: Advances In Theory and Research* (pp. 61–90). Mahwah, NJ: Erlbaum.

Gershon, R. A. (1993). International deregulation and the rise of transnational media corporation. *Journal of Media Economics*, 6(2), 3–22.

——. (1997). *The Transnational Media Corporation: Global Messages And Free Market Competition*. Mahwah, NJ: Lawrence Erlbaum Associates.

Giddens, A. (1991). *The Consequences of Modernity*. Cambridge: Polity Press.

Gilbey, R. (2008, December 10). I'm not shocked by Italy's bowdlerised Brokeback. Retrieved from http://www.guardian.co.uk/film/filmblog/2008/dec/10/brokeback-mountain-gay-censorship

Gill, R. and Pratt, A. (2008). In the social factory? Immaterial labour, precariousness and cultural work. *Theory, Culture & Society*, 25(7–8), 1–30.

Gillan, J. (2010). *Television and New Media: Must-Click TV*. New York: Routledge.

Gillespie, M. (1995). *Television, Ethnicity and Cultural Change*. London: Routledge.

——. (2002). Television, ethnicity and cultural change. In W. Brooker and D. Jermyn (Eds), *The Audience Studies Reader* (pp. 315–321). New York, NY: Routledge.

Gitlin, T. (1983). *Inside Prime Time*. New York: Pantheon Press.

——. (2001). *Media Unlimited: How the Torrent of Images and Sounds Overwhelms Our Lives*. New York, NY: Metropolitan Books.

Global Entertainment & Media Outlook. (2011–2015). Retrieved from http://www.pwc.com/gx/en/global-entertainment-media-outlook/data-insights.jhtml

Goff, P. M. (2007). *Limits to Liberalization: Local Culture in a Global Marketplace*. Ithaca, NY: Cornell University.

Golding, P. and Murdock, G. (1991). Culture, communication and political economy. In J. Curran and M. Gurevitch (Eds), *Mass Media and Society* (pp. 15–32). London: Edward Arnold.

Goldman, S. (1993, July 4). Reborn in the USA. *Sunday Times*. p.6.

Goldsmith, B. (2008, November 8). Beijing opening night lures 15 percent of world. Retrieved from www.reuters.com/article/2008/08/11/us_olympics_viewers_idUSPEK15134720080811.

Goldsmith, B., and O'Regan, T. (2003). *Cinema Cities, Media Cities: The Contemporary International Studio Complex*. Screen Industry, Culture and Policy Research Series. Sydney: Australian Film Commission.

——. (2005). *The Film Studio: Film Production in the Global Economy*. Lanham, MD: Rowman and Littlefield.

——. (2009). International film production: interests and motivations. In J. Wasko and M. Erikson (Eds). *Cross Border Cultural Production: Economic Runaway or Globalization* Amhorst: Cambria Press.

Gomery, D. (2000a). Interpreting media ownership. In B. M. Compaine and D. Gomery (Eds), *Who Owns the Media? Competition and Concentration in the Mass Media Industries*, (pp. 507–536). Mahwah, NJ: Lawrence Erlbaum Associates, Inc.

——. (2000b). The Hollywood film industry. Theatrical exhibition, pay TV and home video. In B.M. Compaine and D. Gomery (Eds), *Who Owns the Media? Competition and Concentration in the Mass Media Industries* (pp. 359–436). Mahwah NJ: Lawrence Erlbaum Associates, Inc.

Gordon, N. S. A. (2009). Globalization and cultural imperialism in Jamaica. *International Journal of Communication*, 3, 307–331.

Goundry, N. (2011, June 29). New Zealand and India sign co-production location filming deal. Retrieved from http://www.thelocationguide.com/blog/2011/06/new-zealand-and-india-sign-co-production-location-filming-deal/

Government of Singapore. (2010, August 12). Singapore awards $2.7 million in creative industries scholarships and bursaries. Retrieved from http://www.thegovmonitor.com/world_news/asia/singapore-awards–2–7-million-in-creative-industries-scholarships-and-bursaries–36986.html

Graber, D. (2009). Looking at the United States through distorted lenses: entertainment television versus public diplomacy. *American Behavioral Scientist*, 52(5), 735–754.

Grainge, P. (2008). *Brand Hollywood: Selling Entertainment In A Global Media Age*. New York, NY: Routledge.

Gray, C. (2007). Commodification and Instrumentality in Cultural Policy. *International Journal of Cultural Policy*, 13(2), 203–215.

Gramsci, A. (1971). *Selections from the Prison Notebooks*. International Publishers Co.

Grant, P. S. and Wood, C. (2004). *Blockbusters and Trade Wars: Popular Culture in a Globalized World*. Vancouver: Douglas & McIntyre.

Gray, J. (1998). *False Dawn: The Delusions of Global Capitalism*. London; Granta Publications.

Gray, J. (2007). Imagining America: *The Simpsons* go global. *Popular Communication*, 5(2), 129–148.

Green, E. (2010, March 31). Kick-Ass banned in Korea. Retrieved from http://www.frontrow-reviews.co.uk/news/kick-ass-banned-in-korea/4633

Green, P. S. (2003, July 30). Prague is fighting to remain in the picture. Retrieved from http://www.nytimes.com/2003/07/30/business/prague-is-fighting-to-remain-in-the-picture.html

Greenberg, A. (2012, 9 May). HBO's Game of Thrones on track to be crowned most pirated show of 2012. Retrived from http://www.forbes.com/sites/andygreenberg/2012/05/09/hbos-game-of-thrones-on-track-to-be-crowned-most-pirated-show-of-2012/

Greenslade, R. (2011, September 12,). Bangladesh introduces TV censorship. Retrieved from http://www.guardian.co.uk/media/greenslade/2011/sep/12/bangladesh-freedom-of-speech

Grixti, J. (2006). Symbiotic transformations: youth, global media and indigenous culture in Malta. *Media, Culture & Society*, 28(1), 105–122.

Guback, T. H. (1969). *The International Film Industry*. Bloomington: Indiana University Press.

Gulder, E. (2011, January 1). Studios focusing on co-financing high-profile tv series with foreign broadcasters. Retrieved from http://www.hollywoodreporter.com/news/studios-focusing-financing-high-profile-75607

Habann, F. (2000). Management of core resources: The case of media enterprises. *The International Journal on Media Management*, 2(1), 14–24.

Hafez, K. (2007). *The Myth of Media Globalization*. Cambridge: Polity Press.

Hagey, K. (2011, May 6). Most of the highest paid CEOs lead media companies. Retrieved from http://www.politico.com/blogs/onmedia/0511/Most_of_the_highestpaid_CEOs_lead_media_companies.htm

Hall, S. (1991). The local and the global: globalization and ethnicity. In A. King (Ed.), *Culture, Globalization and the World System*. London: MacMillan.

——. (1996a). Introduction: who needs "identity"? In S. Hall and P. du Gay (Eds), *Questions of Cultural Identity* (pp. 19–38). London: Sage.

——. (1996b). The West and the Rest: discourse and power. In S. Hall et al. (Eds), *Modernity* (pp. 184–224). Cambridge: Polity Press.

——. (1997). Introduction. In S. Hall (Ed.), *Representation: Cultural Representations and Signifying Practices* (1–12). London: Sage.

——. (2000). 'Encoding/Decoding'. In M.G. Durham and D.M. Kellner (Eds), *Media and Cultural Studies: Keyworks* (pp. 116–76). Blackwell: New York.

——. (2011). The march of the neoliberals. *The Guardian*, Retrieved from http://www.guardian.co.uk/politics/2011/sep/12/march-of-the-neoliberals

Halle, R. (2002). German film, aufgehoben: ensembles of transnational cinema. *New German Critique*, 87, 7–46.

Halter, M. (2002). *Shopping for Identity: The Marketing of Ethnicity*. New York: Shocken Books.

Hamelink, C. J. (1983). *Cultural Autonomy in Global Communications*. New York, NY: Longman.

——. (1997). MacBride with hindsight. In P. Golding and P. Harris (Eds), *Beyond Cultural Imperialism: Globalization, Communication and the New International Order* (pp. 69–94). London: Sage.

——. (2002). The civil society challenge to global media policy. In M. Raboy (Ed), *Global Media Policy in the New Millennium* (pp. 251–260). Luton: University of Luton Press.

Hamelink, C. J and Hoffmann, J. (2008). The state of the right to communicate. *Global Media Journal: American Edition*, 7(Fall). Retrieved from http://lass.calumet.purdue.edu/cca/gmj/fa08/gmj-fa08-hamelink-hoffman.htm

Hancock, D. and Zhang, X. (2010). Europe's top 100 film distributors. Retrieved from http://www.screendigest.com/reports/2010116a/10_11_europes_top_100_film_distributors/view.html

Hannerz, U. (1989). Notes on the global ecumene. *Public Culture*, 1(2), 66–75.

——. (1996). *Transnational Connections: Culture, People, Places*. New York: Routledge.

——. (1997). Scenarios for peripheral cultures. In A. King (Ed.), *Culture, Globalization and the World-system* (pp. 107–128). Minneapolis: University of Minnesota Press.

Harabi, N. (2009). *Creative industries: case studies from Arab countries*. Retrieved from http://mpra.ub.uni-muenchen.de/15628/1/MPRA_paper_15628.pdf

Hardware Top Ten. (2011). Retrieved from http://www.hardwaretop100.org/hardware-companies-top–100–2010-edition.php

Hardy, J. (2010). *Cross-Media Promotion*. New York: Peter Lang Publishing.

Harindranath, R. (2003). Reviving cultural imperialism: international audiences, global capitalism, and the transnational elite. In L. Parks and S. Kumar (Eds), *Planet TV: A Global Television Reader* (pp. 155–168). New York: New York University Press.

Harrington, C. L. and Bielby, D. D. (1995). *Soap Fans: Pursuing Pleasure and Making Meaning in Everyday Life*. Philadelphia: Temple University Press.

Harris, J. (2009, April 1). TV advertising is dying and PVRs are the culprit. Retrieved from http://www.backbonemag.com/Magazine/2009–04/tv-advertising-is-dying.aspx

Harris, N. (2007, March 1). Why Fifa's claim of one billion TV viewers was a quarter. Retrieved from right.http://www.independent.co.uk/sport/football/news-and-comment/why-fifas-claim-of-one-billion-tv-viewers-was-a-quarter-right–438302.html

——. (2011, May 9). REVEALED: Royal Wedding TV audience closer to 300m than 2bn (because sport, not royalty, reigns)". Retrieved from http://www.sportingintelligence.com/2011/05/08/revealed-royal-wedding's-real-tv-audience-closer-to–300m-than–2bn-because-sport-not-royalty-reigns–080501/

Hartlaub, P. (2002, July 16). Spanish-language TV war/competition fierce among Bay Area stations on Espanol. Retrieved from http://articles.sfgate.com/2002–07–16/entertainment/17552374_1_sabado-gigante-univision-tv-azteca-english-language-networks

Hartley, J. (Ed.) (2005). *Creative Industries*. Malden, MA: Blackwell.

Harvey, D. (1990). *The Condition of Postmodernity: An Enquiry into the Origins of Cultural Change*. Cambridge MA and Oxford UK: Blackwell.

——. (2004). The new imperialism of our time. In L. Panitch and C. Leys (Eds), *The New Imperial Challenge: Socialist Register 2004* (pp. 63–88). London: Merlin Press.

——. (2005a). *A Brief History of Neoliberalism*. New York: Oxford.

——. (2005b). *The New Imperialism*. New York: Oxford University Press.

——. (2006). *Spaces of Global Capitalism: Towards a Theory of Uneven Geographical Development*. London: Verso.

——. (2007). Neoliberalism as creative destruction. *The ANNALS of the American Academy of Political and Social Science*, 610(1), 21–44.

——. (2010). *The Enigma of Capital: and the Crises of Capitalism*. London: Profile Books.

Harvey, S. (Ed.). (2006). *Trading Culture: Global Traffic and Local Cultures in Film and Television*. East Leigh: John Libbey Publishing.

Haselton, T. (2011, June 27). Consumers will spend $2.1 trillion on digital information and entertainment products in 2011, Gartner says. Retrieved from http://www.bgr.com/2011/06/27/consumers-will-spend–2–1-trillion-on-digital-information-and-entertainment-products-in–2011-gartner-says/

Havens, T. (2001). Subtitling rap: appropriating The Fresh Prince of Bel-Air for youthful identity formation in Kuwait. *Gazette: The International Journal for Communication Studies*, 63(1), 57–72.

——. (2003). On exhibiting global television: the business and cultural functions of television fairs. *Journal of Broadcasting & Electronic Media*, 47(1), 18–35.

——. (2008). *Global Television Marketplace*. London: British Film Institute.

Havens, T., Lotz, A. D., and Tinic, S. (2009). Critical media industry studies: a research approach. *Communication, Culture & Critique*, 2(1), 234–253.

Hay, C. and Lister, M. (2006). Introduction: theories of the state. In C. Hay, M. Lister, and D. Marsh, (Eds), *The State: Theories and Issues* (pp. 1–20). New York: Palgrave Macmillan.

Hayek, F. A. (2007). *The Road to Serfdom: Texts and Documents*. Chicago: University of Chicago Press.

Headrick, D. (1981). *The Tools of Empire: Technology and European Imperialism in the Nineteenth Century*. New York and Oxford: Oxford University Press.

——. (1988). *The Tentacles of Progress: Technology Transfer in the Age Of Imperialism, 1850–1940*. New York and Oxford: Oxford University Press.

——. (1991). *The Invisible Weapon: Telecommunications and International Politics 1851–1945*. New York, NY: Oxford University Press.

Heath, J. and Potter, A. (2004). *The Rebel Sell: Why Counterculture Became Consumer Culture*. New York: HarperCollins.

Heaven, C. and Tubridy, M. (2003). Global youth culture and youth identity. In J. Arvanitakis (Ed.), *Highly Affected, Rarely Considered: The International Youth Parliament Commission's Report on the Impacts of Globalisation on Young People* (pp. 149–160). Sydney, Australia: Oxfam/International Youth Parliament.

Held, D. and McGrew, A. (Eds). (2000). *The Global Transformations Reader*. Cambridge: Polity Press.

Helewitz, J. and Edwards, L. (2004). *Entertainment Law*. New York: Thomson-Delmar.

Hellmann, C. (2006). *On Location: Cities of the World in Film*. Munach: C.J. Bucher.

Herman, E. and McChesney, R. (1997). *The Global Media: The New Missionaries of Corporate Capitalism*. London: Continuum Press.

Hesmondhalgh, D. (2005). Media and cultural policy as public policy: The case of the British Labour Government. *International Journal of Cultural policy*, 1(1), 1–13.

——. (2007). *The Cultural Industries*. (2nd ed.). Thousand Oaks, CA: Sage.

——. (2008). Neoliberalism, imperialism and the media. In D. Hesmondhalgh and J. Toynbee (Eds), *The Media and Social Theory* (pp. 95–111). New York: Routledge.

Hicks, D. (2007). The Right to communicate: past mistakes and future possibilities. *Dalhousie Journal of Information and Management* 3(1). Retrieved from http://djim.management.dal.ca/issues/issue3_1/hicks/index.htm

Hilderbrand, L. (2007). Where cultural memory and copyright converge. *Film Quarterly*, 61(1), 48–57.

Hills, J. (2007). *Tele-Communications and Empire*. Urbana and Chicago: University of Illinois Press.

Hirst, P. and Thompson, G. (1999). *Globalization in Question: The International Economy and the Possibilities of Governance*. Cambridge: Polity Press.

Hobsbawm, E. (1994). *Age of Extremes: The Short Twentieth Century, 1914–1991*. Great Britain: Abacus.

Hoggart, R. (1957). *The Uses of Literacy*. London: Chatto & Windus.

Ho Kim, P. and Shin, H. (2009). The birth of 'rok' cultural imperialism, nationalism, and the glocalization of rock music in South Korea, 1964–1975. *Positions: East Asia Cultures Critique*, 18(1), 199–230.

Holdsworth, N. (2009, April 9). Film production competition heats up in Eastern Europe. Retrieved from http://www.variety.com/article/VR1118002301

Holloway, K. (2009, April 7). Twilight stars filming New Moon at Vancouver high school. Retrieved from http://www.vancouversun.com/entertainment/Twilight+stars+filming+Moon+Vancouver+high+school/1471218/story.html.

Holson, L. M. (2004, July 5). International actors as passport to prosperity. Retrieved from http://www.nytimes.com/2004/07/05/business/media-international-actors-a-passport-to-profitability.html?pagewanted=1

Holt, J. and Perren, A. (Eds). (2009). *Media Industries: History, Theory and Method*. Malden, MA: Wiley-Blackwell.

Hopewell, J. (2007). EU court backs Spain's TV quota: Ruling throws out union's 2007 action. Retrieved from http://www.variety.com/article/VR1118000878?refCatId=14

Hopkins, K. (2010, February 8). Indian tribe appeals for Avatar director's help to stop Vedanta. Retrieved from http://www.guardian.co.uk/business/2010/feb/08/dongria-kondh-help-stop-vedanta

Hopper, D. (2007). *Understanding Cultural Globalization*. Cambridge: Polity Press.

Horkheimer, M. and Adorno, T. W. (1972). The culture industry: enlightenment as mass deception. *Dialectic of Enlightenment*. New York, NY: Herder and Herder.

Hoskins, C. and Mirus, R. (1990). Television fiction made in the USA. In P. Larsen (Ed). *Import/Export: International Flow of Television Fiction*. (pp.83–90) Paris: UNESCO.

Hoskins, C. and McFadyen, S. (1993). Canadian participation in international co-productions and co-ventures in television programming. *Canadian Journal of Communication*, 18(2). Retrieved from http://www.cjc-online.ca/index.php/journal/article/view/745/651

Hoskins, C. and Mirus, R. (1988). Reasons for the U.S. dominance of the international trade in television programmes. *Media, Culture & Society*, 10(4), 499–515.

Hoskins, C., McFadyen, S., and Finn, A. (1997). *Global Television and Film: An Introduction To the Economics of the Business*. Oxford, England: Clarendon.

——. (2004). *Media Economics: Applying Economics to New and Traditional Media*. London: Sage Publications.

Hough, A. (2011, 15 April). Chinese censors attack frivolous time travel dramas. Retrieved from http://www.telegraph.co.uk/culture/culturenews/8452907/Chinese-censors-attack-frivolous-time-travel-dramas.html

Howe, J. (2006). The rise of crowdsourcing. Retrieved from http://www.wired.com/wired/archive/14.06/crowds.html

Howes, D. (Ed.). (1996). *Cross-Cultural Consumption: Global Markets, Local Realities*. New York: Routledge.

Howkins, J. (2007). *The Creative Economy: How People Make Money From Ideas*. New York: Penguin.

Huang, A. (2002 April 7). *Taiwan fights Starbucks with teahouses*. Associated Press.

Huffington Post. (2010, January 12). Evo Morales praises "Avatar." Retrieved from http://www.huffingtonpost.com/2010/01/12/evo-morales-praises-avata_n_420663.html

Huws, U. (2003). *The Making of the Cybertariat: Virtual World in a Real World*. New York: Monthly Review Press.

——. (Ed.). (2007). The Creative Spark in the Engine: Special Issue of *Work, Organization, Labour & Globalization*, (1), 1–12.

I-chia, L. (2011, October 24). Block media merger, say academics. Retrieved from http://www.taipeitimes.com/News/taiwan/archives/2011/10/24/2003516555

IMAGI (2012, 27 March). IMAGI signs second broadcast agreement with Disney Channel. Retrieved from http://en.acnnewswire.com/press-release/english/8966/imagi-signs-second-broadcast-agreement-with-disney-channel

InfoComm International. (2010, February 2). Commercial audiovisual industry grows worldwide. Retrieved from http://www.infocomm.org/cps/rde/xchg/infocomm/hs.xsl/12811.htm

Innis, H. A. (1950). *The Bias of Communication*. Toronto: University of Toronto Press.

——. (1972). *Empire and Communication*. Toronto: University of Toronto Press.

——. (1995). Great Britain, the United States, and Canada. In D. Drache (Ed.), *Staples, Markets and Cultural Change: Harold A. Innis, Selected Essays* (pp. 271–289). Montreal and Kingston: McGill-Queen's University Press.

International Telecommunications Unions (ITU) (2011). *The world in 2011: ITC facts and figures*. Retrieved from http://www.itu.int/ITU-D/ict/facts/2011/index.html

Izon, L. (2010). That beautiful scenery in Brokeback Mountain was Alberta. Ready to Travel Canada? Start by Exploring the Canada Cool Map Which Will Help You Discover Fascinating Facts, Intriguing Sites and Hundreds of Reasons Why Canada Is Cool. Retrieved from http://www.canadacool.com/COOLFACTS/ALBERTA/BrokebackMountain.html

Jaffe, G. (2011, March 24). Will the great film quota wall of China come down? Retrieved from http://www.guardian.co.uk/business/2011/mar/24/china-film-quota

James, M. (2011, May 29). Viacom execs at top in media pay. Retrieved from http://articles.latimes.com/2011/may/29/business/fi-executive-pay-media-20110529

Jameson, F. (1979). Reification and Utopia in mass culture. *Social Text*, 1(1): 130–48.

——. (1998). Preface. In F. Jameson and M. Miyoshi (Eds), *The Cultures of Globalization* (pp. xi–xvi). Durham and London: Duke University Press.

Jancovich, M. and Lyons, J. (Eds). (2008). *Quality Popular Television: Cult TV, the Industry and Fans*. London: British Film Institute.

Jap. (2011, January 1). Anti-Semitic Turkish blockbuster denied release in Germany. Retrieved from http://www.spiegel.de/international/germany/0,1518,741780,00.html

Jenkins, H. (1988). Star Trek rerun, reread, rewritten: Fan writing as textual poaching. *Critical Studies in Mass Communication*, 5(2), 85–107.

——. (1992). *Textual poachers: Television Fans & Participatory Culture*. New York, NY: Routledge.

——. (2004). The cultural logic of media convergence. *International Journal of Cultural Studies*, 7(1), 33–43.

——. (2006a). *Fans, Bloggers and Gamers: Media Consumers in a Digital Age*. New York, NY: New York University Press.

——. (2006b). *The Wow Climax: Tracing the Emotional Impact of Popular Culture*. New York: New York University Press.

——. (2008). *Convergence Culture*. New York: New York University Press.

——. (2010, September 18). Avatar activism: pick your protest. Retrieved from http://www.theglobeandmail.com/news/opinions/avatar-activism-pick-your-protest/article1712766/

Jensen, R. and Oster, E. (2008, September 23). The power of TV: cable television and women's status in India. Retrieved from http://home.uchicago.edu/~eoster/tvwomen.pdfhttp://home.uchicago.edu/~eoster/tvwomen.pdf

Jenson, J. (1992). Fandom as pathology. In L. A. Lewis (Ed.), *The Adoring Audience: Fan Culture And Popular Media* (pp. 9–29). London: Routledge.

Jessop, B. (2002). *The Future of the Capitalist State*. London: Polity Press.

——. (2012). Marxist approaches to power. In E. Amenta, K. Nash, and A. Scott, (Eds), *The Wiley-Blackwell Companion to Political Sociology* (pp. 3–15). Malden, MA: Blackwell Publishing.

Jha, S. K. (2009, December 31). Directors' choice: Paa, 3 Idiots, Avatar! Retrieved from http://articles.timesofindia.indiatimes.com/2009–12–31/news-interviews/28060568_1_avatar-idiots-balki

Jhally, S. (1987). *The Codes of Advertising: Fetishism and the Political Economy of Meaning in the Consumer Society*. New York, NY: Routledge.

——. (2000). Advertising at the edge of the Apocalypse. In R. Anderson and L. Strate (Eds), *Critical Studies in Media Commercialism* (pp. 27–39). Oxford: Oxford University Press.

Jhunjhunwala, U. (2011, November 5). Competition fierce but there's no Khan-test. Retrieved from http://www.hindustantimes.com/Entertainment/Bollywood/Competition-fierce-but-there-s-no-Khan-test/Article1–765265.aspx

Jiang, Q, and Leung, L. (2012). Lifestyles, gratifications sought, and narrative appeal: American and Korean TV drama viewing among internet users in urban China. *The International Communication Gazette*, 74(20), 159–180.

Jimbo, M. (2010, January 20). Why Did China Kill Avatar? Retrieved from http://www.theatlantic.com/business/archive/2010/01/why-did-china-kill-avatar/33817/

Jin, D. Y. (2007). Reinterpretation of cultural imperialism: emerging domestic market vs. continuing U.S. dominance. *Media, Culture & Society*, 29(5), 753–771.

——. (2011a). A critical analysis of U.S. cultural policy in the global film market: nation-states and FTAs. *The International Communication Gazette*, 73(8), 651–669.

———. (2011b). Deconvergence and deconsolidation in the global media industries. In D. Winseck and D. Y. Jin (Eds), *The Political Economies of the Media: The Transformation of the Global Media Industries*. New York: Bloomsbury Academic.

Jockel, S. and Dobler, T. (2009). The Event Movie: Filmed Entertainment for Transnational Media Corporations. *The International Journal on Media Management*, 8(2), 84–91.

Johnson-Yale, C. (2008). So-called runaway film production: countering Hollywood's outsourcing narrative in the Canadian press. *Critical Studies in Media Communication*, 25(2), 113–134.

———. (2010). *Runaway Film Production: A Critical History of Hollywood Outsourcing Discourse*. Doctoral Dissertation, University of Illinois at Urbana-Champaign.

Johnston, R. (2009, December 11). Review: AVATAR – the most expensive american film ever . . . and possibly the most anti-American one too. Retrieved from http://www.bleedingcool.com/2009/12/11/review-avatar-the-most-expensive-american-film-ever-and-the-most-anti-american-one-too/

Jon Bonné, J. (2003, July 11). Simpsons evolves as an industry. Retrieved from http://today.msnbc.msn.com/id/3403870#.TtK1V2Mk4qQ

Jung, J. and Lee, S. H. (2006). Cross-cultural comparisons of appearance self-scheme, body image, self-esteem and dieting behavior between Korean and U.S. women. *Family and Consumer Sciences Research Journal*, 34(4), 350–365.

Kackman, M. and Binfield, M. (2010). *Flow TV: Television in the Age of Convergence*. New York, NY: Routledge.

Kafka, P. (2006, September 19). Son, Universal land $600 million in film financing. Retrieved from http://www.forbes.com/2006/01/19/sony-universal-0119markets15.html

Kang, G. J. and Morgan, M. (1988). Cultural clash: impact of U.S. television in Korea. *Journalism Quarterly*, 65, 431–438.

Katz, S. (2002). The Migration of Feature Film Production from the U.S. To Canada Year 2001. Production Report Center for Entertainment Industry Data and Research (CEIDR). Retrieved from www.ceidr.org/y2k1report.pdf

Katz, S. (2002). *The migration of feature film production from the U.S. to Canada year 2001 production report*. The Center for Entertainment Industry Data and Research (CEIDR). Retrieved from http://www.ceidr.org/y2k1report.pdf

Kaufman, A. (2006, June 22). Is foreign film the new endangered species? Retrieved from http://www.nytimes.com/2006/01/22/movies/22kauf.html?_r=1

Kazmi, N. (2009, January 15). *Chandni Chowk to China*. Retrieved from http://timesofindia.indiatimes.com/entertainment/movie-reviews/hindi/Chandni-Chowk-to-China/movie-review/3985572.cms

Keane, M. (2002). As a hundred television formats bloom, a thousand television stations contend. *Journal of Contemporary China*, 11(3), 5–16.

———. (2006). Once were peripheral: creating media capacity in East Asia. *Media, Culture & Society*, 28 (6), 835–55.

Keane, M. and Moran, A. (2008). Television's new engines. *Television & New Media*, 9(2), 155–169.

Keane, M., Fung, A., and Moran, A. (2007). *New Television, Globalization, and The East Asian Cultural Imagination*. Hong Kong: Hong Kong University Press.

Keating, J. (2010, January 17). Avatar: an all-purpose allegory. Retrieved from http://blog.foreignpolicy.com/posts/2010/02/16/avatar_an_all_purpose_allegory

Keith W. S. (2002, August 28). Swiss Army goes "XXX" with Vin Diesel. Retrieved from http://www.allbusiness.com/services/museums-art-galleries-botanical-zoological/4358883-1.html.

Kellner, D. and Kahn, R. (2003). Global youth culture. Retrieved from http://www.gseis.ucla.edu/faculty/kellner/essays/globyouthcult.pdf

Kelly, S. (2011). Does Star Wars belong to the fans or George Lucas? Retrieved from http://www.guardian.co.uk/commentisfree/2011/sep/18/star-wars-fans-george-lucas

Kelsky, K. (2001). *Women on the Verge: Japanese women, Western Dreams*. Durham and London: Duke University Press.

Kenny, C. (2009, November/December). Revolution in a Box. Retrieved from http://www.foreignpolicy.com/articles/2009/10/19/revolution_in_a_box?hidecomments=yes

Khattab, U. (2006). Non Mediated Images: Public Culture and (State) Television in Malaysia. *The International Communication Gazette*, 68(4), 347–61.

Khurshid, S. (2011, September 3). What the bleep is happening? Retrieved from http://www.hindustantimes.com/Entertainment/Television/What-the-bleep-is-happening/Article1–741294.aspx

King, G. (2000). *Spectacular Narratives: Hollywood in the Age of the Blockbuster*. London: I.B. Tauris.

—— (2002). *New Hollywood Cinema: An Introduction*. New York: I.B. Tauris.

King, R. (2007, July 31). Foreign remakes fuelling Hollywood. Retrieved from http://www.winnipegfreepress.com/arts-and-life/entertainment/movies/foreign-remakes-fuelling-hollywood–99681144.html

Kivijarv, L. (2005). *Product Placement Spending In Media 2005: History, Analysis and Forecast, 1975–2009*. Stamford, CT: PQ Media.

Klein, C. (2004, April 30). *The hollowing out of Hollywood*. Retrieved from http://yaleglobal.yale.edu

Klein, N. (2000). *No Logo: Taking Aim at the Brand Name Bullies*. Toronto: Vintage.

——. (2007). *The Shock Doctrine: The Rise of Disaster Capitalism*. Toronto: Alfred A. Knopf Canada.

Knee, J. A., Greenwald, B. C., and Seave, A. (2009). *The Curse of the Media Mogul: What's Wrong with the World's Leading Media Companies*. New York, NY: Portfolio.

Kornbluh, P. (2003). *The Pinochet File: A Declassified Dossier on Atrocity and Accountability*. New York: The New Press.

Kraidy, M. (1999). The global, the local, and the hybrid: a native ethnography of globalization. *Critical Studies in Mass Communication*, 16(4), 456–476.

——. (2002). Hybridity in cultural globalization. *Communication Theory*, 12(3), 316–339.

——. (2004). From culture to hybridity in international communication. In M. Semati (Ed.), *New Frontiers in International Communication Theory* (pp. 247–262). London: Rowman & Littlefield.

——. (2005). *Hybridity or the Cultural Logic of Globalization*. Philadelphia: Temple University Press.

Krajewski, A. (2011, November 1). UPDATE 2-Canal+ to gain foothold in TVN, merge pay TVs. Retrieved from http://www.reuters.com/article/2011/11/01/tvn-idUSN1E7A01YV20111101

Krashinksy, S. (2011, May 17). NBC joins forces with Global to launch TV series. Retrieved from http://m.theglobeandmail.com/report-on-business/nbc-joins-forces-with-global-to-launch-tv-series/article2024187/?service=mobile

Kuhner, J. T. (22 Feb 2009). Hollywood's culture of death. Retrieved from http://www.washingtontimes.com/news/2009/feb/22/hollywoods-culture-of-death/?page=all

Kumaravadivelu, B. (2008). *Cultural Globalization and Language Education*. New Haven, CT: Yale University

Kunz, W. M. (2007). *Culture Conglomerates*. Lanham, MD: Rowman & Littlefield.

Kunzle, D. (1991). Introduction to the English Edition. A. Dorfmann and A. Mattelart, *How to Read Donald Duck: Imperialist Ideology in the Disney Comic* (pp. 11–24). Hungary: I.G. Editions.

Laborde, A. and Perrot, M. (2000). Programme making across borders: the Eurosud news magazine. In J. Wietan, G. Murdock, and P. Dahlgren (Eds), *Television Across Europe* (pp. 94–112). London: Sage Publications.

Landers, D. E. and Chan-Olmsted, S. M. (2004). Assessing the changing network TV market: A resource-based analysis of broadcast television networks. *Journal of Media Business Studies*, 1(1), 1–26.

Landry, C (2000). *The Creative City: A Toolkit For Urban Innovators*. London: Earthscan,

La Pastina, A. C. (2003). Now that you're going home, are you going to write about the natives you studied? Telenovela reception, adultery and the dilemmas of ethnographic practice. In P. Murphy and M. Kraidy (Eds), *Global Media Studies: Ethnographic Perspectives* (pp. 125–146). New York: Routledge.

Lash, S. and Lury, C. (2007). *Global Culture Industry*. Cambridge: Polity Press.

Lash, S. and Urry, J. (1987). *The End of Organized Capitalism*. Madison, WI: University of Wisconsin Press.

Lazarus, N. (2002). The Fetish of the West in postcolonial theory. In C. Bartolovich and N. Lazarus (Eds), *Marxism, Modernity, and Postcolonial Studies* (pp. 43–65). Cambridge, MA: Cambridge University Press.

Lee, B. and Bae, H-S. (2004). The effect of screen quotas on the self-sufficiency ratio in recent domestic film markets. *Journal of Media Economics*, 17(3), 163–173.

Lee, C. C. (1980). *Media Imperialism Reconsidered: The Homogenizing Of Television Culture*. Beverly Hills: Sage.

Lee, H-S. (2007). Hybrid media, ambivalent feelings, media co-productions and cultural negotiations. *Spectator*, 27(2), 5–10.

Lee, J-Y. (2011, March 1). CJ consolidates media operations: CJ E&M hopes to maximize synergy in film, music, broadcasting and gaming. Retrieved from http://koreajoongangdaily. joinsmsn.com/news/article/article.aspx?aid=2932840

Lee, J. and Rytina, N. (2009). Naturalizations in the United States: 2008. Annual Flow Report. Office of Immigration Statistics. Retrieved from http://www.dhs.gov/xlibrary/assets/statistics/ publications/natz_fr_2008.pdf

Leeds, J. (2007, February 2). Democracy rules, and pop culture depends on it. Retrieved from http://www.nytimes.com/2007/02/02/business/media/02idol.html

Legrain, P. (2003, Summer). In defense of globalization: why cultural exchange is still an overwhelming force for good. *The International Economy*, 62–65.

Lemish, D., Drotner, K., Liebes, T., Maigret, E., and Stald, G. (1998). Global culture in practice. a look at children and adolescents in Denmark, France and Israel. *European Journal of Communication*, 13(4), 539–556.

Lessig, L. (2004). *Free Culture: How Big Media Uses Technology and the Law to Lock Down Culture and Control Creativity*. New York: Penguin.

Levy, G. (2010, October 1). Top 10 Hollywood remakes. Retrieved from http://entertainment. time.com/2010/10/01/top-10-hollywood-remakes/#let-me-in-2010-let-the-right-one-in-2008

Lewis, J. and Miller, T. (Eds). (2003). *Critical Cultural Policy Studies: A Reader*. Malden MA: Blackwell.

Leys, C. (2001). *Market Driven Politics: Neoliberal Democracy and the Public Interest*. London: Verso.

Liebes, T. (1988). Cultural differences in retelling of television fiction. *Critical Studies in Mass Communication*, 5(4), 277–92.

——. (1996). Notes on the struggle to define involvement in television viewing. In J. Hay, L. Grossberg, E. W artella (Eds). *The Audience and its Landscape*, pp. 177–186. Boulder, CO: Westview.

Liebes, T. and Katz, E. (1990). *The Export of Meaning: Cross-cultural Readings of Dallas*. Oxford: Oxford University Press.

Lipsey, R. and Chrystal, A. (1995). *Positive Economics*. Oxford: Oxford University Press.

Litman, B. R. (1998). *The Motion Picture Mega-Industry*. Boston: Allyn & Bacon.

——. (2000). The structure of the film industry: windows of exhibition. In A. N. Greco (Ed.), *The Media and Entertainment Industries: Readings in mass communications* (pp. 99–121). Boston: Allyn & Bacon.

Liu, F. and Chan-Olmsted, S. M. (2002). Partnership between the old and the new: examining the strategic alliances between broadcast television networks and Internet firms in the context of convergence. *The International Journal of Media Management*, 5(1), 47–56.

Livingstone, S. (1990). Interpreting television narrative: how viewers see a story. *Journal of Communication*, 40(1): 72–82.

——. (1998). *Making Sense of Television: The Psychology Of Audience Interpretation*. New York, NY: Routledge.

——. (2004). The challenge of changing audiences: or, what is the audience researcher do in the age of the internet? *European Journal of Communication*, 19(1), 75–86.

Llosa, M. V. (2001, January 1). The Culture of Liberty. Retrieved from http://www.foreignpolicy.com/articles/2001/01/01/the_culture_of_liberty

Lotz, A. (2007). *The Television Will be Revolutionized*. New York: New York University Press.

——. (Ed.). (2009). *Beyond Prime Time: Television Programming in the Post-Network Era*. New York: Routledge.

Lublin, J. S. (2010, November 14). The Year's Top 10 Highest Paid CEOs. Retrieved from http://online.wsj.com/article/SB10001424052748704393604575614852198144276.html

Luce, H. (1944). *World Communications*. Fortune.

Lukinbeal, C. (2004). The rise of regional film production centers in North America, 1984–1997. *GeoJournal*, 59(1), 307–321.

Lull, J. (2001). Superculture for the communication age. In J. Lull (Ed.), *Culture in the Communication Age* (pp. 132–63). New York: Routledge.

Lule, J. (2011). *Globalization & Media: Global Village of Babel*. Lanham, Maryland: Rowman & Littlefield.

Ma, E. (2000). Rethinking media studies: The case of China. In J. Curran and M. J. Park (Eds), *De-Westernizing Media Studies* (pp. 17–28). New York: Routledge.

MacBride, S. and Roach, C. (2000). The new international information order. In F. J. Lechner and J. Boli (Eds), *The Globalization Reader* (pp. 286–292). Malden: Blackwell Publishers.

McChesney, R. (1999). *Rich Media, Poor Democracy: Communication Politics in Dubious Times*. New York, NY: The New Press.

——. (2002). The global restructuring of media ownership. In M. Raboy (Ed.), *Global Media Policy in the New Millennium* (pp. 149–162). Luton: University of Luton Press.

——. (2003). Theses on media deregulation. *Media, Culture and Society*, 25(1), 125–33.

——. (2004). *The Problem with the U.S. Media: Communication Politics in the 21st Century*. New York: Monthly Review Press.

——. (2004). *The Problem of the Media*. New York, NY: Monthly Review Press.

——. (2005). The new global media. In E. P. Bucy (Ed.), *Living in the Information Age: A New Media Reader* (pp. 92–96). Belmont: Wadsworth Thomson Learning.

——. (2008). *The Political Economy of Media: Enduring Issues, Emerging Dilemmas*. New York: Monthly Review Press.

McChesney, R. and Schiller, D. (2003). *The Political Economy of International Communications: Foundations for the Emerging Global Debate about Media Ownership and Regulation*. United Nations Research Institute for Social Development (Technology, Business and Society Programme Paper Number 11).

Macdonald, P. and Wasko, J. (Eds). (2005). *The Contemporary Hollywood Film Industry*. Malden, MA: Blackwell.

McGuigan, J. (2003). Cultural policy studies. In J. Lewis and T. Miller (Eds), *Critical Cultural Policy Studies: A Reader* (pp. 23–42). Malden MA: Blackwell.

——. (2004). *Rethinking Cultural Policy*. England: Open University Press.

——. (2005). Neoliberalism, culture and policy. *International Journal of Cultural Policy*, 11(3), 229–41.

——. (2009). *Cool Capitalism*. London: Pluto.

——. (2010). Doing a Florida thing: the creative class thesis and cultural policy. *International Journal of Cultural Policy* 16(3), 323–335.

McKenzie, W. (1994). *Virtual Geography: Living with Global Media Events*. Indiana University Press.

McKinley, J. C. (2004, September 28). No, the Conquistadors are not back. It's just Wal-Mart. Retrieved from http://www.nytimes.com/2004/09/28/international/americas/28mexico.html?_r=0

McLean, I. and McMillan, A. (2003). *Oxford Concise Dictionary of Politics.* New York: Oxford

McLuhan, M. (1964). *Understanding Media: The Extensions of Man.* New York: McGraw Hill.

McLuhan, M. and Nevitt, B. (1972). *Take Today: The Executive as Dropout.* New York: Harcourt Brace Jovanovich.

McLuhan, M. and Powers, B. R. (1989). *The Global Village: Transformations in World Life and Media In The 21st Century.* New York, NY: Oxford University Press.

McMillan, D. C. (2007). *International Media Studies.* Malden, MA: Blackwell Publishing.

McNary, D. (22 June 2010). Study: bring shoots back to Cali: Milken study says $2.4 billion lost since 1997. Retrieved from http://www.variety.com/article/VR1118022060

McPhail, T. L. (1987) *Electronic Colonialism: The Future of International Broadcasting and Communication.* Newbury Park, CA: Sage.

McQuail, D. (1992). *Media Performance.* London: Sage.

——. (1997). *Audience Analysis.* London: Sage.

Madger, T. (2006). International agreements and the principles of world communication. In J. Curran and D. Morley (Eds), *Media and Cultural Theory* (pp. 164–76). New York: Routledge.

Magro, M. (2011, January 13). Brazil's communications minister wants rule that limits regional media ownership. Retrieved from http://knightcenter.utexas.edu/blog/brazils-communications-minister-wants-rule-limits-regional-media-ownership

Maltby, R. (2003). *Hollywood Cinema.* Oxford, England: Blackwell.

Mansell, R. and Raboy, M. (2011). *The Handbook of Global Media and Communication Policy.* Malden, MA: Wiley-Blackwell.

Marks, V. (2011, March 30). India v Pakistan: ultimate cricket derby brings two countries to a standstill. Retrieved from http://www.guardian.co.uk/sport/2011/mar/30/india-pakistan-ultimate-cricket-derby

Markusen, A. (2006). Urban development and the politics of a creative class: evidence from a study of artists. *Environment and Planning A*, 38 (1), 1921–1940.

Marlow, I. (2010, September 10). BCE-CTV deal remakes media landscape. Retrieved from http://www.theglobeandmail.com/globe-investor/bce-ctv-deal-remakes-media-landscape/article1702385/

Marlowe, A. (2009, December 23). The most neo-con movie ever made. Retrieved from http://www.forbes.com/2009/12/23/avatar-neo-con-military-opinions-contributors-ann-marlowe.html

Marx, K. (1848). *The Communist Manifesto.* New York, NY: International, 1995 [1848].

——. (1976). *Capital,* 1, 777–80. London: Penguin.

——. (1977). *Capital,* 1, 125. New York, NY: Vintage.

Marx, K. and Engels, F. (1978). Manifesto of the Community Party. In R. C. Tucker (Ed.), *The Marx-Engels Reader* (pp. 489–500). New York and London: W.W. Norton Company.

Massey, D. (1991). A global sense of place. *Marxism Today*, 38, 24–29.

——. (1992). A place called home, *New Formations*, 17, 3–15.

Mastrini, G. and Becerra, M. (2011). Media ownership, oligarchies, and globalization: media concentration in South America. In D. R. Winseck and D. Y. Jin (Eds), *The Political Economies of Media: The Transformation of the Global Media Industries.* New York: Bloomsbury Academic. Retrieved from http://www.bloomsburyacademic.com/view/PoliticalEconomies Media_9781849664264/chapter-ba–9781849664264-chapter–003.xml?print

Mattelart, A. (1979). *Multinational Corporations and the Control of Culture: The Ideological Apparatuses of Imperialism.* Brighton: Harvester.

——. (1994). *Mapping World Communication.* Minneapolis: University of Minnesota.

Mattelart, M. and Mattelart, A. (1998). *Theories of Communication: A Short Introduction.* London: Sage.

Matthews, S. (2007, Feb. 1). Strike Devastating Film Industry. Retrieved from http://urbantoronto.ca/forum/showthread.php/3451-Strike-devastating-Toronto-film-industry

Maxwell, R. (2003). *Herbert Schiller*. New York: Rowman & Littlefield.

Mayer, V. (2008). Where production takes place. *Velvet Light Trap* 63, 1, 71–73.

Mayer, V., Banks, M., and Caldwell, J., (Eds). (2009). *Production Studies: Cultural Studies of Media Industries*. New York: Routledge.

Mead, B. (November 28, 2011). Digital vanguard: Asian market leads the way in D-cinema deployments. Retrieved from http://www.filmjournal.com/filmjournal/content_display/news-and-features/features/technology/e3i5068fd91e4de2296429587e935e04817

Media Centre for National Development of Sri Lanka. Retrieved from http://www.development.lk/about_us.php

Meehan, E. R. (1990). Why we don't count: the commodity audience. In P. Mellencamp (Ed.), *Logics Of Television: Essays In Cultural Criticism* (pp. 117–137). London: BFI Press.

——. (2005). *Why Tv is Not Our Fault: Tv Programming Viewers and Who's Really in Control*. Lanham, MD: Rowman & Littlefield.

——. (2007). Understanding how the popular becomes popular: the role of political economy in the study of popular communication. *Popular Communication*, 5(3), 161–170.

——. (2010). Media empires: corporate structures and lines of control. *Jump Cut: A Review of Contemporary Media*, 52, 1–14. Retrieved from http://www.ejumpcut.org/currentissue/MeehanCorporate/text.html

Meyrowitz, J. (1986). *No Sense of Place: The Impact of Electronic Media on Social Behavior*. New York: Oxford University Press.

Meza, E. (2009, September 11). Nordmedia brings projects to Lower Saxony, Bremen. Retrieved from http://www.variety.com/article/VR1118008496

Miller, D. E. (2011, July 20). Saudi Arabia's 'Anti-Witchcraft Unit' breaks another spell. Retrieved from http://www.jpost.com/MiddleEast/Article.aspx?id=230183

Miller, D. and Shamsie, J. (1996). The resource-based view of the firm in two environments: The Hollywood film studios from 1936 to 1965. *Academy of Management Journal*, 39(3), 519–543.

Miller, J. L. (2010). *Ugly Betty* goes global: global networks of localized content in the telenovela industry. *Global Media and Communication*, 6(2), 198–217.

Miller, M. (2005, August 27). Hollywood on the Vltava: Cheap labour, historic architecture, and local talent bring filmmakers to Prague. Retrieved from http://www.filmcommission.cz/medialinks.php?i–20

Miller, T. (2005). Anti-Americanism and popular culture. Retrieved from http://cps.ceu.hu/publications/working-papers/antiamericanism-and-popular-culture

——. (2010a). Culture + labour = precariat. *Communication and Critical/Cultural Studies*, 7, (10), 99.

——. (2010b). *Television Studies: The Basics*. New York: Routledge.

Miller, T. and Yudice, G. (2002). *Cultural Policy*. London: Sage Publications.

Miller, T., Govil, N., McMurria, J., Maxwell, R., and Wang, T. (2005). *Global Hollywood 2*. London: British Film Institute.

Mills, C. W. (2000). *The Power Elite*. New York: Oxford University Press.

Ministry of Mass Media and Information. Retrieved from http://www.media.gov.lk/about_the_ministry.php

Mody, B. (2003). Foreword: global and local influences on the shape of media institutions. In B. Mody (Ed.) *International and Development Communication: A 21st Century Perspective* (pp. vii–xi). London: Sage Publications.

Mohamed, K. (2009). Chandni Chowk to China. Retrieved from http://www.hindustantimes.com/Entertainment/Reviews/Review-Chandni-Chowk-To-China/Article1-367433.aspx

Mohammadi, A. (1995). Cultural imperialism and cultural identity. In J. Downing, A. Mohammadi, and A. Srebery-Mohammadi (Eds). *Questioning the media: A critical introduction* (pp. 362–378). London: Sage.

Molly, M. (2005, October 21). UN body endorses cultural protection: US objections are turned aside. Retrieved from http://www.globalpolicy.org/globaliz/cultural/2005/1021 body.htm

Moore, J. (2011, February 17). Arts, culture and delivering results from Canada. *Canadian Media Production Association Prime Time Conference*. Ottawa, Ontario, Canada. Retrieved from http://www.jamesmoore.org/PT11Speech/

Moore, R. (2007). Friends don't let friends listen to corporate rock: punk as a field of cultural production. *Journal of Contemporary Ethnography*, 1(36), 438–474.

Moran, A. (1998). *Copycat Television: Globalization, Program Formats and Cultural Identity*. Luton: University of Luton Press.

——. (2004). Television formats in the world/the world of television formats. In A. Moran & M. Keane (Eds), *Television across Asia: Television Industries, Programme Formats and Globalization* (pp. 1–8). London: Routledge.

——. (2009). Global franchising, local customizing: the cultural economy of TV program formats. *Continuum: Journal of Media & Cultural Studies*, 23 (2), 115–125.

Moran, A. and Keane, M. (2006). Cultural power in international tv format markets. *Continuum: Journal of Media & Cultural Studies*, 20 (1), 71–86.

Morawetz, N., Hardy, J., Haslam, C., and Randle, K. (2007). Finance, policy and industrial dynamics–the rise of co-productions in the film industry. *Industry & Innovation*, 14 (4), 421–443.

Morley, D. (1980). *The Nationwide Audience*. London: BFI.

——. (1992). *Television, Audiences and Cultural Studies*. New York: Routledge.

——. (1994). Postmodernism: the highest stage of cultural imperialism In M. Perryman (Ed.), *Altered States: Postmodernism Politics, Culture*. London: Lawrence and Wishart.

——. (1996). The geography of television: ethnography, communications and community. In J. Hay, L. Grossberg & E. Wartella (Eds), *The Audience and its Landscape* (pp. 317–42). Boulder, CO: Westview.

——. (2000). *Home Territories: Media, Mobility, and Identity*. New York, NY: Routledge.

——. (2006). Globalization and cultural imperialism reconsidered: old questions in new guises. In J. Curran and D. Morley (Eds), *Media and Cultural Theory* (pp. 31–43). New York, NY: Routledge.

Morley, D. and Robins, K. (1995). *Spaces of Identity: Global Media, Electronic Landscapes and Cultural Boundaries*. New York, NY: Routledge.

Morris, N. (2002). The myth of unadulterated culture meets the threat of imported media. *Media, Culture & Society*, 24(2), 278–289.

Mosco, V. (1996). *The Political Economy of Communication*. London: Sage.

——. (2004). *The Digital Sublime*. London: MIT Press.

——. (2008). Current trends in the political economy of communication. *Global Media Journal: Canadian Edition*, 1(1), 45–63.

——. (2009). *The Political Economy of Communication*. London: Sage.

Mowlana, H. (1996). *Global Communication in Transition*. Thousand Oaks, CA: Sage.

Motion Picture Association of America (MPAA). (2007). *Theatrical Market Statistics 2007*. Retrieved from www.mpaa.org/2007-US-Theatrical-Market-Statistics-Report.pdf

——. (2009). Theatrical Market Statistics. Retrieved from http://www.womeninfilm.ca/_Library/docs/MPAATheatricalMarketStatistics2009.pdf

——. (2010). Trade Barriers to Exports of U.S. Filmed Entertainment. Retrieved from http://www.mpaa.org/resources/69721865-ac82–4dc4–88ec–01ee84c651a1.pdf

——. (2011). Advancing a unique american industry. Retrieved from http://www.mpaa.org/policy

——. (2005). Glickman expresses disappointment at outcome of cultural diversity discussions. Retrived from http://www.mpaa.org/press_releases/2005_10_21.pdf

Mukherjee, D. (2011, September 16). Why animation outsourcing to India is good for you. Retrieved from http://vepro.articlesnare.com/software-articles/why-animation-outsourcing-to-india-is-good-for-you.htm

Munro, J. R. (1990, February 14). Good-bye to Hollywood. *Delivered to Town Hall of California*. Los Angeles, California.

Murdock, G. (2006a). Cosmopolitans and conquistadors: Empires, nations and networks. In O. Boyd-Barrett (Ed.), *Communications Media, Globalization and Empire*. (pp. 17–32). Eastleigh, UK: John Libbey.

——. (2006b). Notes from the number one country. *International Journal of Cultural Policy*, 12(2), 209–227.

Murdock, G. and Golding, P. (1977). Capitalism, communication and class relations. In J. Curran, M. Gurevitch, and J. Woollacott (Eds), *Mass Communication and Society* (pp. 12–43). London: Arnold.

——. (2005). Culture, Communications and Political Economy. In J. Curran and M. Gurvitch (Eds), *Mass Media and Society* (pp. 60–83). London: Arnold.

Murphy, P. D. (2005). Fielding the study of reception: notes on "negotiation" for global media studies. *Popular Communication*, 3(3), 167–180.

Murray, S. (2005). Brand loyalties: rethinking content within global corporate media. *Media, Culture & Society*, 27(3), 415–435.

Naficy, H. (1993). *The Making of Exile Cultures: Iranian Television in Los Angeles*. Minneapolis: University of Minnesota Press.

Nain, Z. (2000). Globalized theories and national controls: the state, the market and the Malaysian media. In J. Curran and M. J. Park (Eds), *De-Westernizing Media Studies* (124–136). New York: Routledge.

Napoli, P. M. (2006). *Bridging cultural policy and media policy in the U.S.: challenges and opportunities*. Working paper, The Donald McGannon Communication Research Centre, September 6, 2006.

——. (2009). Media economics and the study of media industries. In J. Holt and L. Perren (Eds), *Media Industries: History, Theory, and Method* (pp. 161–170). Malden, MA: Wiley-Blackwell.

Neff, G., Wissinger, E., and Zukin, S. (2005). Entrepreneurial labor among cultural producers: 'cool' jobs in 'hot' industries. *Social Semiotics*, 15(3), 307–334.

Netherby, J. (2009, March 17). Twilight sets on Oregon as film moves to Canada. Retrieved from http://www.oregonbusiness.com/articles/17-march–2009/180-twilight-sets-on-oregon-as-film-heads-to-canada

Newell, J., Salmon, C.T., and Chang, S. (2006). The Hidden History of Product Placement. *Journal of Broadcasting & Electronic Media*, 50(4), 575–594.

Newitz, A. (2009, December 18). When will white people stop making movies like Avatar? Retrieved from http://io9.com/5422666/when-will-white-people-stop-making-movies-like-avatar

News Editor. (2008, April 10). Singapore censors fine Cable TV operator $10,000 for ad featuring lesbian kiss. Retrieved from http://www.fridae.asia/newsfeatures/2008/04/10/2040.singapore-censors-fine-cable-tv-operator-s–10000-for-ad-featuring-lesbian-kiss

New Zealand. (2009, December 16). Weta Technology inspires "Avatar" world. Retrieved from http://www.newzealand.com/travel/media/pressreleases/2009/12/film&television_weta-technology-inspires-avatar_press-release.cfm

Nielsen. (2011a). Top 10 Internet. Retrieved from http://www.nielsen.com/us/en/insights/top10s/internet.html

—— (2011b). Global advertising rebounded 10.6% in 2010. Retrieved from: http://www.nielsen.com/us/en/insights/press-room/2011/global-advertising-rebound–2010.html

Nielsenwire. (2008, November 3). In praise of cinema advertising. Retrieved from http://blog.nielsen.com/nielsenwire/consumer/in-praise-of-in-cinema-advertising/

Noam, E. M. (2009). *Media Ownership and Concentration in America*. New York, NY: Oxford University Press.

No Author. (2011a, May 6). Chinese TV: a history of bans and censorship. Retrieved from http://www.telegraph.co.uk/news/worldnews/asia/china/8496823/Chinese-TV-a-history-of-bans-and-censorship.html

——. (2011b, June 4). Paid TV market and fierce competition. Retrieved from http://www.vneconomynews.com/2011/06/paid-tv-market-potential-and-fierce.html

Nolte, J. (2009, December 13). REVIEW: Cameron's 'Avatar' is a big, dull, America-hating, pc revenge fantasy. Retrieved from http://www.freerepublic.com/focus/f-chat/2406793/posts

Nordenstreng, K. and Schiller, H. (Eds). (1979). *National Sovereignty and International Communication*. Norwood, NJ: Ablex.

Nordenstreng, K, and Varis, T. (1974). *Television traffic: a one-way street?* Reports and papers on Mass Communication # 70. Paris: UNESCO.

Nrkumah, K. (1965). *Neo-Colonialism: the Last Stage of Imperialism*. London: Thomas Nelson & Sons, Ltd.

Nurse, K. (2007, February 12). Creative industries as growth engine. policy innovations. Retrieved from http://www.policyinnovations.org/ideas/innovations/data/creative_cultural

Nye, J. (2004). *Soft Power: The Means to Success in World Politics*. Toronto: Harper Collins.

Nye, J. (2008). *Public diplomacy and soft power*. The ANNALS of the American Academy of Political and Social Science 616(1), 94–109.

Oba, G. and Chan-Olmsted, S. (2007). Video strategy of transnational media corporations: a resource-based examination of global alliances and patterns. *Journal of Media Business Studies*, 4(2), 1–25.

Ofcom. (2010). International communications market report. London: Ofcom. stakeholders. Retrieved from ofcom.org.uk/binaries/research/cmr/753567/. . ./ICMR_2010.pdf

Ogan, C. (1988). Media imperialism and the video cassette recorder: The case of Turkey. *Journal of Communication*, 38, 93–106.

O'Hara, K. and Stevens, D. (2006). *Inequality.Com: Power, Poverty and the Digital Divide*. Oxford: OneWorld Books.

Ohmae, K. (1995). *The Borderless World: Power and Strategy in an Interdependent Economy*. New York, NY: Harper Business.

Oliveira, O. S. (1986). Satellite tv and dependency: an empirical approach. *Gazette*, 38, 127–145.

Oliver, C. (2012, February 10). South Korea's K-pop takes off in the west. Retrieved from http://www.ft.com/intl/cms/s/0/ddf11662–53c7–11e1–9eac–00144feabdc0.html#axzz2BbbSjopO

Oliver, L. V. (2005, October 20). Explanation of vote of the United States on the convention on the protection and promotion of the diversity of cultural expressions. Retrieved from http://geneva.usmission.gov/Press2005/2010Oliver.htm

Olsen, M. (2008, September 8). Hurt Locker a soldier's-eye view of the Iraq war. Retrieved from http://articles.latimes.com/2008/sep/08/entertainment/et-hurt8

Olsen, S. (2008, July 22). Viacom CEO: 'Great' content is king. Retrieved from http://news.cnet.com/8301–1023_3–9996614–93.html

Olson, S. R. (2000). The globalization of Hollywood. *International Journal on World Peace*, XVII (4), 3–17.

Olson, S. R. (1999). *Hollywood Planet: Global Media and the Competitive Advantage of Narrative Transparency*. Mahway, N.J.: Lawrence Erlbaum.

O'Neill, M. J. (1993). *The Roar of The Crowd: How Television and People Power are Changing the World*. New York, NY: Times Books Randomhouse.

Pacenti, J. (2011, April 26). Disney, Hanna Barbera sue Costume World. Retrieved from http://www.dailybusinessreview.com/PubArticleDBR.jsp?id=1202491697931&Disney_Hanna_Barbera_sue_Costume_World&slreturn=1iew

Pacheco, W. (2010, August 12). Walt Disney faces $200,000 lawsuit in alleged Donald Duck groping case. Orlando Sentinel. Retrieved from http://articles.orlandosentinel.com/2010–08–12/travel/os-disney-donald-duck-groping-lawsuit20100812_1_michael-c-chartrand-lawsuit-federal-court

Pagello, F. (2010). The *Lord of the Rings* as global phenomenon: a review of the Frodo franchise, watching the Lord of the Rings and studying the film event. *New Review of Film and Television Studies*, 8(2), 233–245.

Palfrey, D. H. (2010, March 19). New media park opens gateway to Chapalawood. Retrieved from http://www.focusonmexico.com/New-Media-Park-opens-Gateway-to-Chapalawood.html

Panitch, L. (1996). Rethinking the role of the state. In J. Mittelman, (Ed.), *Globalization: Critical Reflections* (pp. 83–113). Boulder: Lynn Rienner.

Panitch, L. and Gindin, S. (2004). Global capitalism and American Empire. In L. Panitch and C. Leys (Eds), *The New Imperial Challenge: Socialist Register 2004* (1–45). London: Merlin Press.

Parameswaran, R. (1999). Western romance fiction as English-language media in postcolonial India. *Journal of Communication*, 49(3), 84–105.

Parks, L. and Kumar, S. (Eds). (2003). *Planet TV: A Global Television Reader*. New York, NY: New York University Press.

Pathania-Jain, G. (2001). Global parents, local partners: A value-chain analysis of collaborative strategies of media firm in India. *Journal of Media Economics*, 14(3), 169–187.

Patton, T. (2006). Hey girl, am I more than my hair? African American women and their struggles with beauty, body image, and hair. *NWSA Journal*, 18(2), 24–51.

Pauwels, C. and Loisen, J. (2003). The WTO and the Audiovisual Sector: Economic Free Trade vs Cultural Horse Trading? *European Journal of Communication*, 18 (3), 291–313.

Pauwelyn, J. (2005, November 15). The UNESCO Convention on Cultural Diversity, and the WTO: Diversity in International Law-Making? ASIL Inside. The American Society of International Law.

Pellerin, B. (2006). Can pop-cultural imperialism be stopped? Give us this day our daily Brad Pitt. Retrieved from http://www.globalenvision.org/library/33/775

Pendakur, M. (1990). *Canadian Dreams and American Control: The Political Economy of the Canadian Film Industry*. Toronto: Garamond Press.

Perry, A. (2011, April 10). Africa's starring role. Retrieved from http://www.time.com/time/magazine/article/0,9171,2063730,00.html#ixzz1JJH35vZi

Petrazzini, B. (1995). *The Political Economy of Telecommunications Reform in Developing Countries: Privatization and Liberalization in Perspective*. Praeger Westport, Connecticut and London.

Pevere, G. (2009, May 2). Homer Simpson goes to mosque. Retrieved from http://www.thestar.com/comment/columnists/article/627746

Phillips, M. (2010, January 10). Why is Avatar a film of Titanic proportions? Retrieved from http://articles.chicagotribune.com/2010–01–08/entertainment/1001070518_1_critics-avatar-james-cameron

Phillips, R. (2004). The global export of risk: finance and the film business. *Competition & Change*, 8 (2), 105–136.

Phillipson, R. (2003). *English-Only Europe?* New York: Routledge.

Pickard, V. (2010). Reopening the postwar settlement for U.S. media: the origins and implications of the social contract between media, the state, and the polity. *Communication, Culture & Critique*, 3(1), 170–189.

Pierce, B. (2009, September 28). How is Family Guy a threat to the Bolivarian Revolution? Retrieved from http://blog.foreignpolicy.com/posts/2009/09/28/how_is_peter_griffin_a_threat_to_the_bolivarian_dream

Pieterse, J. N. (2003). *Global Mélange: Globalization and culture*. Lanham: Rowman & Littlefield.

Pike, R., and Winseck, D. (2004). The politics of global media reform, 1907–23. *Media Culture & Society*, 26(5), 643–675.

Pomerantz, D. (2010, April 4). Why Hollywood loves a remake. Retrieved from http://www.forbes.com/2010/04/07/hollywood-remakes-business-entertainment-remakes_print.html

Porter, M. (1985). *Competitive Advantage: Creating and Sustaining Superior Performance*. London: Collier MacMillan.

Potts, J. (2008). Creative industries & cultural science: a definitional odyssey. *Cultural Science*, 1(1). Retrieved from http://cultural-science.org/journal/index.php/culturalscience/article/viewArticle/6/16

Powers, L. (2011, March 17). Lady Gaga's 'Born This Way' lyrics censored in Malaysia. Retrieved from http://www.hollywoodreporter.com/news/lady-gagas-born-way-lyrics–168800

Price, M. (2002). *Media and Sovereignty: The Global Information Revolution and Its Challenge to State Power*. Cambridge, MA: The MIT Press.

Prigge, M. (2010, September 14). Six foreign remakes of American films. Retrieved from http://www.philadelphiaweekly.com/screen/Six-Foreign-Remakes-of-American-Films.html

Pryke, S. (1995). Nationalism as Culturalism. *Politics*, 15(1), 63–70.

PTI. (2010, May 9). Finmin advisors moots incentive for film industry. Retrieved from http://articles.economictimes.indiatimes.com/2010–05–09/news/27602262_1_service-tax-tax-subsidy-film-industry

Puente, M. (2008, February 27). The Oscars had a strong foreign accent this year. Retrieved from http://www.usatoday.com/life/movies/movieawards/oscars/2008–02–27-oscar-international_N.htm

Punter, J. (2010, May 7). New studio planned for Toronto. Retrieved from http://www.variety.com/article/VR1118018909

Puppis, M. (2008). National media regulation in the era of free trade: the role of global media governance. *European Journal of Communication*, 23(4), 405–424.

Pye, L. (Ed.). (1963). *Communications and Political Development*. Princeton NJ: Princeton University Press.

Raboy, M. (2002). Media policy in the new communications environment. In M. Raboy (Ed.), *Global Media Policy in the New Millennium* (pp. 3–16). Luton: University of Luton Press.

Raboy, M. (2007). Global media policy – defining the field. *Global Media and Communication*, 3 (3), 343–361.

Raboy, M. and Padovani, C. (2010). Mapping global media policy: concepts, frameworks, methods. *Communication, Culture & Critique*, 3(1), 150–169.

Raboy, M. and Shtern, J. (2010). *Media Divides: Communication Rights and the Right to Communicate in Canada*. Vancouver: University of British Columbia Press.

Rainwater-McClure, R., Reed, W., and Kramer, E. (2003). A world of cookie-cutter faces. In E. Kramer (Ed.), *The Emerging Monoculture: Assimilation and the "Model Minority"* (pp. 221–233). Westport CT: Praeger.

Ramachandran, N. (2011, May 27). Star, Zee merge distrib'n arms. Retrieved from http://www.variety.com/article/VR1118037701?refCatId=1442

Rantanen, R. (2005). *The Media and Globalization*. London: Sage.

Rao, N. (2010, January 7). Anti-imperialism in 3-D. Retrieved from http://socialistworker.org/2010/01/07/anti-imperialism-in–3D

Rea, S. (2009, January 16). A Slumdog this one surely is not. Retrieved from http://articles.philly.com/2009–01–16/entertainment/24984723_1_akshay-kumar-deepika-padukone-chandni-chowk

Reel Toronto. (2008). The Incredible Hulk. Retrieved from http://torontoist.com/2008/11/reel_toronto_the_incredible_hulk.php

Reeves, G. (1993). *Communications and the Third World*. London; Sage.

Reeves, T. (2006). *The Worldwide Guide to Movie Locations*. London: Titan Books.

Rehlin, G. (2010, April 9). Scandinavia unites to lure filmmakers: Nordic nations develop resources, promote production. Retrieved from http://www.variety.com/article/VR1118017421

Reich, R. B. (2010). *Aftershock: The Next Economy and America's Future*. New York: Knopf.

Renton, D. (2001). *Marx on Globalization*. London: Lawrence and Wishart.

Reuters (2010, May 11). Disney forms joint venture in South Korea. Retrieved from http://www.reuters.com/article/2010/05/12/disney-southkorea-idUSN1113600020100512

——. (2011, May 31). Telmex: DISH no substitute for Mexico TV license. Retrieved from http://www.reuters.com/article/2011/05/31/telmex-idUSN3110210120110531

Ribes, A. J. (2010). Theorizing global media events: cognition, emotions and performances. *New Global Studies*, 4(3), 3.

Rigney, M. (2009, June 24). Chinese fans celebrate Bumblebee and Transformers 2 release. Retrieved from http://www.motorauthority.com/news/1021703_chinese-fans-celebrate-bumblebee-and-transformers–2-release

Riordan, M. H. and Salant, D. J. (1994). *Exclusion and Integration in the Market for Video Programming Delivered to the Home*. Boston: Boston University, Industry Studies Program.

Ritzer, G. (Ed.). (2002). *McDonaldization: The Reader*. Thousand Oaks: Pine Forge Press.

Roach, C. (1997). Cultural imperialism and resistance in media theory and literary theory. *Media, Culture & Society*, 19, 47–66.

Robertson, R. (1995). Glocalization: Time-Space and Homogeneity-Heterogeneity. In M. Featherstone et al. (Eds). *Global Modernities* (pp. 25–44). London: Sage.

Robertson, W. (2007, August 14). Viacom backs MLK memorial. Retrieved from http://www.variety.com/article/VR1117970248

Robinson, W. I. (2004) *A Theory of Global Capitalism: Production, Class and State in a Transnational World*. The John Hopkins University Press.

Rodney, W. (1981). *How Europe Underdeveloped Africa*. Howard University Press.

Rogers, E. M. (1962). *Diffusion of Innovations*. New York, NY: Free Press.

——. (1965). Mass media exposure and modernization among Colombian peasants. *The Public Opinion Quarterly*, 29(4), 614–625.

——. (1976). Communication and development: the passing of the dominant paradigm. *Communication Research*, 3(2), 213–240.

Rosenberg, E. S. (1982). *Spreading the American Dream: American Economic and Cultural Expansion 1890–1945*. New York: Hill and Wang.

Ross, A. (2004). *No-Collar: The Humane Workplace and its Hidden Consequences*. Philadelphia, PA: Temple University Press.

——. (2008). The new geography of work. *Theory, Culture & Society*, 25(7–8), 31–48.

——. (2009). *Nice Work If You Can Get It: Life and Labor in Precarious Times*. New York and London: New York University Press.

Rothkopf, D. (1997). In praise of cultural imperialism? *Foreign Policy*, (103, Summer), 38–53.

Rowell, A. (2010, March 5). Welcome to Canada's AvaTAR Sands. Retrieved from http://priceofoil.org/2010/03/05/welcome-to-canadas-avatar-sands/

Ruiz, E. G. (2004 2 July). The Bush family's murky dealings in Venezuela. Retrieved from http://www.trinicenter.com/articles/020704.html

Ryall, J. (2008, December 3). Brutal Japanese reality TV formats set to invade Britain. Retrieved from http://www.telegraph.co.uk/news/worldnews/asia/japan/3543957/Brutal-Japanese-reality-TV-formats-set-to-invade-Britain.html

Ryan, M. P. (1998). *Knowledge Diplomacy: Global Competition and the Politics of Intellectual Property*. Washington, D.C.: Brookings Institute.

Ryan, M. T. (2007). Consumption. In G. Ritzer (Ed.), *The Blackwell Encyclopaedia of Sociology* (pp. 701–705). Blackwell Publishing.

Rydell, R. and Kroes, R. (2005). *Buffalo Bill in Bologna. The Americanization of the World, 1869–1922*. Chicago and London: University of Chicago Press.

Ryoo, W. (2009). Globalization, or the logic of cultural hybridization: the case of Korean Wave. *Asian Journal of Communication*, 19(2), 137–51.

Said, E. (1979). *Orientalism*. New York: Vintage.

——. (1993). *Culture and Imperialism*. New York, NY: Vintage.

Saltzman, M. (2011, December 26). The most pirated TV shows of 2011. Retrieved from http://www.moneyville.ca/blog/post/1107072–the-most-pirated-tv-shows-of-2011

Sapa. (2011, November 9). Bollywood censorship sparks Tibetan protest. Retrieved from http://www.timeslive.co.za/entertainment/movies/2011/11/09/bollywood-censorship-sparks-tibetan-protest

Sarikakis, K. (2004). *Media and communication policy: a definition*. Retrieved from http://ics.leeds.ac.uk/papers/vp01.cfm?outfit=ks&folder=4&paper=25

Sauve, P. (2006). Introduction. Trends in Audiovisual Markets: Regional Perspectives from the South. United Nations Educational, Scientific and Cultural Organization. Retrieved from http://www.unesco.org/new/en/communication-and-information/resources/publications-and-communication-materials/publications/full-list/trends-in-audiovisual-markets-regional-perspectives-from-the-south/

Schatz, T. (1992). The new Hollywood. In J. Collins et al. (Eds), *Film Theory Goes to the Movies* (pp. 15–20). New York, NY: Routledge.

Scherer, K. (2010, December 3). The Big Picture. Retrieved from http://www.nzherald.co.nz/business/news/article.cfm?c_id=3&objectid=10691502

Schiller, D. (1996). *Theorizing Communication: A History*. Oxford: Oxford University Press.

——. (2000). *Digital Capitalism: Networking in the Global Market System*. Cambridge, MA: The MIT Press.

——. (2008). Review of *Media Policy and Globalization: History, Culture, Politics*, by Paula Chakravarty and Katherine Sarikakis. *Political Communication*, 25(1), 99.

——. (2010). *How to Think About Information*. Champaign, Illinois: University of Illinois Press.

Schiller, H. (1969). *Mass Communication and American Empire*. New York, NY: Augustus M. Kelley.

——. (1976). *Communication and Cultural Domination*. White Plains, NY: International Arts and Sciences Press.

——. (1979). Transnational media and national development. In K. Nordenstreng and H. Schiller. (Eds), *National Sovereignty and International Communication*, Norwood, NJ: Ablex.

——. (1989). *Culture, Inc.: The Corporate Takeover of Public Expression*. New York: Oxford University Press.

——. (1991). Not yet the post-imperial era. *Critical Studies in Mass Communication*, 8(1), 13–28.

——. (1992). *Mass Communication and American Empire*. New York: August M. Kelley Publishers.

——. (2000). *Living in the Number One Country: Reflections of a Critic of American Empire*. New York, NY: Seven Stories Press.

Schlesinger, P. (1991). Media, the political order and national identity. *Media, Culture & Society*, 13(1), 297–308.

Schlussel, D. (2009). Don't Believe the Hype: Avatar Stinks (Long, boring, uber-left). Retrieved from http://www.debbieschlussel.com/13898/dont-believe-the-hype-avatar-stinks-long-boring-unoriginal-uber-left/#more-13898

Schramm, W. (1954). *The Process and Effects of Mass Communication*. Urbana: University of Illinois Press.

——. (1963). Communication development and the development process. In Lucien Pye (Ed.), *Communications and Political Development* (pp. 30–57). Princeton, NJ: Princeton University Press.

——. (1964). *Mass Media and National Development: The Role Of Information In The Developing Countries*. Sanford, CA; Stanford University Press.

Schreiber, A. L. and Lenson, B. (2000). *Multicultural Marketing*. New York: McGraw-Hill.

Schrøder, K. (2000). Making sense of audience discourses: towards a multidimensional model of mass media reception. *European Journal of Cultural Studies*, 3(2), 233–58.

Schrodt, P. (2011, June 6). First Class: the latest chapter in the X-Men gay-rights parable. Retrieved from http://www.theatlantic.com/entertainment/archive/2011/06/first-class-the-latest-chapter-in-the-x-men-gay-rights-parable/239959/

Schudson, M. (1994). Culture and the integration of national societies. *International Social Science Journal*, 46 (1), 63–81.

Schuker, L. A. (2010, August 2). Plot change: foreign forces transform Hollywood films. Retrieved from http://online.wsj.com

Scott, A. (1999). Regional motors of the world economy. In W.E. Halal and K. B. Taylor (Eds), *Twenty First Century Economics: Perspectives of Socio-Economics for a Changing World* (pp. 77–105). New York: St Martin's.

Scott, A. J. (2004a). The other Hollywood: the organizational and geographic bases of television-program production. *Media, Culture and Society*, 26(2), 183–205.

——. (2004b). Hollywood and the world: The geography of motion-picture distribution and marketing. *Review of International Political Economy*, 11(1), 33–61.

——. (2005). *On Hollywood; The Place, the Industry*. Princeton, NJ: Princeton University Press.

Scott, A. J. and Pope, N. E. (2007). Hollywood, Vancouver, and the world: employment relocation and the emergence of satellite production centers in the motion picture industry. *Environment and Planning A*, 39, 1364–1381.

Scott, A. O. (2000, January 30). The whole world isn't watching. *The New York Times Magazine*.

——. (2011, January 26). A golden age of foreign films, mostly unseen. Retrieved from http://www.nytimes.com/2011/01/30/movies/awardsseason/30scott.html?pagewanted=all

Scott, J. (2012). Studying power. In E. Amenta, K. Nash, Kate and A. Scott, (Eds), *The Wiley-Blackwell Companion to Political Sociology* (pp. 69–94). Malden, MA: Blackwell Publishing.

Scottish Government. (2011, March 21). Government strategy for creative industries published. Retrieved from http://www.scottish-enterprise.com/news/2011/03/government-strategy-for-the-creative-industries.aspx

Segrave, K. (1997). *American Films Abroad: Hollywood's Domination of the World's Movie Screens*. North Carolina: McFarland & Company, Inc. Publishers.

——. (1998). *American Television Abroad: Hollywood's Attempt to Dominate World Television*. Jefferson: Mcfarland & Company.

——. (1996). Notes on children as a television audience. In J. Hay, L. Grossberg and E. Wartella (Eds). *The Audience and its Landscape* (pp.131–44). Boulder, CO: Westview Press.

Seiter, E. (1999). *Television and New Media Audiences*. Oxford: Clarendon Press.

Seitz, P. (2011, October 31). Disney's streaming deals show content is king. Retrieved from http://news.investors.com/article/589905/201110311056/Disneys-Streaming-Deals-Show-Content-Is-King.htm

Selznick, B. J. (2008). *Global Television: Co-Producing Culture*. Philadelphia, PA: Temple University Press.

Sen, A. (1993). The impact of American pop culture in the Third World. *Media Asia*, 20(4), 208–17.

Sengupta, M. (2010, February 3). Will Avatar's racial politics both Oscar voters? Retrieved from http://www.alternet.org/story/145490/will_avatar's_proindigenous_narrative_bother_oscar_voters?page=3

Shackle, S. (2008, November 17). U.S. will not air climate change episode of Frozen Planet. Retrieved from http://www.newstatesman.com/blogs/star-spangled-staggers/2011/11/episode-climate-series-bbc

Shefrin, E. (2004). *Lord of the Rings, Star Wars*, and Participatory Fandom: Mapping New Congruencies between the Internet and Media Entertainment Culture. *Critical Studies in Media Communication*, 21(3), 261–281.

Shim, D. (2006). Hybridity and the rise of Korean popular culture in Asia. *Media, Culture & Society*, 28(1), 25–44.

Shimpack, S. (2005). The immortal cosmopolitan: the international co-production and global circulation of Highlander: The Series. *Cultural Studies*, 19(3), 338–371.

Shirky, C. (2008). *Here Comes Everybody: The Power of Organizing without Organizations*. New York: Penguin Press.

Shoard, C. (2011, November 11). Nun Sues Disney for "stealing Sister Act". Retrieved from http://www.guardian.co.uk/film/2011/nov/11/nun-sues-disney-sister-act

Sigismondi, P. (2011). *The Digital Glocalization of Entertainment: New Paradigms in the 21st Century Global Mediascape*. New York: Springer.

Signorielli, N. (1990). Television's mean and dangerous world: A continuation of the cultural indicators perspective. In N. Signorielli and M. Morgan (Eds), *Cultivation Analysis: New Directions in Media Effects Research* (pp. 85–106). Newbury Park: Sage.

Sinclair, J. (2003). The Hollywood of Latin America: Miami as a regional center in television trade. *Television & New Media*, (3), 211–229.

Sinclair, J., Jacka, E., and Cunningham, S. (1996). *New Patterns in Global Television: Peripheral Vision*. Oxford, UK. Oxford University Press.

Sivanandan, T. (2004). Anticolonialism, national liberation and postcolonial nation formation. In N. Lazarus (Ed.), *Postcolonial Literary Studies* (pp. 41–65). Cambridge: Cambridge University Press.

Sklair, L. (2001). *The Transnational Capitalist Class*. Oxford: Blackwell Publishers.

——. (2002). *Globalization: Capitalism and its Alternatives*. Oxford: Oxford University Press.

Smith, Anthony. (1980). *The Geopolitics of Information: How Western Culture Dominates the World*. New York, NY: Oxford University Press.

Smith, Adam. (2012). *The Wealth of Nations*. New York, NY: Simon & Brown.

Smith, B. (2010). *Re-narrating globalization: hybridity and resistance* in Amores Perros, Santitos and El Jardín del Edén. *Rupkatha Journal on Interdisciplinary Studies in Humanities*, 2 (3), 268–281.

Smith, D. (2009, August 20). *District 9*: South Africa and apartheid come to the movies. Retrieved from http://www.guardian.co.uk/film/2009/aug/20/district-9-south-africa-apartheid

Smythe, D. (1981). *Dependency Road: Communications, Capitalism, Consciousness, and Canada*. Norwood, NJ: Ablex.

Smythe, D. (2001). On the Audience Commodity and its Work. In M.G. Durham and D. Kellner (Eds), *Media and Cultural Sudies: Keyworks* (pp. 253–279). Malden, MA: Blackwell.

Snider, M. (2011, June 13). Entertainment, media spending hits $433B in 2010. Retrieved from http://www.usatoday.com/tech/news/2011-06-14-entertainment-spending-rises_n.htm

Snow, N. (2009). Rethinking public diplomacy. In N. Snow and P.M. Taylor (Eds), *Routledge Handbook of Public Diplomacy* (pp. 3–11). New York: Routledge.

Sonwalker, P. (2001). India: makings of little cultural/media imperialism? *The International Communication Gazette*, 63 (6), 503–519.

Sood, S, and Dreze, X. (2006). Brand extensions of experiential goods: movie sequel, evaluations. *Journal of Consumer Research*, 33, 352–360.

Sowards, S. K. (2003). MTV Asia: localizing the global media. In L. Artz and Y. R. Kamalipour (Eds), *The Globalization of Corporate Media Hegemony* (pp. 229–243). New York, NY: State University of New York Press.

Sparks, C. (2007). *Globalization, Development and the Mass Media*. Los Angeles: Sage.

——. (2009). Keyword: Imperialism. Retrieved from http://iamcr.org/latest-news/523-keywords-iamcrs-intervention-at-ica-2009

——. (2012). Resurrecting media imperialism. Retrieved from http://www.icavirtual.com/2012/04/21/conference-paper-resurrecting-media-imperialism/

Spivak, G. (1993). *Outside in the Teaching Machine*. London: Routledge.

Sreberny, A. (2006). The global and the local in international communications. In M.G. Durham & D. Kellner (Eds). *Media and Cultural Studies: Key Works* (pp. 604–625). Malden, MA: Blackwell.

Sreberny, A., Winseck, D. McKenna, J. and Boyd-Barrett, O. (Eds). (1997). *Media in Global Context: A Reader*. London: Arnold.

Sreberny-Mohammadi, A. (1996). Globalization, communication and transnational civil society: introduction. In S. Braman and A. Sreberny-Mohammadi (Eds), *Globalization, Communication and Transnational Civil Society*. Cresskill, NJ: Hampton Press.

——. (1997). The many faces of cultural imperialism. In P. Golding and P. Harris (Eds), *Beyond Cultural Imperialism: Globalization, Communication, and the New International Order* (pp. 49–64). London: Sage.

Sri Lanka Broadcasting Corporation. Retrieved from http://www.slbc.lk/index.php/services

Stableford, D. (2011, August 3). 'The Daily Show' censored by British television for using Parliament footage. Retrieved from http://news.yahoo.com/blogs/cutline/daily-show-censored-british-television-using-parliament-footage-174241780.html

Staff and Agencies. (2008, Nov. 3). Stuntman died filming Batman car chase. Retrieved from http://www.guardian.co.uk/film/2008/nov/03/dark-knigh-stuntman

Staff Writer. (2006, November 15). Consumer is king in the content and demand marketplace. Retrieved from http://www.telecomasia.net/node/4355

Steele, S. (2008, July 9). How much do television shows cost to produce? Retrieved from http://www.associatedcontent.com/article/869035/how_much_do_television_shows_cost_to_pg2.html?cat=31

Steger, M.B. (2009). *Globalization: A Very Short Introduction* (2nd ed.). New York, NY: Oxford University Press.

Steinmetz, G. (2003). The state of emergency and the revival of American imperialism: toward an authoritarian post-Fordism. *Public Culture*, 15(2), 323–345.

Stenger, J. (1997). Consuming the Planet: Planet Hollywood, stars, and the global consumer culture. *The Velvet Light Trap*, 40(Fall), 42–55.

Steven, P. (2010). *No-Nonsense Guide to Global Media* (2nd ed.). Toronto: Between the Lines.

Stiglitz, J. (2002). *Globalization and its Discontents*. New York, NY: W. W. Norton.

Stiglitz, J. E. (2011). Of the 1%, by the 1%, for the 1%. Retrieved from http://www.vanityfair.com/society/features/2011/05/top-one-percent-201105#gotopage2

Storper, M. (1989). The transition to flexible specialization in the U.S. film industry: external economics, the division of labour and the crossing of industrial divides. *Cambridge Journal of Economics*, 13, 273–305.

——. (1993). Flexible specialization in Hollywood: a response to Aksoy and Robins. *Cambridge Journal of Economics*, 17, 479–484.

Storper M. and Christopherson, S. (1987). Flexibilize specialization and regional industrial agglomerations: the case of the U.S. motion-picture industry. *Annals of the Association of American Geographers*, 77 (1), 260–282.

Storper, M. and Venabels, A. J. (2004). Buzz: face-to-face contact and the urban economy. *Journal of Economic Geography*, 4(1), 351–370.

Strandberg, K. W. (2002, August 28). Swiss Army Goes "*XXX*" with Vin Diesel. Retrieved from http://www.allbusiness.com/services/museums-art-galleries-botanical-zoological/4358883-1.html

Strangelove, M. (2010). *Watching YouTube: Extraordinary Videos by Ordinary People*. Toronto: University of Toronto Press.

Straubhaar, J. (1991). Beyond media imperialism: asymmetrical interdependence and cultural proximity. *Critical Studies in Mass Communication*, 8(1), 39–59.

——. (1997). Distinguishing the global, regional and national levels of world television. In A. Srebery-Mohammadi, D. Winseck, J. McKenna, and O. Boyd-Barrett (eds) *Media in a Global Context: A Reader* (pp. 284–98). London: Edward Arnold.

Straubhaar, J. and Duarte, L. (2005). Adapting U.S. transnational television channels to a complex world: from cultural imperialism to localization and hybridization. In J. K. Chalaby (Ed.), *Transnational Television Worldwide* (pp. 216–253). New York: I.B. Tauris.

Strelitz, L. N. (2002). Media consumption and identity formation: The case of the "Homeland" viewers. *Media, Culture & Society*, 24, 459–480.

——. (2003). Where the global meets the local: South African youth and their experience of global media. In P. Murphy and M. Kraidy (Eds), *Global Media Studies* (pp. 234–256). New York, NY: Routledge.

——. (2004). Against cultural essentialism: media reception among South African youth. *Media, Culture & Society*, 26(5), 625–641.

Style News Wire (20 Oct. 2011). New African American network has competition. Retrieved from http://www.stylemagazine.com/new-african-american-network-has-competition/

Sui-Nam Lee, P. (1995). A case against the thesis of communication imperialism: The audience's response to foreign TV in Hong Kong. *Australian Journal of Communication*, 22, 63–81.

——. (1988). Communication imperialism and dependency: A conceptual clarification. *Gazette: The International Journal of Mass Communication Studies*, 41, 69–83.

Synder, S. J. (2010, January 13). The politics of Avatar: America bad. Retrieved from http://techland.time.com/2010/01/13/the-politics-of-avatar-america-bad/

Szalai, G. (2011a, March 17). U.S. advertising spending rose 6% to $131 billion in 2010. Retrieved from http://www.hollywoodreporter.com/news/us-advertising-spending-rose-65-168793

——. (2011b, April 11). HBO to top $1 billion in international revenue this year. Retrieved from http://www.hollywoodreporter.com/news/hbo-top-1-billion-international-176907

——. (2011c, July 29). Hollywood conglomerates on track for banner year of dividends, stock buybacks. Retrieved from http://www.hollywoodreporter.com/news/hollywood-conglomerates-track-banner-year-217304

Takaku, J. (2011, September 20). Korean Drams bite deep into Japanese TV market. Retrieved from http://www.asahi.com/english/TKY201109200340.html

Takeuchi, C. (2008, March 13). Canadian films seek more screen time. Retrieved from http://www.straight.com/article-135700/canadian-films-seek-more-screen-time

Tang, Y. (2011). *Avatar*: A Marxist saga on the far distant planet. *Triple-c*, 9(2), 657–667.

Tapscott, D. and Williams, A. (2010). *Wikinomics: How Mass Collaboration Changes Everything*. New York: Portfolio Trade.

Taylor, P. M. (1997). *Global Communications, International Affairs, and the Media Since 1945*. New York: Routledge.

Taylor, P. W. (1995). Co-productions—content and change: international television in the Americas. *Canadian Journal of Communication*, 20(3).

Teague, E. (2010, February 2). Avatar is real say tribal people. Retrieved from http://www.survivalinternational.org/news/5466\

The Canadian Press. (2009a, March 9). Ottawa announces Canada media fund. Retrieved from http://toronto.ctv.ca/servlet/an/local/CTVNews/20090309/canadian_tv_090309/20090309/?hub=TorontoNewHome

—— (2009b, March 22). Vancouver island hosts Twilight movie sequel shoot. Retrieved from http://www.ctv.ca/CTVNews/Entertainment/20090322/twilight_shoot_090322/

The Daily Bits (2012, May 21). Top 10 most pirated movies of all time. Retrieved from http://www.dailybits.com/top-10-most-pirated-movies-of-all-time/

——. (2001). Harry Potter and the Synergy Test. Retrieved from http://www.forbes.com/global2000/#p_1_s_arank_BroadcastingCable_All_All

The Economist (11 April 2002). Think local: cultural imperialism doesn't sell. Retrieved from http://www.economist.com/node/1066620

——. (2003, September 11). Media regulation outside america. Retrieved from http://www.economist.com/node/2054812

——. (2008, October 8). Economies of scale. Retrieved from http://www.economist.com/node/12446567

——. (2011a, June 9). Unilateral disarmament. Retrieved from http://www.economist.com/node/18805941

——. (2011b, October 15). Branding Japan as 'cool.' No limits, now laws. Retrieved from http://www.economist.com/node/21532297

——. (2011c, November 5). Entertainers to the world. Retrieved from http://www.economist.com/node/21536602

——. (2011d, February 1). Hollywood goes global. Retrieved from http://www.economist.com/node/18178291

The Nation. (2009, April 22). Thailand's film censors block Zack and Miri Make a Porno. Retrieved from http://www.asiaone.com/News/Latest%2BNews/Showbiz/Story/A1Story20090422-136716.html

The Nielsen Company. (2008). Cinema advertising demystified. Retrieved from http://www.widescreenmedia.com/nielsen.pdf

The Statesman. (2007, April 16). Is Ghana a victim of cultural imperialism? Retrieved from http://www.thestatesmanonlin.com/pages/editorial_detail.php?newsid+172&section=0

Thierer, A. and Eskelsen, G. (2008). Media Metrics: The True State of the Modern Media Marketplace. The Progress Freedom Foundation Special Report. Retrieved from http://www.pff.org/mediametrics/

Thiong'o, N. W. (1986). *Writing Against Neo-Colonialism*. Vita Books.

Thomas, P. N. (1997). An inclusive NWICO: cultural resilience and popular resistance. In P. Golding and P. Harris (Eds), *Beyond Cultural Imperialism: Globalization, Communication and the New International Order* (pp. 163–164). London: Sage.

Thomas, P. N. and Nain, Z. (Eds). (2004). *Who Owns the Media: Global Trends and Local Resistances*. London and New York: Zed Books.

Thompson, A. K. (2010). Co-opting capitalism: *Avatar* and the thing itself. *Upping the Anti*, 10, 77–96.

Thompson, J. B. (1995). The Media and Modernity: A Social Theory of the Media. Stanford, CA: Stanford University Press.

Thompson, K. (2003). Fantasy, franchises and Frodo Baggins: The Lord of the Rings and modern Hollywood. *The Velvet Light Trap*, 52 (Fall), 45–63.

——. (2007a). The Frodo Franchise: *The Lord of the Rings* and Modern Hollywood. Berkley: University of California Press.

——. (2007b, February 28). World rejects Hollywood blockbusters? Retrieved from http://www.davidbordwell.net/blog/2007/02/28/world-rejects-hollywood-blockbusters/

Throsby, D. (2008). Modelling the cultural industries. *International Journal of Cultural Policy*, 14 (3), 217–232.

——. (2010). *The Economics of Cultural Policy*. Cambridge: Cambridge University Press.

Thussu, D. K. (Ed.) (1998). *Electronic Empires: Global Media and Local Resistance*. London: Arnold.

——. (2000). *International Communication: Continuity and Change*. London: Arnold Press.

——. (2005). The transnationalization of television: the Indian experience. In J.K. Chalaby (Ed.), *Transnational Television Worldwide* (pp. 156–172). New York, NY: I.B. Tauris.

——. (2006). *International Communication: Continuity and Change*. London: Arnold Press.

——. (Ed.). (2007a). *Media on the Move: Global Flow and Contra-Flow*. New York, NY: Routledge.

——. (2007b). *News as Entertainment: The Rise of Global Infotainment*. Los Angeles: Sage.

Tinic, S. (2003). Going global: international co-productions and the disappearing domestic audience in Canada. In L. Parks, and S. Kumar (Eds), *Planet TV: A Global Television Reader* (pp. 169–186). New York: New York University Press.

——. (2004). Global vistas and local identities: negotiating place and identity in Vancouver television. *Television and New Media*, 7 (2), 154–83.

——. (2005). *On Location: Canada's Television Industry in a Global Market*. Toronto: University of Toronto Press.

——. (2008). Mediated spaces: cultural geography and the globalization of production. *Velvet Light Trap*, 62 (1), 74–75.

——. (2010). Walking a tightrope: the global cultural economy of Canadian television. In N. Beaty, D. Briton, G. Filax and R. Sullivan (Eds), *How Canadians Communicate III: Contexts of Canadian Popular Culture* (pp. 95 115). Edmonton, AB: Athabasca University Press.

Tizard, W. (2010, January 4). Czechs set film rebates. Retrieved from http://www.variety.com/article/VR1118013276?refCatId=1279

Toffler, A. (1984). *The Third Wave*. New York: Bantam.

Tomlinson, J. (1991). Cultural Imperialism. Baltimore: The Johns Hopkins University Press.

———. (1996). Cultural Globalization: placing and displacing the West. In H. Mackay and T. O'Sullivan (Eds), *The Media Reader: Continuity and Transformation* (pp. 165–177). London: Sage.

———. (1999). *Globalization and Culture*. Chicago: The University of Chicago Press.

———. (2002). The discourse of cultural imperialism. In D. McQuail (Ed.), *Mcquail's Reader in Mass Communication Theory* (pp. 223–237). London: Sage Publications.

Torre, P. J. (2009). Block booking migrates to television: the rise and fall of the international output deal. *Television & New Media*, 10(6), 501–520.

Toumarkine, T. (2004). Going for the gold. Retrieved from http://allbusiness.com/services/motion_pictures/4426146-1.html

Tracy, M. (1988). Popular culture and the economics of global television. *Intermedia*, 16 (1), 9–25.

Tracey, M. (1998). *The Decline and Fall of Public Service Broadcasting*. Oxford: Oxford University Press.

Trumpbour, J. (2003). *Selling Hollywood to the World: U.S. and European Struggles for Mastery of the Global Film Industry, 1920–1950*. Cambridge: Cambridge University Press.

Tucker, I. B. (2004). *Microeconomics for Today*. Mason, OH: South-Western CENGAGE Learning.

Tunstall, J. (1977). *The Media are American*. London: Constable.

———. (2000). *The Anglo-American Media Connection*. Oxford: Oxford University Press.

———. (2007). International-regional-national: The national media system as the lead player. *Global Media and Communication*, 3(3), 321–342.

———. (2008). *The Media Were American: U.S. Mass Media in Decline*. New York, NY: Oxford University Press.

Turner, T. (2004). My beef with big media. Retrieved from http://www.washingtonmonthly.com/features/2004/0407.turner.html

UNCTAD. (2010). Creative economy report 2010: creative economy: a feasible development option. Retrieved from http://www.unctad.org/Templates/WebFlyer.asp?intItemID=5763&lang=1

UNWTO. (2012, May 7). World Tourism Organization UNWTO: International tourism receipts surpass U.S. $1 trillion. Retrieved from http://media.unwto.org/en/press-release/2012-05-07/international-tourism-receipts-surpass-us-1-trillion-2011

Ursell, G. (2000). Television production: issues of exploitation, commodification and subjectivity in UK television labour markets. *Media, Culture & Society* 22(1), 805–825.

USITC. (2011). Recent Trends in US Services Trade: 2011. Annual Report, Investigation No: 332–345; Publication No: 4243. Washington DC: United States International Trade Commission.

van Elteren, M. (2003). U.S. cultural imperialism today: only a chimera? *SAIS Review*, XXIII(2), 169–188.

van Kooten, M. (2011). Global Software Top 100 – Edition 2011. Retrieved from http://www.softwaretop100.org/global-software-top-100-edition-2011

Vang, J. and Chaminade, C. (2007). Cultural clusters, global-local linkages and spillovers: theoretical and empirical insights from an exploratory study of Toronto's film cluster. *Industry and Innovation*, 14(4), 401–420.

Varis, T. (1974). Global traffic in television. *Journal of Communication*, 24(1), 102–109.

———. (1984). The international flow of television programs. *Journal of Communication*, 34(1), 134–152.

Visiting Arts. (2008, February 26). Japan cultural profile. Retrieved from http://www.cultural-profiles.net/japan/Directories/Japan_Cultural_Profile/-6036.html

Vivarelli, N. (2010, Feb 16). Cinecitta campaign: Italian studio looks to lure U.S. Productions. Retrieved from http://www.variety.com/article/VR1118015312

Vogel, H. L. (2007). *Entertainment Industry Economics: A Guide for Financial Analysis*. Cambridge: Cambridge University Press.

Voxy. (January 24, 2010). Avatar delivers $307 million to New Zealand economy. Retrieved from http://www.voxy.co.nz/entertainment/avatar-delivers-307m-new-zealand-economy/5/36156

Wagneleitner, R. (1999). The empire of the fun, or talkin' Soviet Union blues: the sound of freedom and U.S. cultural hegemony in Europe. In. M. J. Hogan, (Ed.). *The Ambiguous Legacy: U.S. Foreign Relations in the "American Century"* (pp. 463–499). New York: Cambridge University Press.

Waisbord, S. (2004). McTV: understanding the global popularity of television formats. *Television & New Media*, 5(4), 359–383.

Waisbord, S. and Morris, N. (2001). Introduction: rethinking media globalization and state power. In Morris, N. and Waisbord, S.R, (Eds). *Media and Globalization: Why the State Matters* (pp.vi–xvi). Lanham: Rowman & Littlefield Publishers, Inc.

Wallerstein, I. (1961). *Africa, The Politics of Independence*. New York: Vintage Books.

——. (1974). *The Modern World System*. New York/London: Academic Press.

——. (1979). *The Capitalist World-Economy*. Cambridge: Cambridge University Press.

Ward, S. and O'Regan, T. (2007). Servicing 'the other Hollywood': The vicissitudes of an international television production location. *International Journal of Cultural Studies*, 10(2), 167–185.

Warf, B. (2007). Oligopolization of Global Media and Telecommunications and its Implications. *Democracy, Ethics, Place and Environment*, 10(1), 89–105.

Wark, M. (1994). *Virtual Geography: Living with Global Media Events*. Bloomington: Indiana University Press.

Wasko, J. (2003). *How Hollywood Works*. London: Sage Publications.

Wasko, J. and Erikson, M., (Eds). (2009). *Cross border cultural production: economy runaway or globalization?* New York: Cambria Press.

Wasser, F. (1995). Is Hollywood America? The trans-nationalization of the American film industry. *Critical Studies in Mass Communication*, 12 (4), 423–37.

Waterman, D. (2005). *Hollywood's road to riches*. Cambridge, MA: Harvard University Press.

Waterman, D. and Weiss, A. A. (1997). *Vertical Integration in Cable Television*. Cambridge, MA: MIT Press.

Waxman, S. (1990, Oct. 26). Hollywood attuned to world markets. Retrieved from http://www.washingtonpost.com/wp-srv/inatl/longterm/mia/part2.htm

——. (1998). Hollywood Tailors its Movies to Sell in Foreign Markets. Washington Post. A1

Wayne, M. (2003). Post-Fordism, monopoly capitalism, and Hollywood's media industrial complex. *International Journal of Cultural Studies*, 6(1), 82–103.

Weeks, E. (2010). Where is there? The Canadianization of the American media landscape. *International Journal of Canadian Studies*, 39–40 (1), 83–107.

Wei, R. and Pan, Z. (1999). Mass media and consumerist values in the People's Republic of China. *International Journal of Public Opinion Research*, 11, 75–96.

Weil, D. (2011, October 4). At Time Warner, Content is Still King. Retrieved from http://www.moneynews.com/Companies/TWX-media-cable-stocks/2011/10/04/id/413217

Wellemeyer, J. (2006). Hollywood and the spread of anti-Americanism. Retrieved from http://www.npr.org/templates/story/story.php?storyId=6625002

Wen, W. (2010, January 28). Avatar juggernaut crushes opposition to U.S. soft power. Retrieved from http://www.globaltimes.cn/opinion/commentary/2010-01/501921.html

WENN. (2011, March 6). Director admits 'Transformers 2' was no good. Retrieved from http://movies.msn.com/movies/article.aspx?news=633946&affid=100055

WENN.COM. (2011, July 8). Lucas Quashes 'Star Wars' fan event. Retrieved from http://www.torontosun.com/2011/07/08/lucas-quashes-star-wars-fan-event

Westcott, T. (October 20, 2011). Comcast Leads U.S. dominated Audio-visual Business in 2010. Retrieved from http://www.isuppli.com/Media-Research/News/Pages/Comcast-Leads-US-Dominated-Audiovisual-Business-in-2010.aspx?PRX

White, T. R. (1990). Hollywood's attempt at appropriating television. The case of paramount pictures. In T. Balio (Ed.). *Hollywood in the Age of Television*. Boston: Unwin Hyman.

Wike, R. (2007, September 11). From hyperpower to declining power. *Pew Research Center*. Retrieved from http://www.pewglobal.org/2011/09/07/from-hyperpower-to-declining-power/

Wildman, K. (1994). One-way flows and the economics of audience making. In J. S. Ettema and D. C. Whitney (Eds), *Audience making: How the Media Create the Audience*. (pp. 115–41). Sage: Thousand Oaks.

Will, I. (2009, February 28). Why is New Moon filmed in Vancouver, not Oregon? Retrieved from http://www.newmoonmovie.org/2 009/02/why-is-new-moon-filmed-in-vancouver-not-oregon/

Williams, R. (1974). *Television: Technology and Cultural Form*. London: Fontana.

——. (1976). *Keywords: A Vocabulary of Culture and Society*. London: Fontana.

——. (1977). *Marxism and Literature*. London: Oxford University Press.

——. (1981). *Culture*. London: Fontana.

Wilson, T. (2000). Media Convergence: Watching Television, Anticipating Going On-Line: A Malaysian Reception Study. *Media Asia*, 27(1), 3–9.

——. (2001). On playfully becoming the 'Other': watching Oprah Winfrey on Malaysian television. *International Journal of Cultural studies*, 4(1), 89–110.

Winseck, D. (2008). The state of media ownership and media markets: competition or concentration and why should we care? *Sociology Compass*, 2(1), 34–47.

——. (2011). Introductory essay: the political economies of media and the transformation of the global media industries. In D. Winseck and D. Y. Jin (Eds), *The Political Economies of Media: The Transformation of the Global Media Industries* (pp. 3–48). London and New York: Bloomsbury Academic.

Winseck, D. and Jin, D. Y. (Eds). (2011). *The Political Economies of the Media: The Transformation of the Global Media Industries*. New York: Bloomsbury Academic.

Winseck, D. and Pike. R. M. (2007). *Communication and Empire: Media, Markets and Globalization, 1860–1930*. Durham and London: Duke University Press.

Winseck, D., McKenna, J., and Boyd-Barrett, O. (Eds). (1997). *Media in a Global Context: A Reader*. New York, NY: Arnold.

Wiseman, A. (2011, December 22). Russia primed to embrace world. Retrieved from http://www.screendaily.com/reports/in-focus/russia-primed-to-embrace-world/5035927.article

Wolf, N. (1992). *The Beauty Myth: How Images of Beauty are Used Against Women*. New York, NY: Harper Collins Publishers.

Wong, E. (2012, 2 January). China's president lashes out at western cultural influences. Retrieved from http://www.nytimes.com/2012/01/04/world/asia/chinas-president-pushes-back-against-western-culture.html?_r=0

Wood, E. M. (2002). Global capital, national states. In M. Rupert and H. Smith (Eds), *Historical Materialism and Globalization* (17–39). New York: Routledge.

——. (2003). *Empire of Capital*. New York: Verso.

World Bank. (2009). Growth of the service sector. Retrieved from http://www.worldbank.org/depweb/beyond/beyondco/beg_09.pdf

World Intellectual Property Organization (WIPO). (2010). Creative clusters. Retrieved from http://www.wipo.int/ip-development/en/creative_industry/creative_clusters.html

World Trade Organization (WTO). (2010, January 12). Audiovisual services: background note by the secretariat. Retrieved from http://www.oecd.org/tad/servicestrade/47559464.pdf

Wright, S. (2007, August 20). Competition is fierce in today's cinema. Retrieved from http://www.variety.com/article/VR1117970526?refCatId=13

Wu, H. and Chan, J. M. (2007). Globalizing Chinese martial arts cinema: The global-local alliance and the production of Crouching Tiger, Hidden Dragon. *Media, Culture & Society*, 29(2), 195–217.

Wu, T. (2010). *The Master Switch: The Rise and Fall of Information Empires*. New York, NY: Alfred A Knopf.

Wyatt, J. (1994). *High Concept: Movies and Marketing in Hollywood*. Austin: Texas University Press.

Yong, J. (2007) Reinterpretation of cultural imperialism: emerging domestic market vs. continuing U.S. dominance. *Media, Culture & Society*, 29 (5), 753–71.

Young, R. C. (2001). *Postcolonialism: An Historical Introduction*. Malden, MA: Blackwell.

Za'Za', B. (2002, March 21). Arab speakers see threat to culture by globalization. Retrieved from gulfnews.com/news/gulf/uae/general/speakers-see-threat-to-culture-by-globalization-1.381604